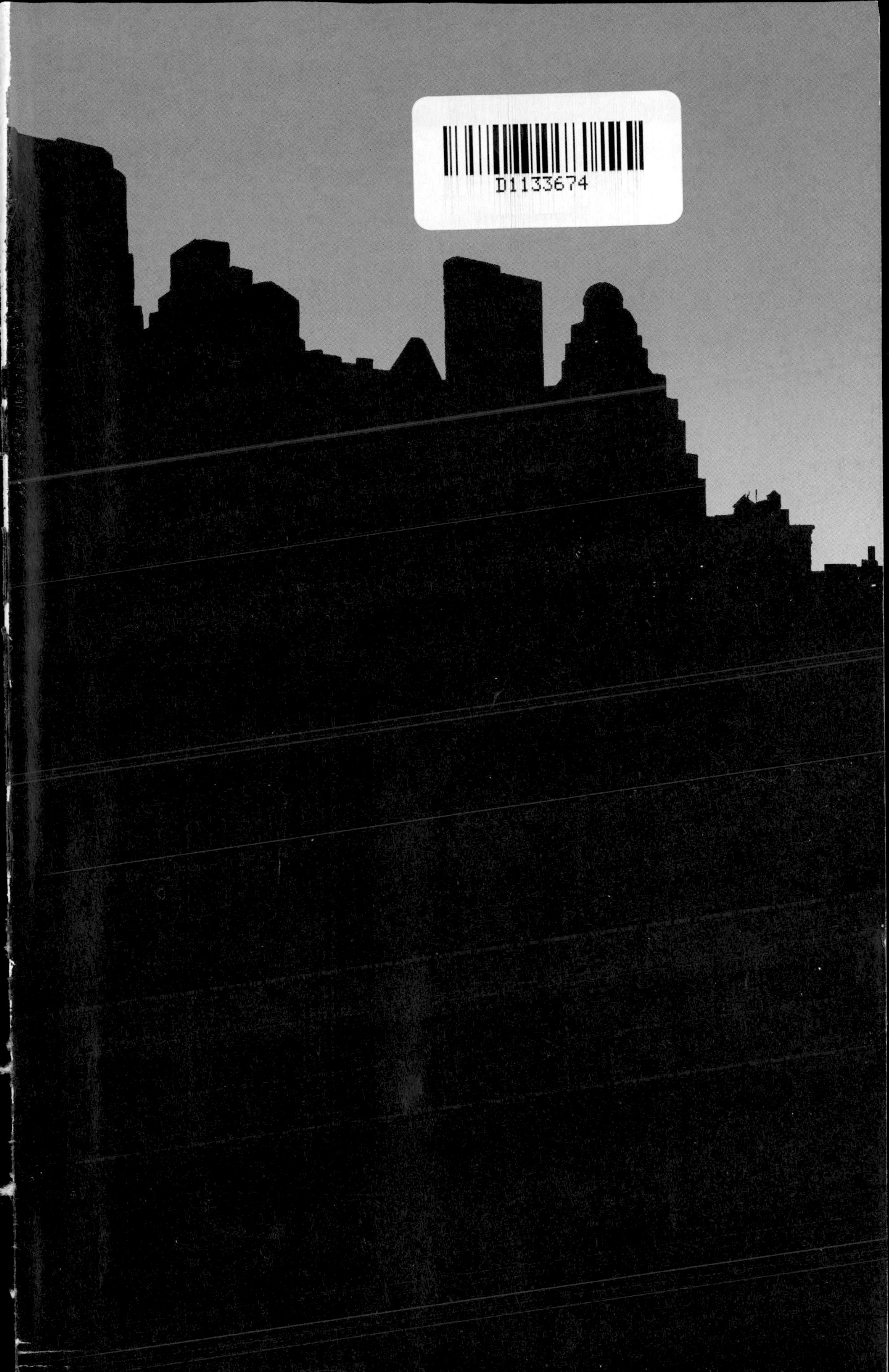

D1133674

POW ★★★ BUR

CREATED AND PRODUCED
BY
BRIAN MICHAEL BENDIS
AND
MICHAEL AVON OEMING

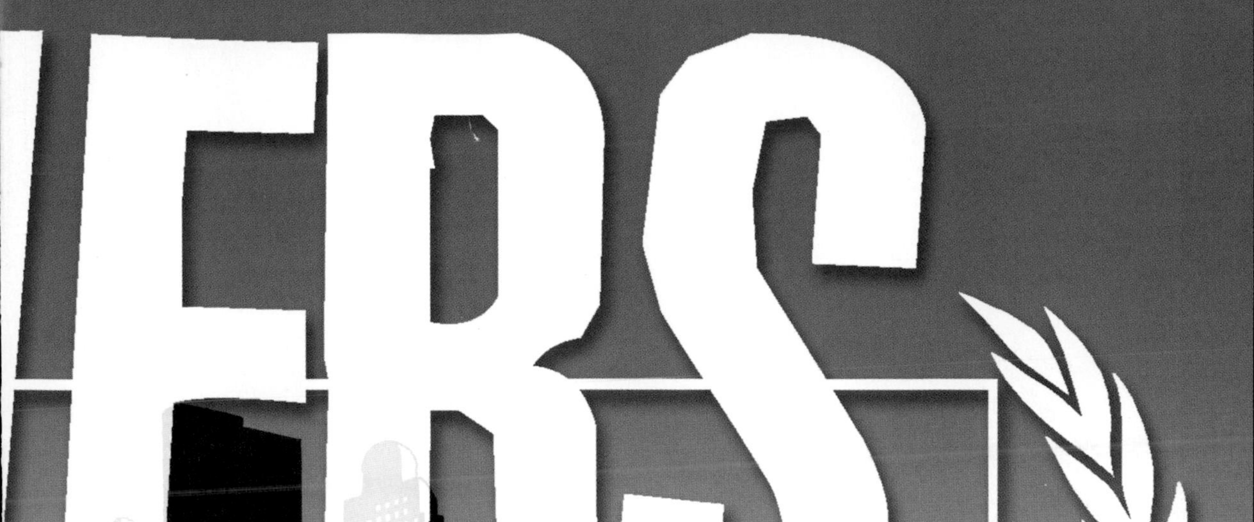
ERS
EAU

COLORING
NICK FILARDI

LETTERS
CHRIS ELIOPOULOS

EDITING AND PRODUCTION
JENNIFER GRÜNWALD

BUSINESS AFFAIRS
ALISA BENDIS

COLLECTION DESIGNER
PATRICK McGRATH

Previously in Powers:

Federal agents Christian Walker, Deena Pilgrim, and Enki Sunrise used to be homicide detectives who focused on cases specific to powers, but after a powers-related disaster, the government declares all powers cases are federal cases.

During their last case, Walker went undercover, ultimately resulting in the arrest of Erika Broglia, the daughter of a major crime family that Walker and Pilgrim had encountered in the past. Former criminal Nick Roberts aided the agents in this case and in the process revealed the armor that Triphammer had bequeathed him.

Meanwhile, Agent Pilgrim is keeping a big secret...

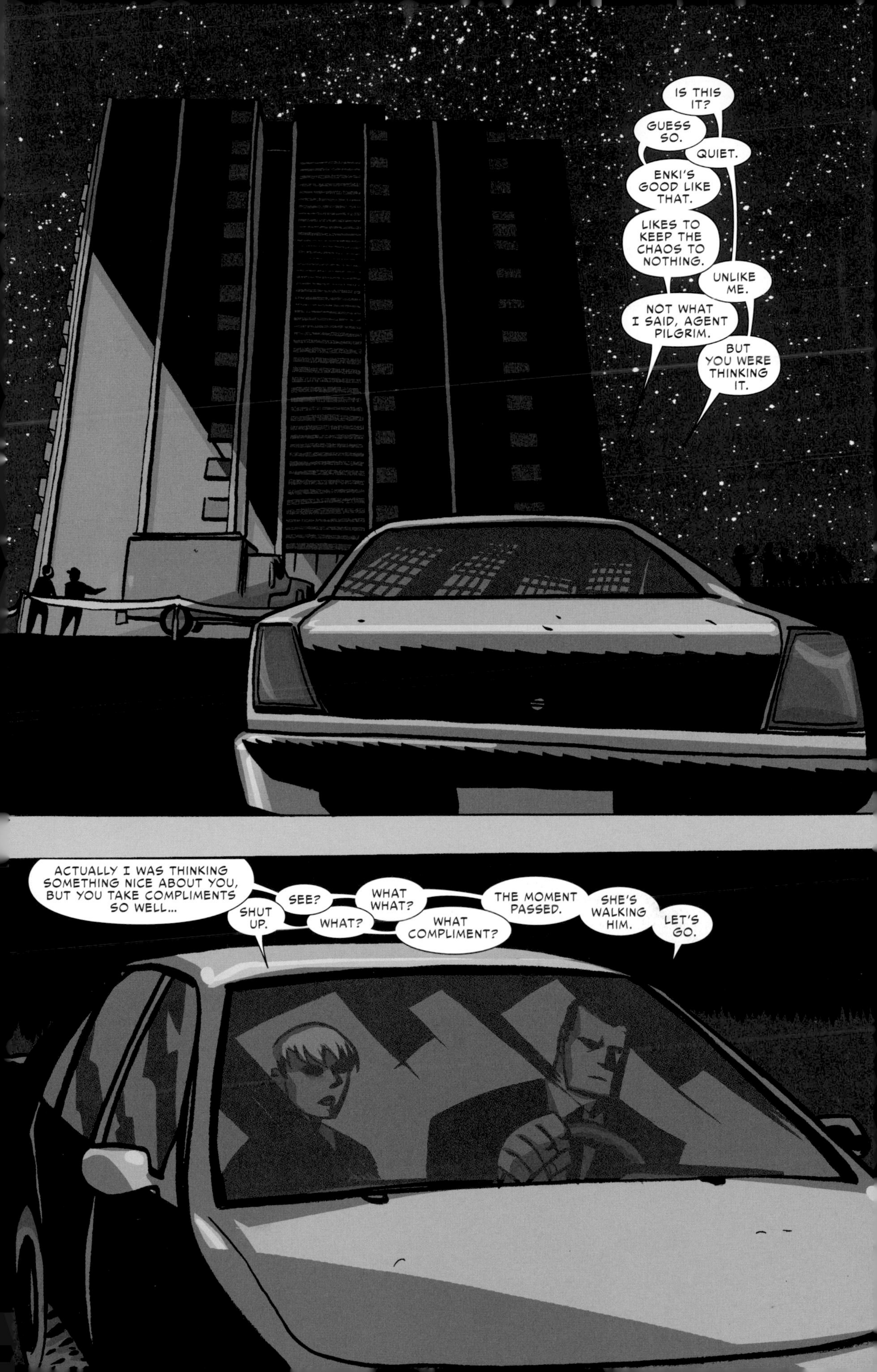
IS THIS IT?
GUESS SO.
QUIET.
ENKI'S GOOD LIKE THAT.
LIKES TO KEEP THE CHAOS TO NOTHING.
UNLIKE ME.
NOT WHAT I SAID, AGENT PILGRIM.
BUT YOU WERE THINKING IT.
ACTUALLY I WAS THINKING SOMETHING NICE ABOUT YOU, BUT YOU TAKE COMPLIMENTS SO WELL...
SHUT UP.
SEE?
WHAT?
WHAT WHAT?
WHAT COMPLIMENT?
THE MOMENT PASSED.
SHE'S WALKING HIM.
LET'S GO.

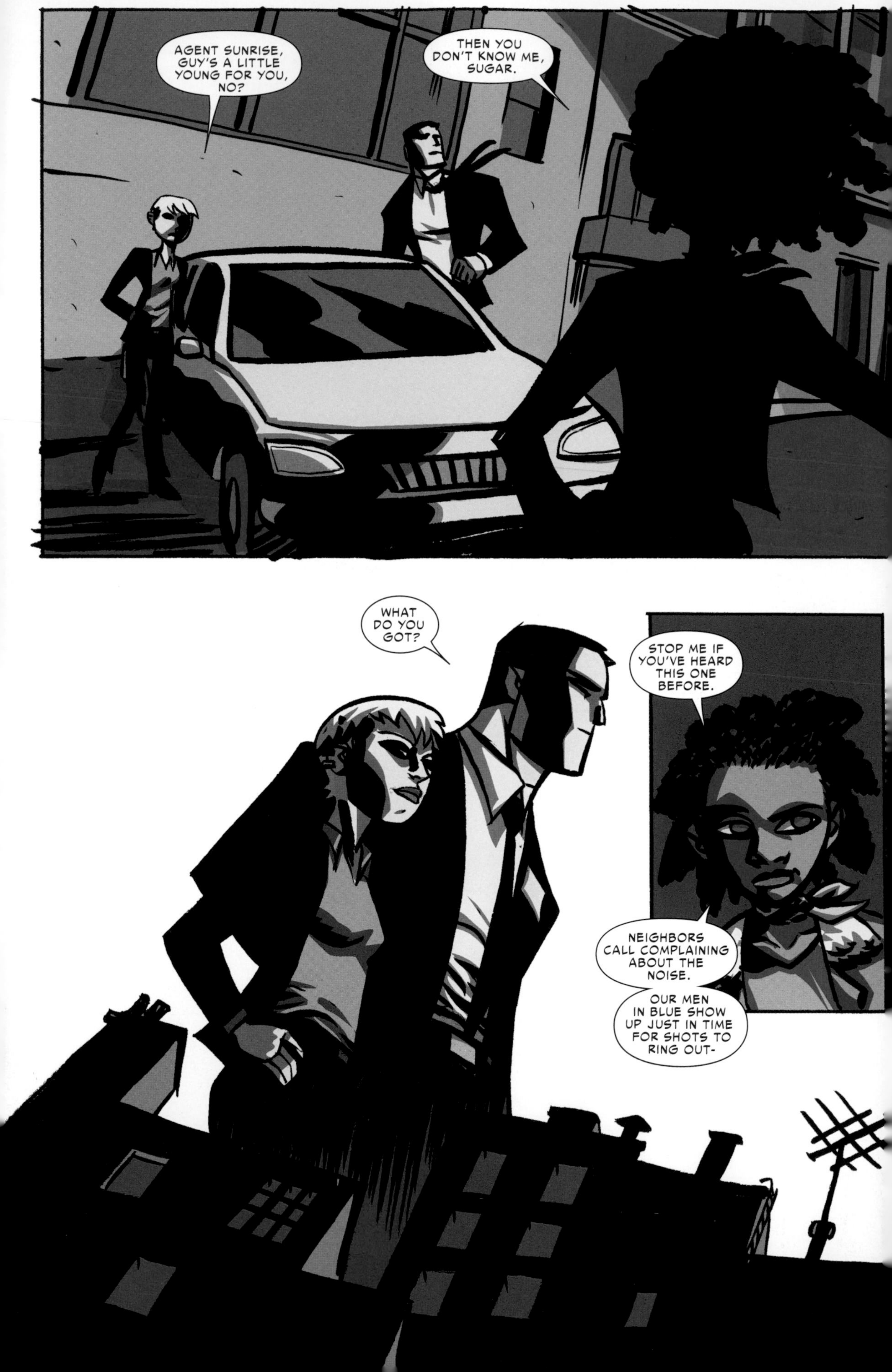
AGENT SUNRISE, GUY'S A LITTLE YOUNG FOR YOU, NO?
THEN YOU DON'T KNOW ME, SUGAR.
WHAT DO YOU GOT?
STOP ME IF YOU'VE HEARD THIS ONE BEFORE.
NEIGHBORS CALL COMPLAINING ABOUT THE NOISE.
OUR MEN IN BLUE SHOW UP JUST IN TIME FOR SHOTS TO RING OUT-

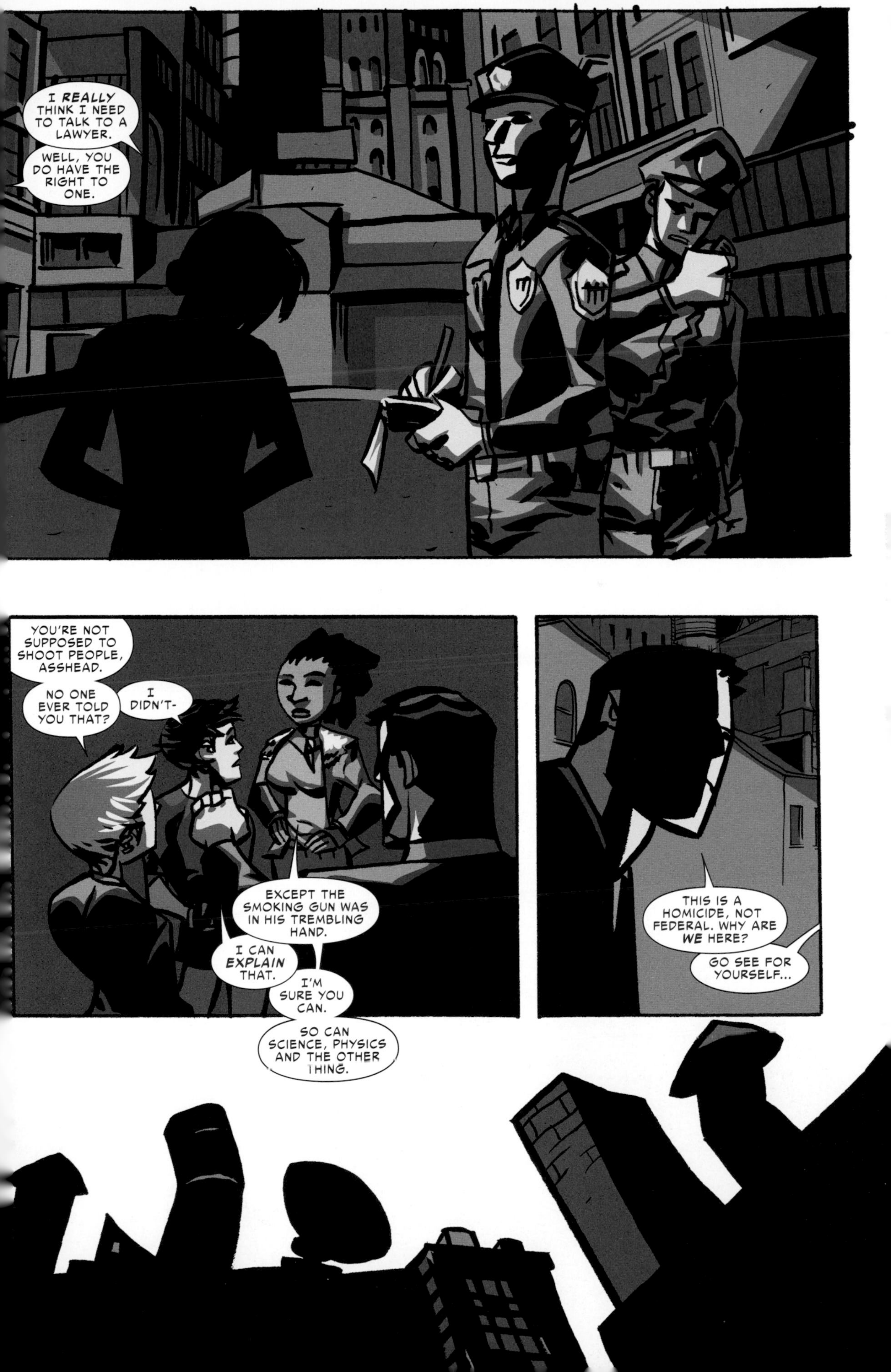
I REALLY THINK I NEED TO TALK TO A LAWYER.
WELL, YOU DO HAVE THE RIGHT TO ONE.
YOU'RE NOT SUPPOSED TO SHOOT PEOPLE, ASSHEAD.
NO ONE EVER TOLD YOU THAT?
I DIDN'T-
EXCEPT THE SMOKING GUN WAS IN HIS TREMBLING HAND.
I CAN EXPLAIN THAT.
I'M SURE YOU CAN.
SO CAN SCIENCE, PHYSICS AND THE OTHER THING.
THIS IS A HOMICIDE, NOT FEDERAL. WHY ARE WE HERE?
GO SEE FOR YOURSELF...

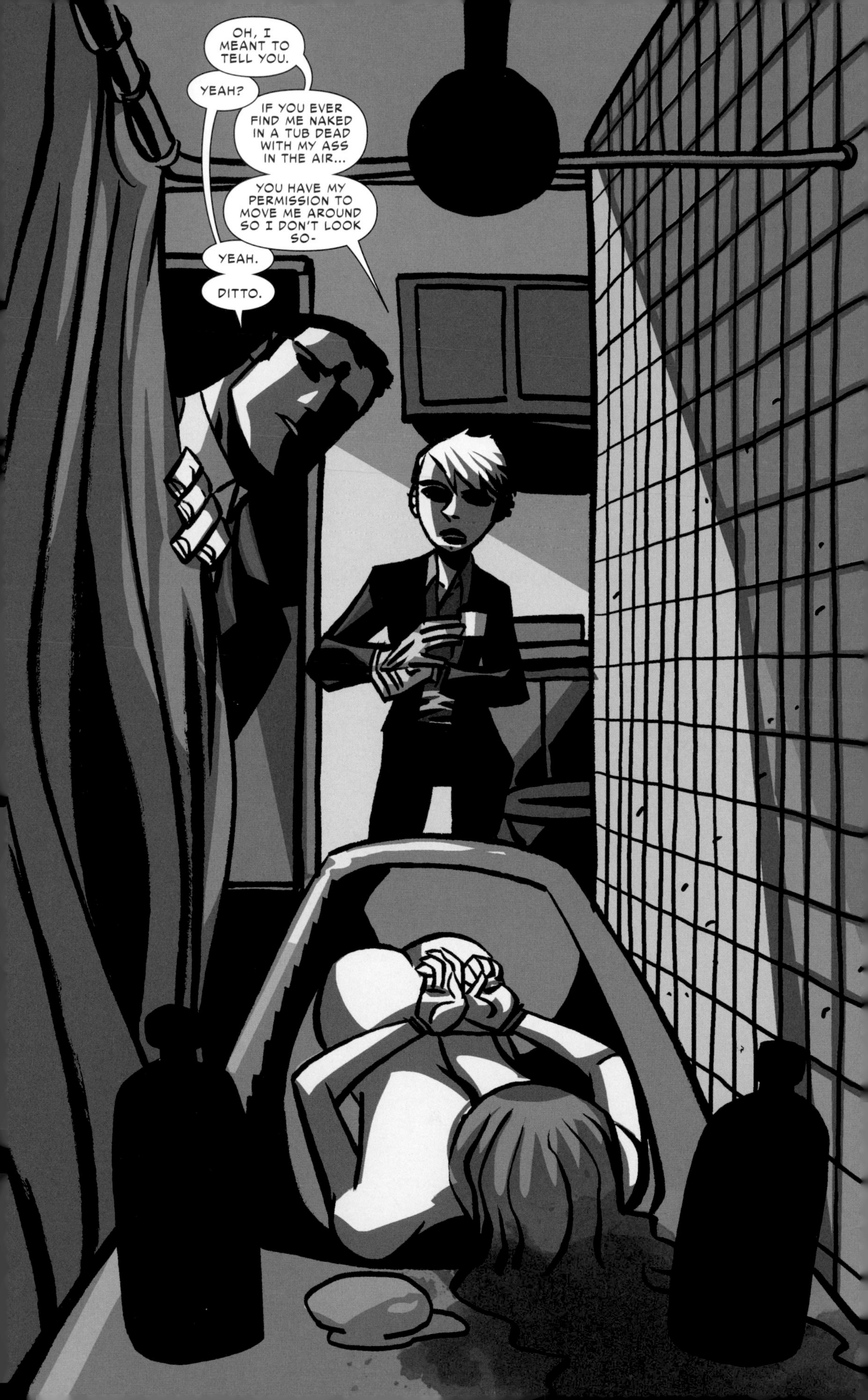
OH, I MEANT TO TELL YOU.
YEAH?
IF YOU EVER FIND ME NAKED IN A TUB DEAD WITH MY ASS IN THE AIR...
YOU HAVE MY PERMISSION TO MOVE ME AROUND SO I DON'T LOOK SO-
YEAH.
DITTO.

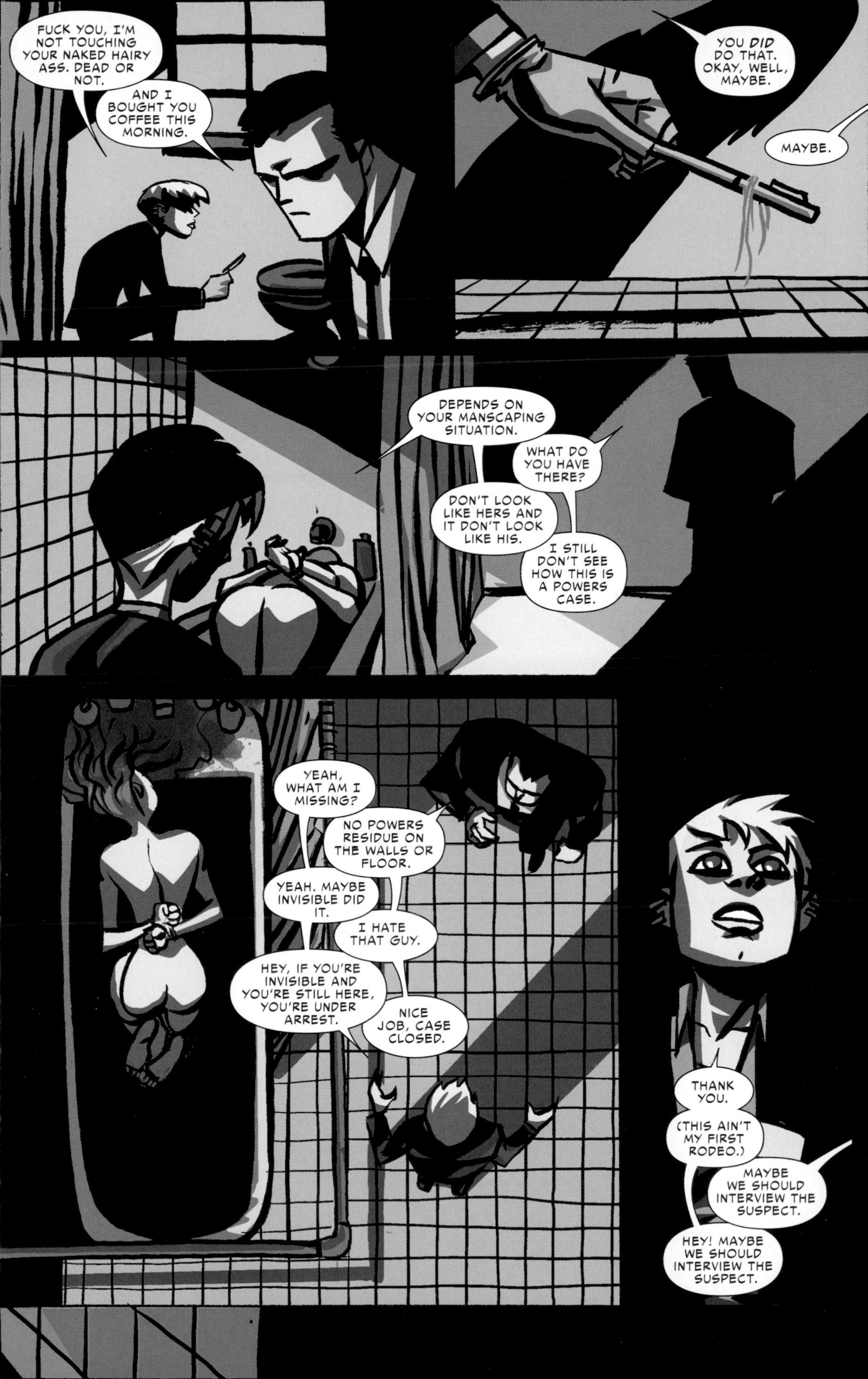
FUCK YOU, I'M NOT TOUCHING YOUR NAKED HAIRY ASS. DEAD OR NOT.
AND I BOUGHT YOU COFFEE THIS MORNING.
YOU DID DO THAT. OKAY, WELL, MAYBE.
MAYBE.
DEPENDS ON YOUR MANSCAPING SITUATION.
WHAT DO YOU HAVE THERE?
DON'T LOOK LIKE HERS AND IT DON'T LOOK LIKE HIS.
I STILL DON'T SEE HOW THIS IS A POWERS CASE.
YEAH, WHAT AM I MISSING?
NO POWERS RESIDUE ON THE WALLS OR FLOOR.
YEAH. MAYBE INVISIBLE DID IT.
I HATE THAT GUY.
HEY, IF YOU'RE INVISIBLE AND YOU'RE STILL HERE, YOU'RE UNDER ARREST.
NICE JOB, CASE CLOSED.
THANK YOU.
(THIS AIN'T MY FIRST RODEO.)
MAYBE WE SHOULD INTERVIEW THE SUSPECT.
HEY! MAYBE WE SHOULD INTERVIEW THE SUSPECT.

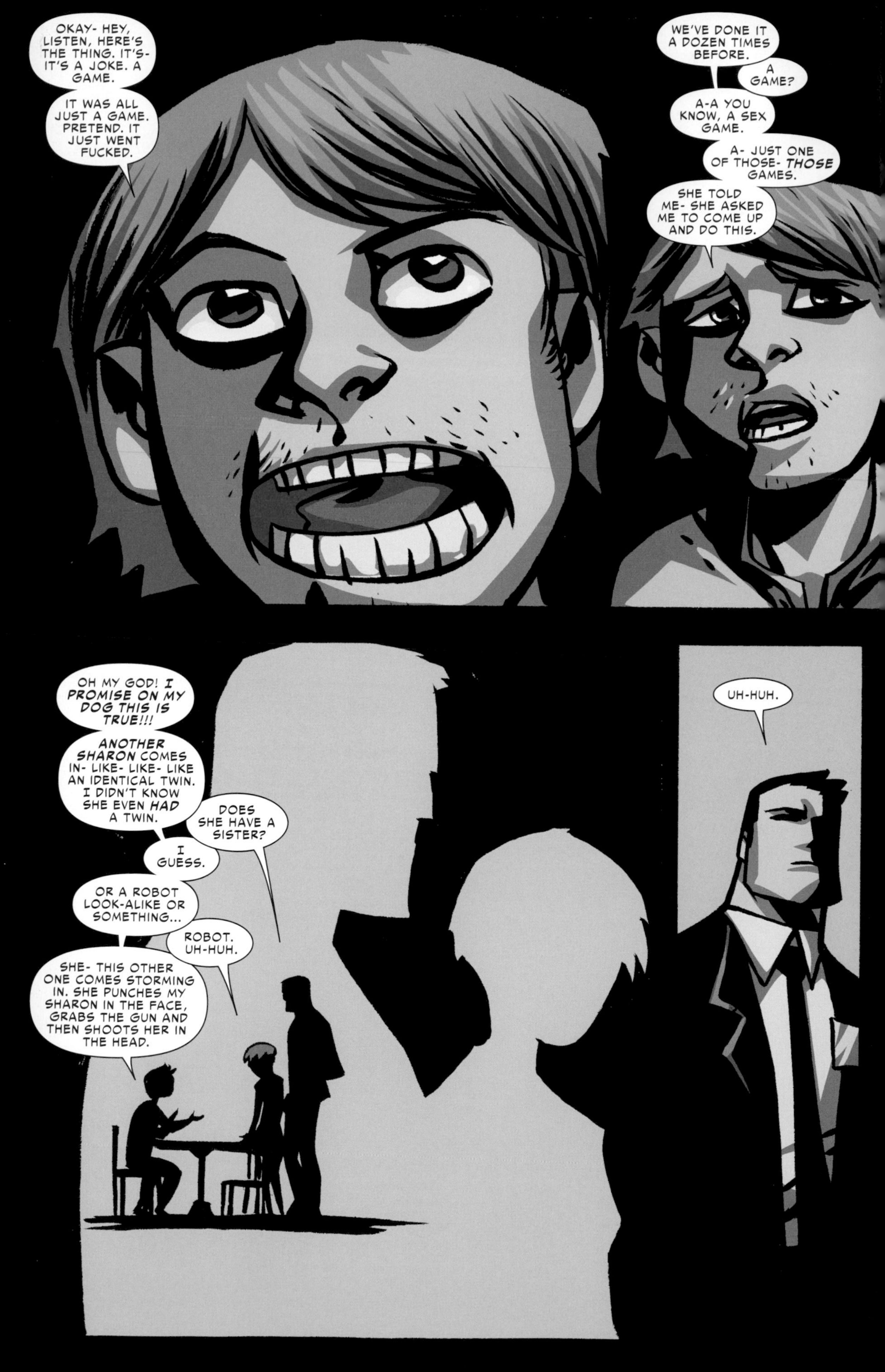
OKAY- HEY, LISTEN, HERE'S THE THING. IT'S- IT'S A JOKE. A GAME.
IT WAS ALL JUST A GAME. PRETEND. IT JUST WENT FUCKED.
WE'VE DONE IT A DOZEN TIMES BEFORE.
A GAME?
A-A YOU KNOW, A SEX GAME.
A- JUST ONE OF THOSE- *THOSE* GAMES.
SHE TOLD ME- SHE ASKED ME TO COME UP AND DO THIS.
OH MY GOD! *I PROMISE ON MY DOG THIS IS TRUE!!!*
ANOTHER SHARON COMES IN- LIKE- LIKE- LIKE AN IDENTICAL TWIN. I DIDN'T KNOW SHE EVEN *HAD* A TWIN.
DOES SHE HAVE A SISTER?
I GUESS.
OR A ROBOT LOOK-ALIKE OR SOMETHING...
ROBOT. UH-HUH.
SHE- THIS OTHER ONE COMES STORMING IN. SHE PUNCHES MY SHARON IN THE FACE, GRABS THE GUN AND THEN SHOOTS HER IN THE HEAD.
UH-HUH.

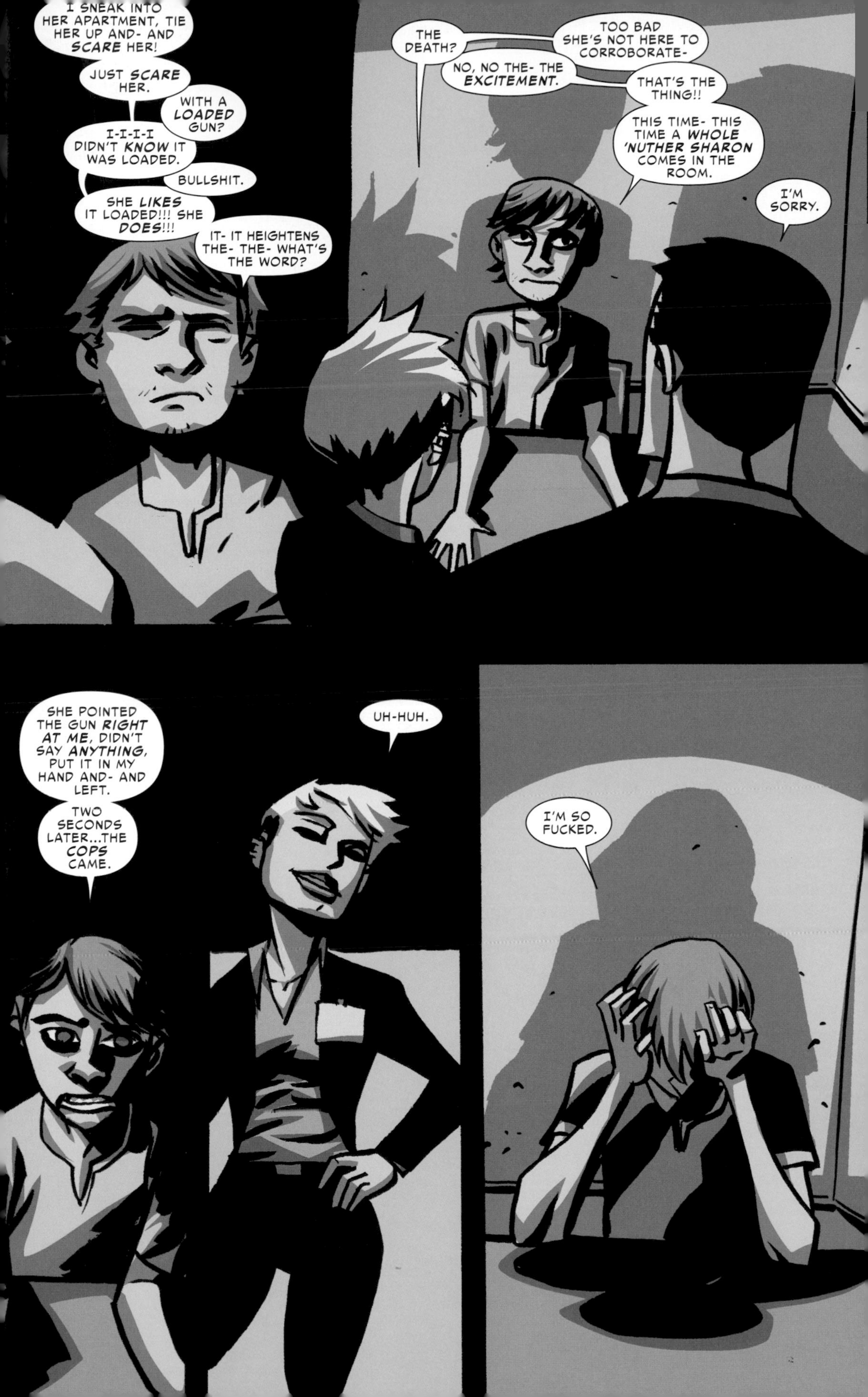
I SNEAK INTO HER APARTMENT, TIE HER UP AND- AND SCARE HER!
JUST SCARE HER.
WITH A LOADED GUN?
I-I-I-I DIDN'T KNOW IT WAS LOADED.
BULLSHIT.
SHE LIKES IT LOADED!!! SHE DOES!!!
IT- IT HEIGHTENS THE- THE- WHAT'S THE WORD?
THE DEATH?
TOO BAD SHE'S NOT HERE TO CORROBORATE-
NO, NO THE- THE EXCITEMENT.
THAT'S THE THING!!
THIS TIME- THIS TIME A WHOLE 'NUTHER SHARON COMES IN THE ROOM.
I'M SORRY.
SHE POINTED THE GUN RIGHT AT ME, DIDN'T SAY ANYTHING, PUT IT IN MY HAND AND- AND LEFT.
TWO SECONDS LATER...THE COPS CAME.
UH-HUH.
I'M SO FUCKED.

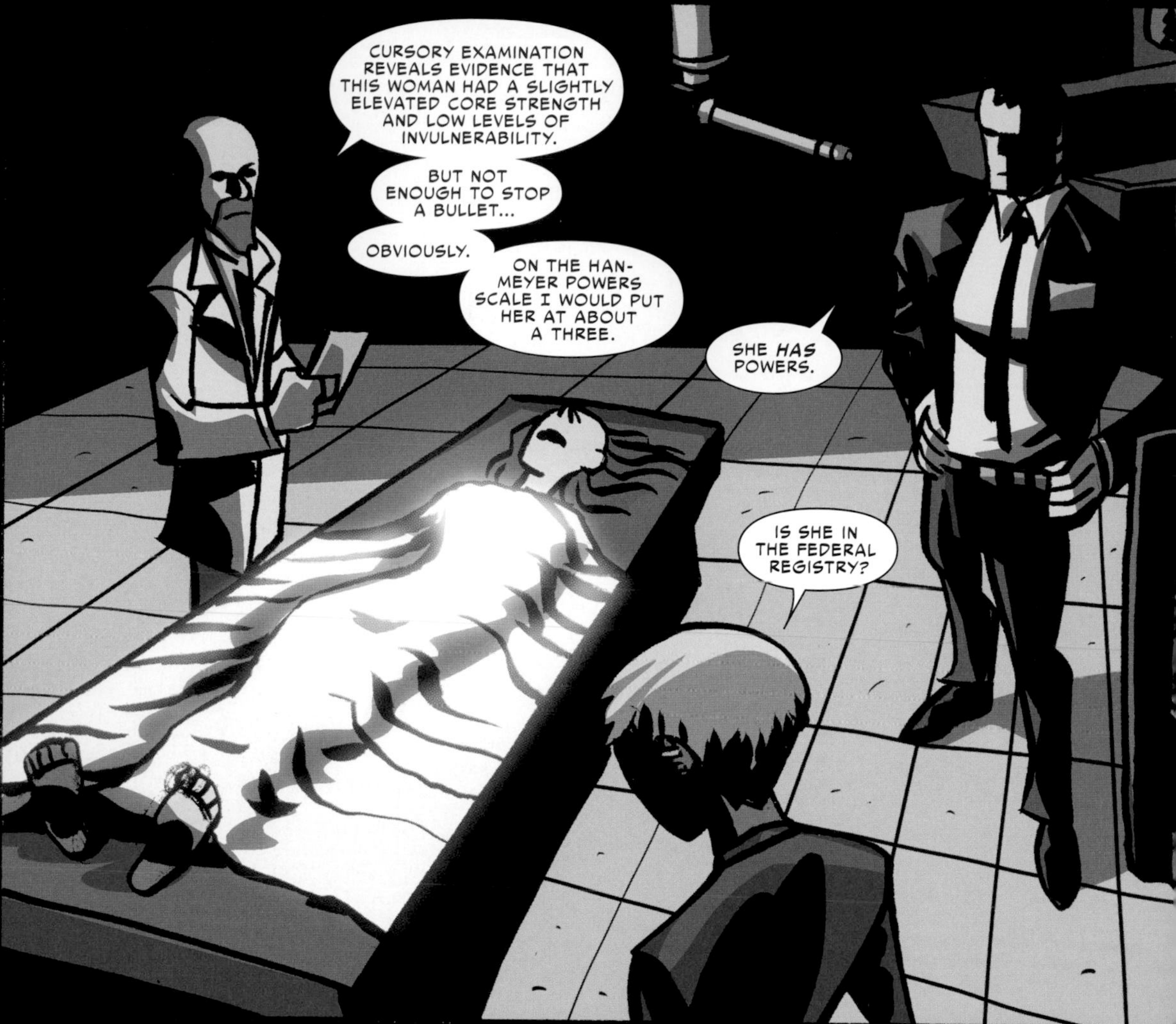
CURSORY EXAMINATION REVEALS EVIDENCE THAT THIS WOMAN HAD A SLIGHTLY ELEVATED CORE STRENGTH AND LOW LEVELS OF INVULNERABILITY.
BUT NOT ENOUGH TO STOP A BULLET...
OBVIOUSLY.
ON THE HAN-MEYER POWERS SCALE I WOULD PUT HER AT ABOUT A THREE.
SHE *HAS* POWERS.
IS SHE IN THE FEDERAL REGISTRY?

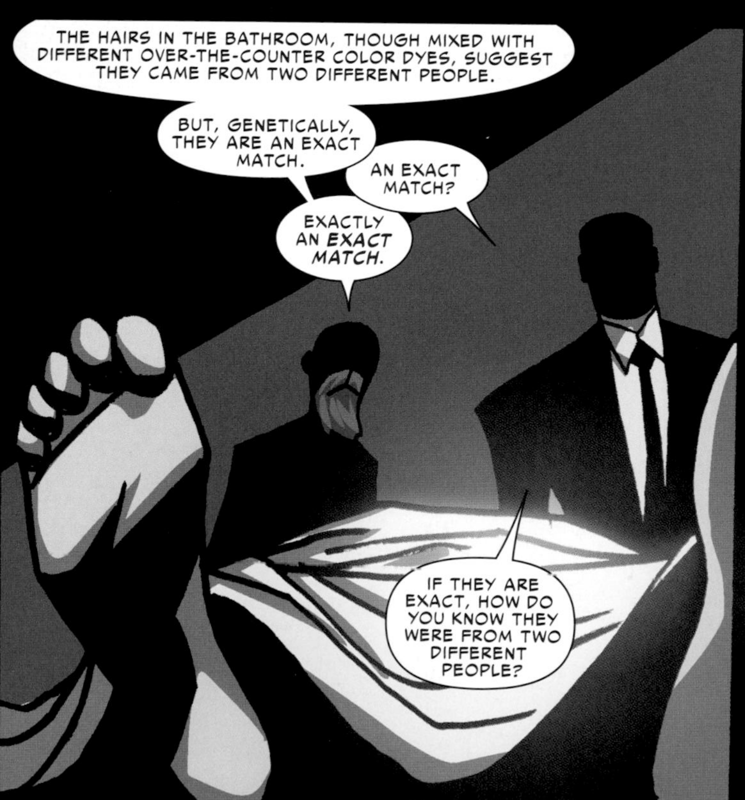
THE HAIRS IN THE BATHROOM, THOUGH MIXED WITH DIFFERENT OVER-THE-COUNTER COLOR DYES, SUGGEST THEY CAME FROM TWO DIFFERENT PEOPLE.
BUT, GENETICALLY, THEY ARE AN EXACT MATCH.
AN EXACT MATCH?
EXACTLY AN *EXACT MATCH*.
IF THEY ARE EXACT, HOW DO YOU KNOW THEY WERE FROM TWO DIFFERENT PEOPLE?

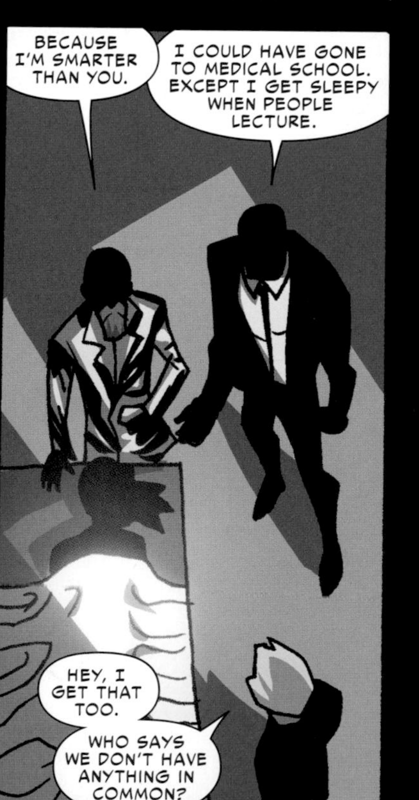
BECAUSE I'M SMARTER THAN YOU.
I COULD HAVE GONE TO MEDICAL SCHOOL. EXCEPT I GET SLEEPY WHEN PEOPLE LECTURE.
HEY, I GET THAT TOO.
WHO SAYS WE DON'T HAVE ANYTHING IN COMMON?

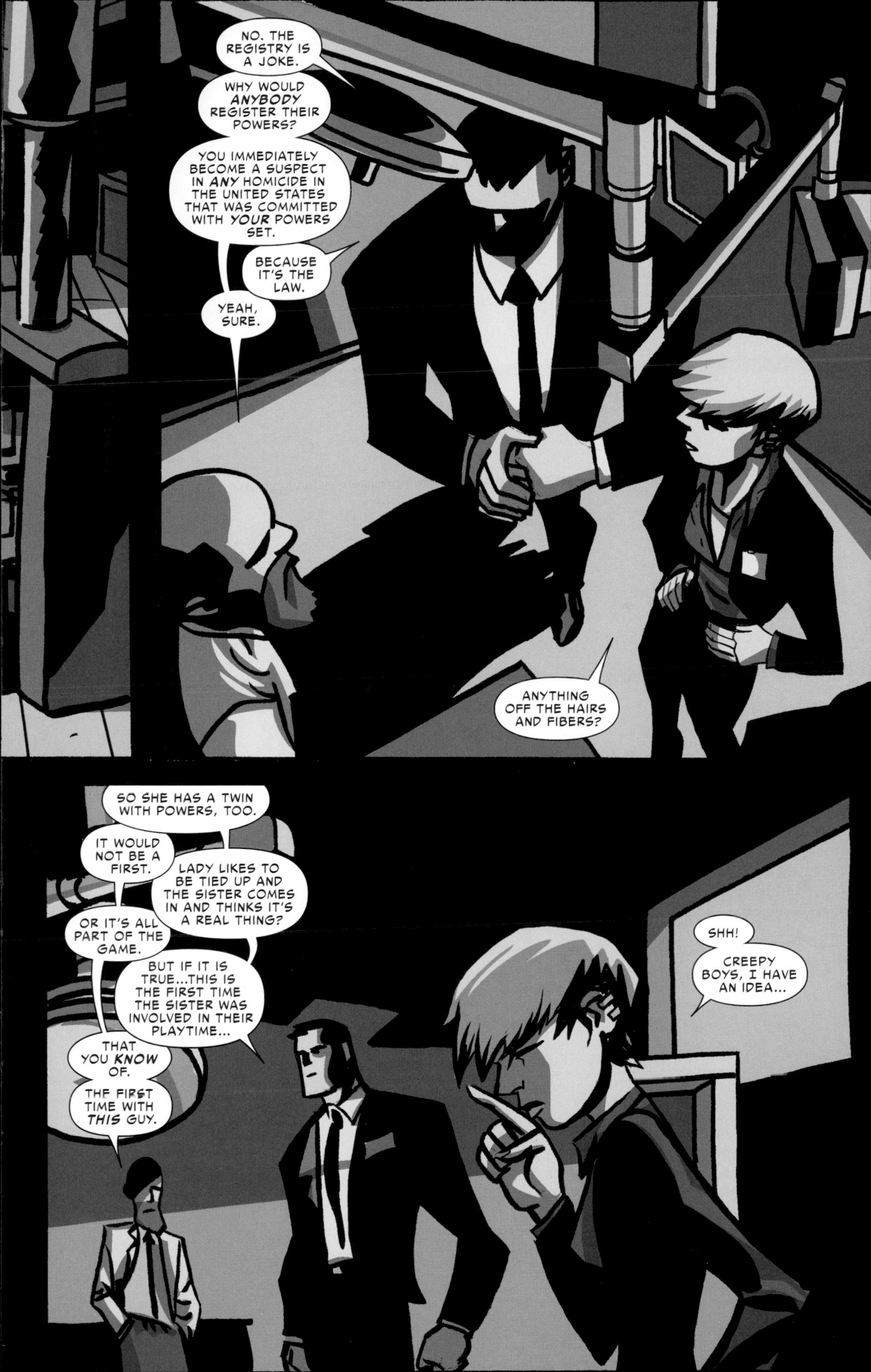
NO. THE REGISTRY IS A JOKE.
WHY WOULD ANYBODY REGISTER THEIR POWERS?
YOU IMMEDIATELY BECOME A SUSPECT IN ANY HOMICIDE IN THE UNITED STATES THAT WAS COMMITTED WITH YOUR POWERS SET.
BECAUSE IT'S THE LAW.
YEAH, SURE.
ANYTHING OFF THE HAIRS AND FIBERS?
SO SHE HAS A TWIN WITH POWERS, TOO.
IT WOULD NOT BE A FIRST.
LADY LIKES TO BE TIED UP AND THE SISTER COMES IN AND THINKS IT'S A REAL THING?
OR IT'S ALL PART OF THE GAME.
BUT IF IT IS TRUE...THIS IS THE FIRST TIME THE SISTER WAS INVOLVED IN THEIR PLAYTIME...
THAT YOU KNOW OF.
THE FIRST TIME WITH THIS GUY.
SHH!
CREEPY BOYS, I HAVE AN IDEA...

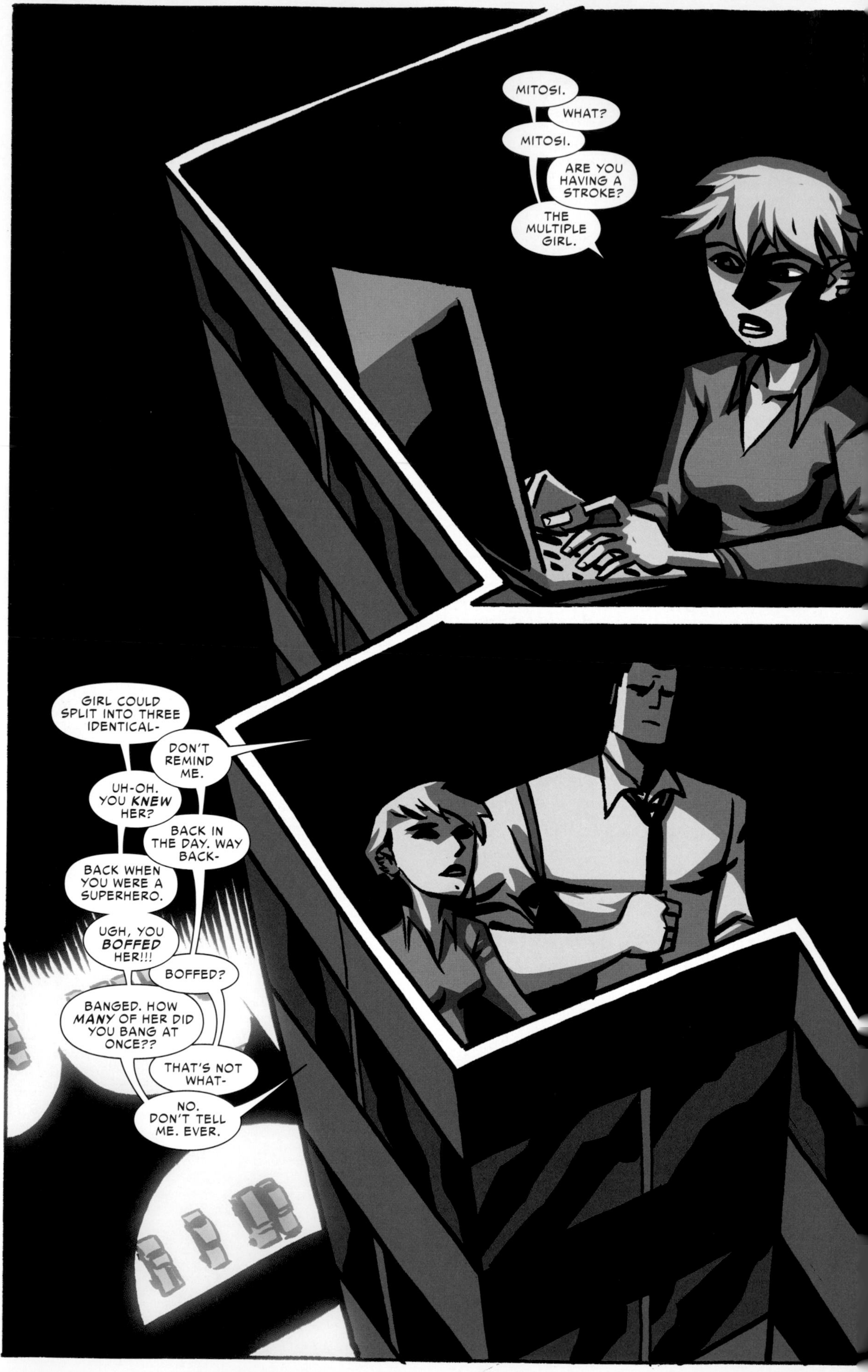

MITOSI.
WHAT?
MITOSI.
ARE YOU HAVING A STROKE?
THE MULTIPLE GIRL.
GIRL COULD SPLIT INTO THREE IDENTICAL-
DON'T REMIND ME.
UH-OH. YOU *KNEW* HER?
BACK IN THE DAY. WAY BACK-
BACK WHEN YOU WERE A SUPERHERO.
UGH, YOU *BOFFED* HER!!!
BOFFED?
BANGED. HOW *MANY* OF HER DID YOU BANG AT ONCE??
THAT'S NOT WHAT-
NO. DON'T TELL ME. EVER.

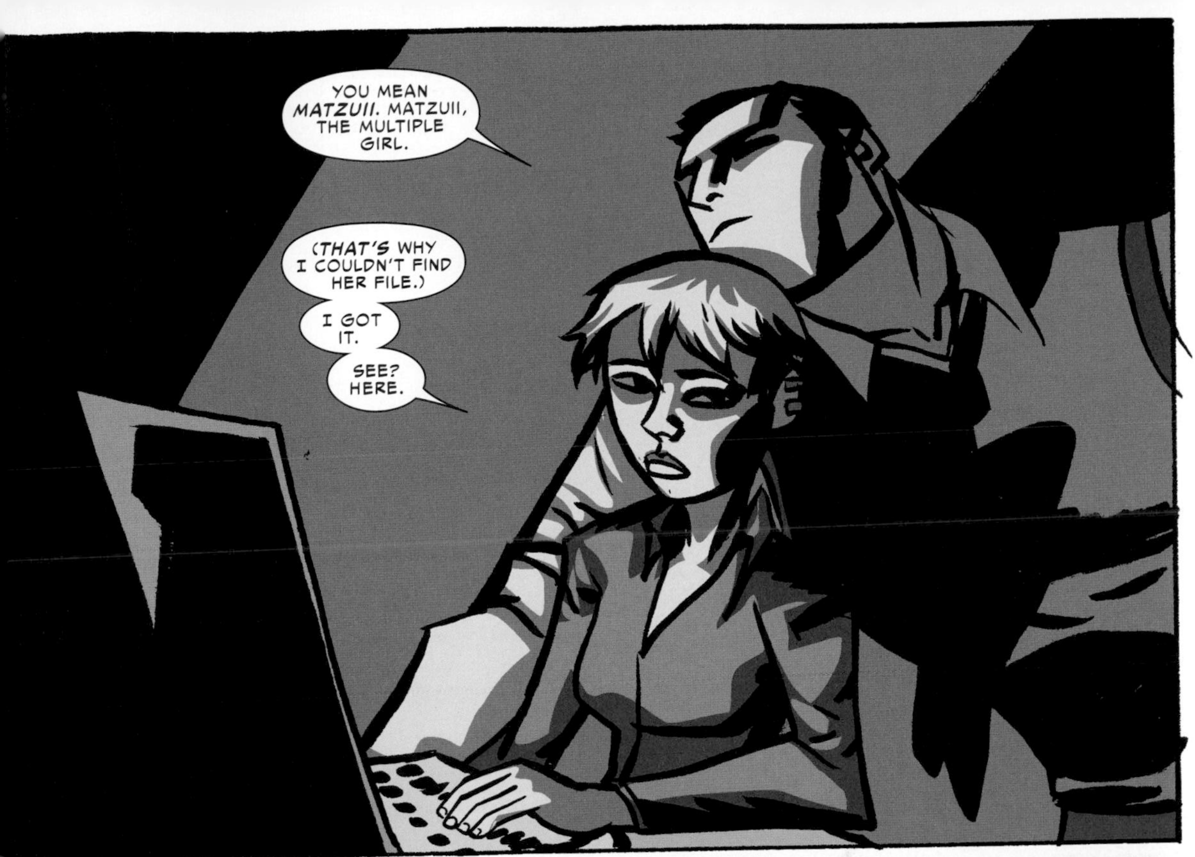
YOU MEAN *MATZUII*. MATZUII, THE MULTIPLE GIRL.
(*THAT'S* WHY I COULDN'T FIND HER FILE.)
I GOT IT.
SEE? HERE.

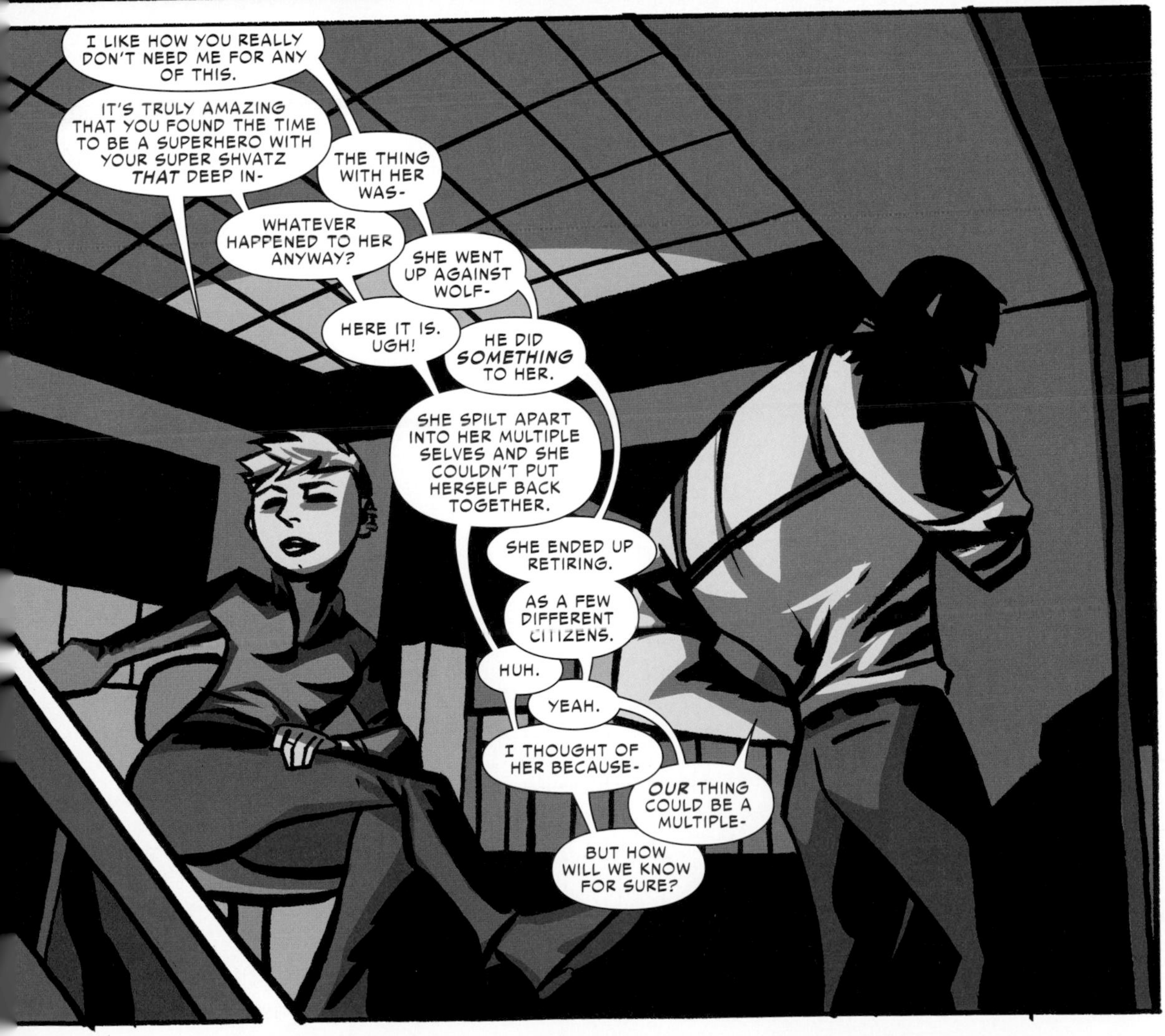
I LIKE HOW YOU REALLY DON'T NEED ME FOR ANY OF THIS.
IT'S TRULY AMAZING THAT YOU FOUND THE TIME TO BE A SUPERHERO WITH YOUR SUPER SHVATZ *THAT* DEEP IN-
THE THING WITH HER WAS-
WHATEVER HAPPENED TO HER ANYWAY?
SHE WENT UP AGAINST WOLF-
HERE IT IS. UGH!
HE DID *SOMETHING* TO HER.
SHE SPILT APART INTO HER MULTIPLE SELVES AND SHE COULDN'T PUT HERSELF BACK TOGETHER.
SHE ENDED UP RETIRING.
AS A FEW DIFFERENT CITIZENS.
HUH.
YEAH.
I THOUGHT OF HER BECAUSE-
OUR THING COULD BE A MULTIPLE-
BUT HOW WILL WE KNOW FOR SURE?

"MY GUESS? WE'RE GOING TO GET A CALL.

"ANOTHER BODY.

"EXCEPT THIS ONE MIGHT BE WORSE. MORE VIOLENT.

"ESCALATION.

"SERIAL KILLER 101."

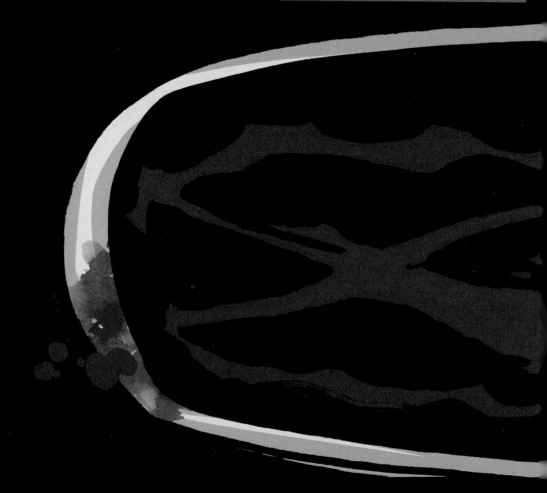

"MY GUESS? WE'RE GOING TO

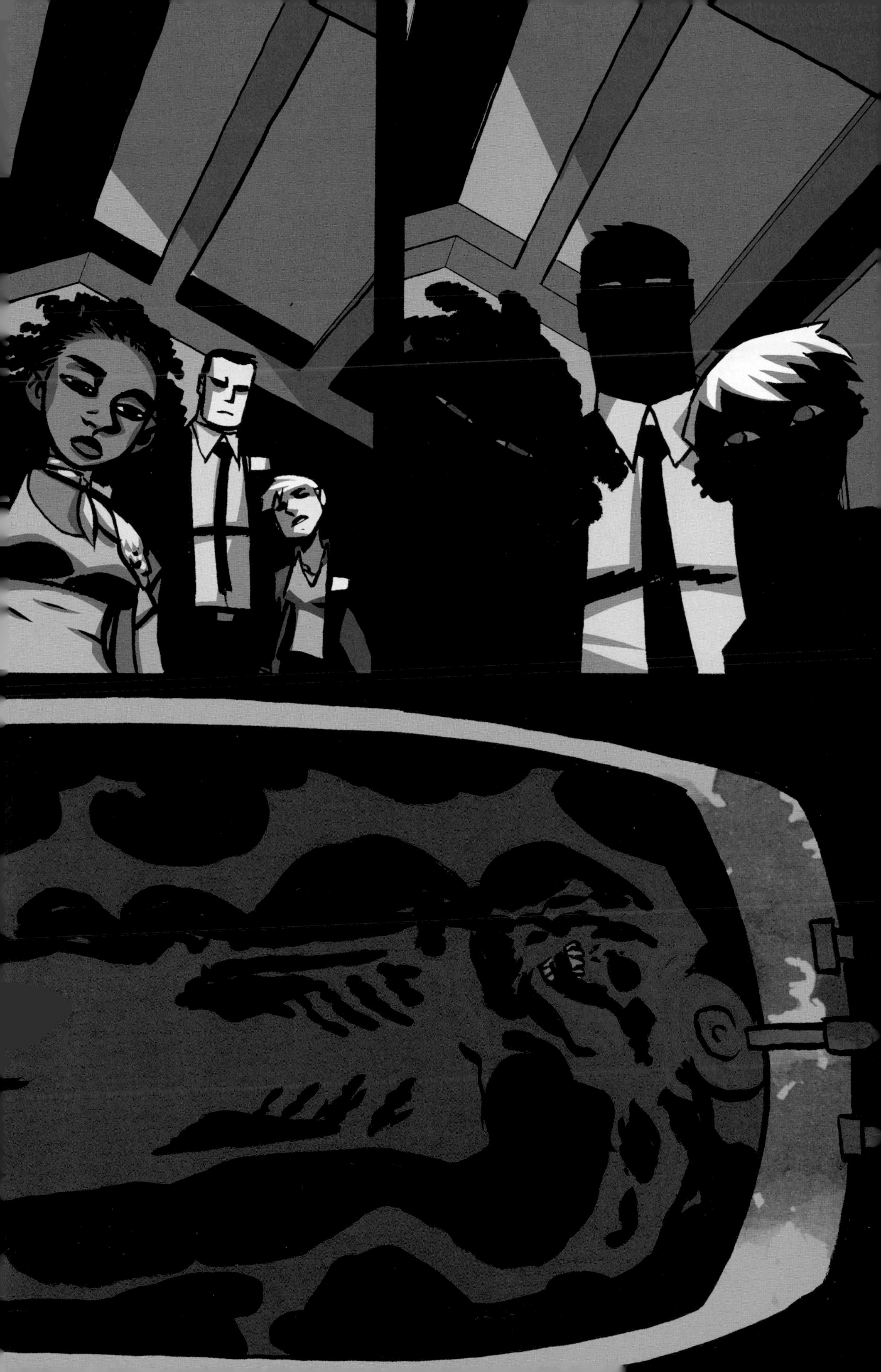

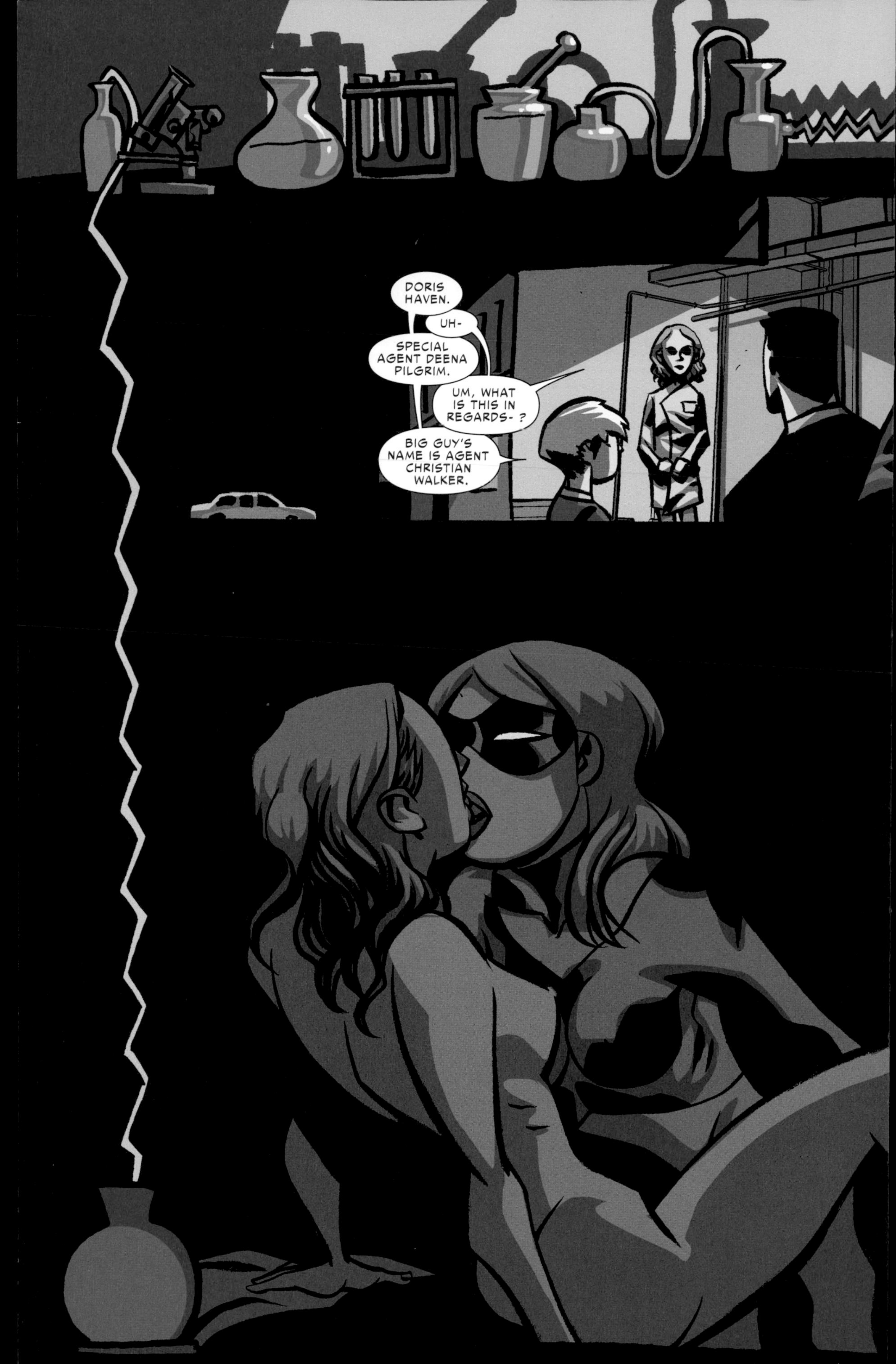
DORIS HAVEN.
UH-
SPECIAL AGENT DEENA PILGRIM.
UM, WHAT IS THIS IN REGARDS- ?
BIG GUY'S NAME IS AGENT CHRISTIAN WALKER.

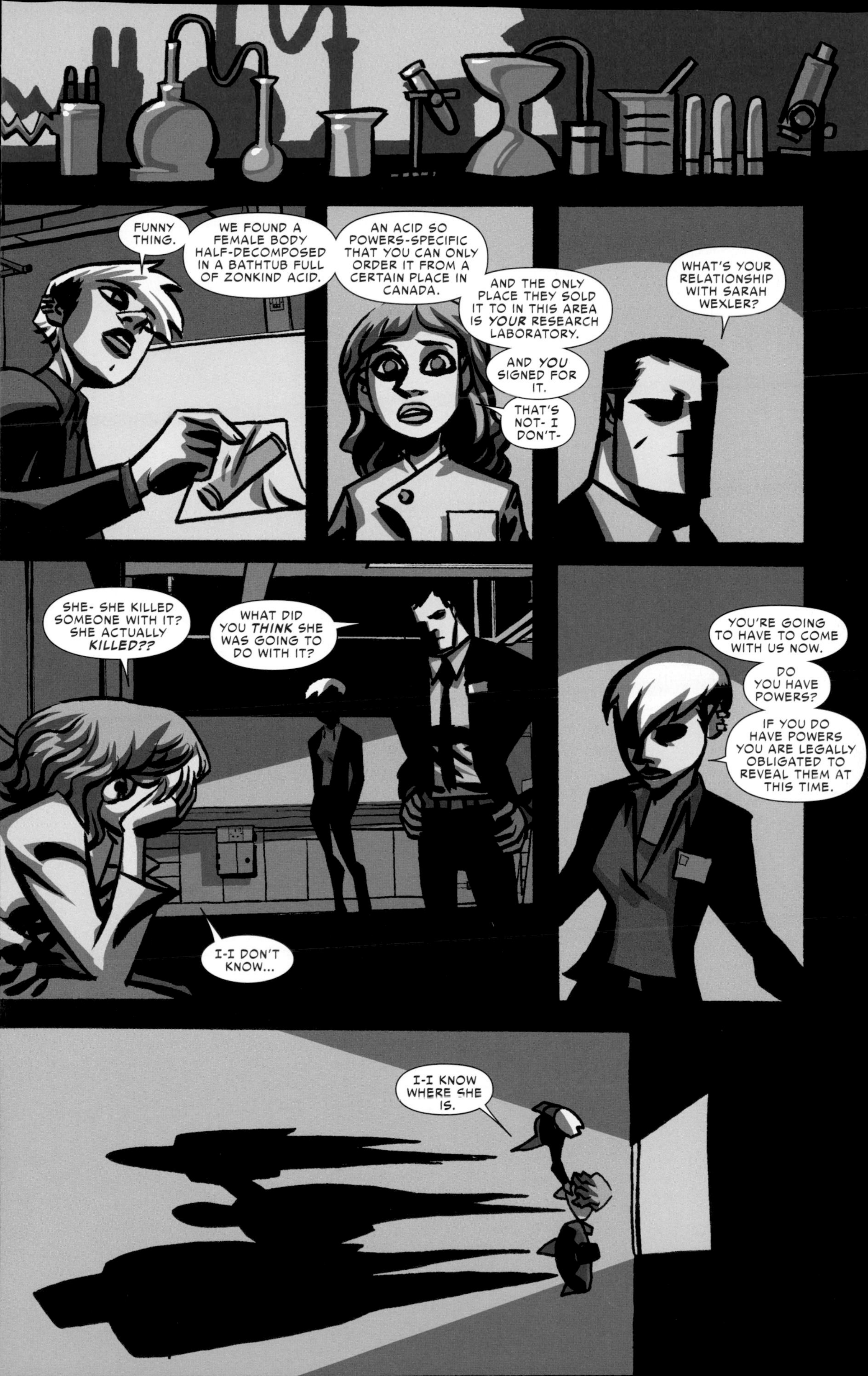
FUNNY THING.
WE FOUND A FEMALE BODY HALF-DECOMPOSED IN A BATHTUB FULL OF ZONKIND ACID.
AN ACID SO POWERS-SPECIFIC THAT YOU CAN ONLY ORDER IT FROM A CERTAIN PLACE IN CANADA.
AND THE ONLY PLACE THEY SOLD IT TO IN THIS AREA IS *YOUR* RESEARCH LABORATORY.
AND *YOU* SIGNED FOR IT.
THAT'S NOT- I DON'T-
WHAT'S YOUR RELATIONSHIP WITH SARAH WEXLER?
SHE- SHE KILLED SOMEONE WITH IT? SHE ACTUALLY *KILLED??*
WHAT DID YOU *THINK* SHE WAS GOING TO DO WITH IT?
I-I DON'T KNOW...
YOU'RE GOING TO HAVE TO COME WITH US NOW.
DO YOU HAVE POWERS?
IF YOU DO HAVE POWERS YOU ARE LEGALLY OBLIGATED TO REVEAL THEM AT THIS TIME.
I-I KNOW WHERE SHE IS.

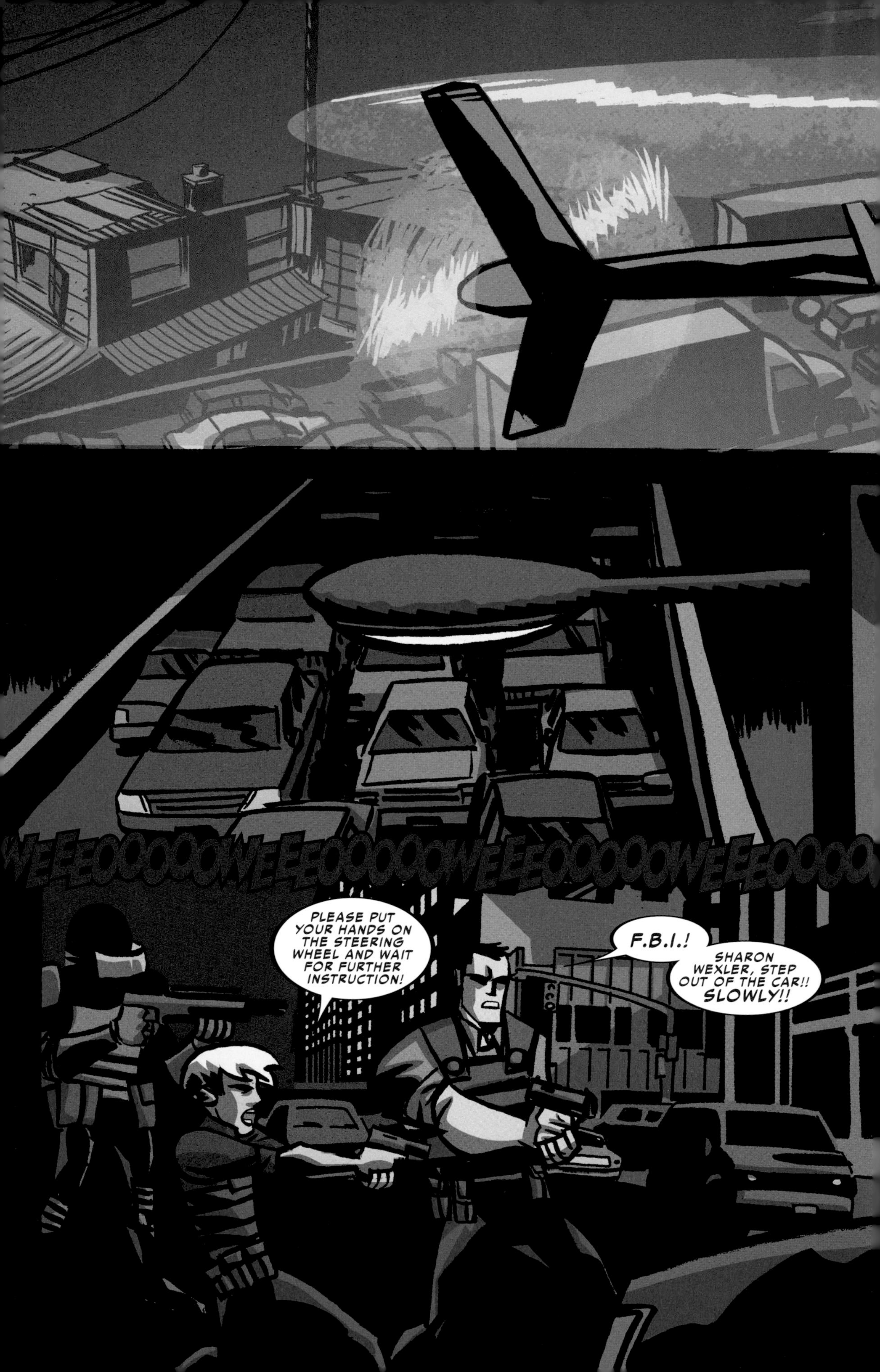
WEEEOOOOOOWEEEOOOOOOOWEEEOOOOOOOWEEEOOOOO
PLEASE PUT YOUR HANDS ON THE STEERING WHEEL AND WAIT FOR FURTHER INSTRUCTION!
F.B.I.!
SHARON WEXLER, STEP OUT OF THE CAR!! SLOWLY!!

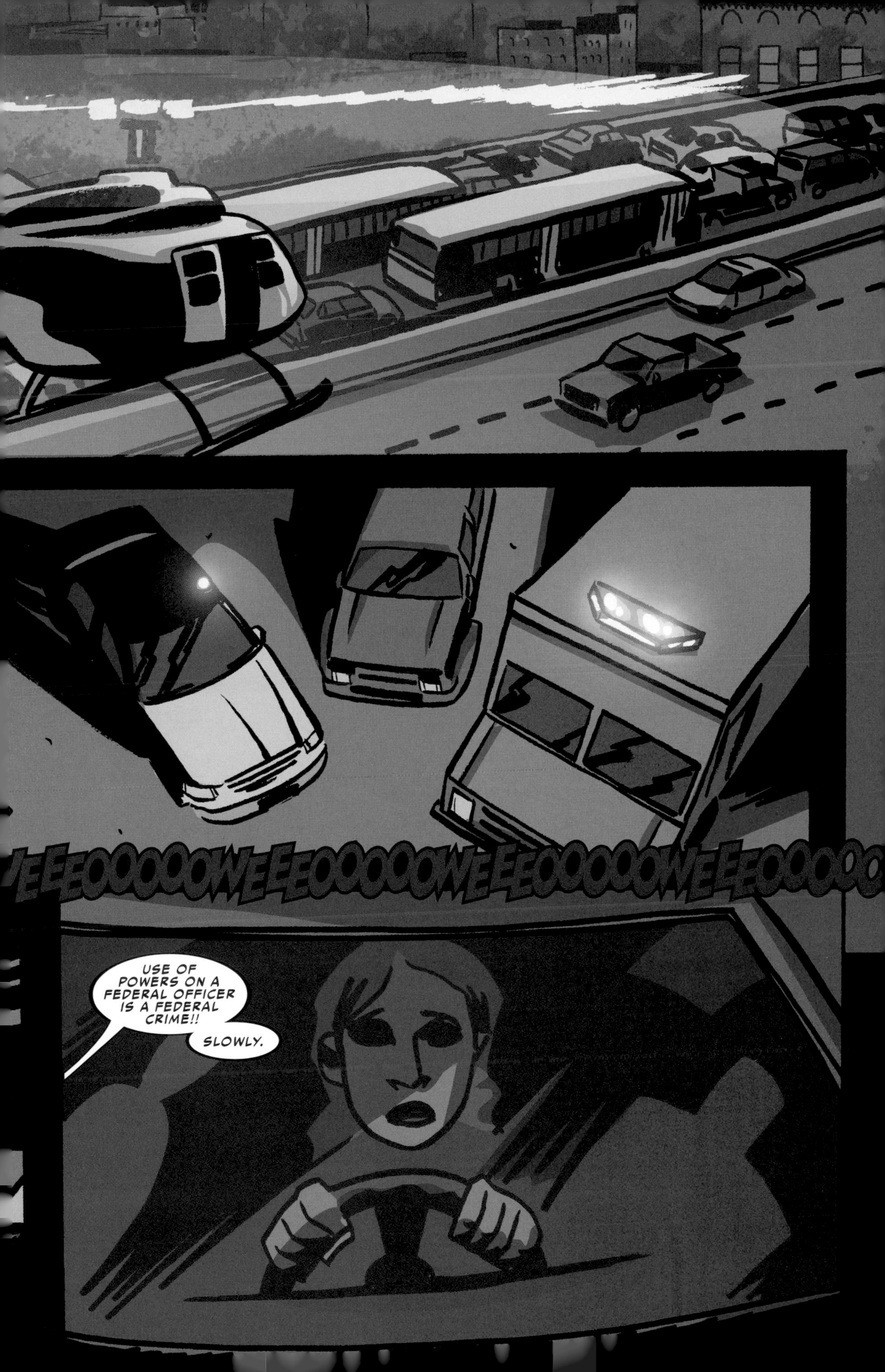
WEEEOOOOOOWEEEOOOOOOWEEEOOOOOOWEEEOOOOOO
USE OF POWERS ON A FEDERAL OFFICER IS A FEDERAL CRIME!!
SLOWLY.

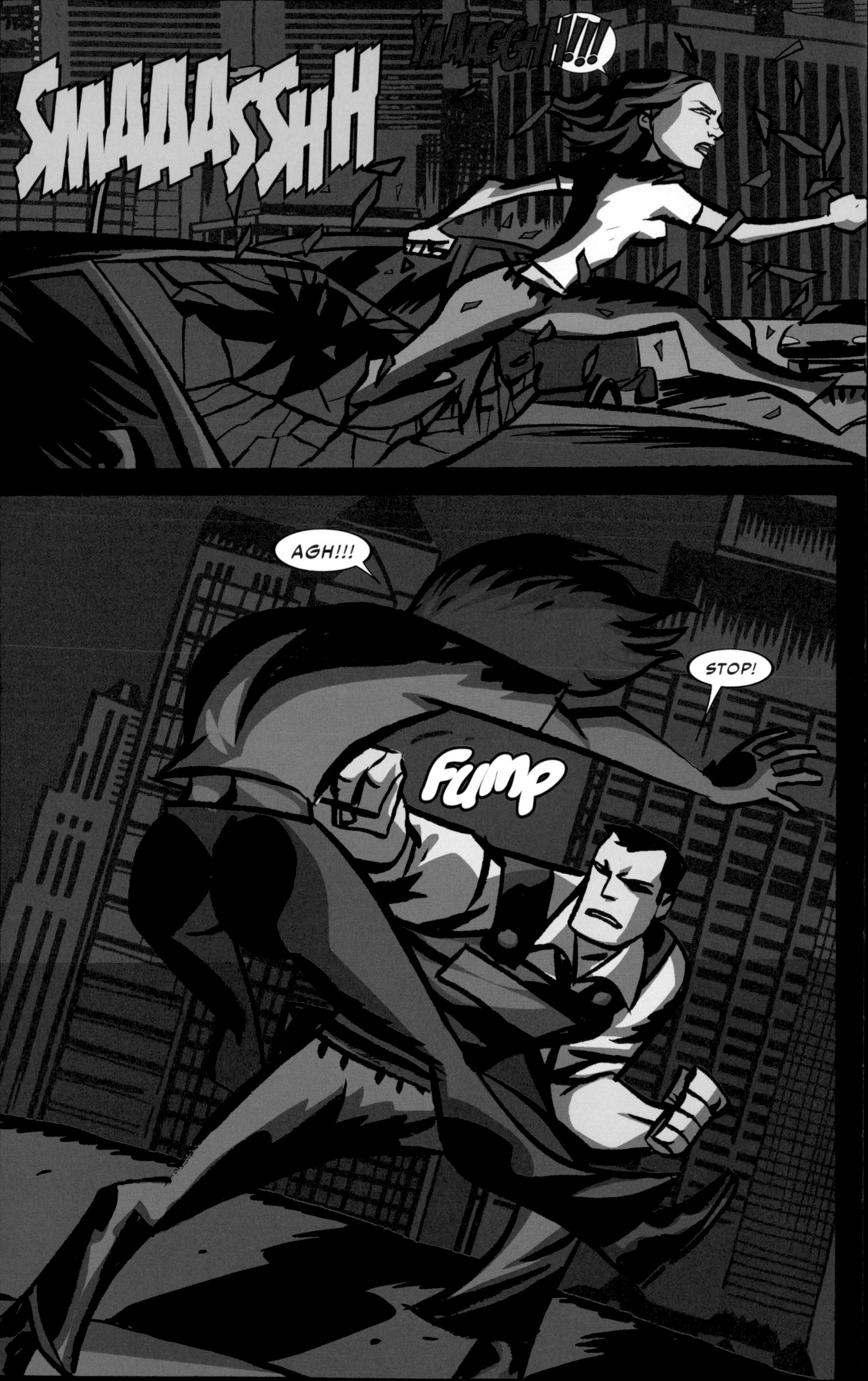

SMAAASSHH
YAAAGGHH!!!
AGH!!!
STOP!
FUMP

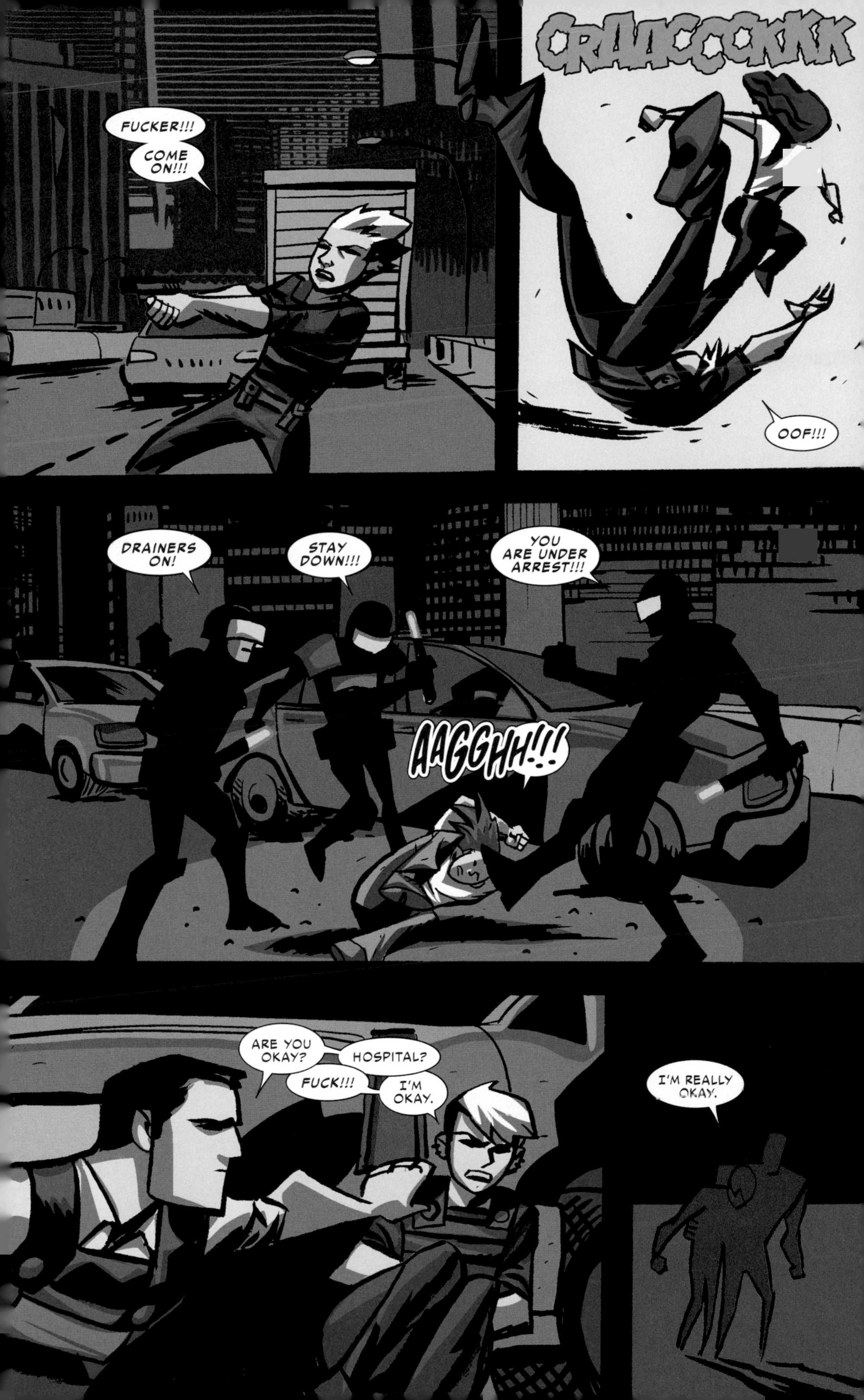
FUCKER!!!
COME ON!!!
CRAAACCCKKK
OOF!!!
DRAINERS ON!
STAY DOWN!!!
YOU ARE UNDER ARREST!!!
AAGGHH!!!
ARE YOU OKAY?
HOSPITAL?
FUCK!!!
I'M OKAY.
I'M REALLY OKAY.

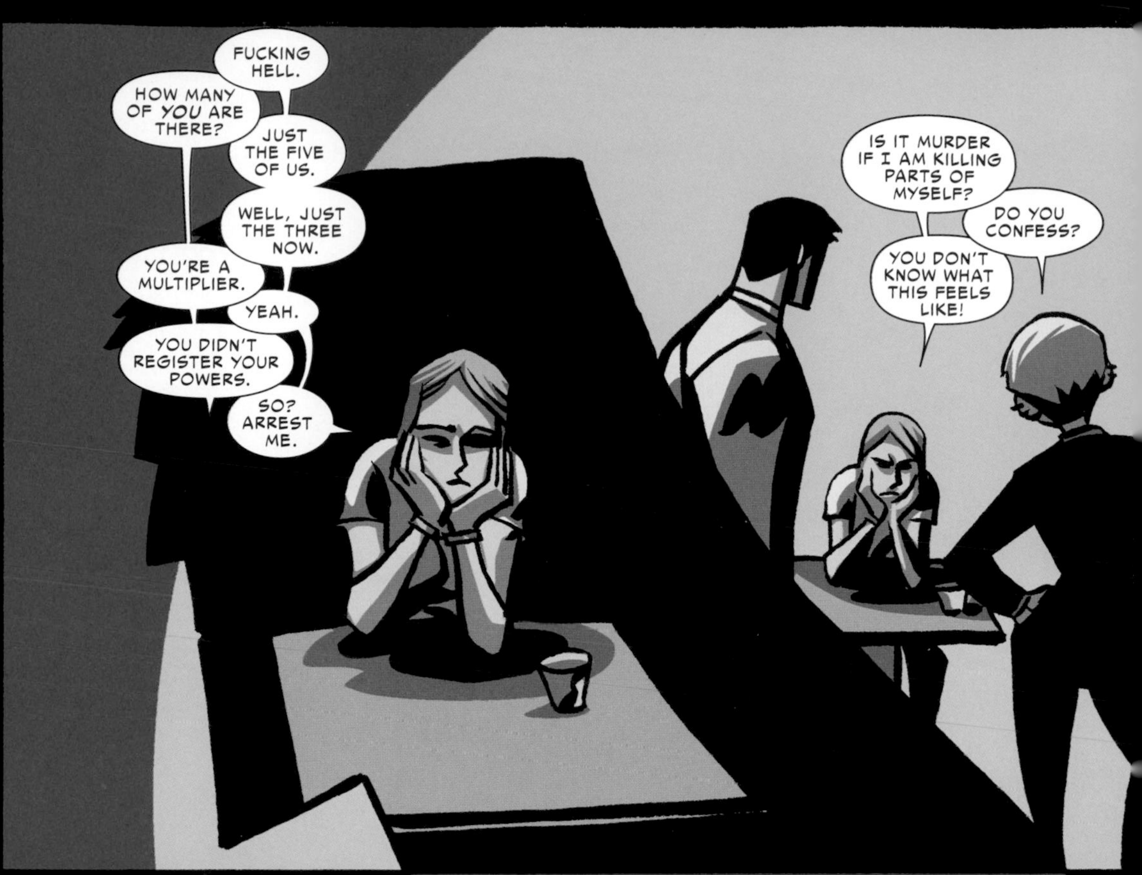
FUCKING HELL.
HOW MANY OF YOU ARE THERE?
JUST THE FIVE OF US.
WELL, JUST THE THREE NOW.
YOU'RE A MULTIPLIER.
YEAH.
YOU DIDN'T REGISTER YOUR POWERS.
SO? ARREST ME.
IS IT MURDER IF I AM KILLING PARTS OF MYSELF?
DO YOU CONFESS?
YOU DON'T KNOW WHAT THIS FEELS LIKE!

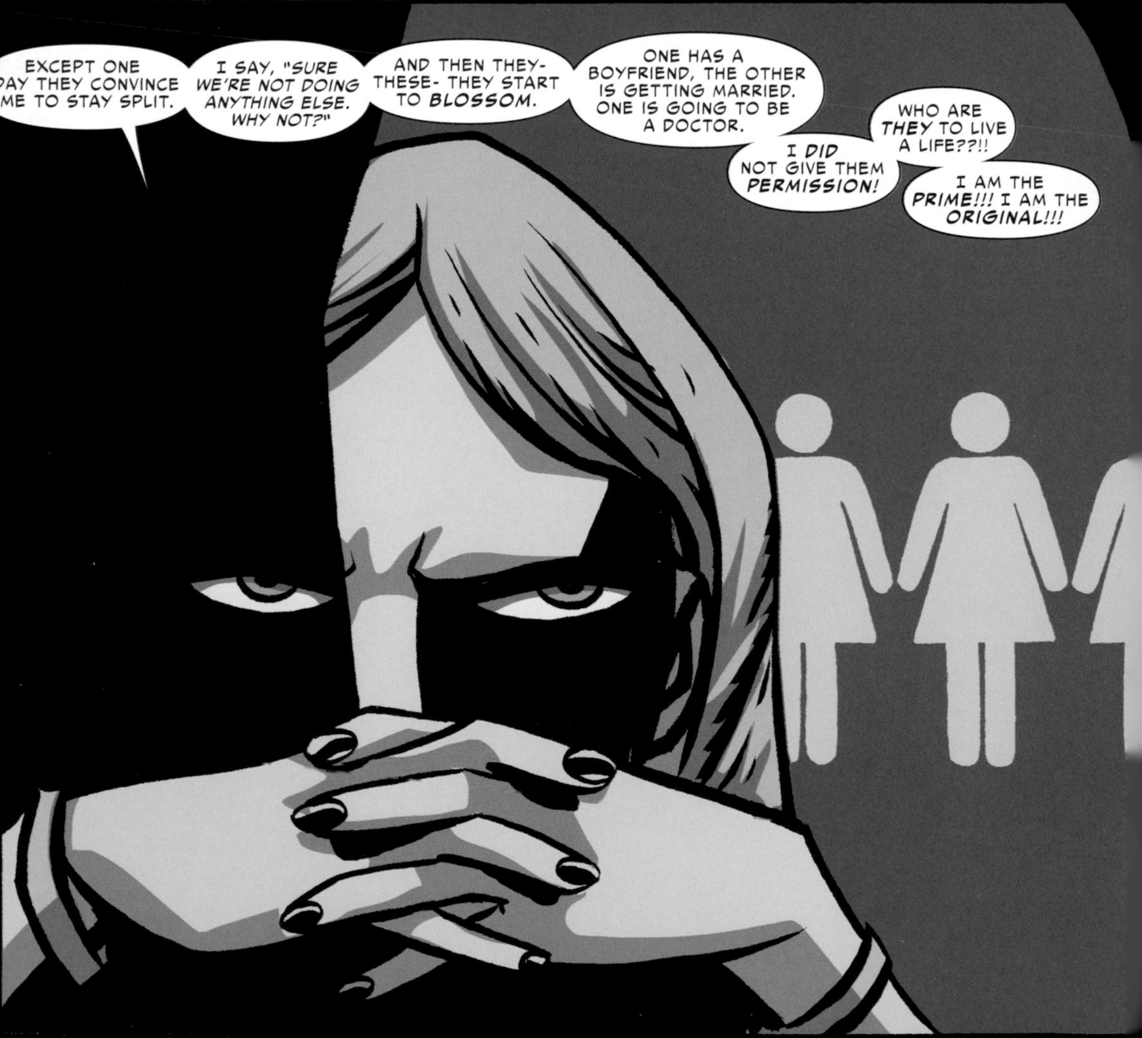
EXCEPT ONE DAY THEY CONVINCE ME TO STAY SPLIT.
I SAY, "SURE WE'RE NOT DOING ANYTHING ELSE. WHY NOT?"
AND THEN THEY- THESE- THEY START TO BLOSSOM.
ONE HAS A BOYFRIEND, THE OTHER IS GETTING MARRIED. ONE IS GOING TO BE A DOCTOR.
I DID NOT GIVE THEM PERMISSION!
WHO ARE THEY TO LIVE A LIFE??!!
I AM THE PRIME!!! I AM THE ORIGINAL!!!

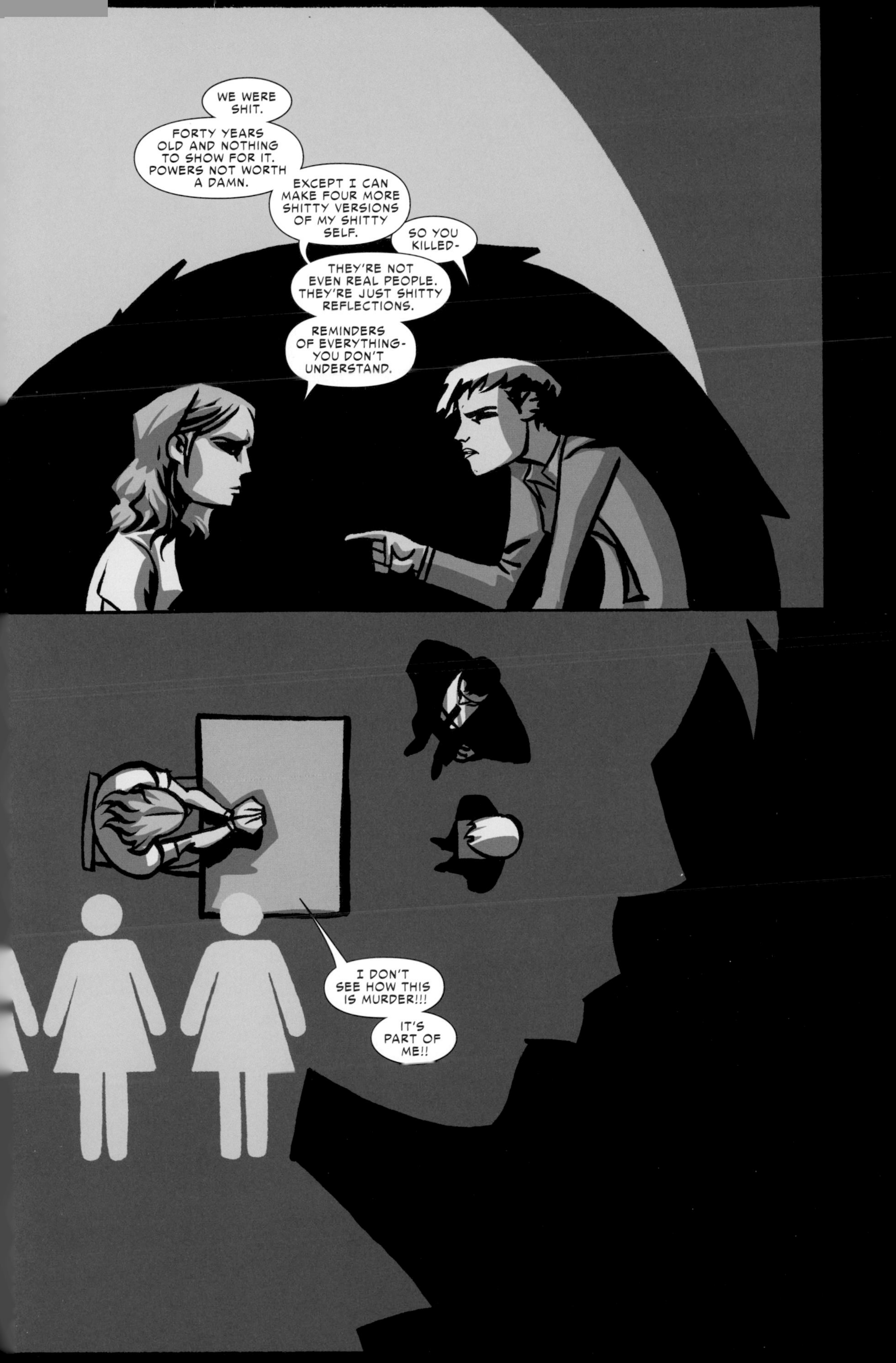
WE WERE SHIT.
FORTY YEARS OLD AND NOTHING TO SHOW FOR IT. POWERS NOT WORTH A DAMN.
EXCEPT I CAN MAKE FOUR MORE SHITTY VERSIONS OF MY SHITTY SELF.
SO YOU KILLED-
THEY'RE NOT EVEN REAL PEOPLE. THEY'RE JUST SHITTY REFLECTIONS.
REMINDERS OF EVERYTHING- YOU DON'T UNDERSTAND.
I DON'T SEE HOW THIS IS MURDER!!!
IT'S PART OF ME!!

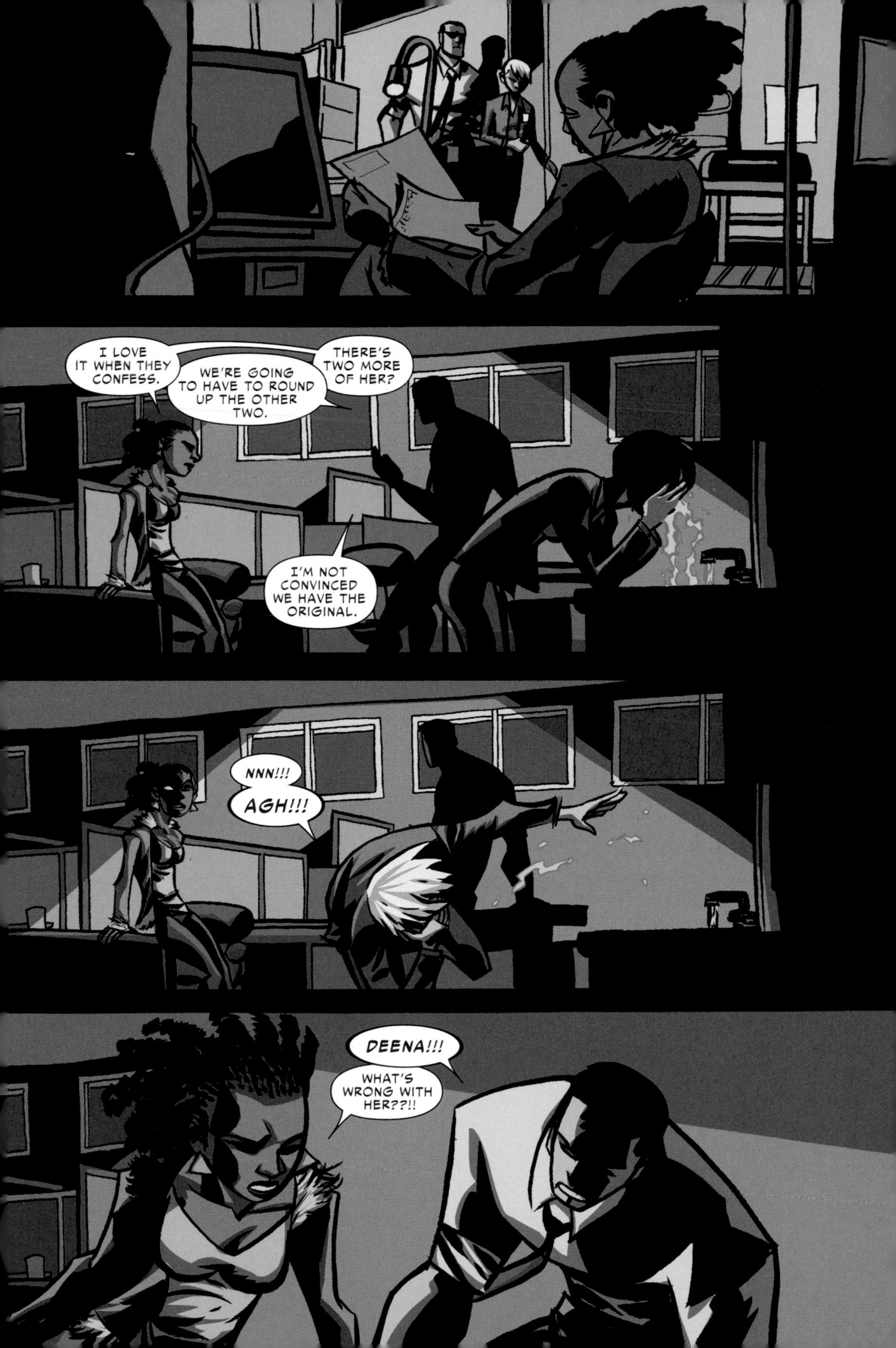
I LOVE IT WHEN THEY CONFESS.
WE'RE GOING TO HAVE TO ROUND UP THE OTHER TWO.
THERE'S TWO MORE OF HER?
I'M NOT CONVINCED WE HAVE THE ORIGINAL.
NNN!!!
AGH!!!
DEENA!!!
WHAT'S WRONG WITH HER??!!

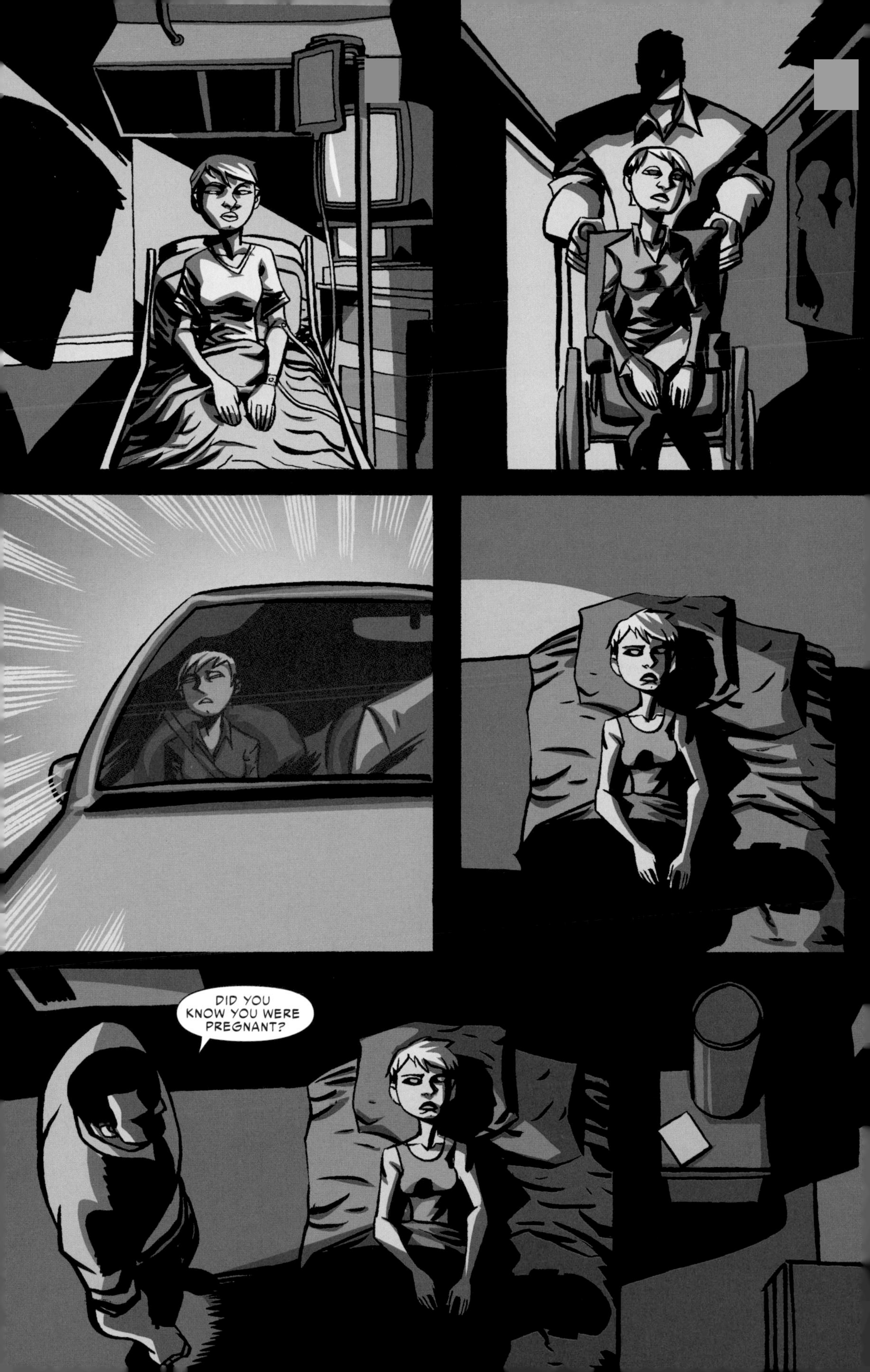
DID YOU KNOW YOU WERE PREGNANT?

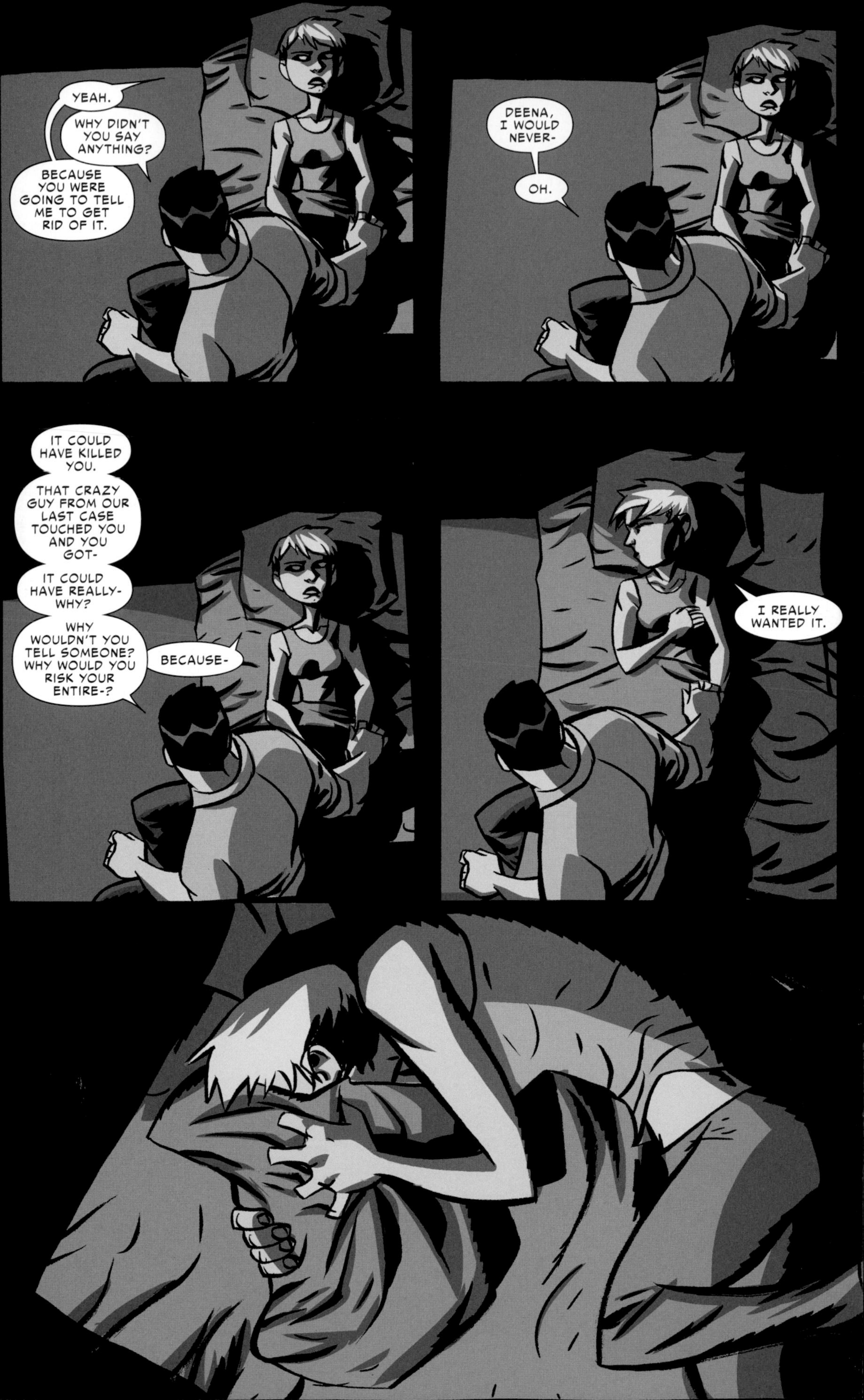
YEAH.
WHY DIDN'T YOU SAY ANYTHING?
BECAUSE YOU WERE GOING TO TELL ME TO GET RID OF IT.
DEENA, I WOULD NEVER-
OH.
IT COULD HAVE KILLED YOU.
THAT CRAZY GUY FROM OUR LAST CASE TOUCHED YOU AND YOU GOT-
IT COULD HAVE REALLY- WHY?
WHY WOULDN'T YOU TELL SOMEONE? WHY WOULD YOU RISK YOUR ENTIRE-?
BECAUSE-
I REALLY WANTED IT.

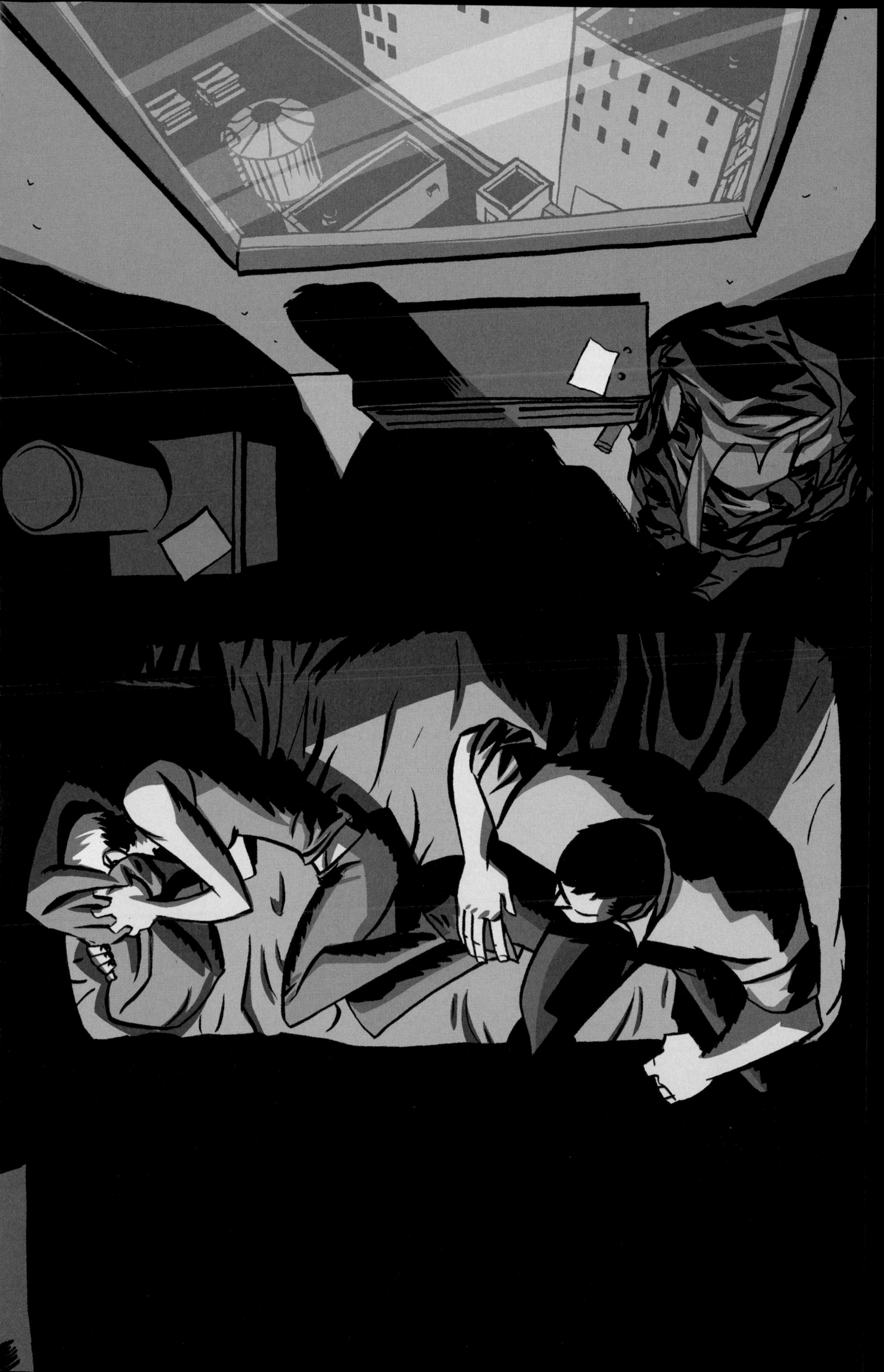

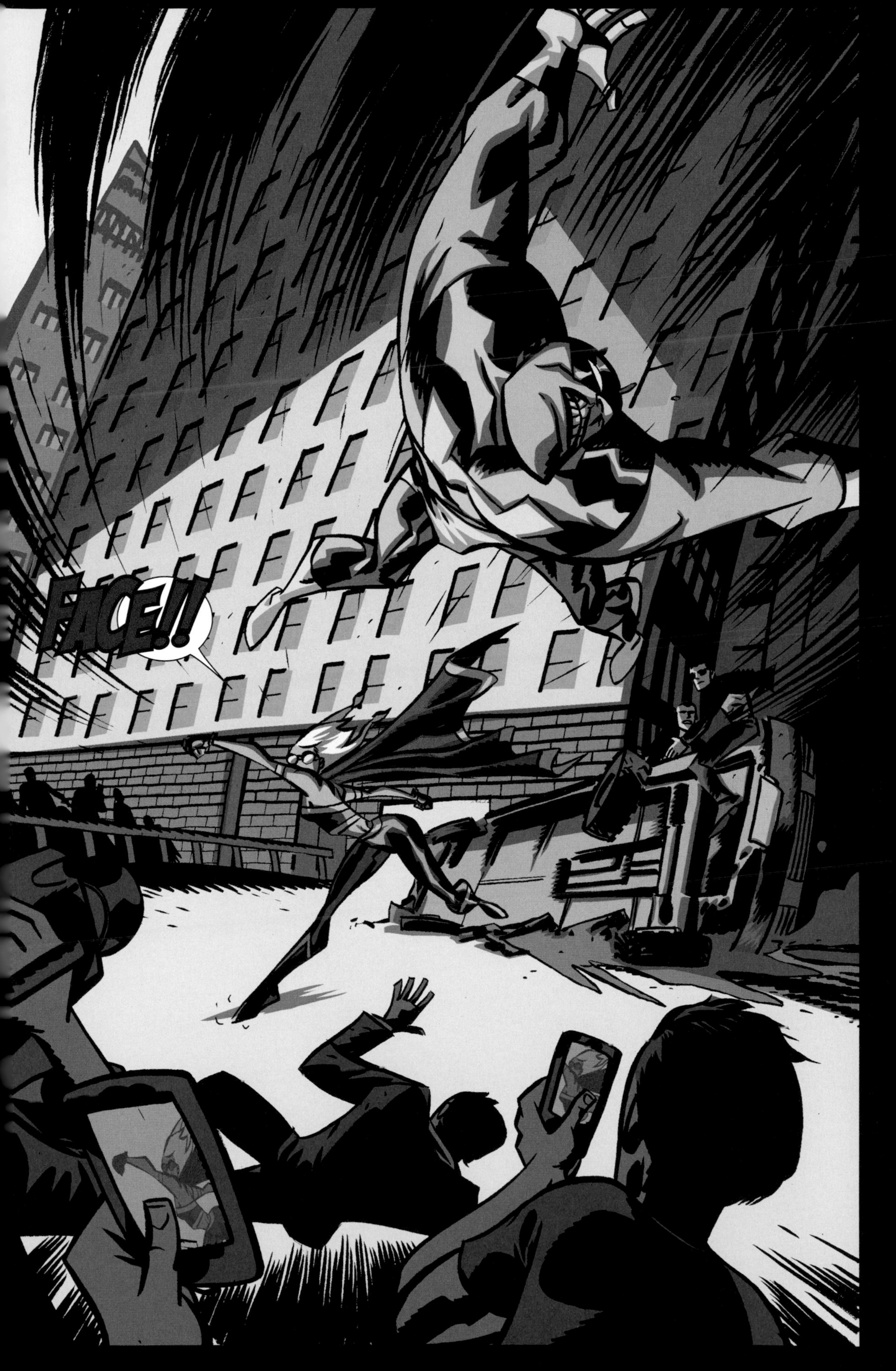
FACE!!

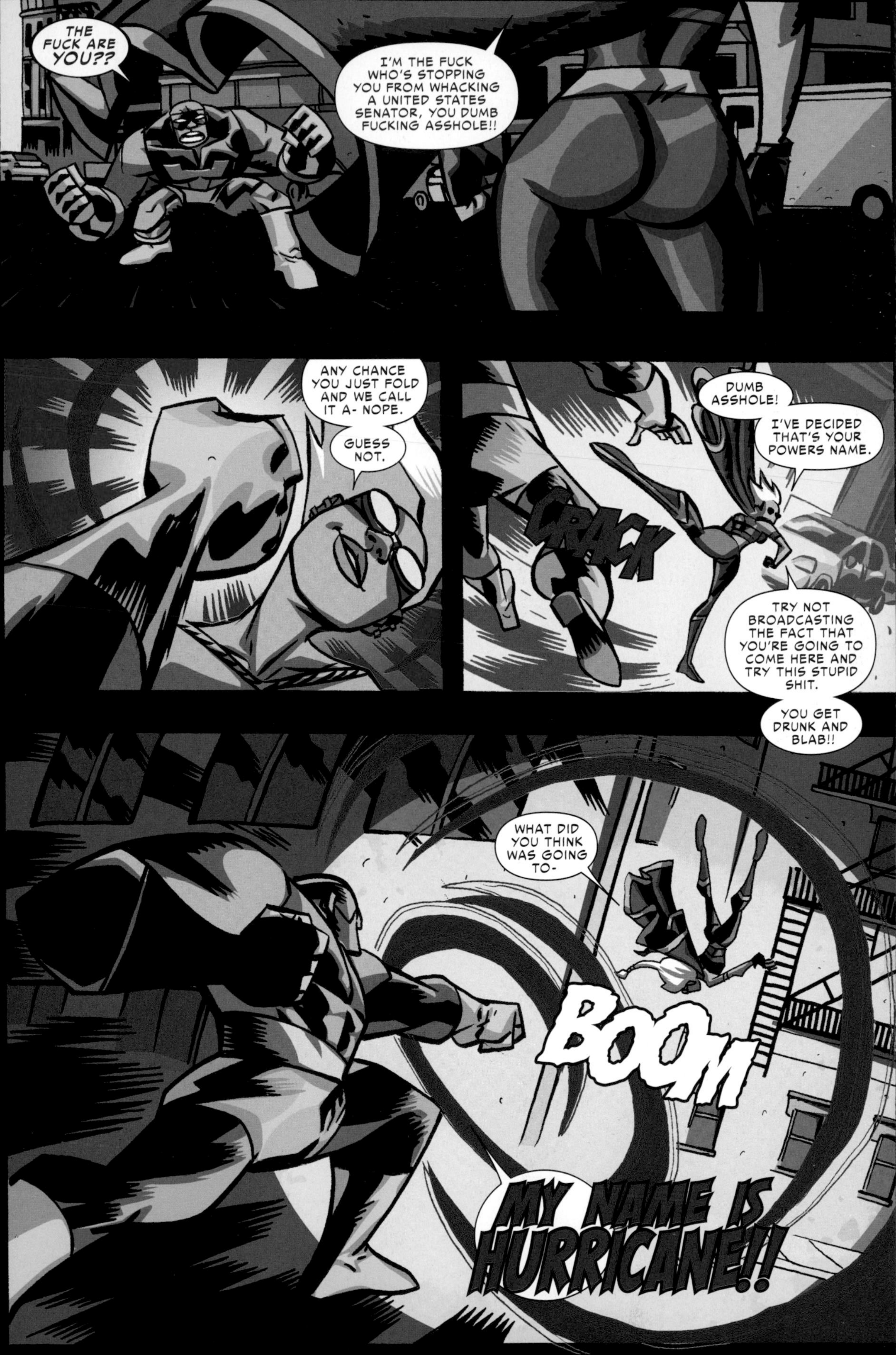
THE FUCK ARE YOU??
I'M THE FUCK WHO'S STOPPING YOU FROM WHACKING A UNITED STATES SENATOR, YOU DUMB FUCKING ASSHOLE!!
ANY CHANCE YOU JUST FOLD AND WE CALL IT A- NOPE.
GUESS NOT.
DUMB ASSHOLE!
I'VE DECIDED THAT'S YOUR POWERS NAME.
CRACK
TRY NOT BROADCASTING THE FACT THAT YOU'RE GOING TO COME HERE AND TRY THIS STUPID SHIT.
YOU GET DRUNK AND BLAB!!
WHAT DID YOU THINK WAS GOING TO-
BOOM
MY NAME IS HURRICANE!!

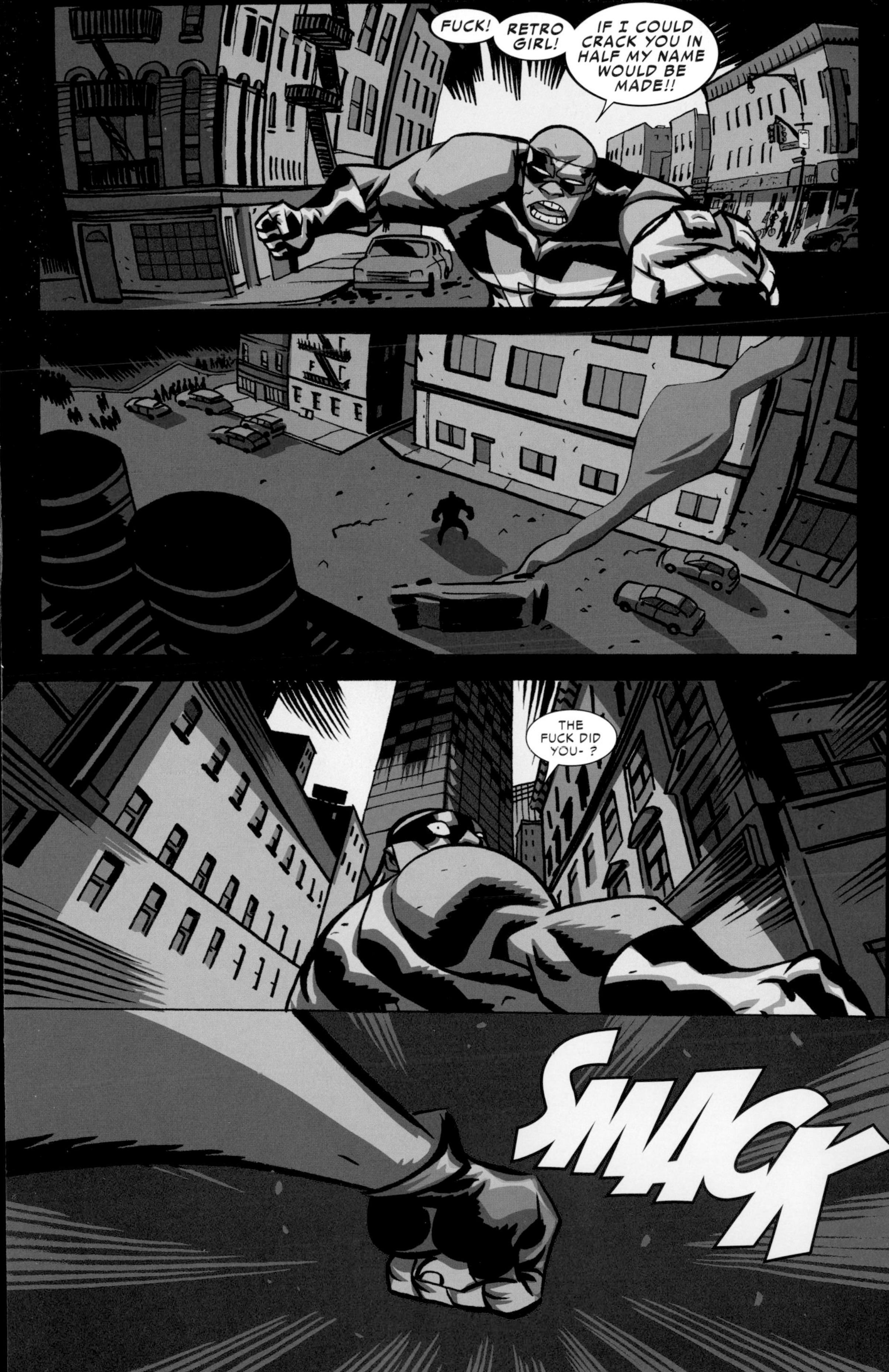
FUCK!
RETRO GIRL!
IF I COULD CRACK YOU IN HALF MY NAME WOULD BE MADE!!
THE FUCK DID YOU- ?
SMACK

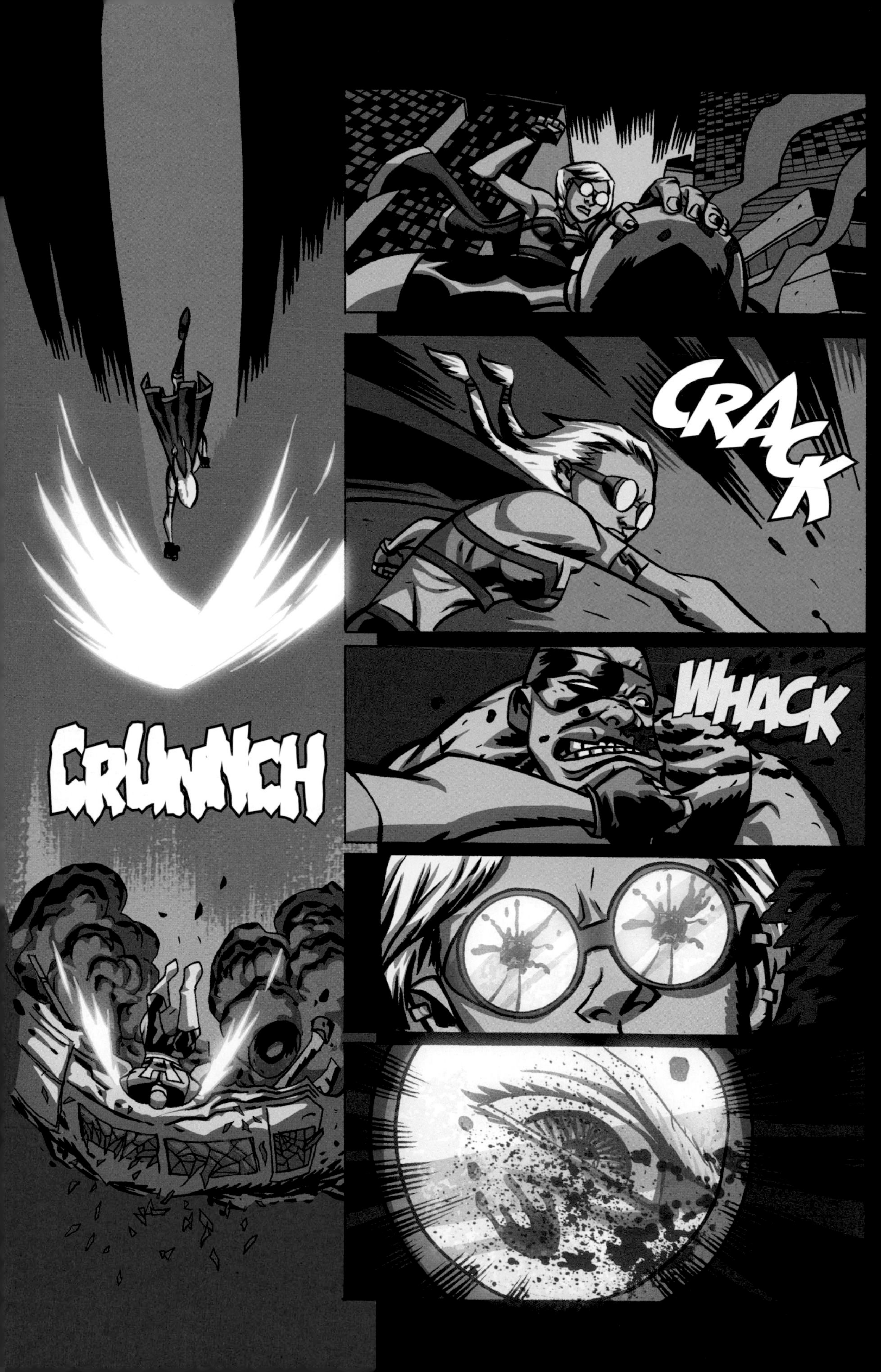
CRACK
WHACK
CRUNNCH

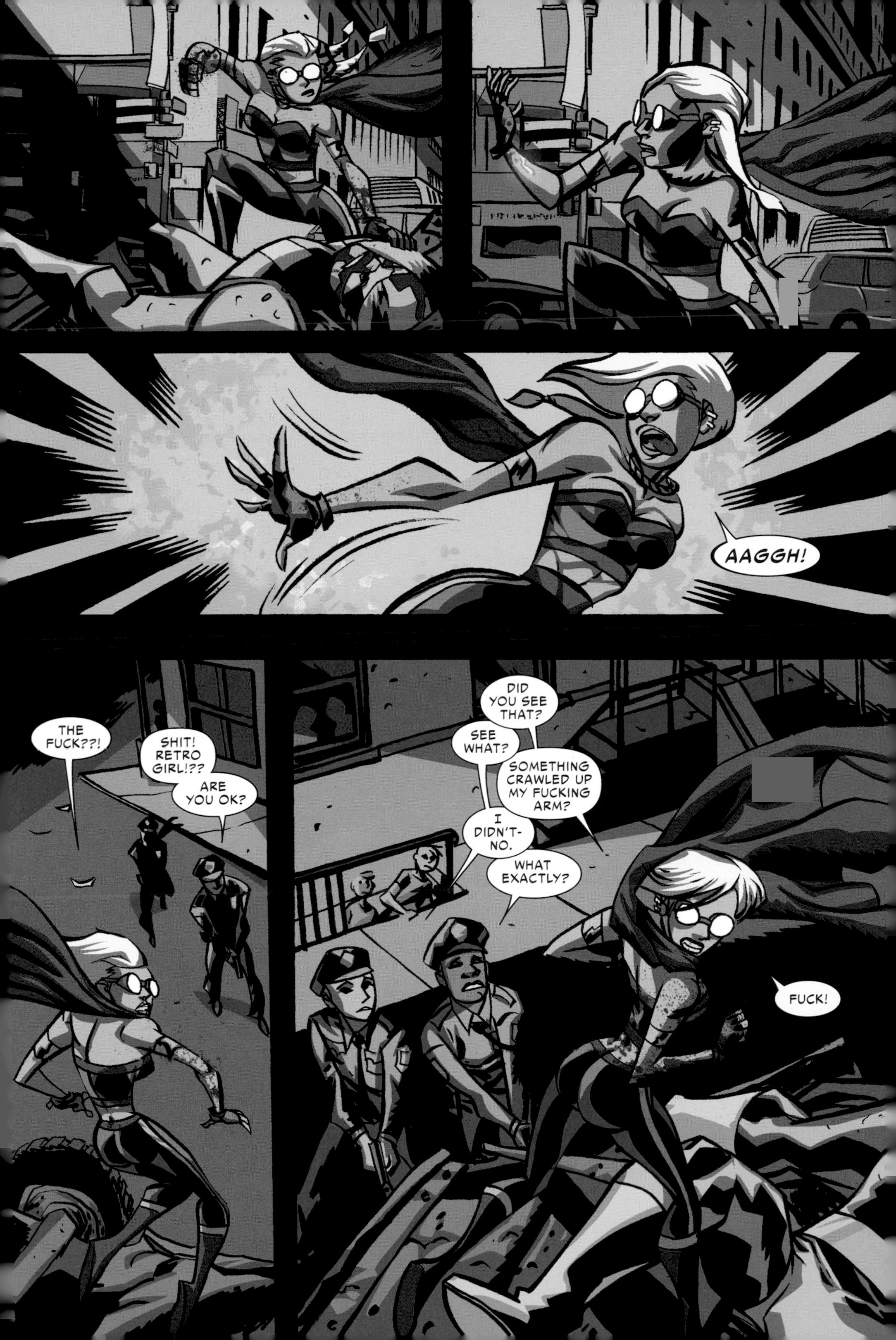
AAGGH!
THE FUCK??!
SHIT! RETRO GIRL!??
ARE YOU OK?
DID YOU SEE THAT?
SEE WHAT?
SOMETHING CRAWLED UP MY FUCKING ARM?
I DIDN'T- NO.
WHAT EXACTLY?
FUCK!

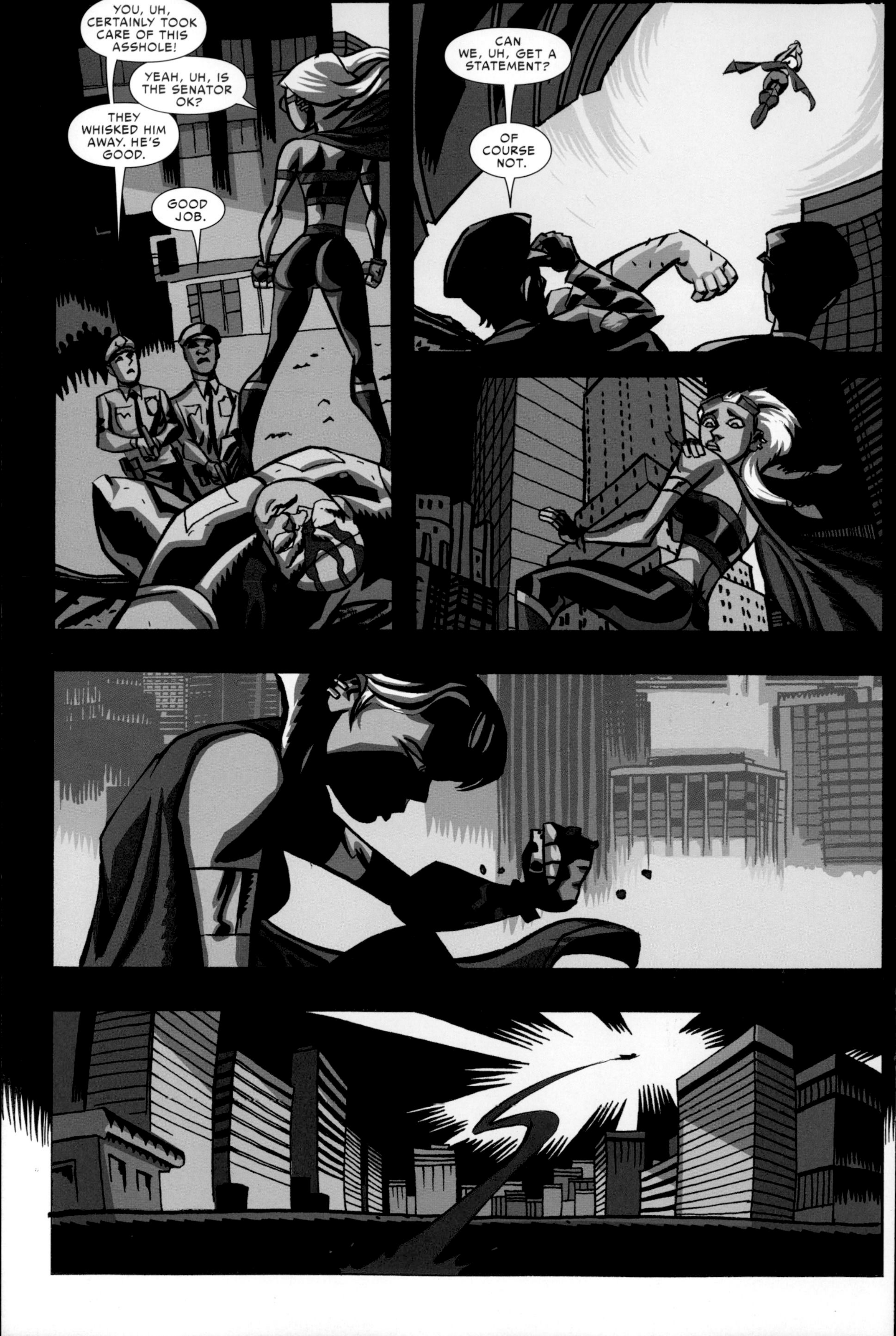
YOU, UH, CERTAINLY TOOK CARE OF THIS ASSHOLE!
YEAH, UH, IS THE SENATOR OK?
THEY WHISKED HIM AWAY. HE'S GOOD.
GOOD JOB.
CAN WE, UH, GET A STATEMENT?
OF COURSE NOT.

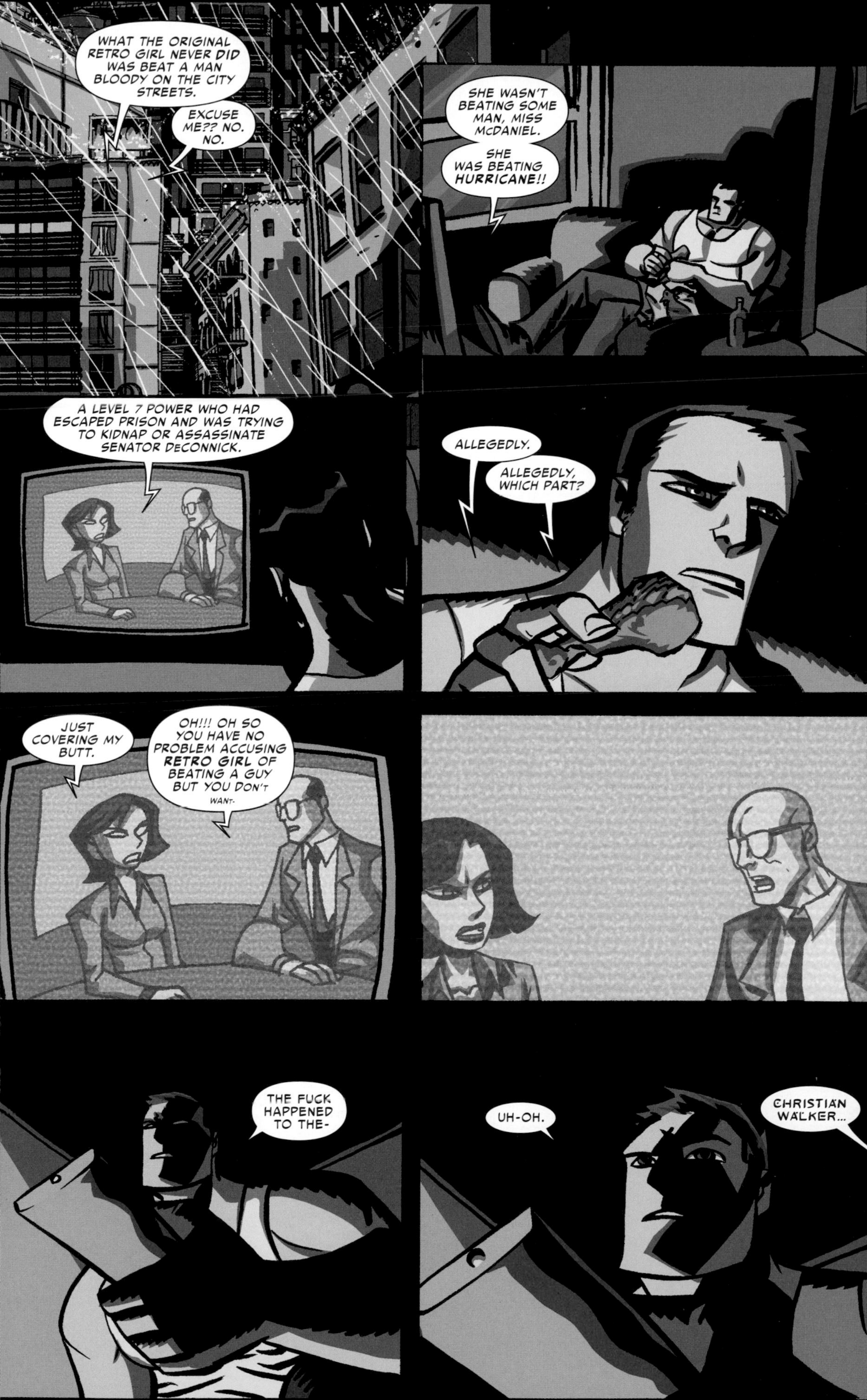
WHAT THE ORIGINAL RETRO GIRL NEVER DID WAS BEAT A MAN BLOODY ON THE CITY STREETS.
EXCUSE ME?? NO. NO.
SHE WASN'T BEATING SOME MAN, MISS McDANIEL.
SHE WAS BEATING HURRICANE!!
A LEVEL 7 POWER WHO HAD ESCAPED PRISON AND WAS TRYING TO KIDNAP OR ASSASSINATE SENATOR DeCONNICK.
ALLEGEDLY.
ALLEGEDLY, WHICH PART?
JUST COVERING MY BUTT.
OH!!! OH SO YOU HAVE NO PROBLEM ACCUSING RETRO GIRL OF BEATING A GUY BUT YOU DON'T WANT-
THE FUCK HAPPENED TO THE-
UH-OH.
CHRISTIAN WALKER...

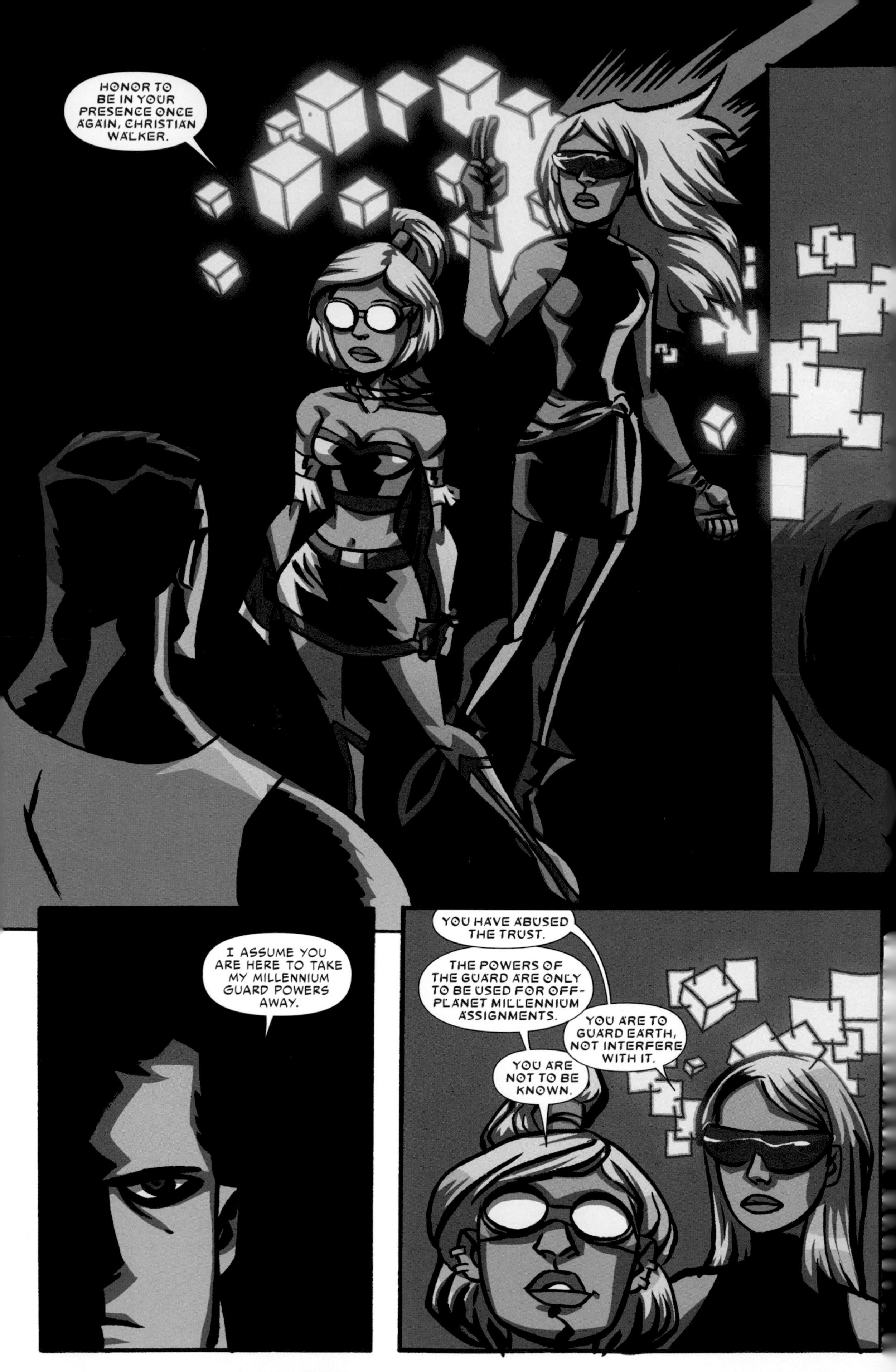
HONOR TO BE IN YOUR PRESENCE ONCE AGAIN, CHRISTIAN WALKER.
I ASSUME YOU ARE HERE TO TAKE MY MILLENNIUM GUARD POWERS AWAY.
YOU HAVE ABUSED THE TRUST.
THE POWERS OF THE GUARD ARE ONLY TO BE USED FOR OFF-PLANET MILLENNIUM ASSIGNMENTS.
YOU ARE NOT TO BE KNOWN.
YOU ARE TO GUARD EARTH, NOT INTERFERE WITH IT.

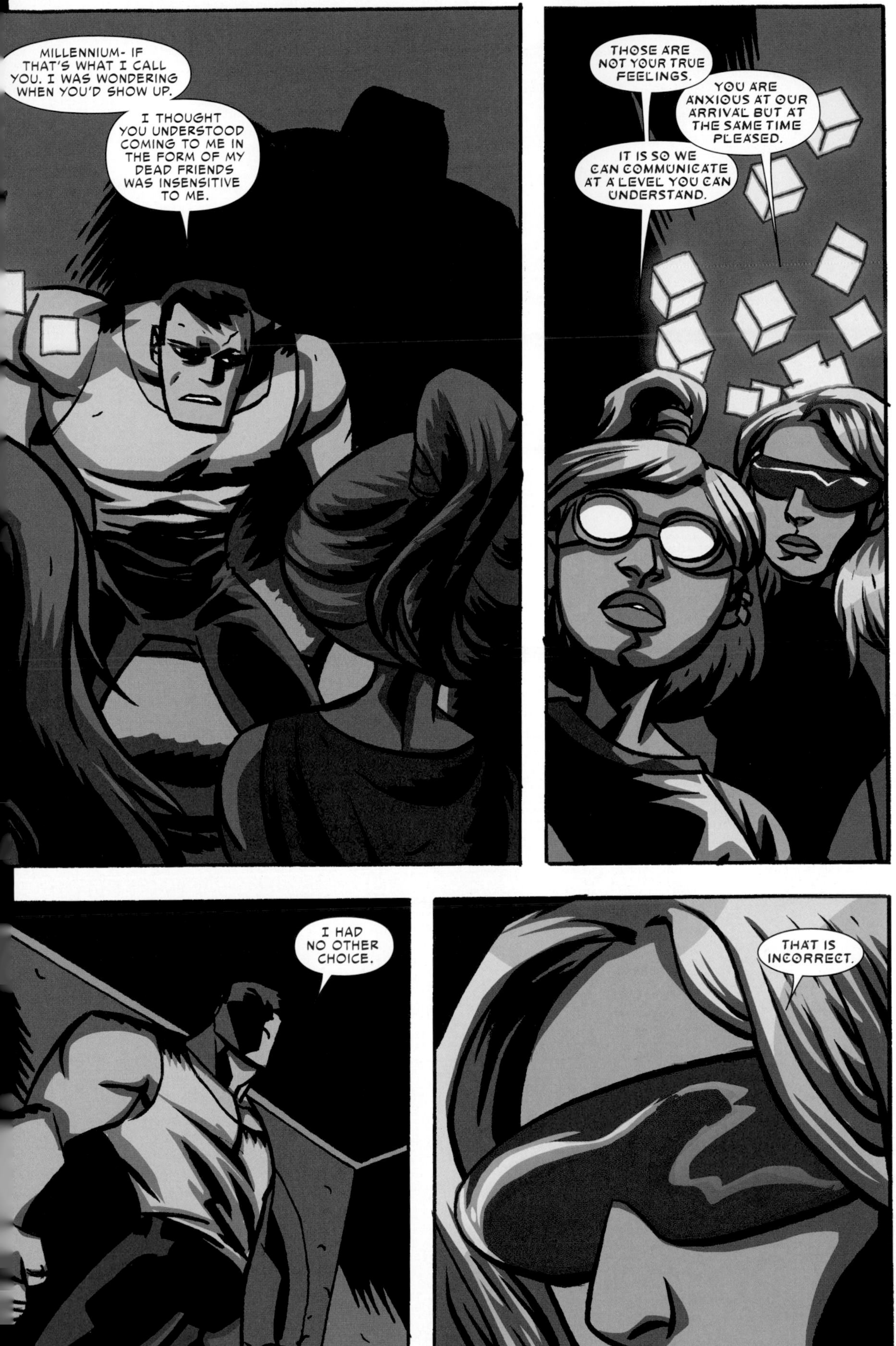
MILLENNIUM- IF THAT'S WHAT I CALL YOU. I WAS WONDERING WHEN YOU'D SHOW UP.
I THOUGHT YOU UNDERSTOOD COMING TO ME IN THE FORM OF MY DEAD FRIENDS WAS INSENSITIVE TO ME.
THOSE ARE NOT YOUR TRUE FEELINGS.
YOU ARE ANXIOUS AT OUR ARRIVAL BUT AT THE SAME TIME PLEASED.
IT IS SO WE CAN COMMUNICATE AT A LEVEL YOU CAN UNDERSTAND.
I HAD NO OTHER CHOICE.
THAT IS INCORRECT.

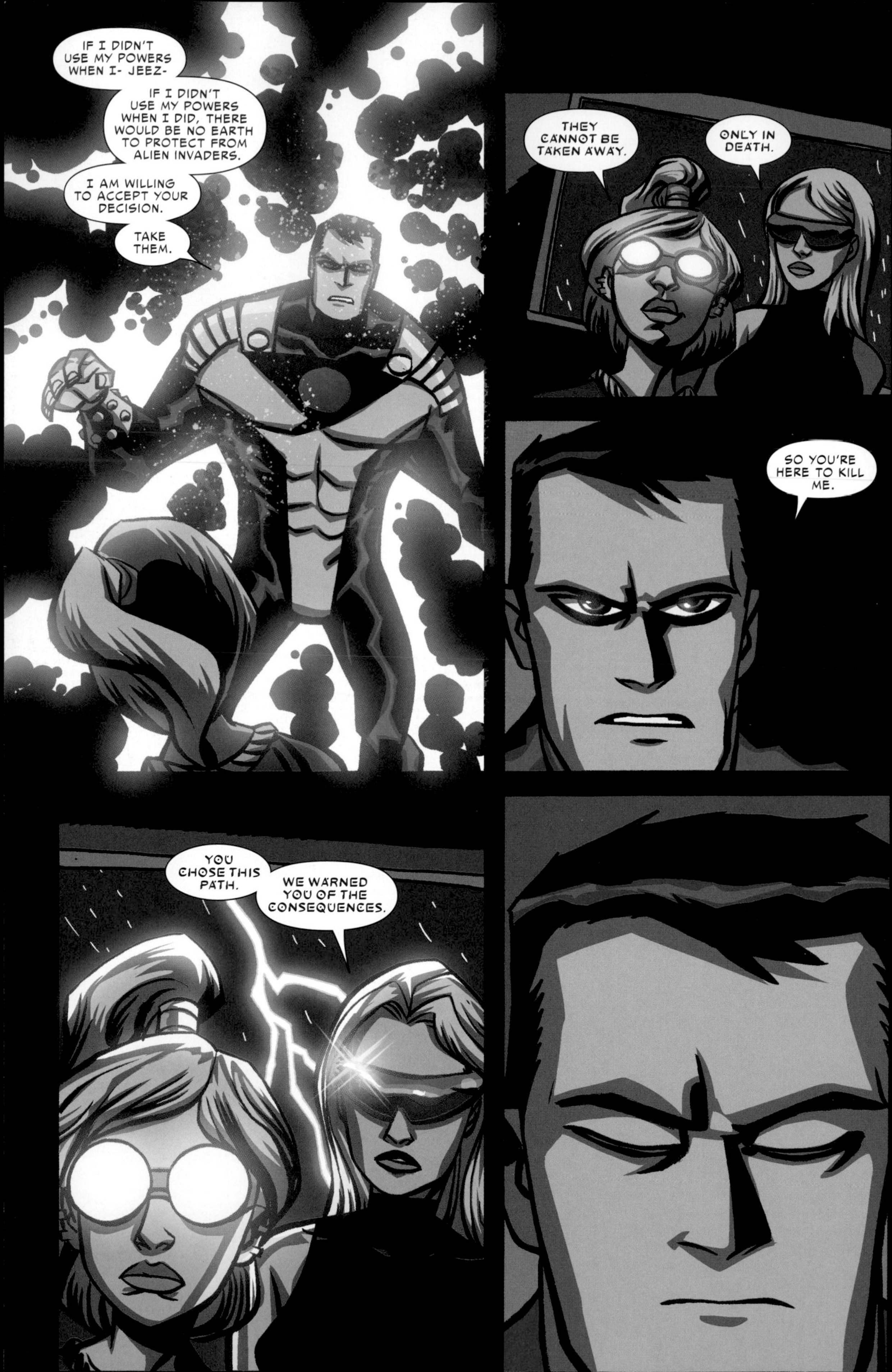

IF I DIDN'T USE MY POWERS WHEN I- JEEZ-
IF I DIDN'T USE MY POWERS WHEN I DID, THERE WOULD BE NO EARTH TO PROTECT FROM ALIEN INVADERS.
I AM WILLING TO ACCEPT YOUR DECISION.
TAKE THEM.
THEY CANNOT BE TAKEN AWAY.
ONLY IN DEATH.
SO YOU'RE HERE TO KILL ME.
YOU CHOSE THIS PATH.
WE WARNED YOU OF THE CONSEQUENCES.

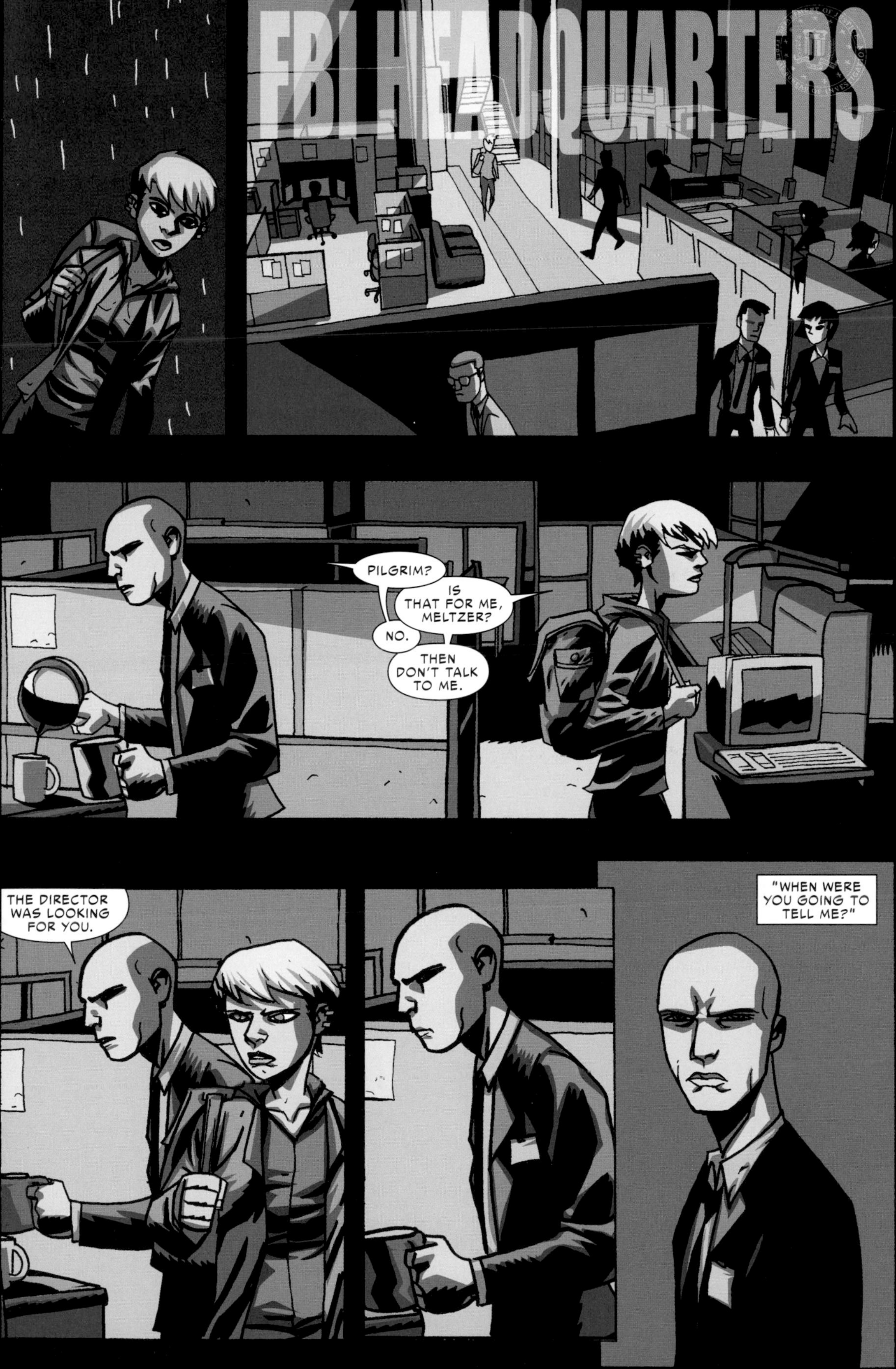
FBI HEADQUARTERS
PILGRIM?
IS THAT FOR ME, MELTZER?
NO.
THEN DON'T TALK TO ME.
THE DIRECTOR WAS LOOKING FOR YOU.
"WHEN WERE YOU GOING TO TELL ME?"

GOOD MORNING, MA'AM. WHEN WERE YOU GOING TO TELL ME YOU WERE PREGNANT?

I'M NOT ANYMORE.

SO I'VE BEEN TOLD.

I DIDN'T KNOW I WAS PREGNANT.

WE BOTH KNOW THAT'S NOT TRUE.

I'M NOT PREGNANT ANYMORE SO...

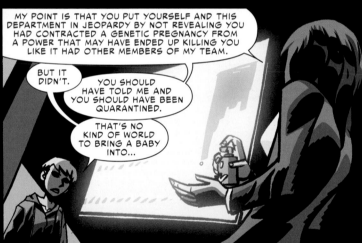

MY POINT IS THAT YOU PUT YOURSELF AND THIS DEPARTMENT IN JEOPARDY BY NOT REVEALING YOU HAD CONTRACTED A GENETIC PREGNANCY FROM A POWER THAT MAY HAVE ENDED UP KILLING YOU LIKE IT HAD OTHER MEMBERS OF MY TEAM.

BUT IT DIDN'T.

YOU SHOULD HAVE TOLD ME AND YOU SHOULD HAVE BEEN QUARANTINED.

THAT'S NO KIND OF WORLD TO BRING A BABY INTO...

ANYTHING ELSE, MA'AM?

I WANT TO FIRE YOU.

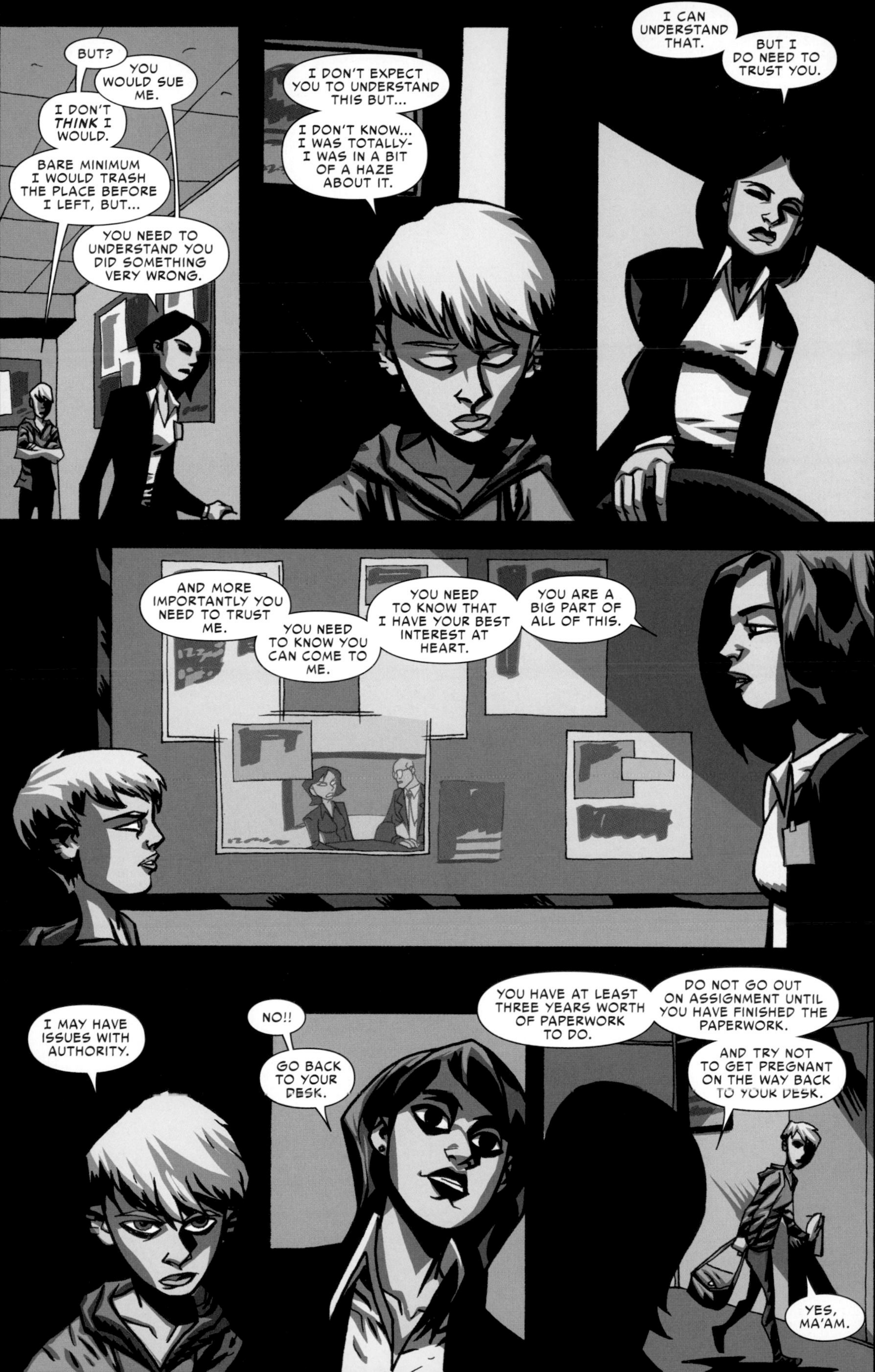
BUT?
YOU WOULD SUE ME.
I DON'T *THINK* I WOULD.
BARE MINIMUM I WOULD TRASH THE PLACE BEFORE I LEFT, BUT...
YOU NEED TO UNDERSTAND YOU DID SOMETHING VERY WRONG.
I DON'T EXPECT YOU TO UNDERSTAND THIS BUT...
I DON'T KNOW... I WAS TOTALLY- I WAS IN A BIT OF A HAZE ABOUT IT.
I CAN UNDERSTAND THAT.
BUT I DO NEED TO TRUST YOU.
AND MORE IMPORTANTLY YOU NEED TO TRUST ME.
YOU NEED TO KNOW YOU CAN COME TO ME.
YOU NEED TO KNOW THAT I HAVE YOUR BEST INTEREST AT HEART.
YOU ARE A BIG PART OF ALL OF THIS.
I MAY HAVE ISSUES WITH AUTHORITY.
NO!!
GO BACK TO YOUR DESK.
YOU HAVE AT LEAST THREE YEARS WORTH OF PAPERWORK TO DO.
DO NOT GO OUT ON ASSIGNMENT UNTIL YOU HAVE FINISHED THE PAPERWORK.
AND TRY NOT TO GET PREGNANT ON THE WAY BACK TO YOUR DESK.
YES, MA'AM.

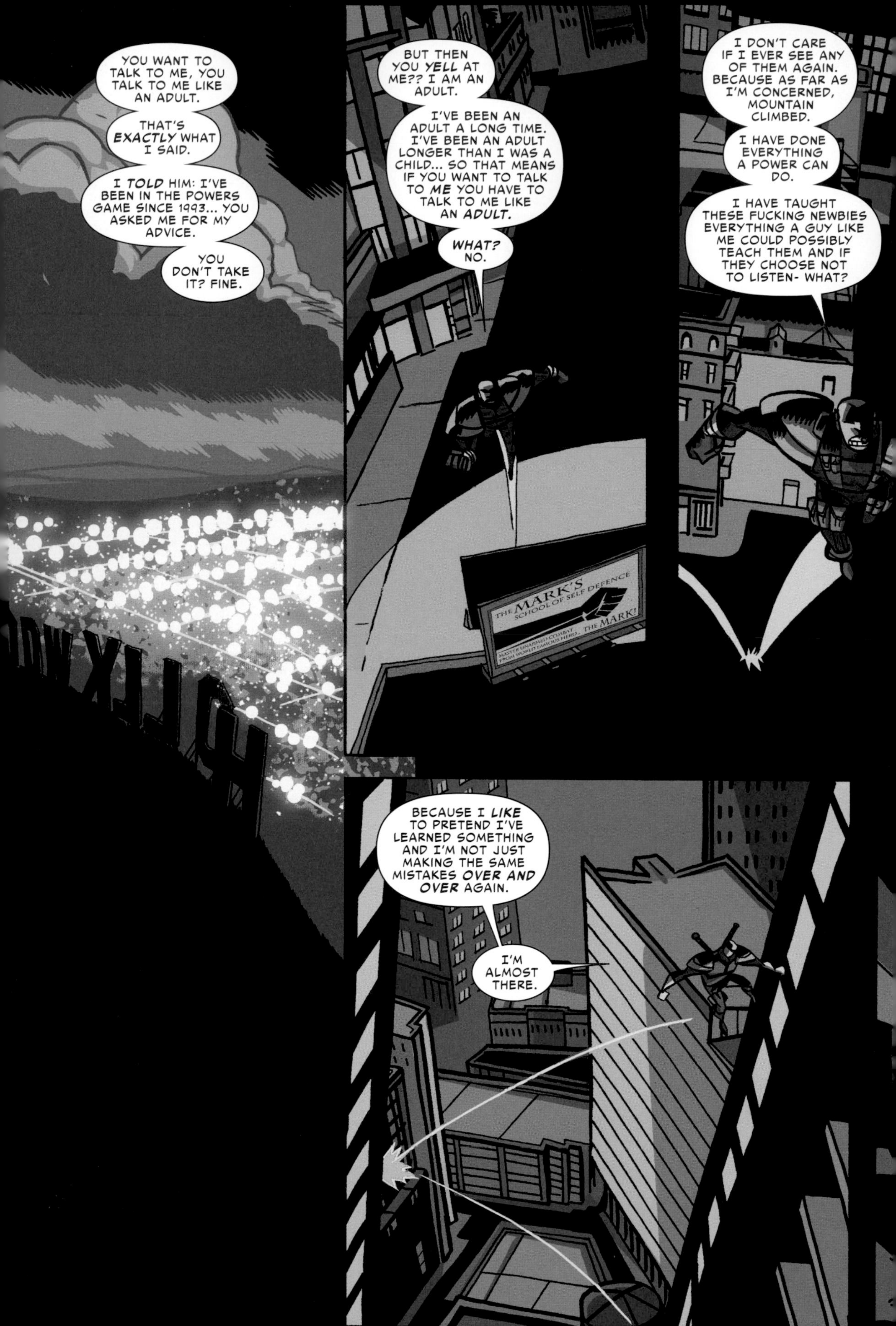

YOU WANT TO TALK TO ME, YOU TALK TO ME LIKE AN ADULT.
THAT'S *EXACTLY* WHAT I SAID.
I *TOLD* HIM: I'VE BEEN IN THE POWERS GAME SINCE 1993... YOU ASKED ME FOR MY ADVICE.
YOU DON'T TAKE IT? FINE.
BUT THEN YOU *YELL* AT ME?? I AM AN ADULT.
I'VE BEEN AN ADULT A LONG TIME. I'VE BEEN AN ADULT LONGER THAN I WAS A CHILD... SO THAT MEANS IF YOU WANT TO TALK TO *ME* YOU HAVE TO TALK TO ME LIKE AN *ADULT.*
WHAT? NO.
THE MARK'S SCHOOL OF SELF DEFENCE
MASTER UNARMED COMBAT FROM WORLD FAMOUS HERO... THE MARK!
I DON'T CARE IF I EVER SEE ANY OF THEM AGAIN. BECAUSE AS FAR AS I'M CONCERNED, MOUNTAIN CLIMBED.
I HAVE DONE EVERYTHING A POWER CAN DO.
I HAVE TAUGHT THESE FUCKING NEWBIES EVERYTHING A GUY LIKE ME COULD POSSIBLY TEACH THEM AND IF THEY CHOOSE NOT TO LISTEN- WHAT?
BECAUSE I *LIKE* TO PRETEND I'VE LEARNED SOMETHING AND I'M NOT JUST MAKING THE SAME MISTAKES *OVER AND OVER* AGAIN.
I'M ALMOST THERE.

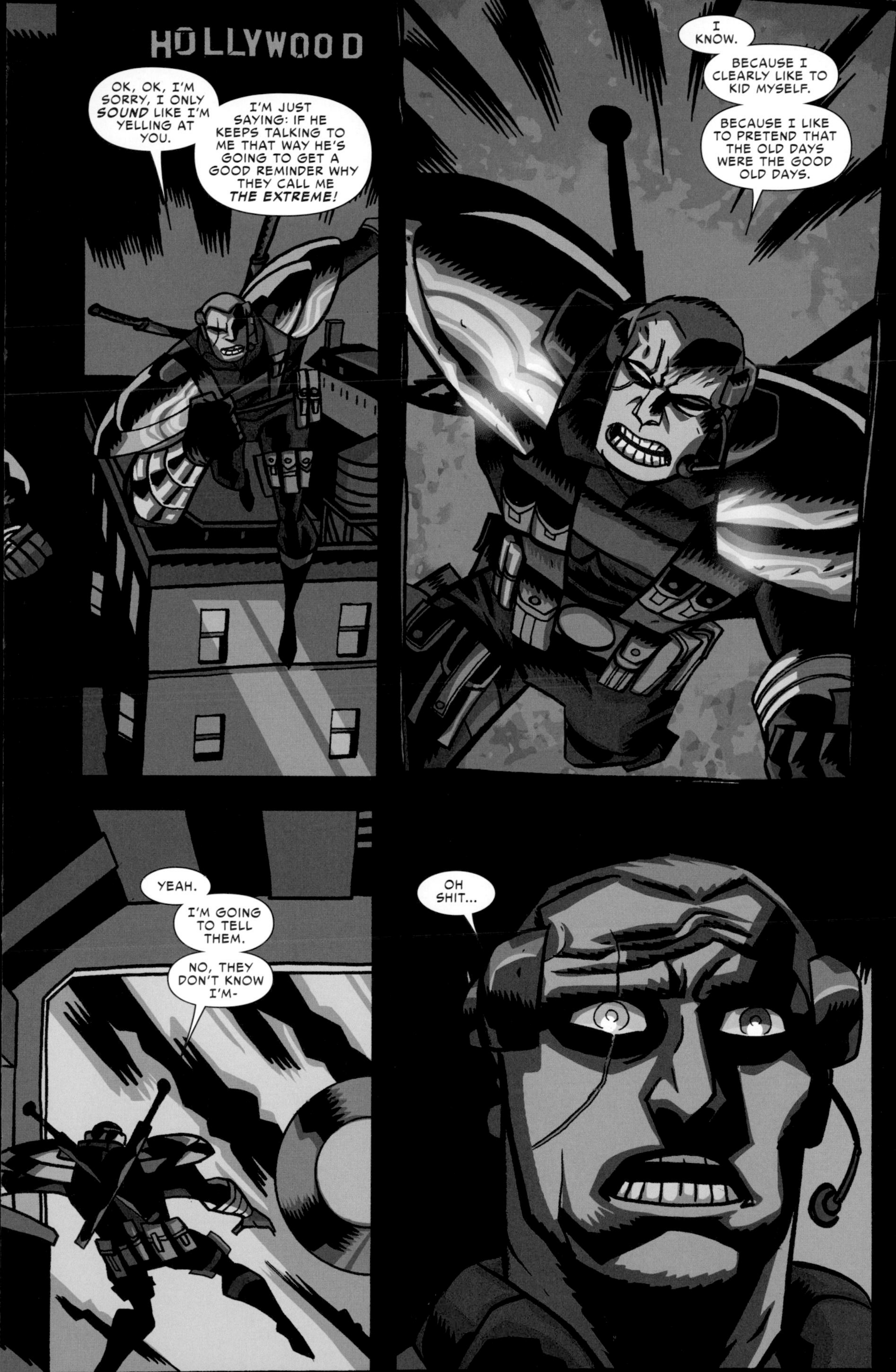
HOLLYWOOD
OK, OK, I'M SORRY, I ONLY SOUND LIKE I'M YELLING AT YOU.
I'M JUST SAYING: IF HE KEEPS TALKING TO ME THAT WAY HE'S GOING TO GET A GOOD REMINDER WHY THEY CALL ME THE EXTREME!
I KNOW.
BECAUSE I CLEARLY LIKE TO KID MYSELF.
BECAUSE I LIKE TO PRETEND THAT THE OLD DAYS WERE THE GOOD OLD DAYS.
YEAH.
I'M GOING TO TELL THEM.
NO, THEY DON'T KNOW I'M-
OH SHIT...

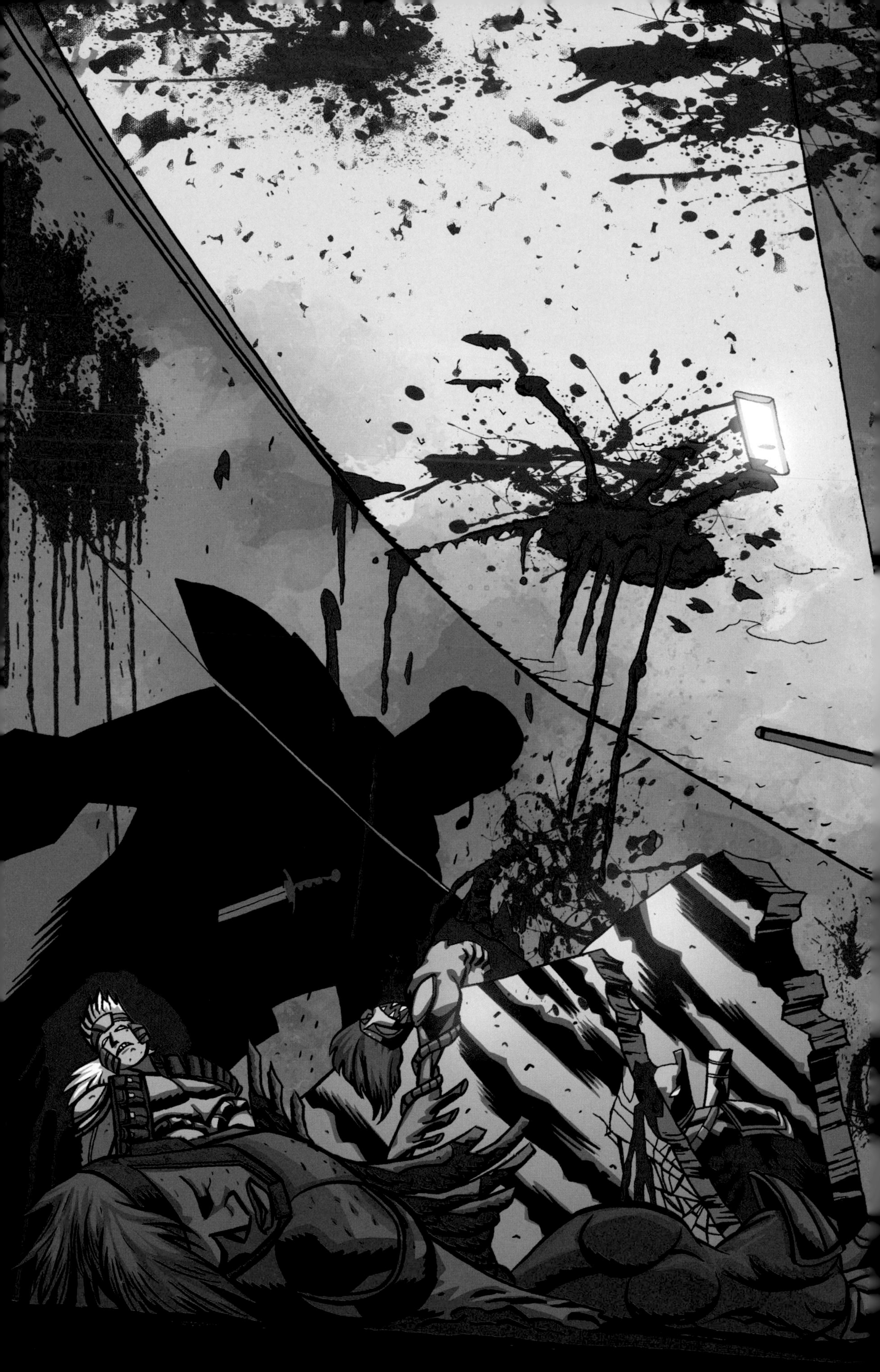

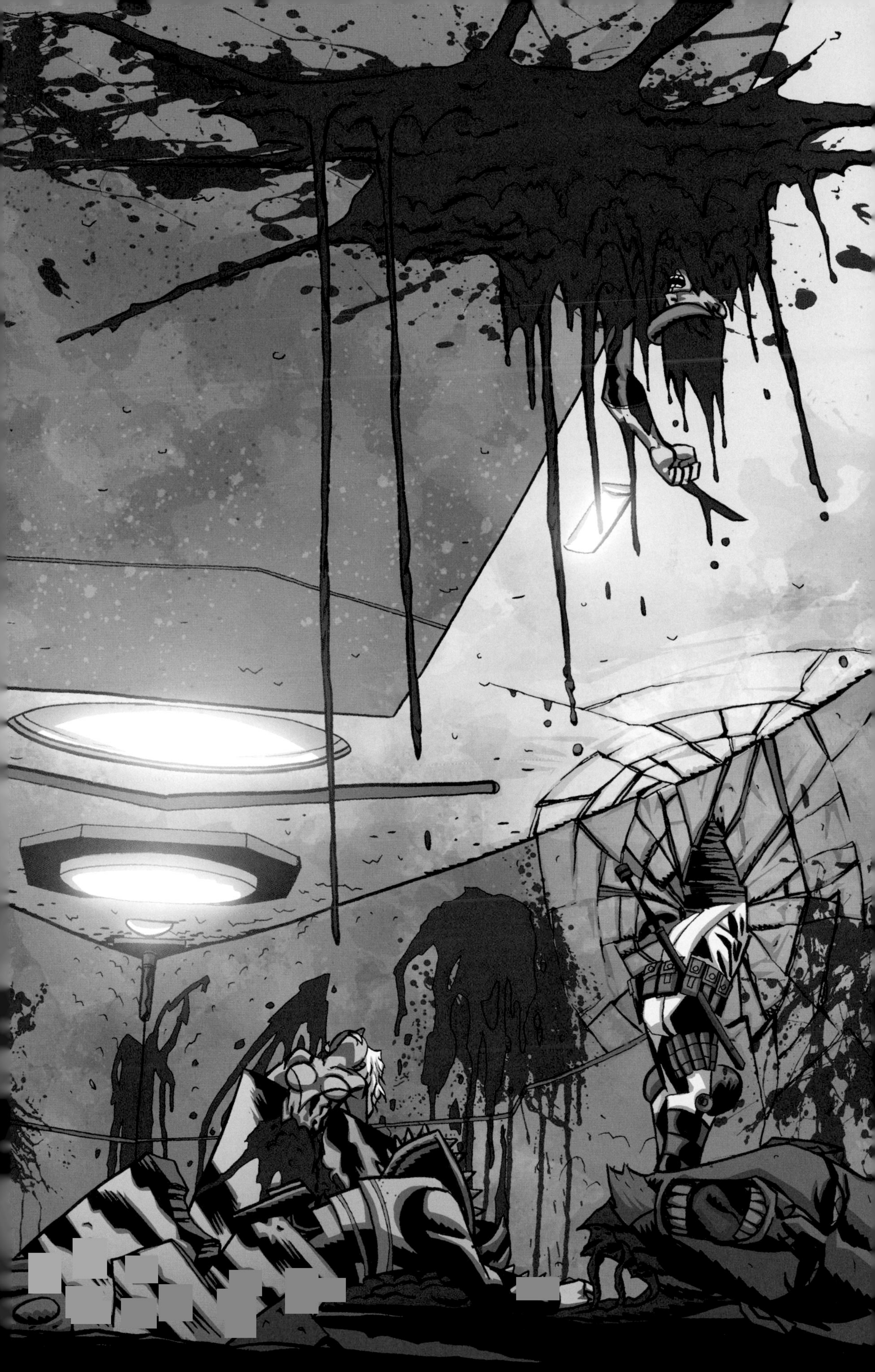

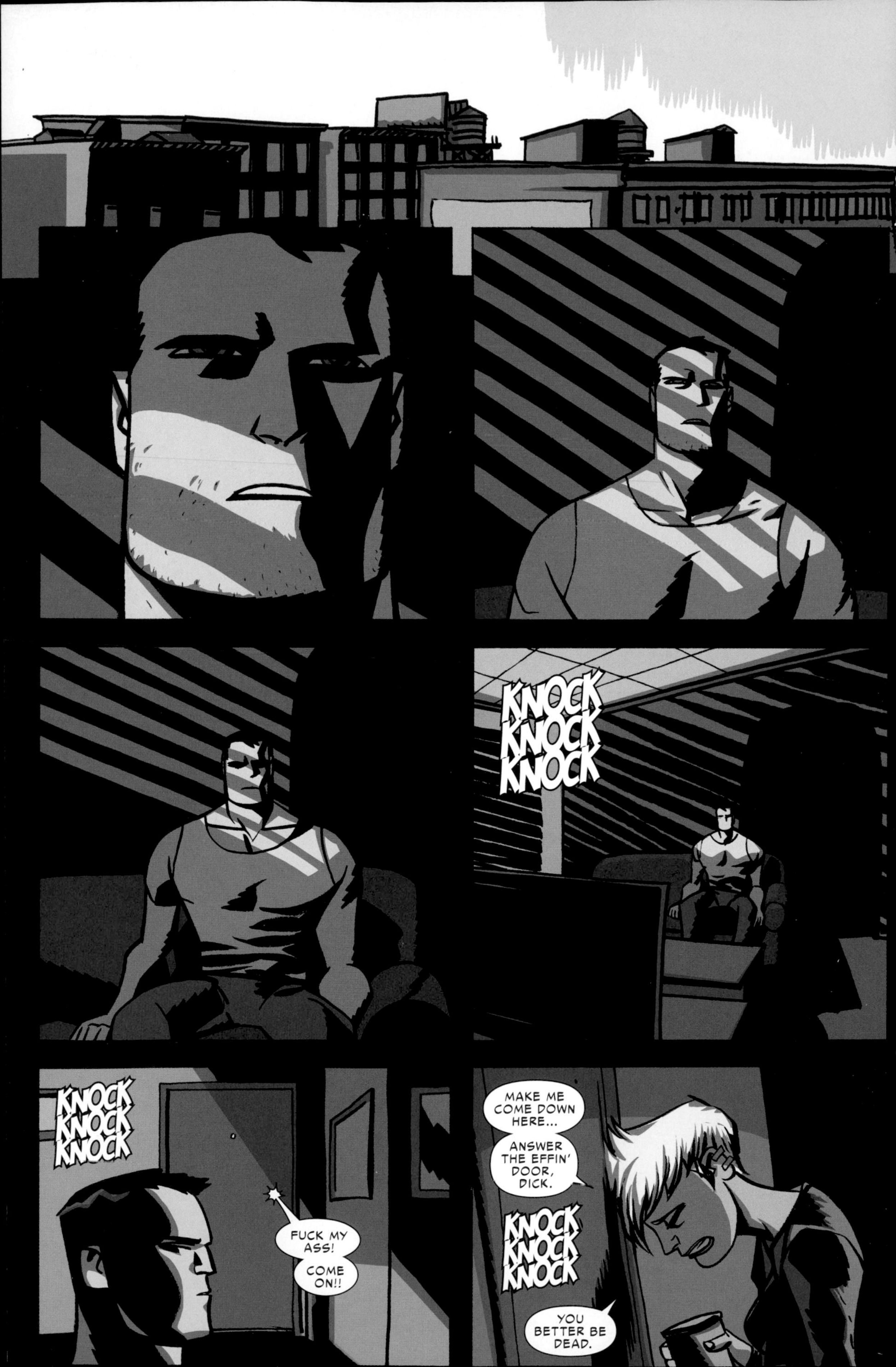
KNOCK KNOCK KNOCK
KNOCK KNOCK KNOCK
FUCK MY ASS!
COME ON!!
MAKE ME COME DOWN HERE...
ANSWER THE EFFIN' DOOR, DICK.
KNOCK KNOCK KNOCK
YOU BETTER BE DEAD.

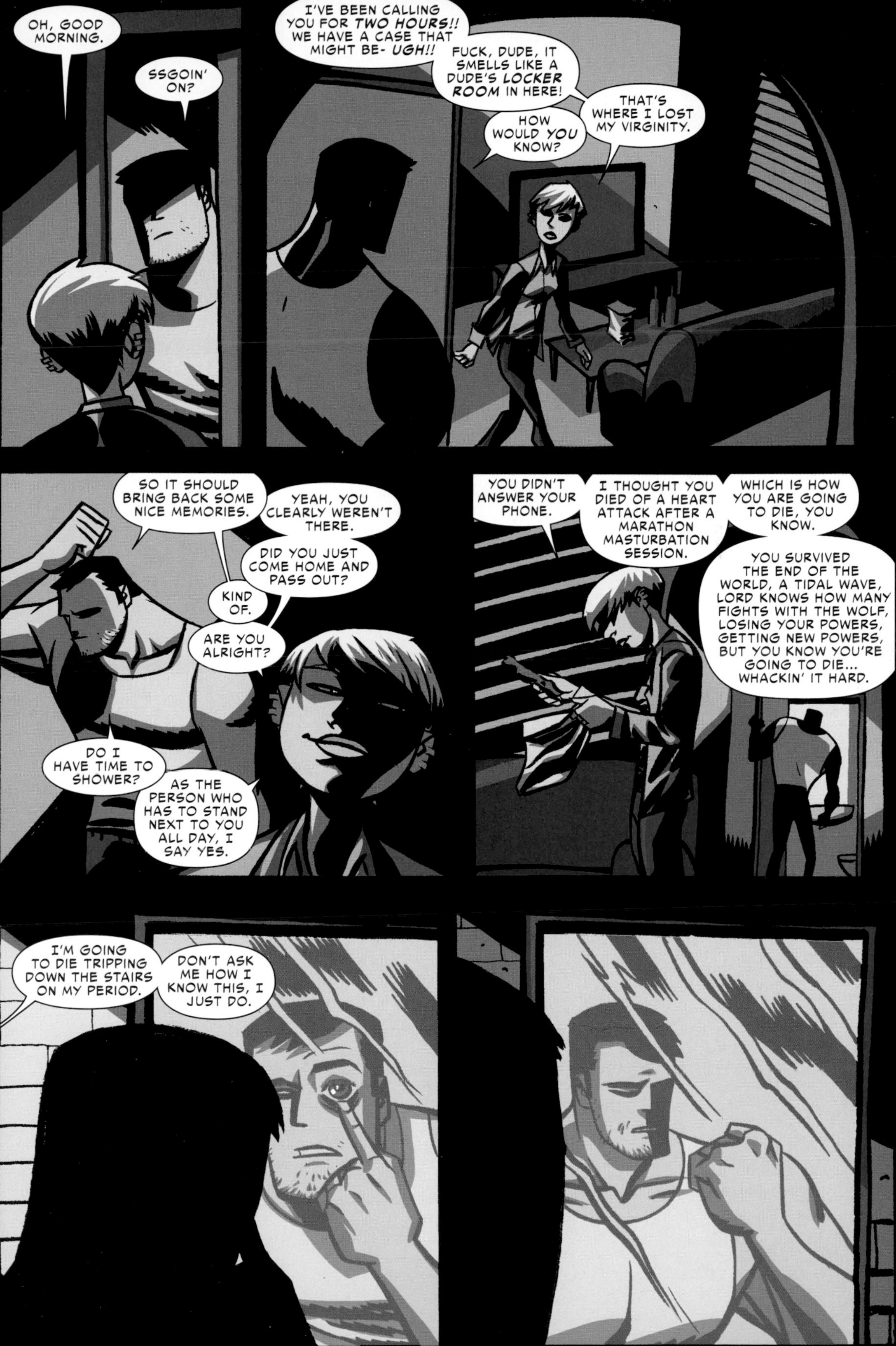

OH, GOOD MORNING.
SSGOIN' ON?
I'VE BEEN CALLING YOU FOR TWO HOURS!! WE HAVE A CASE THAT MIGHT BE- UGH!!
FUCK, DUDE, IT SMELLS LIKE A DUDE'S LOCKER ROOM IN HERE!
THAT'S WHERE I LOST MY VIRGINITY.
HOW WOULD YOU KNOW?
SO IT SHOULD BRING BACK SOME NICE MEMORIES.
YEAH, YOU CLEARLY WEREN'T THERE.
DID YOU JUST COME HOME AND PASS OUT?
KIND OF.
ARE YOU ALRIGHT?
DO I HAVE TIME TO SHOWER?
AS THE PERSON WHO HAS TO STAND NEXT TO YOU ALL DAY, I SAY YES.
YOU DIDN'T ANSWER YOUR PHONE.
I THOUGHT YOU DIED OF A HEART ATTACK AFTER A MARATHON MASTURBATION SESSION.
WHICH IS HOW YOU ARE GOING TO DIE, YOU KNOW.
YOU SURVIVED THE END OF THE WORLD, A TIDAL WAVE, LORD KNOWS HOW MANY FIGHTS WITH THE WOLF, LOSING YOUR POWERS, GETTING NEW POWERS, BUT YOU KNOW YOU'RE GOING TO DIE... WHACKIN' IT HARD.
I'M GOING TO DIE TRIPPING DOWN THE STAIRS ON MY PERIOD.
DON'T ASK ME HOW I KNOW THIS, I JUST DO.

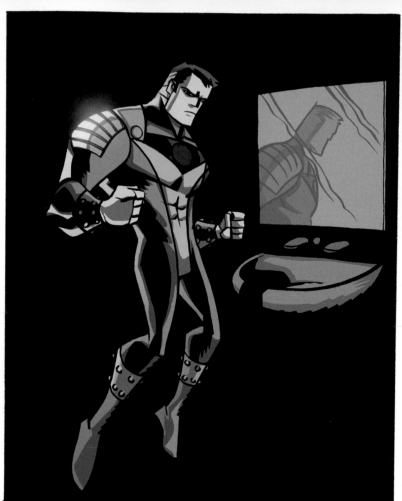

-KEEP HOPING THEY INVENT A CURE FOR OLD AGE BEFORE WE GET THERE, YOU KNOW?

LIKE WHATEVER THAT THING IS THAT MAKES PEOPLE STOP CARING ABOUT POPULAR CULTURE OR TECHNOLOGICAL ADVANCES...

THAT AND CANCER.

I'D LIKE THAT ALL CURED SOON.

DEENA...

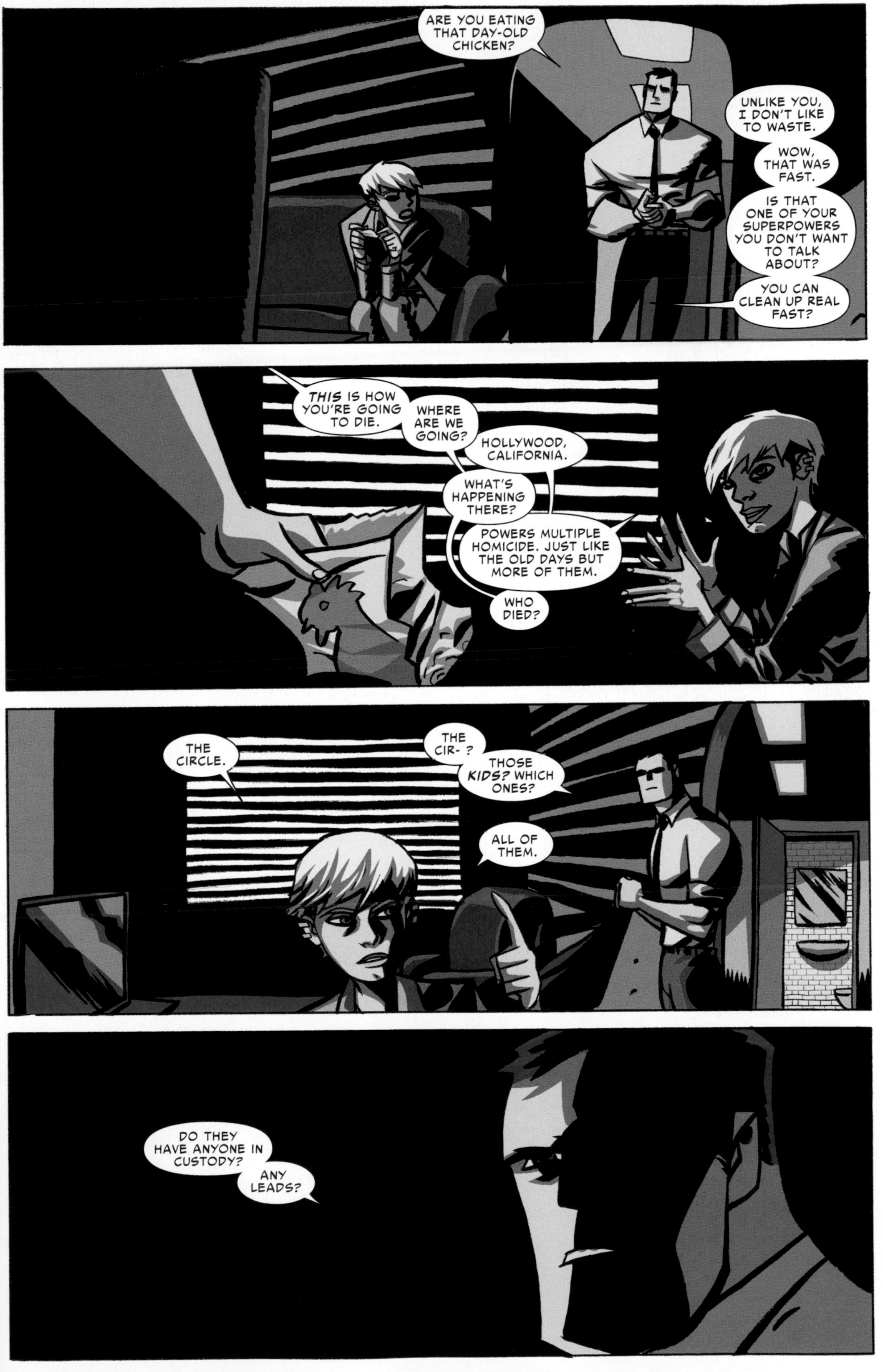
ARE YOU EATING THAT DAY-OLD CHICKEN?
UNLIKE YOU, I DON'T LIKE TO WASTE.
WOW, THAT WAS FAST.
IS THAT ONE OF YOUR SUPERPOWERS YOU DON'T WANT TO TALK ABOUT?
YOU CAN CLEAN UP REAL FAST?
THIS IS HOW YOU'RE GOING TO DIE.
WHERE ARE WE GOING?
HOLLYWOOD, CALIFORNIA.
WHAT'S HAPPENING THERE?
POWERS MULTIPLE HOMICIDE. JUST LIKE THE OLD DAYS BUT MORE OF THEM.
WHO DIED?
THE CIRCLE.
THE CIR- ?
THOSE *KIDS?* WHICH ONES?
ALL OF THEM.
DO THEY HAVE ANYONE IN CUSTODY?
ANY LEADS?

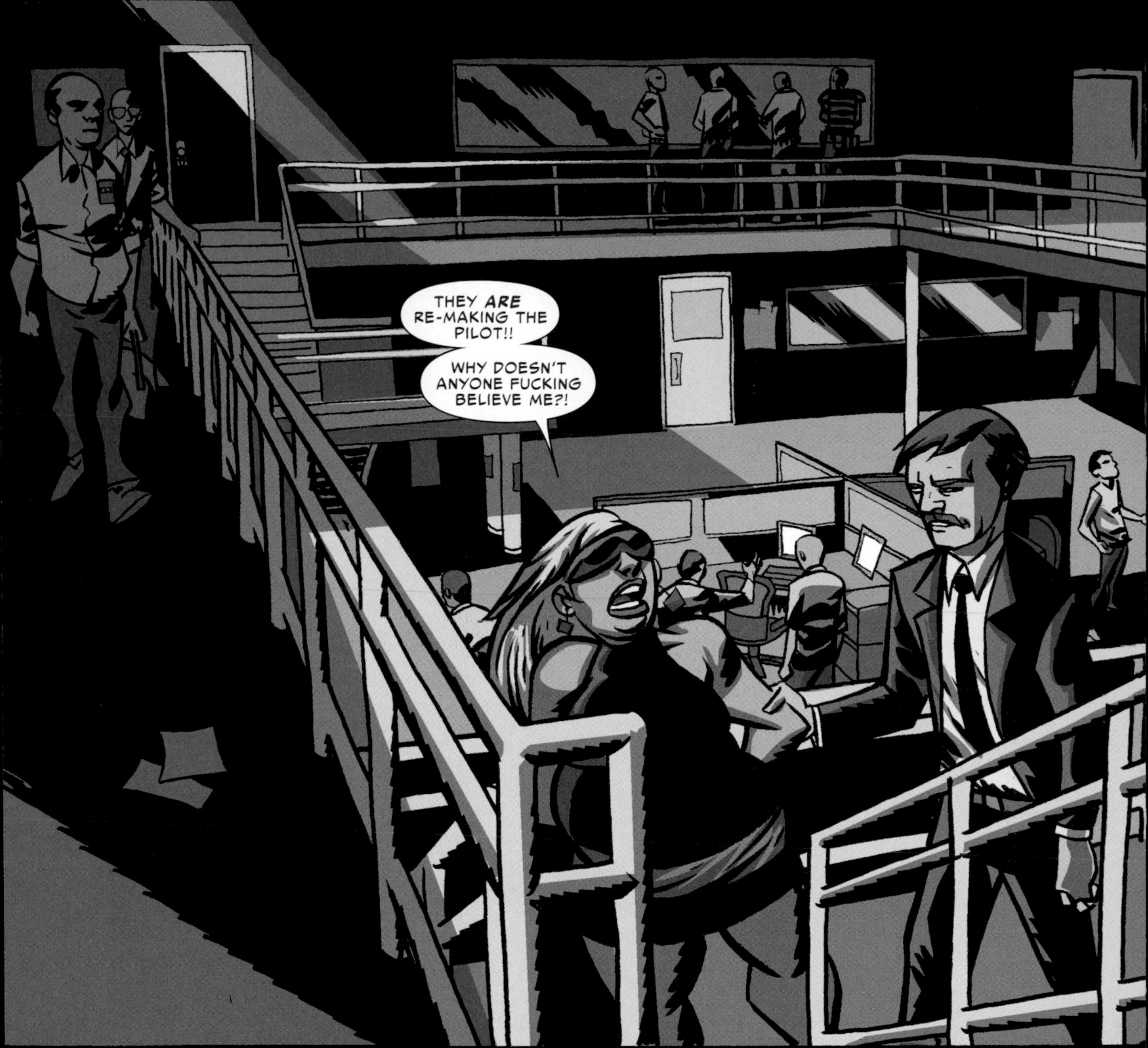
THEY ARE RE-MAKING THE PILOT!!
WHY DOESN'T ANYONE FUCKING BELIEVE ME?!

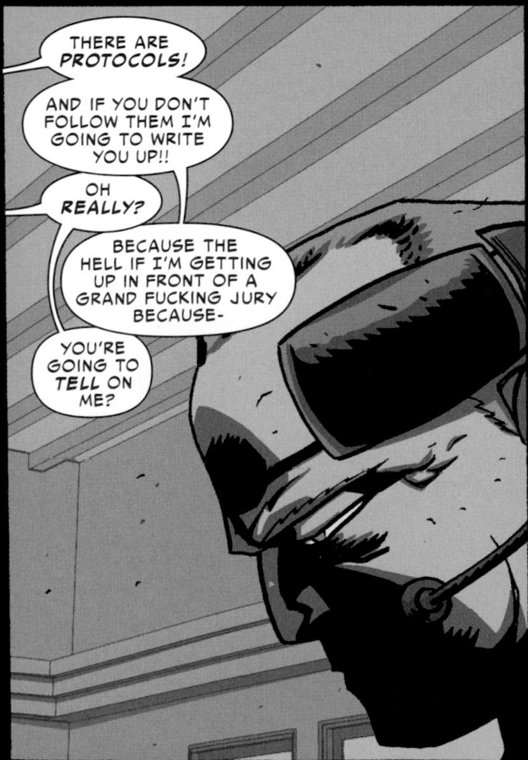
THERE ARE PROTOCOLS!
AND IF YOU DON'T FOLLOW THEM I'M GOING TO WRITE YOU UP!!
OH REALLY?
BECAUSE THE HELL IF I'M GETTING UP IN FRONT OF A GRAND FUCKING JURY BECAUSE-
YOU'RE GOING TO TELL ON ME?

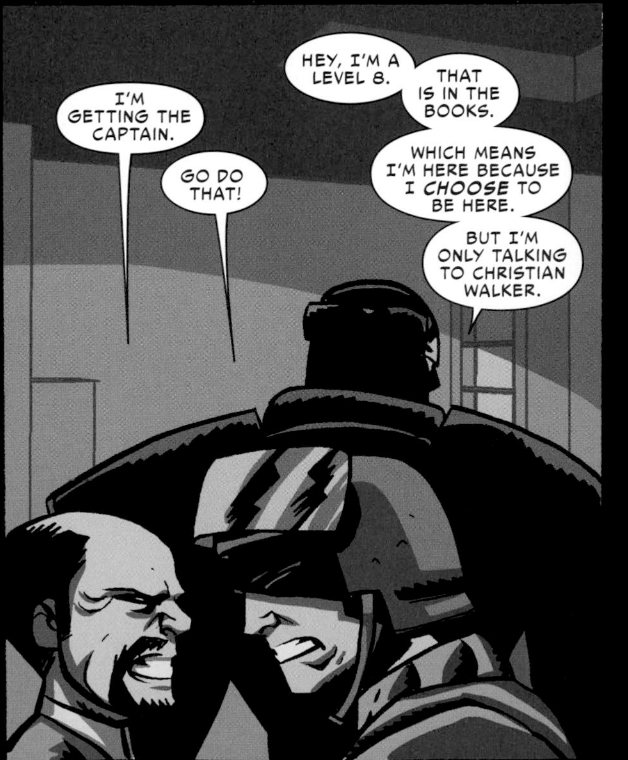
I'M GETTING THE CAPTAIN.
GO DO THAT!
HEY, I'M A LEVEL 8.
THAT IS IN THE BOOKS.
WHICH MEANS I'M HERE BECAUSE I CHOOSE TO BE HERE.
BUT I'M ONLY TALKING TO CHRISTIAN WALKER.

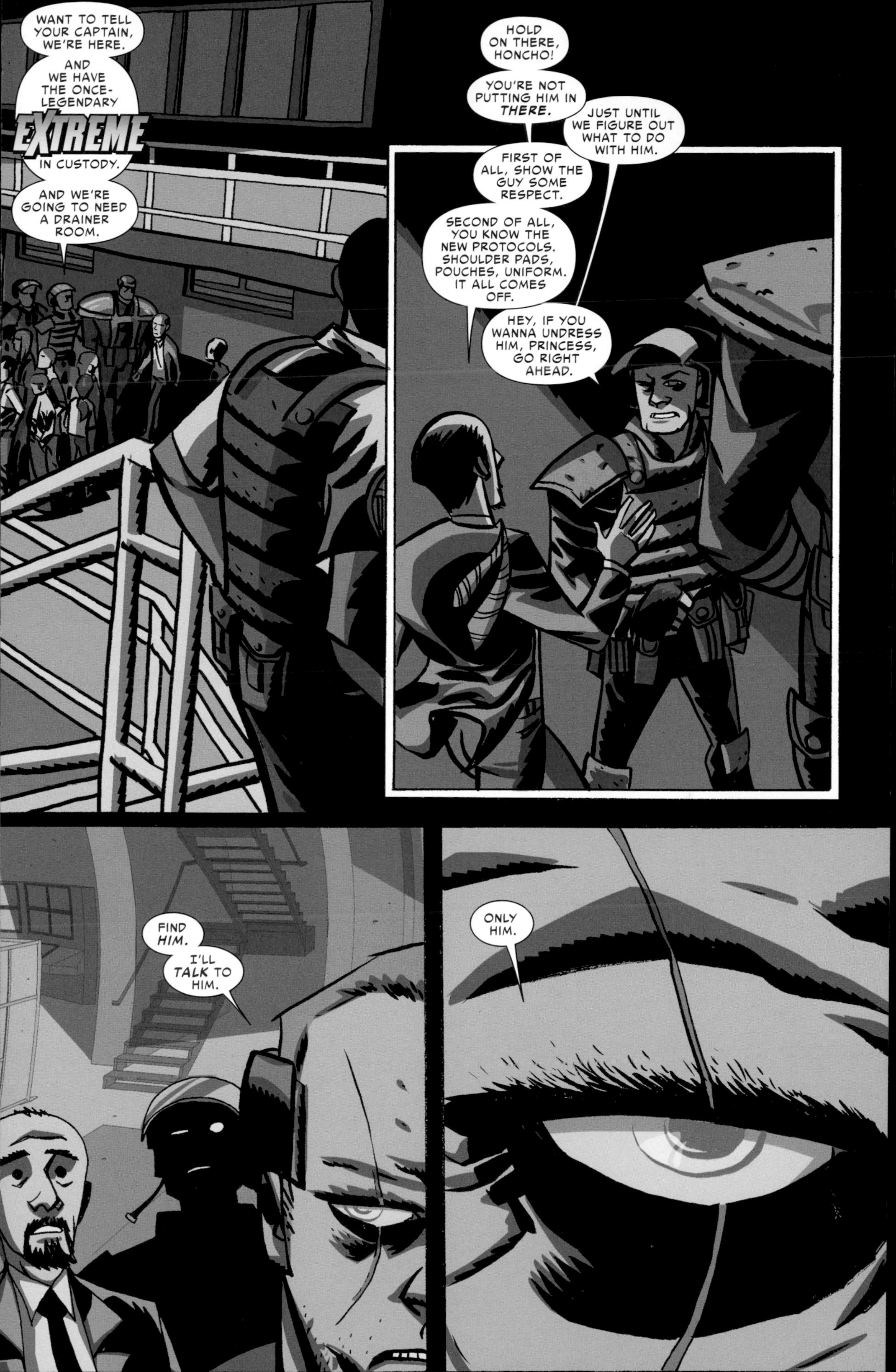

WANT TO TELL YOUR CAPTAIN, WE'RE HERE.
AND WE HAVE THE ONCE-LEGENDARY EXTREME IN CUSTODY.
AND WE'RE GOING TO NEED A DRAINER ROOM.
HOLD ON THERE, HONCHO!
YOU'RE NOT PUTTING HIM IN *THERE.*
JUST UNTIL WE FIGURE OUT WHAT TO DO WITH HIM.
FIRST OF ALL, SHOW THE GUY SOME RESPECT.
SECOND OF ALL, YOU KNOW THE NEW PROTOCOLS. SHOULDER PADS, POUCHES, UNIFORM. IT ALL COMES OFF.
HEY, IF YOU WANNA UNDRESS HIM, PRINCESS, GO RIGHT AHEAD.
FIND *HIM.*
I'LL *TALK* TO HIM.
ONLY HIM.

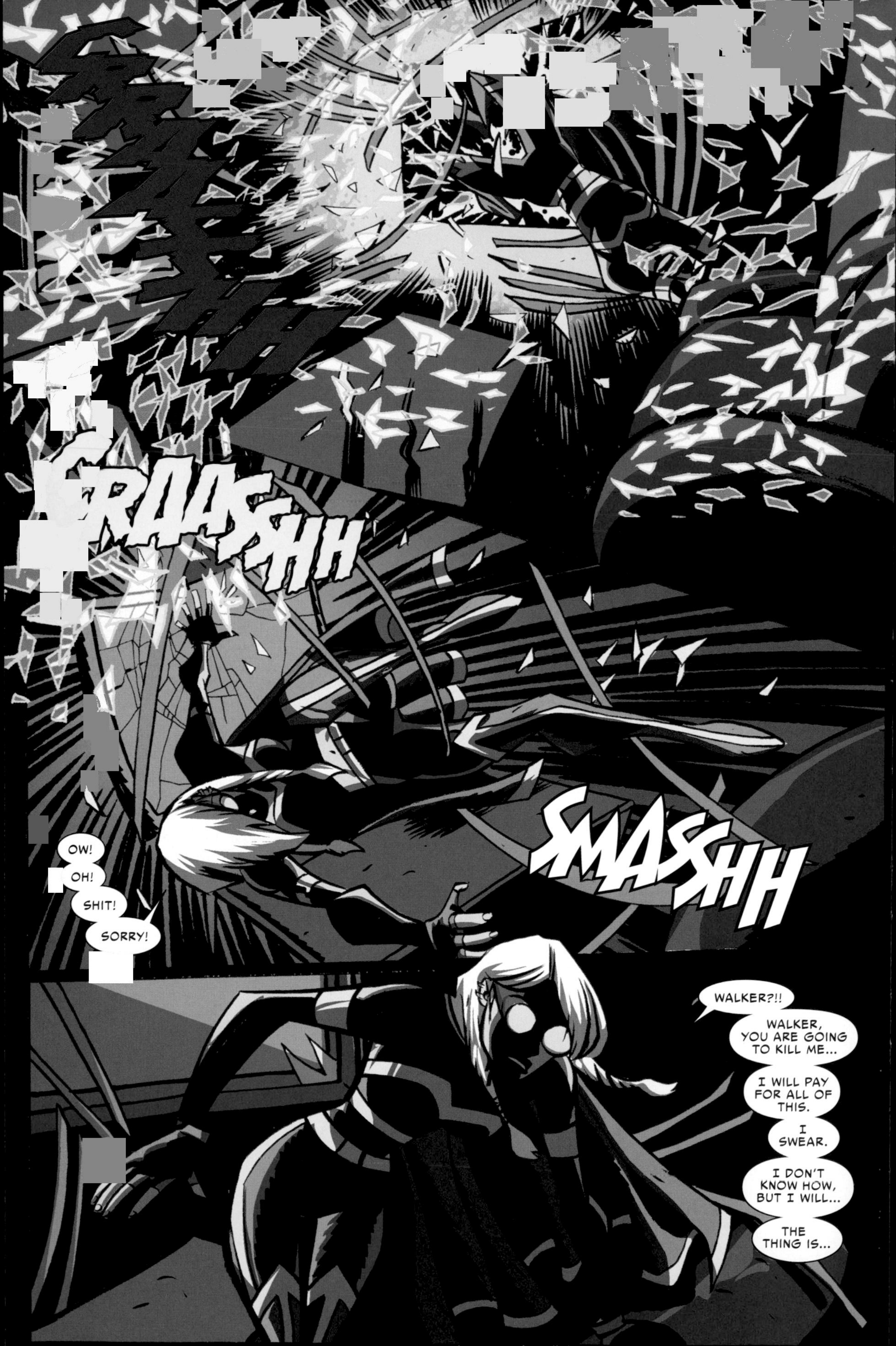
CRAASHH
SMASHH
OW!
OH!
SHIT!
SORRY!
WALKER?!!
WALKER, YOU ARE GOING TO KILL ME...
I WILL PAY FOR ALL OF THIS.
I SWEAR.
I DON'T KNOW HOW, BUT I WILL...
THE THING IS...

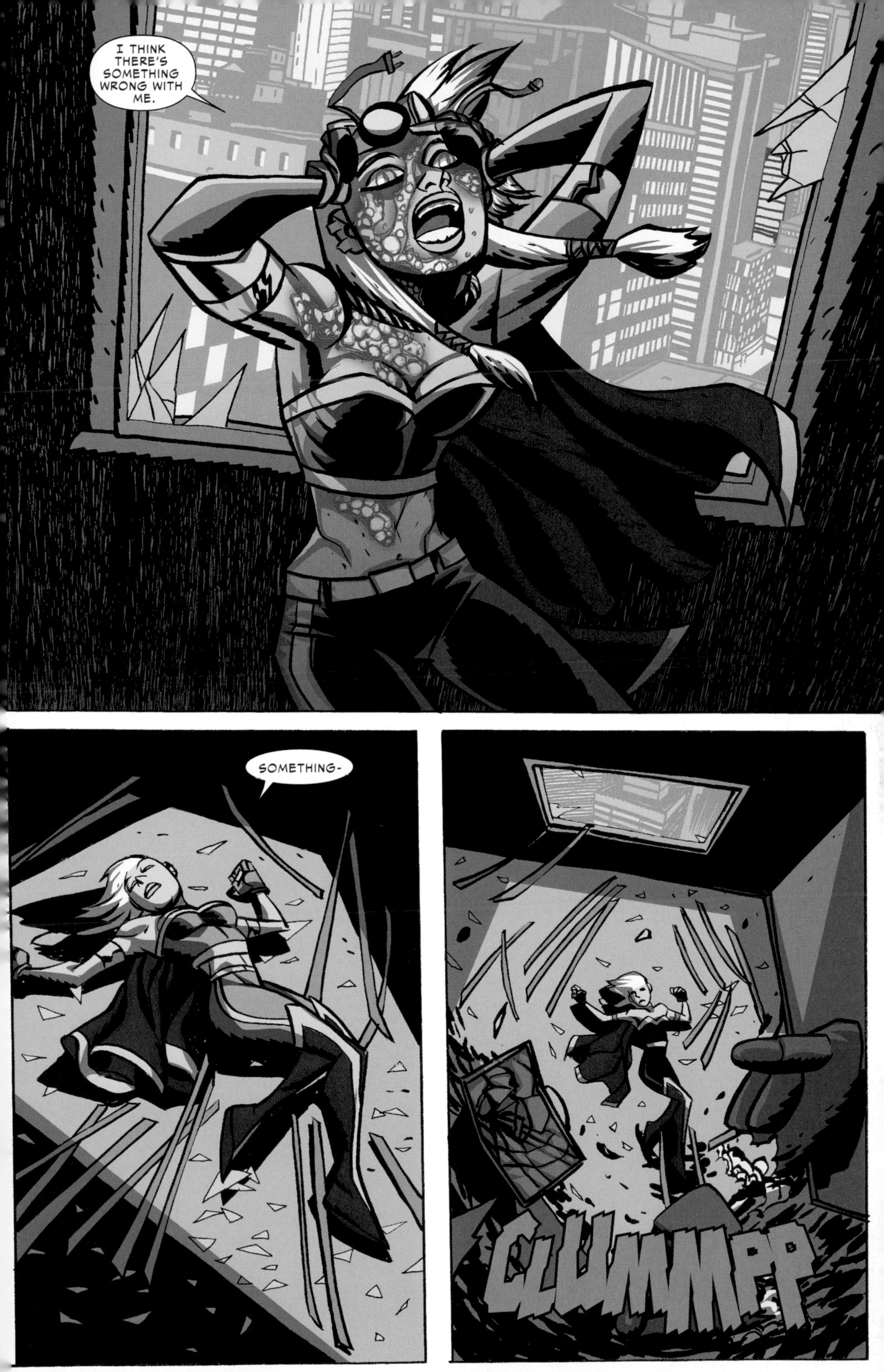
I THINK THERE'S SOMETHING WRONG WITH ME.
SOMETHING-
CLUMMPP

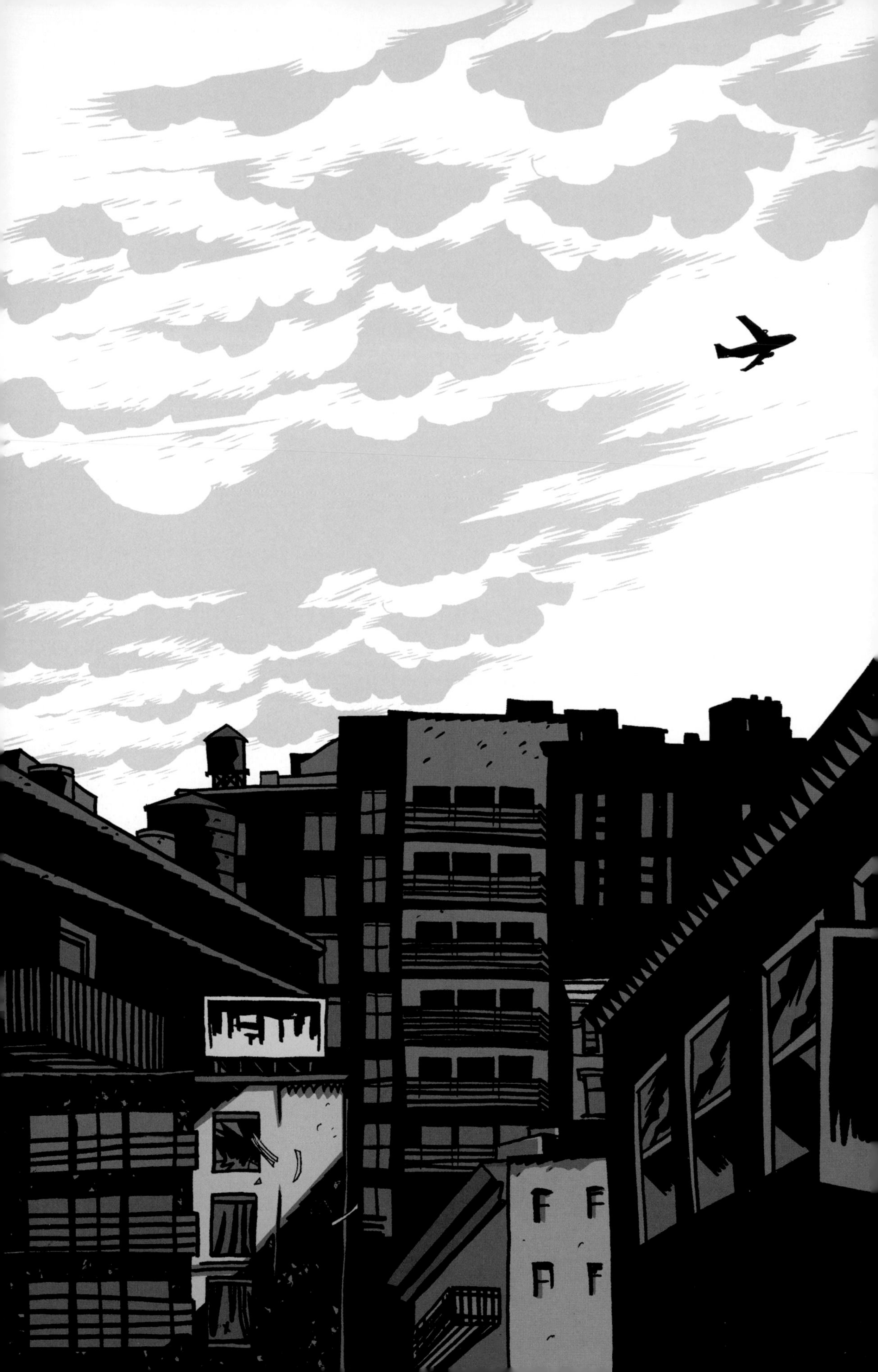

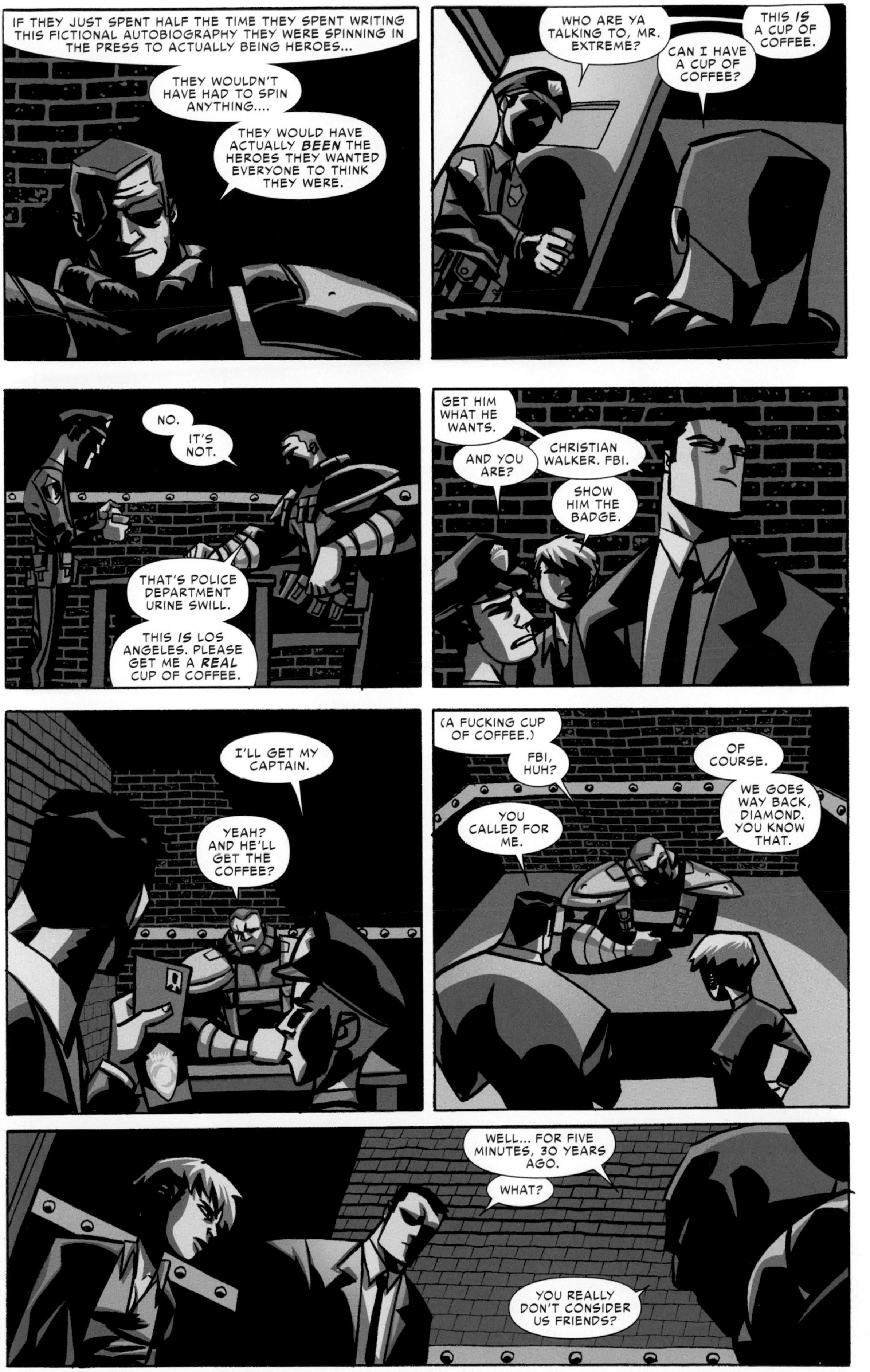
IF THEY JUST SPENT HALF THE TIME THEY SPENT WRITING THIS FICTIONAL AUTOBIOGRAPHY THEY WERE SPINNING IN THE PRESS TO ACTUALLY BEING HEROES...
THEY WOULDN'T HAVE HAD TO SPIN ANYTHING....
THEY WOULD HAVE ACTUALLY BEEN THE HEROES THEY WANTED EVERYONE TO THINK THEY WERE.
WHO ARE YA TALKING TO, MR. EXTREME?
CAN I HAVE A CUP OF COFFEE?
THIS IS A CUP OF COFFEE.
NO.
IT'S NOT.
THAT'S POLICE DEPARTMENT URINE SWILL.
THIS IS LOS ANGELES. PLEASE GET ME A REAL CUP OF COFFEE.
GET HIM WHAT HE WANTS.
AND YOU ARE?
CHRISTIAN WALKER. FBI.
SHOW HIM THE BADGE.
I'LL GET MY CAPTAIN.
YEAH? AND HE'LL GET THE COFFEE?
(A FUCKING CUP OF COFFEE.)
FBI, HUH?
YOU CALLED FOR ME.
OF COURSE.
WE GOES WAY BACK, DIAMOND. YOU KNOW THAT.
WELL... FOR FIVE MINUTES, 30 YEARS AGO.
WHAT?
YOU REALLY DON'T CONSIDER US FRIENDS?

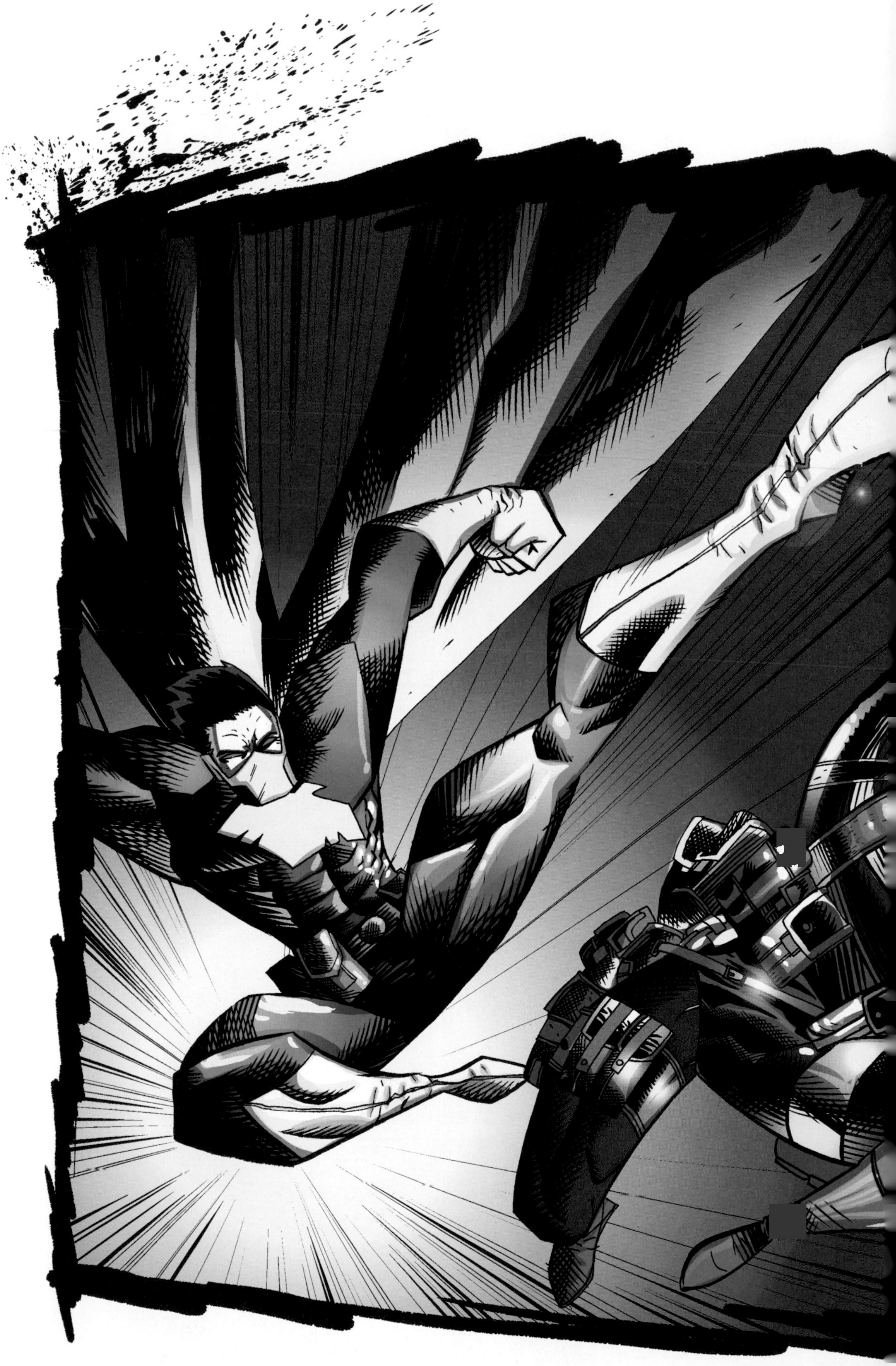

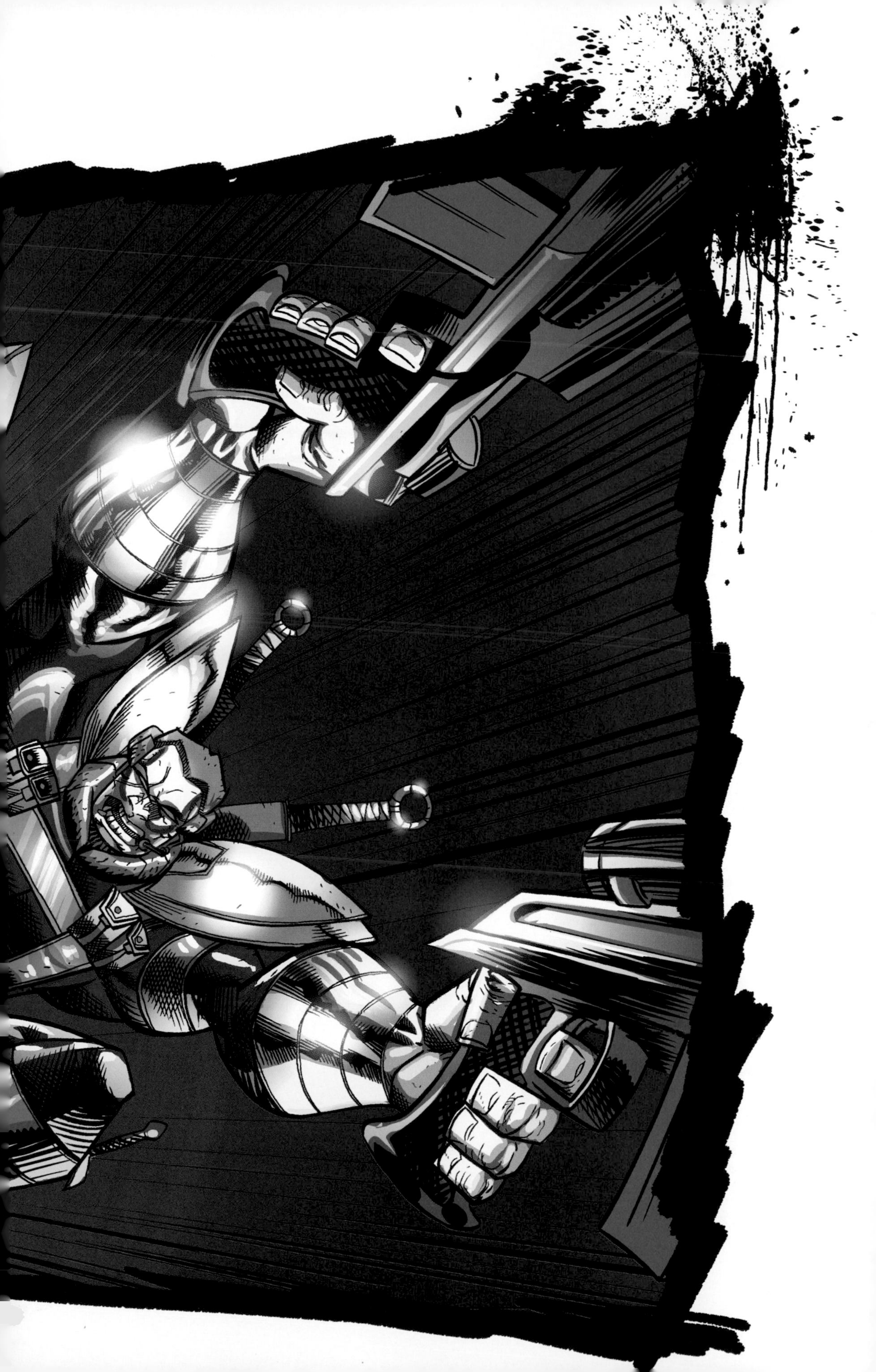

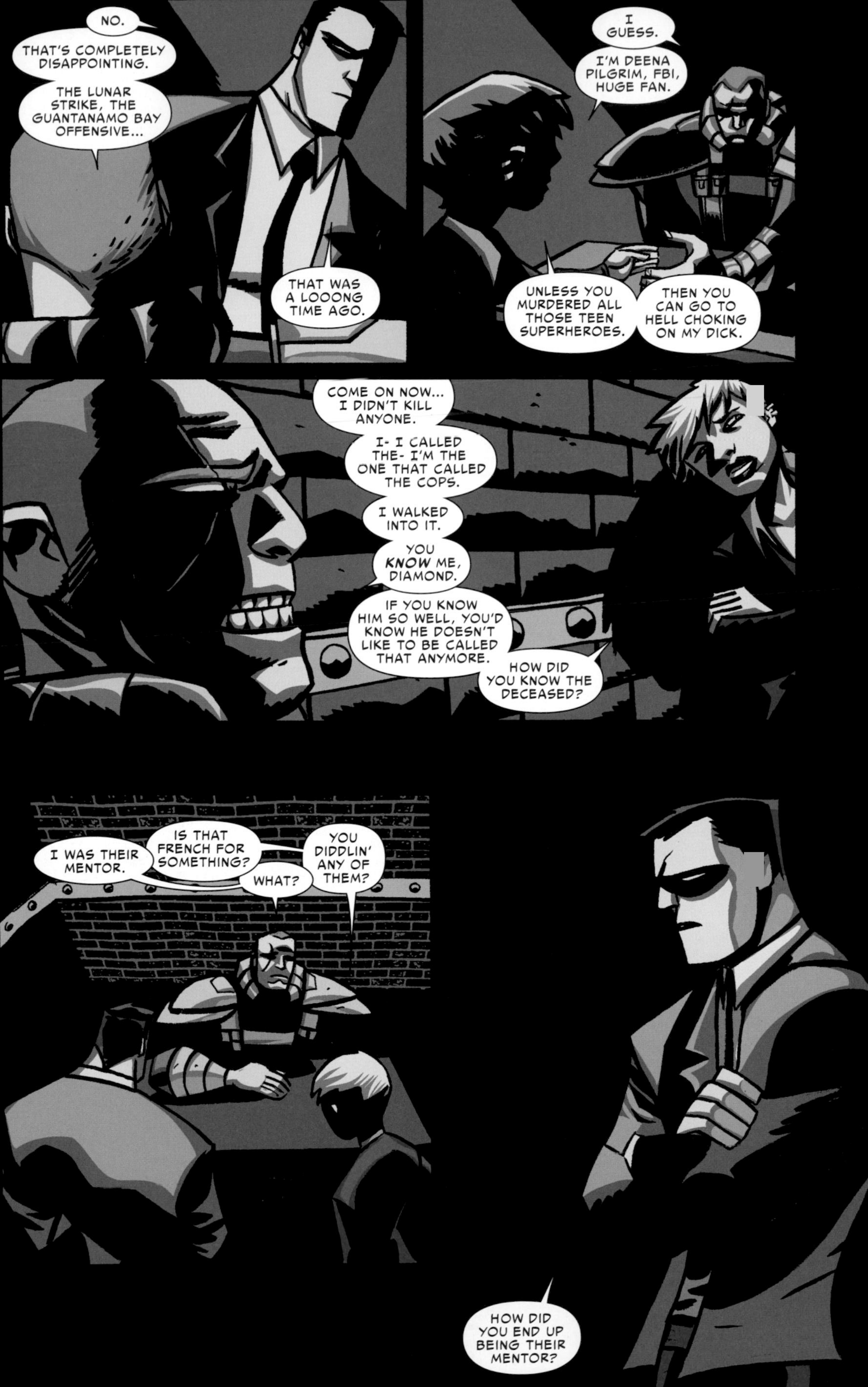
NO.
THAT'S COMPLETELY DISAPPOINTING.
THE LUNAR STRIKE, THE GUANTANAMO BAY OFFENSIVE...
THAT WAS A LOOONG TIME AGO.
I GUESS.
I'M DEENA PILGRIM, FBI, HUGE FAN.
UNLESS YOU MURDERED ALL THOSE TEEN SUPERHEROES.
THEN YOU CAN GO TO HELL CHOKING ON MY DICK.
COME ON NOW... I DIDN'T KILL ANYONE.
I- I CALLED THE- I'M THE ONE THAT CALLED THE COPS.
I WALKED INTO IT.
YOU *KNOW* ME, DIAMOND.
IF YOU KNOW HIM SO WELL, YOU'D KNOW HE DOESN'T LIKE TO BE CALLED THAT ANYMORE.
HOW DID YOU KNOW THE DECEASED?
I WAS THEIR MENTOR.
IS THAT FRENCH FOR SOMETHING?
WHAT?
YOU DIDDLIN' ANY OF THEM?
HOW DID YOU END UP BEING THEIR MENTOR?

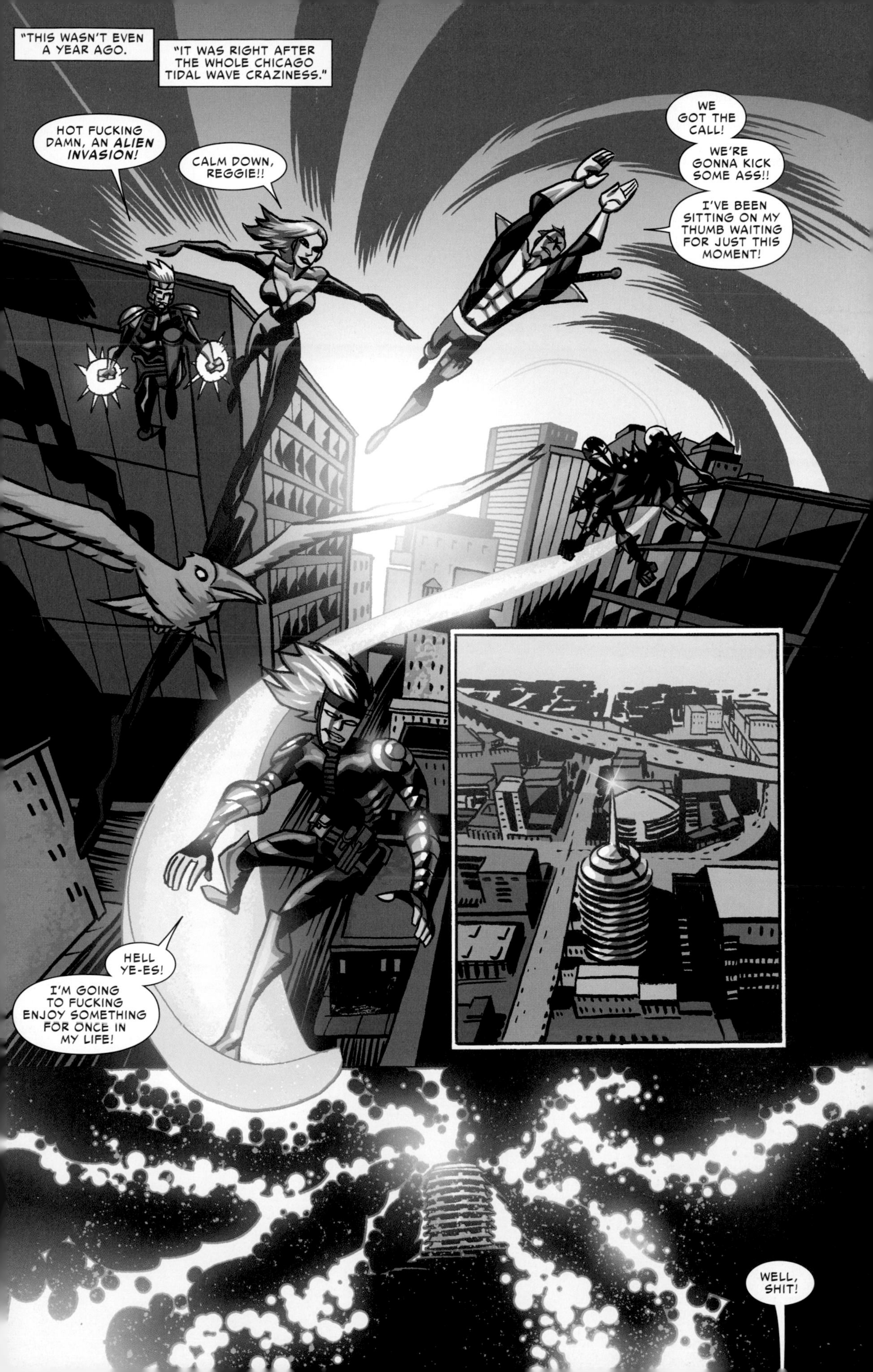
"THIS WASN'T EVEN A YEAR AGO.
"IT WAS RIGHT AFTER THE WHOLE CHICAGO TIDAL WAVE CRAZINESS."
HOT FUCKING DAMN, AN *ALIEN INVASION!*
CALM DOWN, REGGIE!!
WE GOT THE CALL!
WE'RE GONNA KICK SOME ASS!!
I'VE BEEN SITTING ON MY THUMB WAITING FOR JUST THIS MOMENT!
HELL YE-ES!
I'M GOING TO FUCKING ENJOY SOMETHING FOR ONCE IN MY LIFE!
WELL, SHIT!

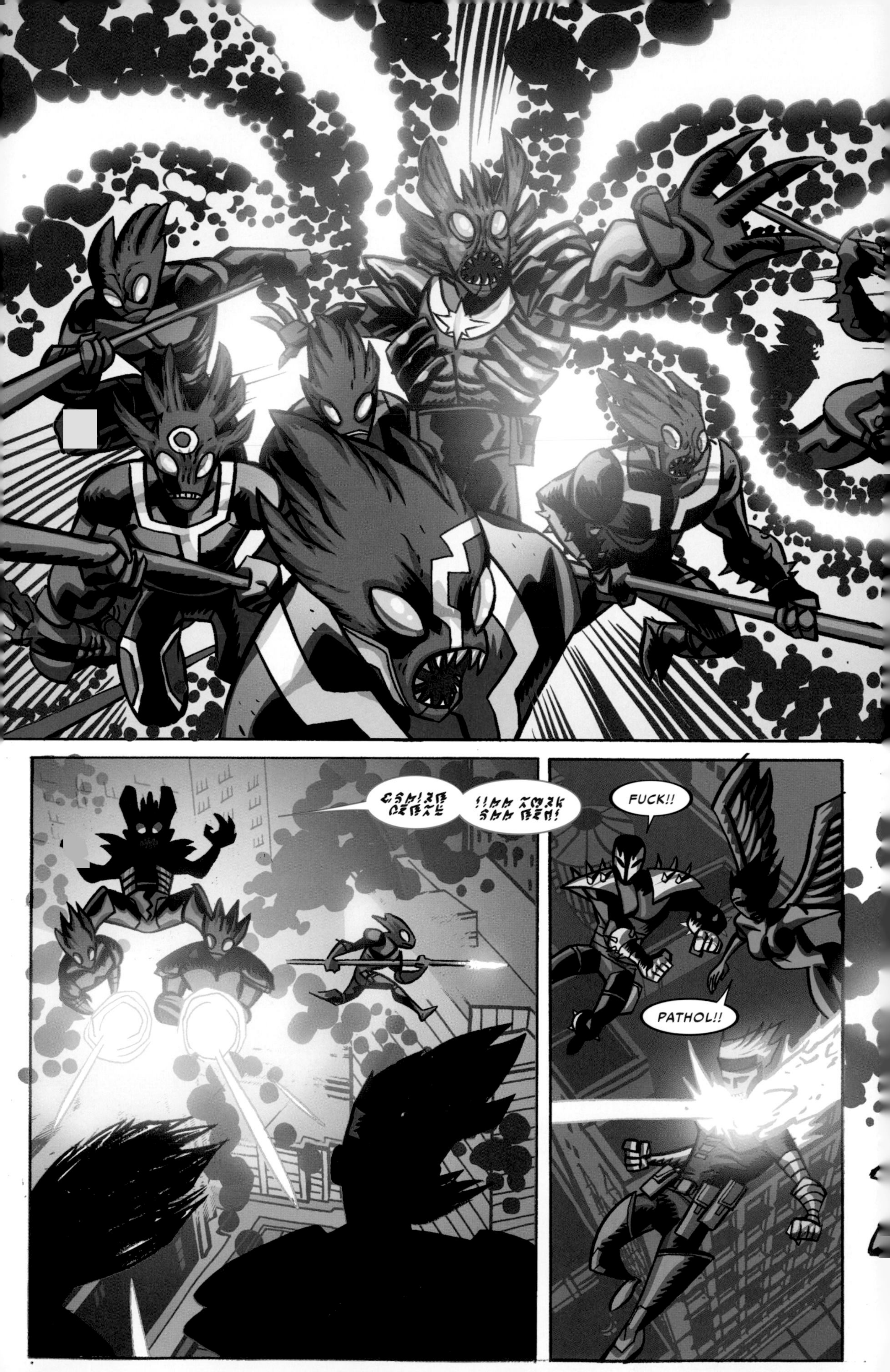
FUCK!!
PATHOL!!

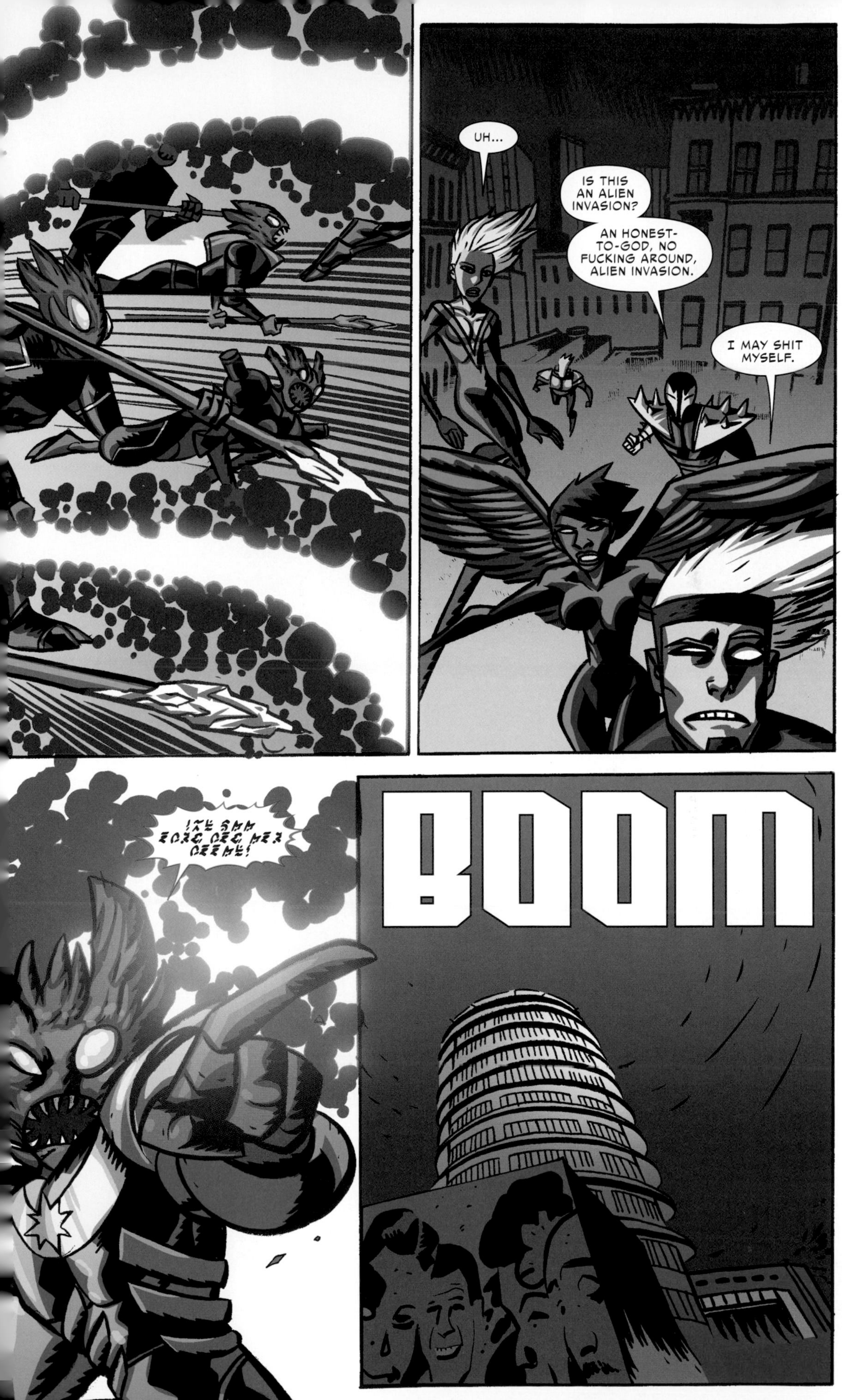
UH...
IS THIS AN ALIEN INVASION?
AN HONEST-TO-GOD, NO FUCKING AROUND, ALIEN INVASION.
I MAY SHIT MYSELF.
BOOM

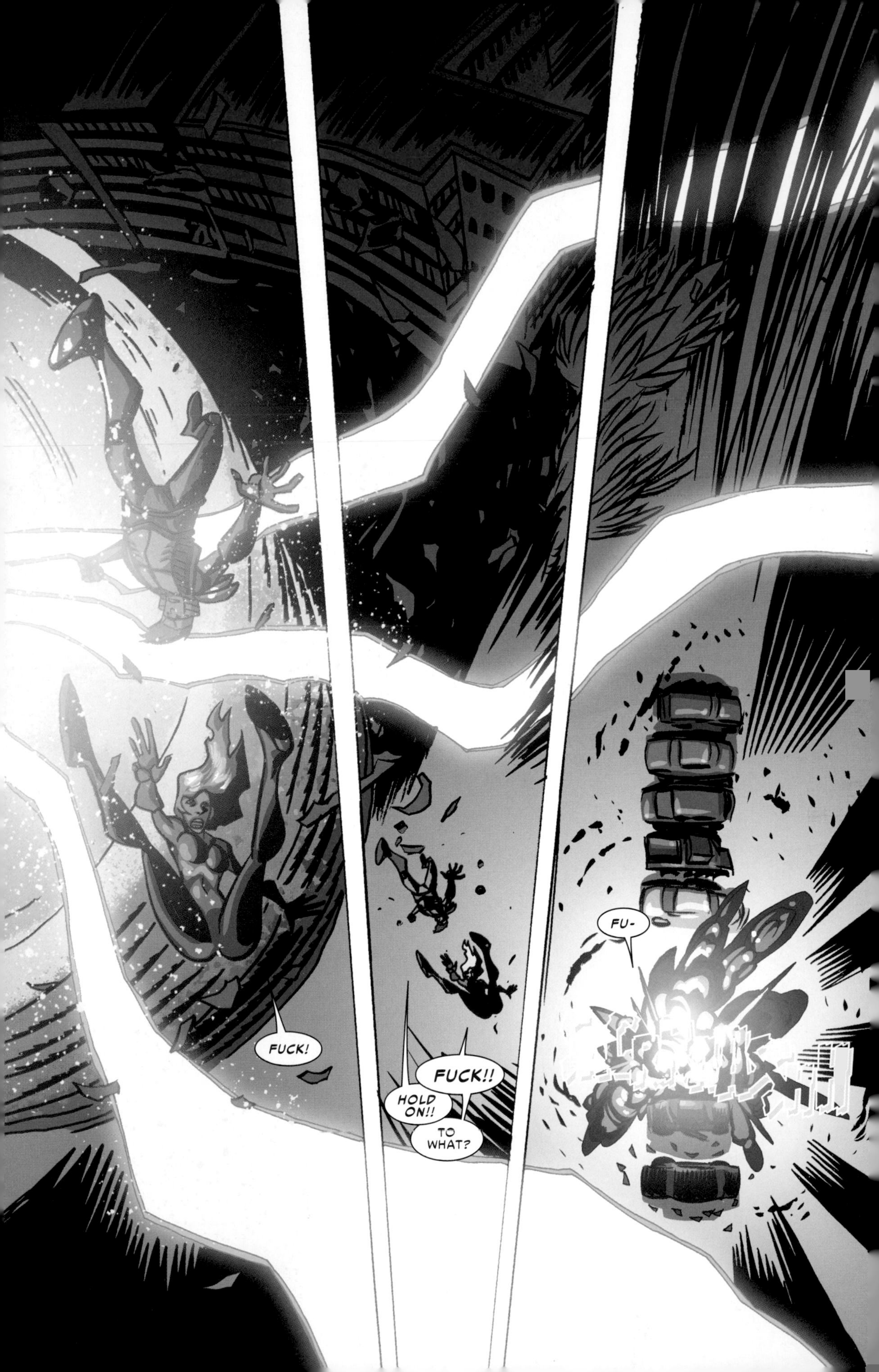
FUCK!
HOLD ON!!
FUCK!!
TO WHAT?
FU-

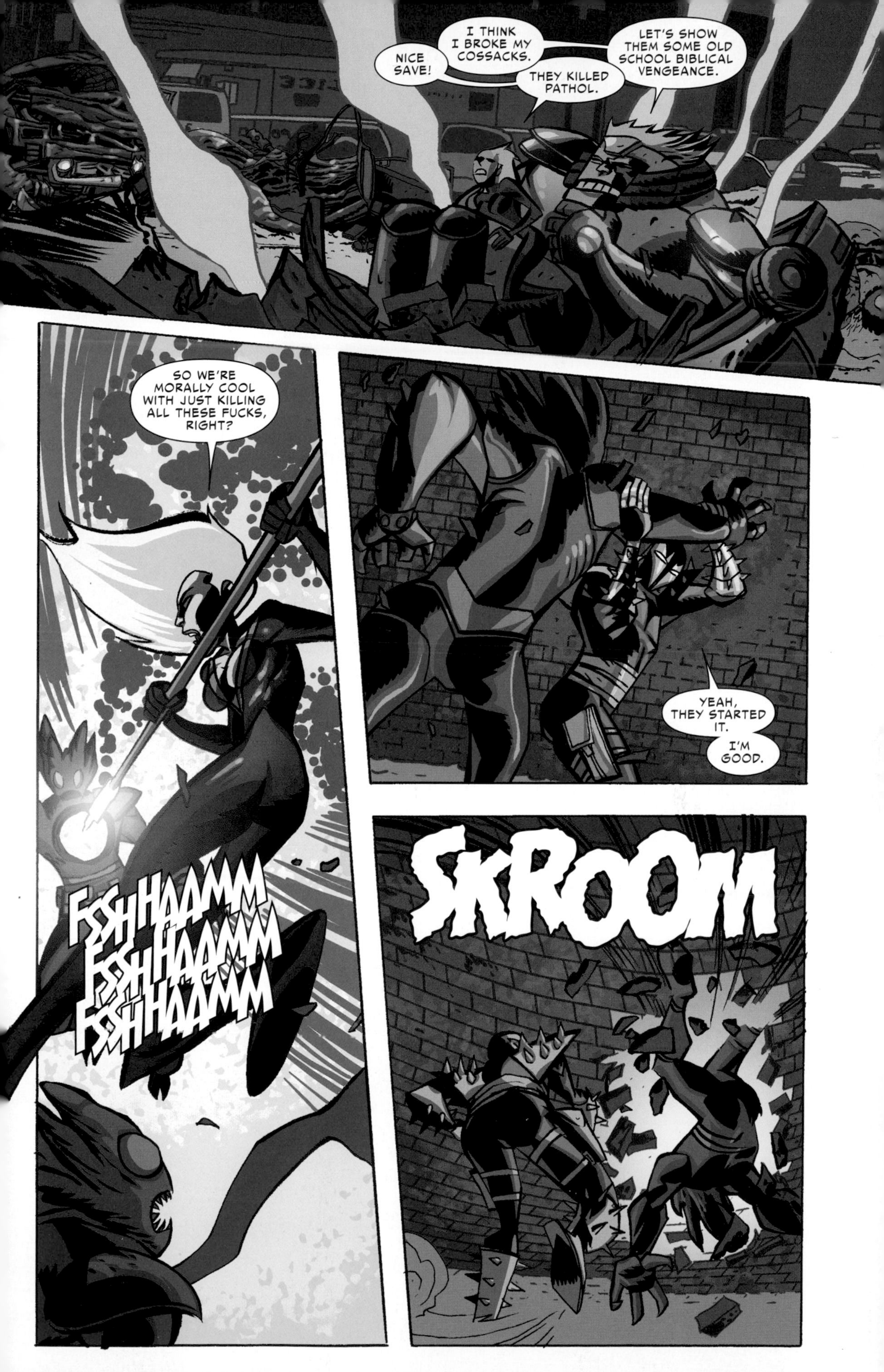
NICE SAVE!
I THINK I BROKE MY COSSACKS.
THEY KILLED PATHOL.
LET'S SHOW THEM SOME OLD SCHOOL BIBLICAL VENGEANCE.
SO WE'RE MORALLY COOL WITH JUST KILLING ALL THESE FUCKS, RIGHT?
FSHHAAMM
FSHHAAMM
FSHHAAMM
YEAH, THEY STARTED IT.
I'M GOOD.
SKROOM

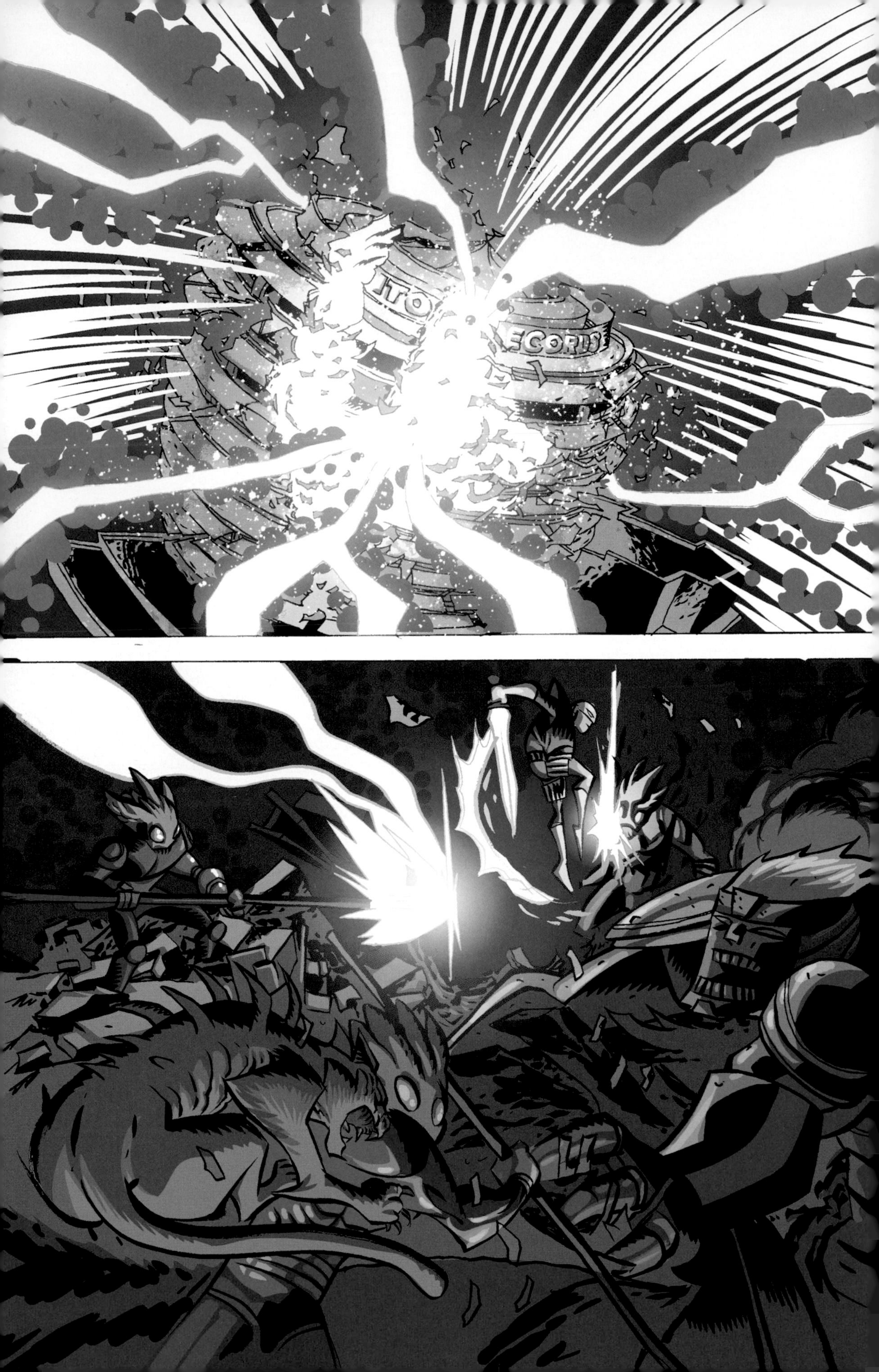

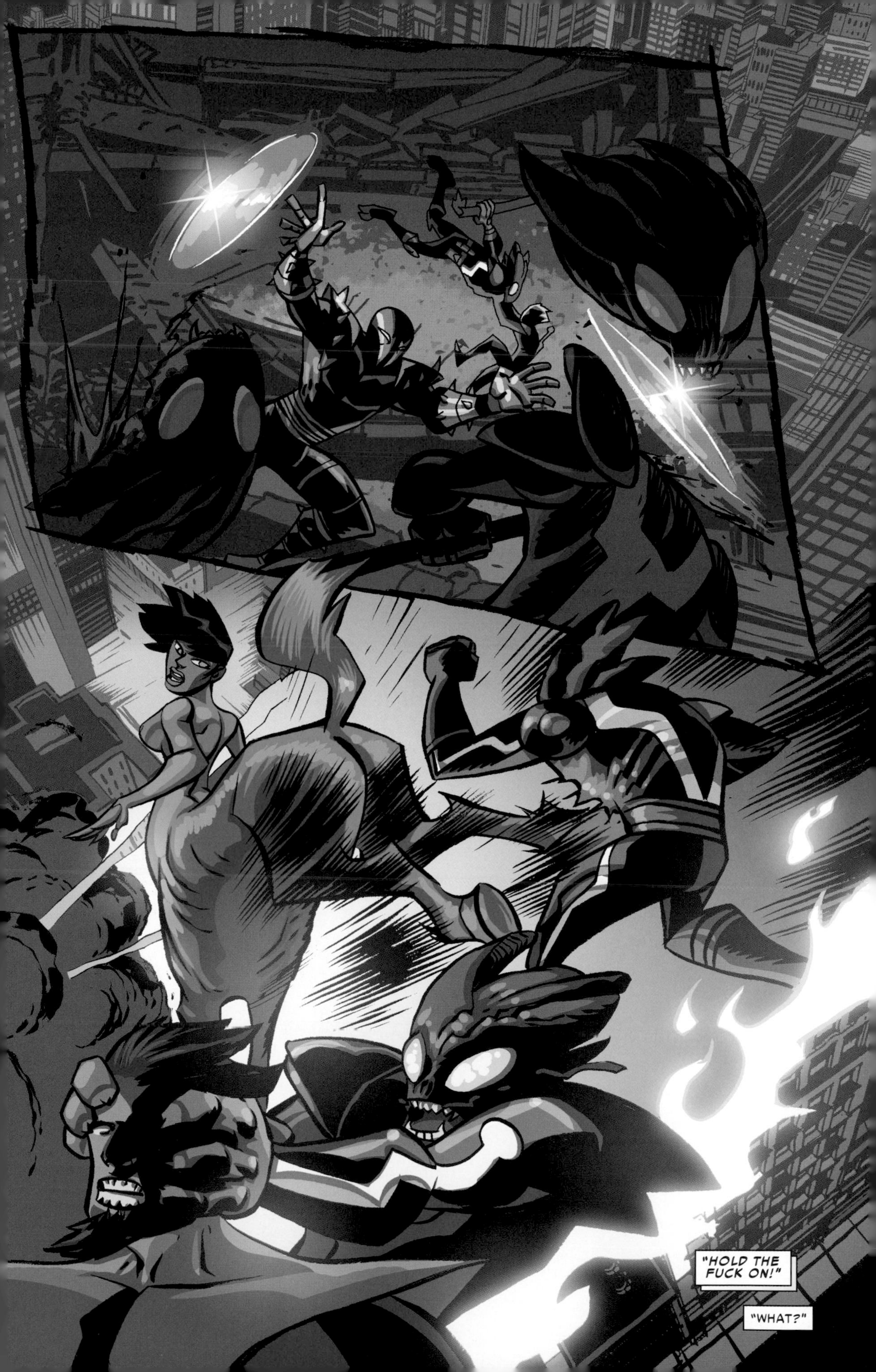
"HOLD THE FUCK ON!"
"WHAT?"

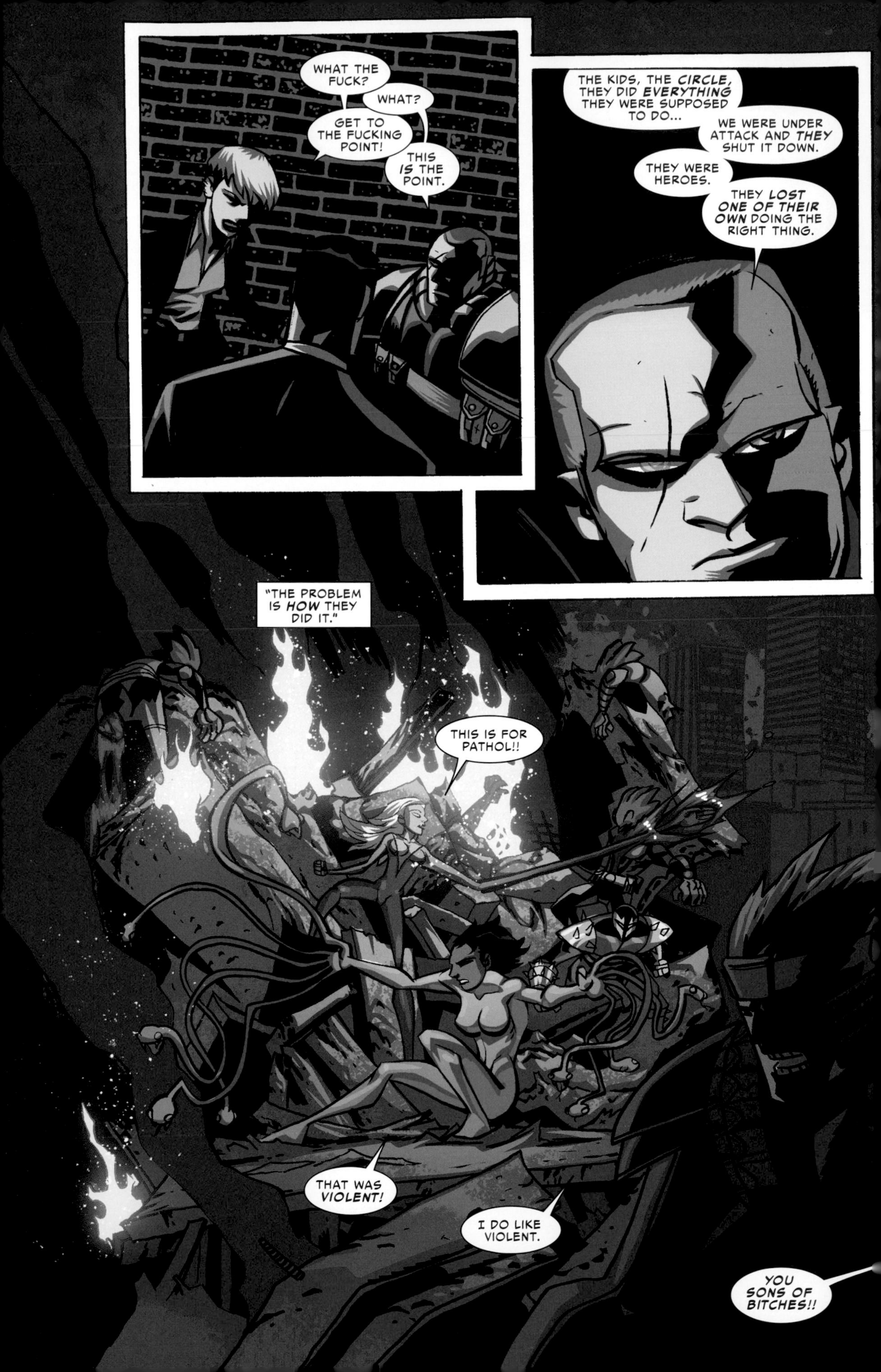
WHAT THE FUCK?
WHAT?
GET TO THE FUCKING POINT!
THIS *IS* THE POINT.
THE KIDS, THE *CIRCLE*, THEY DID *EVERYTHING* THEY WERE SUPPOSED TO DO...
WE WERE UNDER ATTACK AND *THEY* SHUT IT DOWN.
THEY WERE HEROES.
THEY *LOST ONE OF THEIR OWN* DOING THE RIGHT THING.
"THE PROBLEM IS *HOW* THEY DID IT."
THIS IS FOR PATHOL!!
THAT WAS *VIOLENT!*
I DO LIKE VIOLENT.
YOU SONS OF BITCHES!!

WHAT THE FUCK DID YOU JUST DO?

WHO THE HELL ARE YOU SUPPOSED TO BE?

IT'S THE FUCKING TRIPHAMMER FAN CLUB, YO! HA!

YOU'RE UNDER ARREST!!

NUH-UH!! YOU'RE UNDER ARREST!

I AM A FEDERAL AGENT, YOU COMPLETE DUMB SHIT!!

GREAT!

WE ARE MOTHERFUCKING SUPERHEROES AND WE JUST SAVED THE MOTHERFUCKING WORLD FROM A MOTHERFUCKING ALIEN INVASION!!

SO SUCK MY DICK AND SAY THANK YOU!

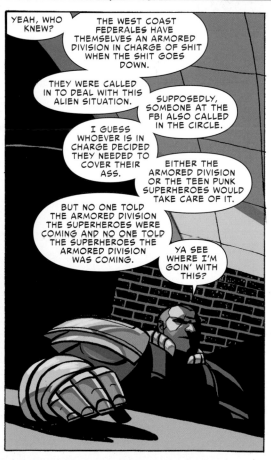

YEAH, WHO KNEW?

THE WEST COAST FEDERALES HAVE THEMSELVES AN ARMORED DIVISION IN CHARGE OF SHIT WHEN THE SHIT GOES DOWN.

THEY WERE CALLED IN TO DEAL WITH THIS ALIEN SITUATION.

SUPPOSEDLY, SOMEONE AT THE FBI ALSO CALLED IN THE CIRCLE.

I GUESS WHOEVER IS IN CHARGE DECIDED THEY NEEDED TO COVER THEIR ASS.

EITHER THE ARMORED DIVISION OR THE TEEN PUNK SUPERHEROES WOULD TAKE CARE OF IT.

BUT NO ONE TOLD THE ARMORED DIVISION THE SUPERHEROES WERE COMING AND NO ONE TOLD THE SUPERHEROES THE ARMORED DIVISION WAS COMING.

YA SEE WHERE I'M GOIN' WITH THIS?

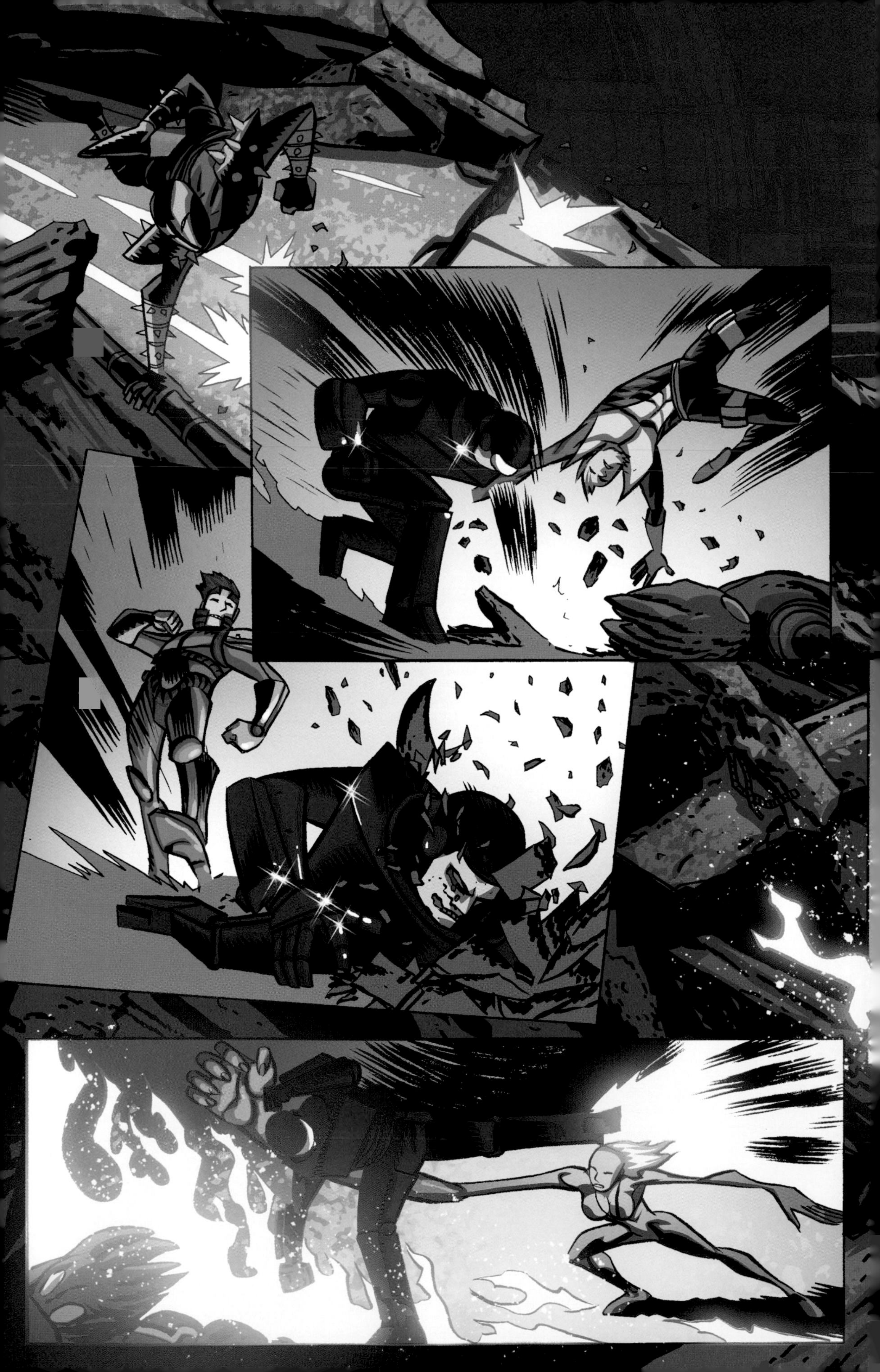

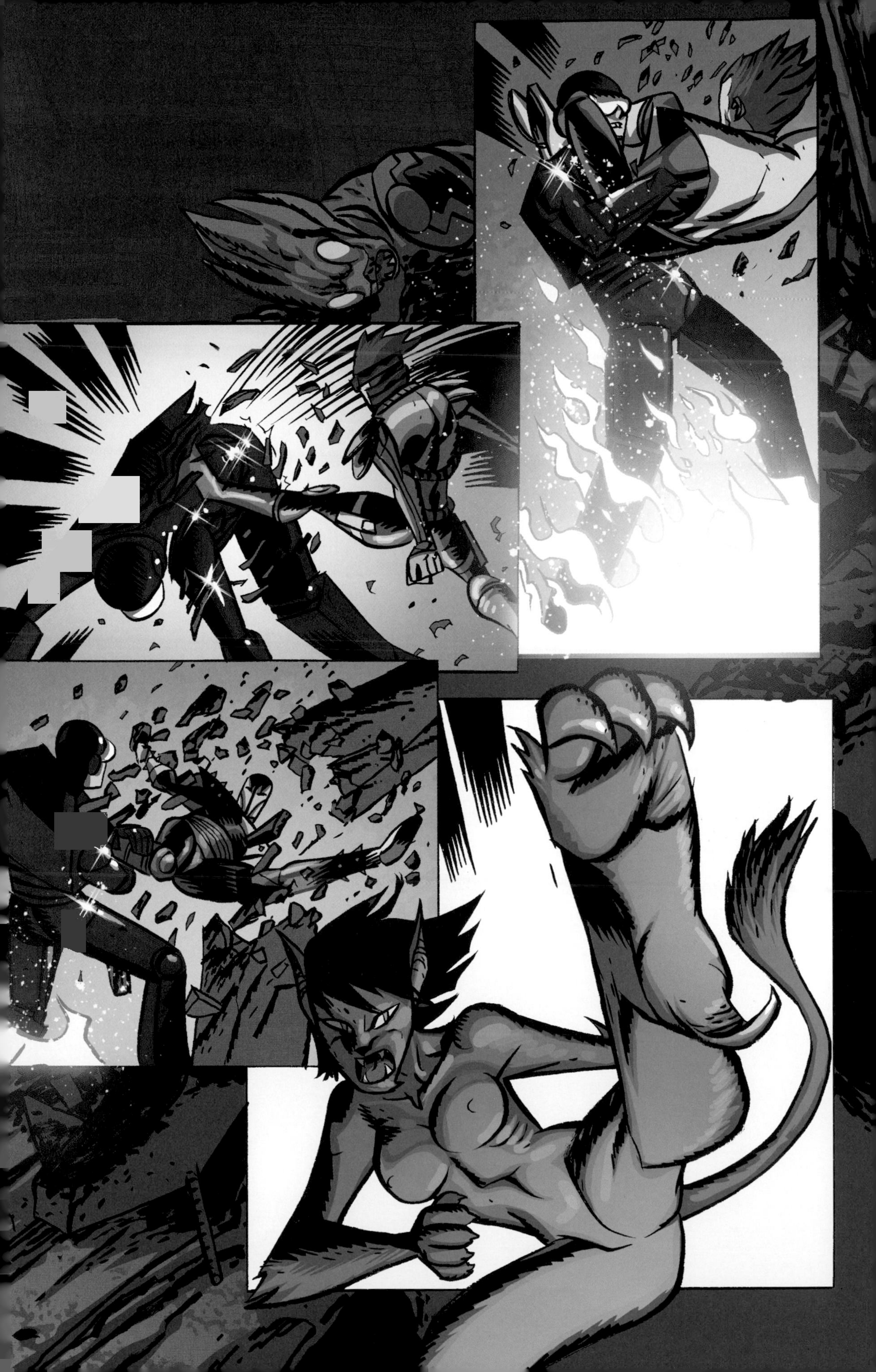

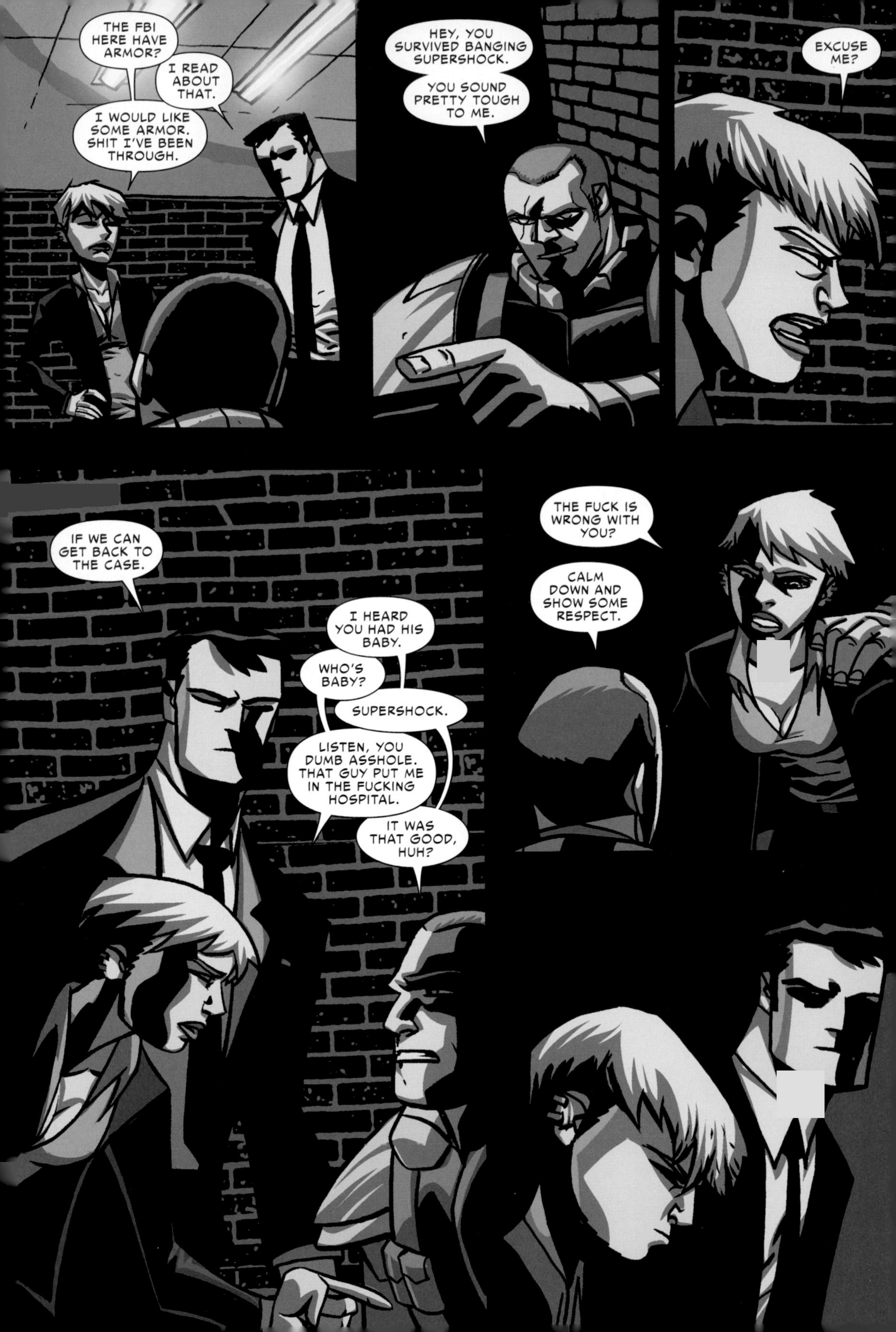

THE FBI HERE HAVE ARMOR?
I READ ABOUT THAT.
I WOULD LIKE SOME ARMOR. SHIT I'VE BEEN THROUGH.
HEY, YOU SURVIVED BANGING SUPERSHOCK.
YOU SOUND PRETTY TOUGH TO ME.
EXCUSE ME?
IF WE CAN GET BACK TO THE CASE.
I HEARD YOU HAD HIS BABY.
WHO'S BABY?
SUPERSHOCK.
LISTEN, YOU DUMB ASSHOLE. THAT GUY PUT ME IN THE FUCKING HOSPITAL.
IT WAS THAT GOOD, HUH?
THE FUCK IS WRONG WITH YOU?
CALM DOWN AND SHOW SOME RESPECT.

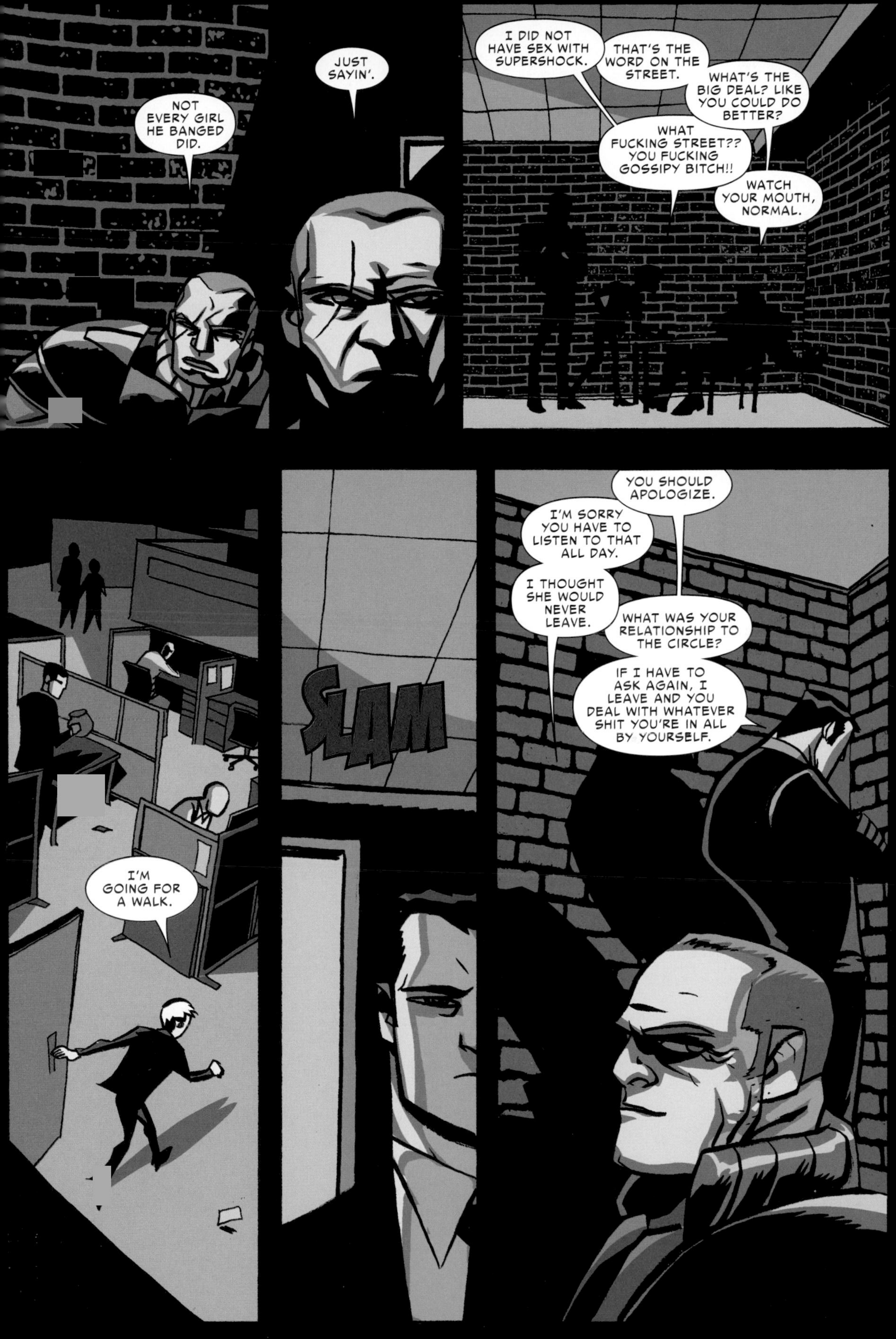
NOT EVERY GIRL HE BANGED DID.
JUST SAYIN'.
I DID NOT HAVE SEX WITH SUPERSHOCK.
THAT'S THE WORD ON THE STREET.
WHAT'S THE BIG DEAL? LIKE YOU COULD DO BETTER?
WHAT FUCKING STREET?? YOU FUCKING GOSSIPY BITCH!!
WATCH YOUR MOUTH, NORMAL.
I'M GOING FOR A WALK.
SLAM
YOU SHOULD APOLOGIZE.
I'M SORRY YOU HAVE TO LISTEN TO THAT ALL DAY.
I THOUGHT SHE WOULD NEVER LEAVE.
WHAT WAS YOUR RELATIONSHIP TO THE CIRCLE?
IF I HAVE TO ASK AGAIN, I LEAVE AND YOU DEAL WITH WHATEVER SHIT YOU'RE IN ALL BY YOURSELF.

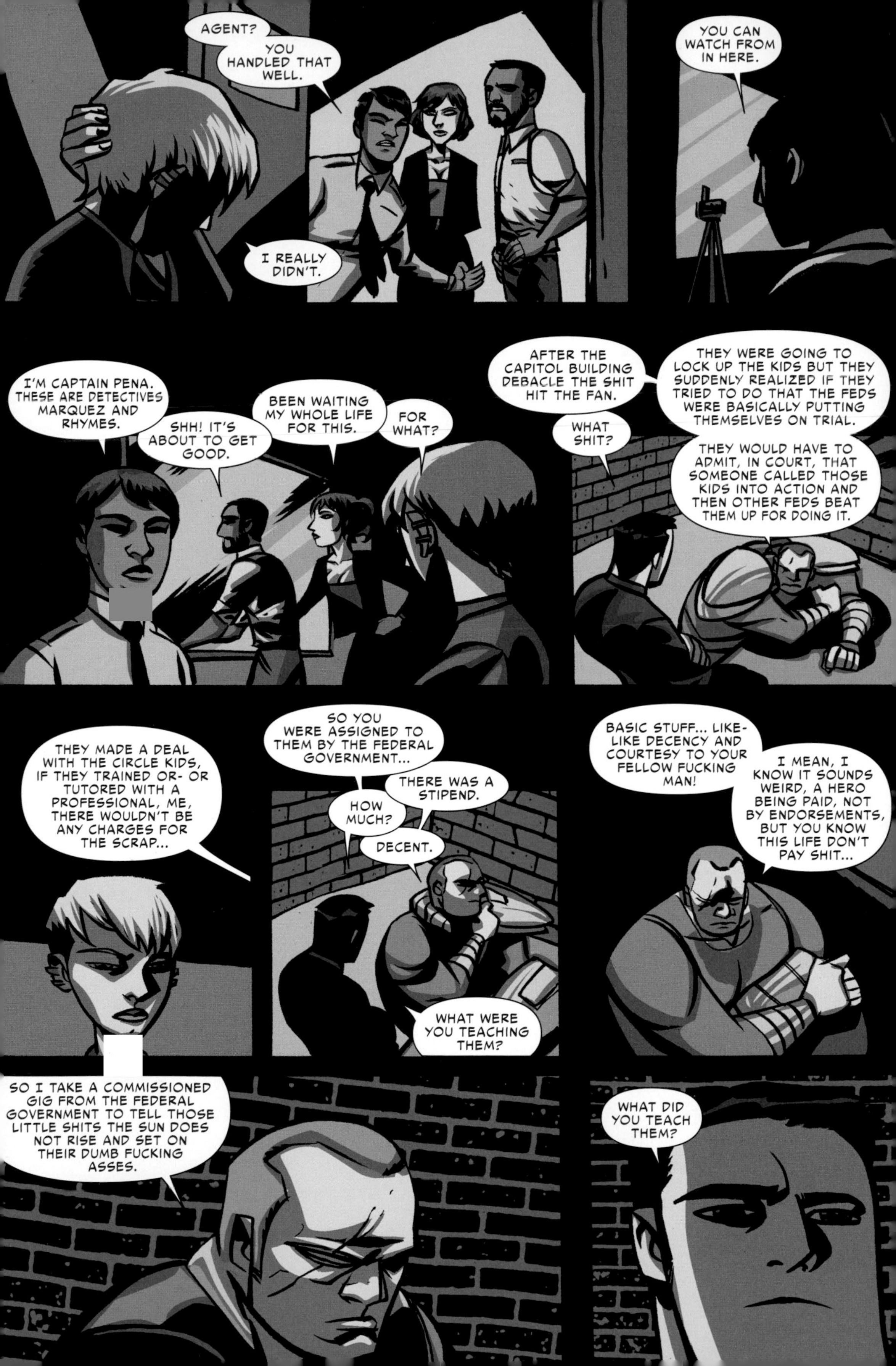
AGENT?
YOU HANDLED THAT WELL.
I REALLY DIDN'T.
YOU CAN WATCH FROM IN HERE.
I'M CAPTAIN PENA. THESE ARE DETECTIVES MARQUEZ AND RHYMES.
SHH! IT'S ABOUT TO GET GOOD.
BEEN WAITING MY WHOLE LIFE FOR THIS.
FOR WHAT?
AFTER THE CAPITOL BUILDING DEBACLE THE SHIT HIT THE FAN.
WHAT SHIT?
THEY WERE GOING TO LOCK UP THE KIDS BUT THEY SUDDENLY REALIZED IF THEY TRIED TO DO THAT THE FEDS WERE BASICALLY PUTTING THEMSELVES ON TRIAL.
THEY WOULD HAVE TO ADMIT, IN COURT, THAT SOMEONE CALLED THOSE KIDS INTO ACTION AND THEN OTHER FEDS BEAT THEM UP FOR DOING IT.
THEY MADE A DEAL WITH THE CIRCLE KIDS, IF THEY TRAINED OR- OR TUTORED WITH A PROFESSIONAL, ME, THERE WOULDN'T BE ANY CHARGES FOR THE SCRAP...
SO YOU WERE ASSIGNED TO THEM BY THE FEDERAL GOVERNMENT...
THERE WAS A STIPEND.
HOW MUCH?
DECENT.
WHAT WERE YOU TEACHING THEM?
BASIC STUFF... LIKE- LIKE DECENCY AND COURTESY TO YOUR FELLOW FUCKING MAN!
I MEAN, I KNOW IT SOUNDS WEIRD, A HERO BEING PAID, NOT BY ENDORSEMENTS, BUT YOU KNOW THIS LIFE DON'T PAY SHIT...
SO I TAKE A COMMISSIONED GIG FROM THE FEDERAL GOVERNMENT TO TELL THOSE LITTLE SHITS THE SUN DOES NOT RISE AND SET ON THEIR DUMB FUCKING ASSES.
WHAT DID YOU TEACH THEM?

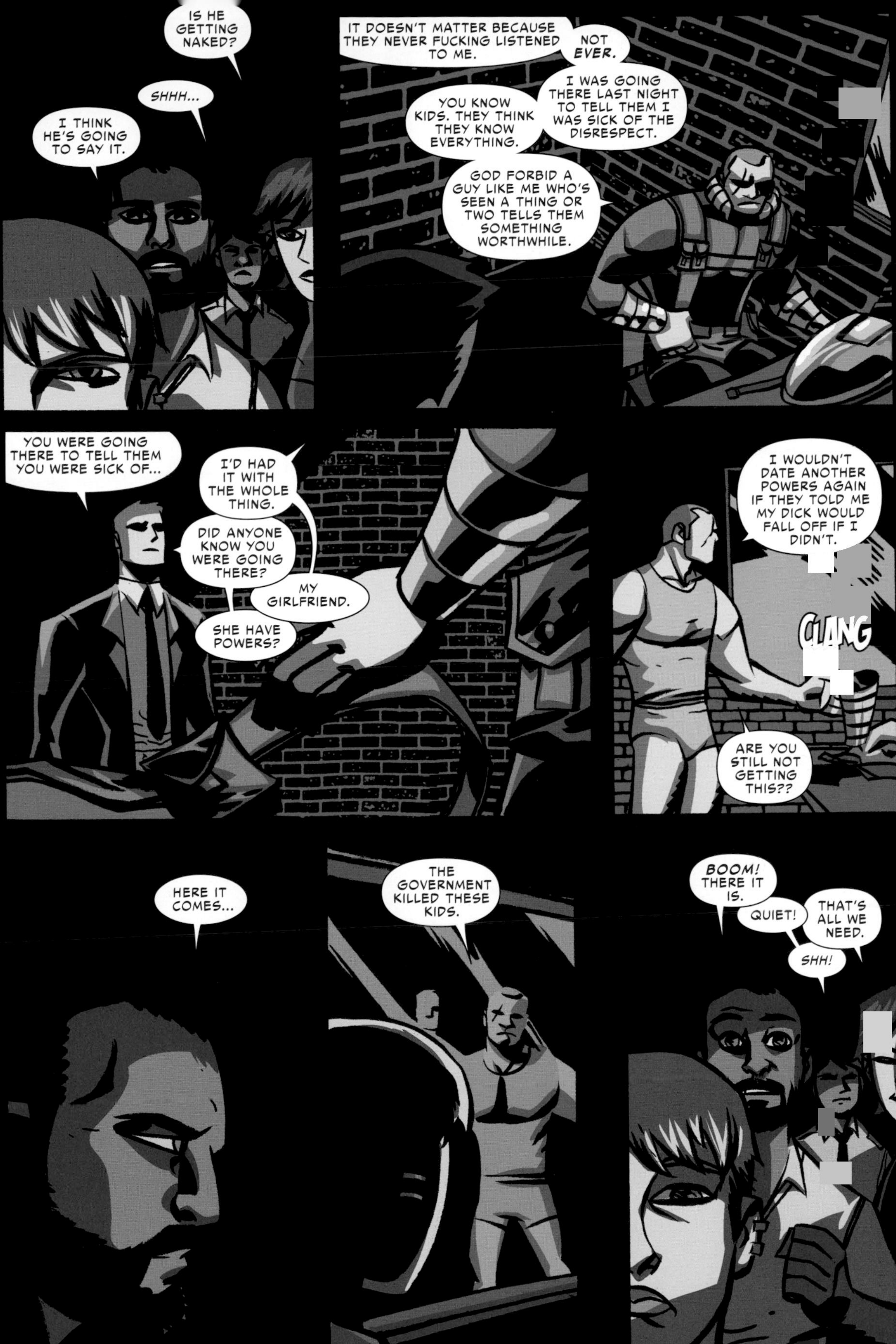

IS HE GETTING NAKED?
SHHH...
I THINK HE'S GOING TO SAY IT.
IT DOESN'T MATTER BECAUSE THEY NEVER FUCKING LISTENED TO ME.
NOT *EVER.*
YOU KNOW KIDS. THEY THINK THEY KNOW EVERYTHING.
I WAS GOING THERE LAST NIGHT TO TELL THEM I WAS SICK OF THE DISRESPECT.
GOD FORBID A GUY LIKE ME WHO'S SEEN A THING OR TWO TELLS THEM SOMETHING WORTHWHILE.
YOU WERE GOING THERE TO TELL THEM YOU WERE SICK OF...
I'D HAD IT WITH THE WHOLE THING.
DID ANYONE KNOW YOU WERE GOING THERE?
MY GIRLFRIEND.
SHE HAVE POWERS?
I WOULDN'T DATE ANOTHER POWERS AGAIN IF THEY TOLD ME MY DICK WOULD FALL OFF IF I DIDN'T.
CLANG
ARE YOU STILL NOT GETTING THIS??
HERE IT COMES...
THE GOVERNMENT KILLED THESE KIDS.
BOOM! THERE IT IS.
QUIET!
THAT'S ALL WE NEED.
SHH!

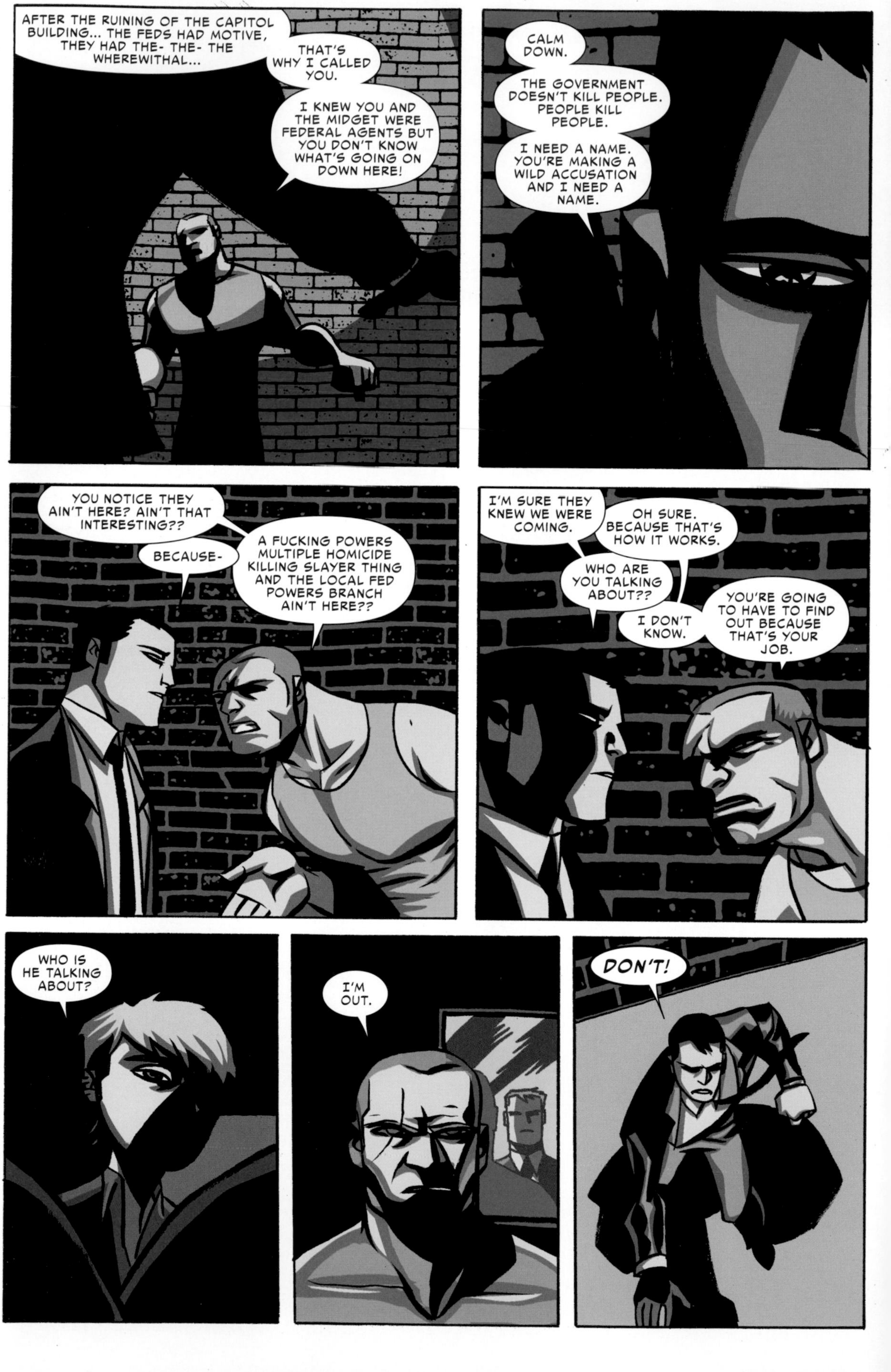
AFTER THE RUINING OF THE CAPITOL BUILDING... THE FEDS HAD MOTIVE, THEY HAD THE- THE- THE WHEREWITHAL...
THAT'S WHY I CALLED YOU.
I KNEW YOU AND THE MIDGET WERE FEDERAL AGENTS BUT YOU DON'T KNOW WHAT'S GOING ON DOWN HERE!
CALM DOWN.
THE GOVERNMENT DOESN'T KILL PEOPLE. PEOPLE KILL PEOPLE.
I NEED A NAME. YOU'RE MAKING A WILD ACCUSATION AND I NEED A NAME.
YOU NOTICE THEY AIN'T HERE? AIN'T THAT INTERESTING??
BECAUSE-
A FUCKING POWERS MULTIPLE HOMICIDE KILLING SLAYER THING AND THE LOCAL FED POWERS BRANCH AIN'T HERE??
I'M SURE THEY KNEW WE WERE COMING.
OH SURE. BECAUSE THAT'S HOW IT WORKS.
WHO ARE YOU TALKING ABOUT??
I DON'T KNOW.
YOU'RE GOING TO HAVE TO FIND OUT BECAUSE THAT'S YOUR JOB.
WHO IS HE TALKING ABOUT?
I'M OUT.
DON'T!

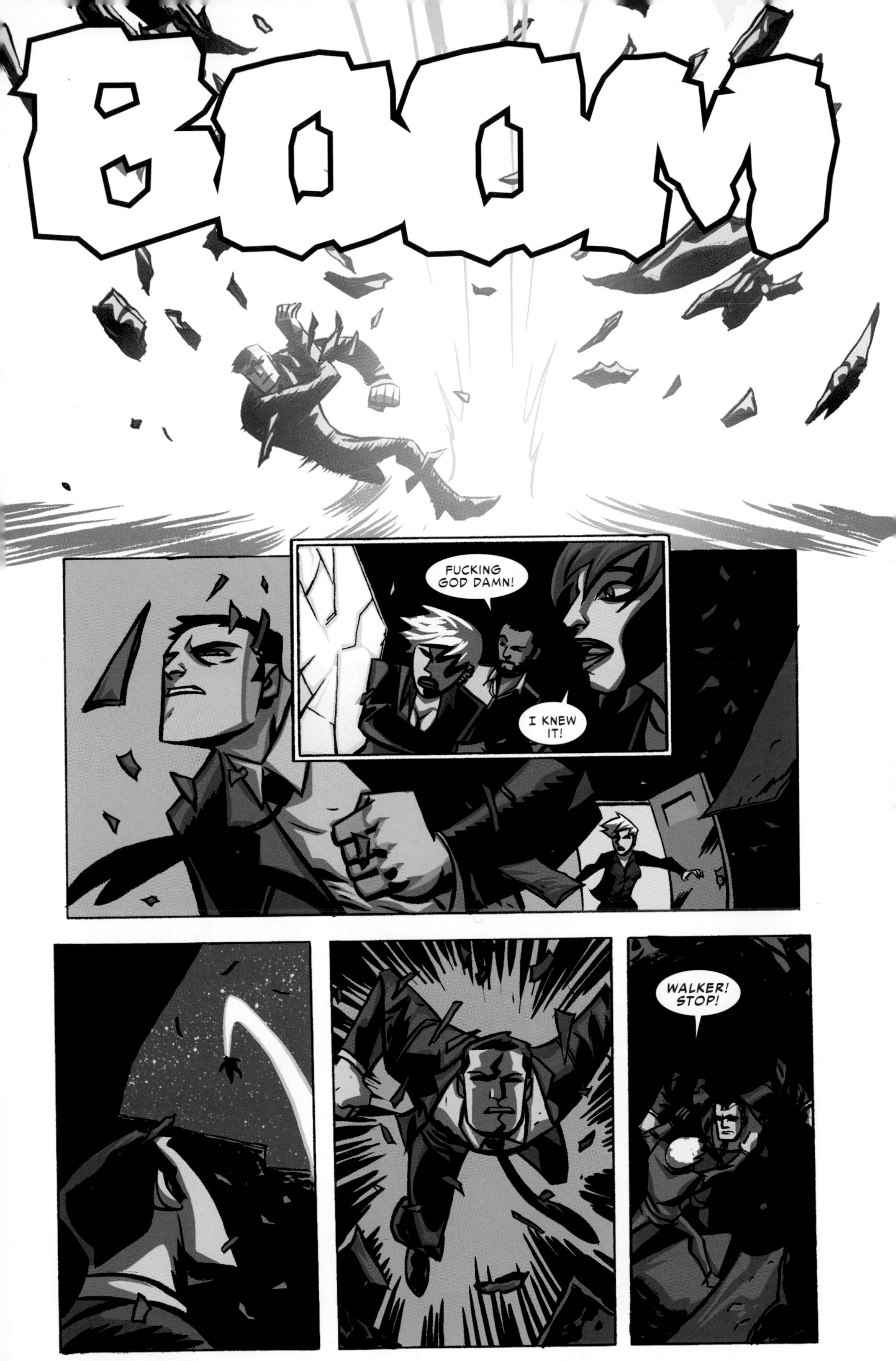
BOOM
FUCKING GOD DAMN!
I KNEW IT!
WALKER! STOP!

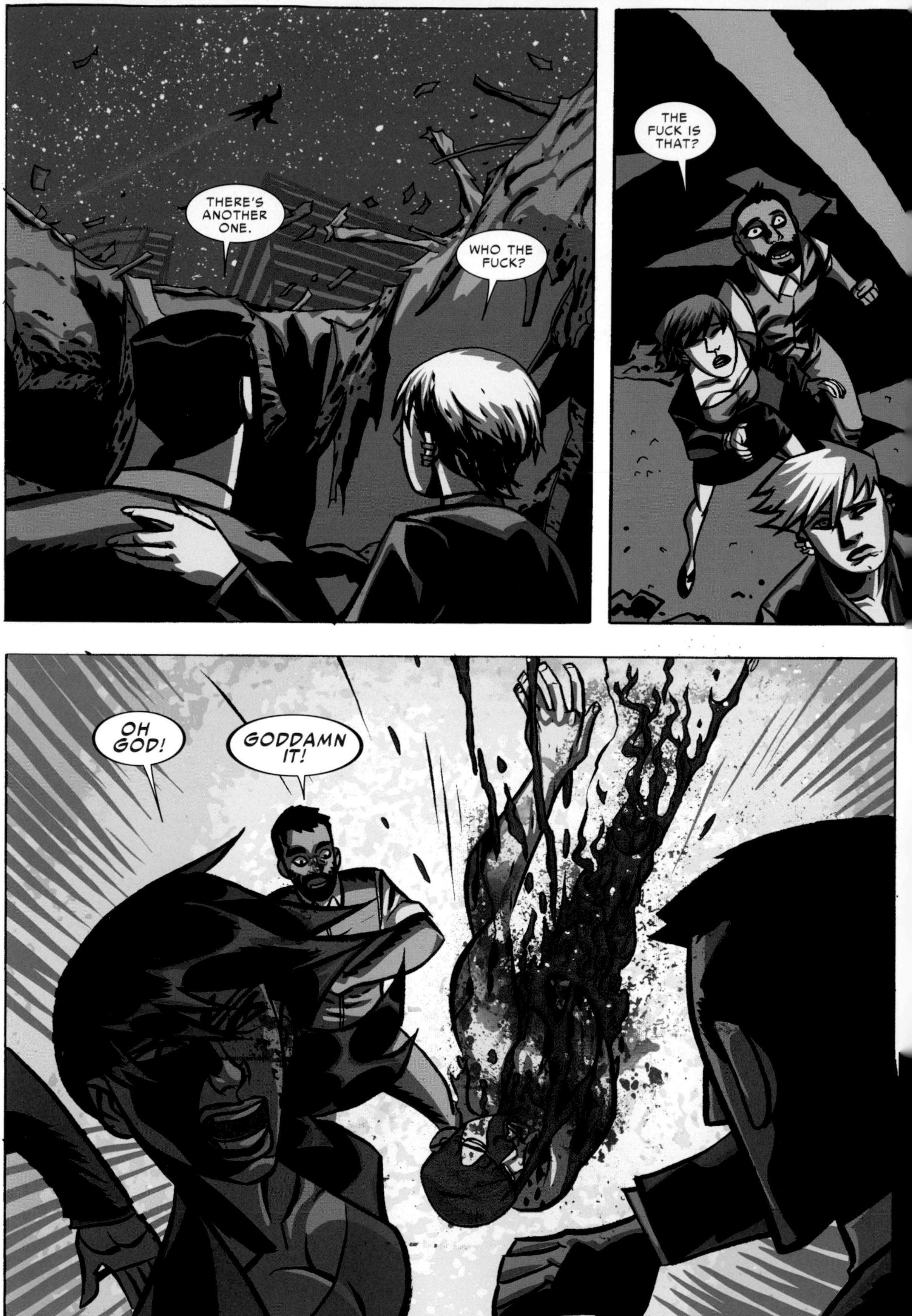
THERE'S ANOTHER ONE.
WHO THE FUCK?
THE FUCK IS THAT?
OH GOD!
GODDAMN IT!

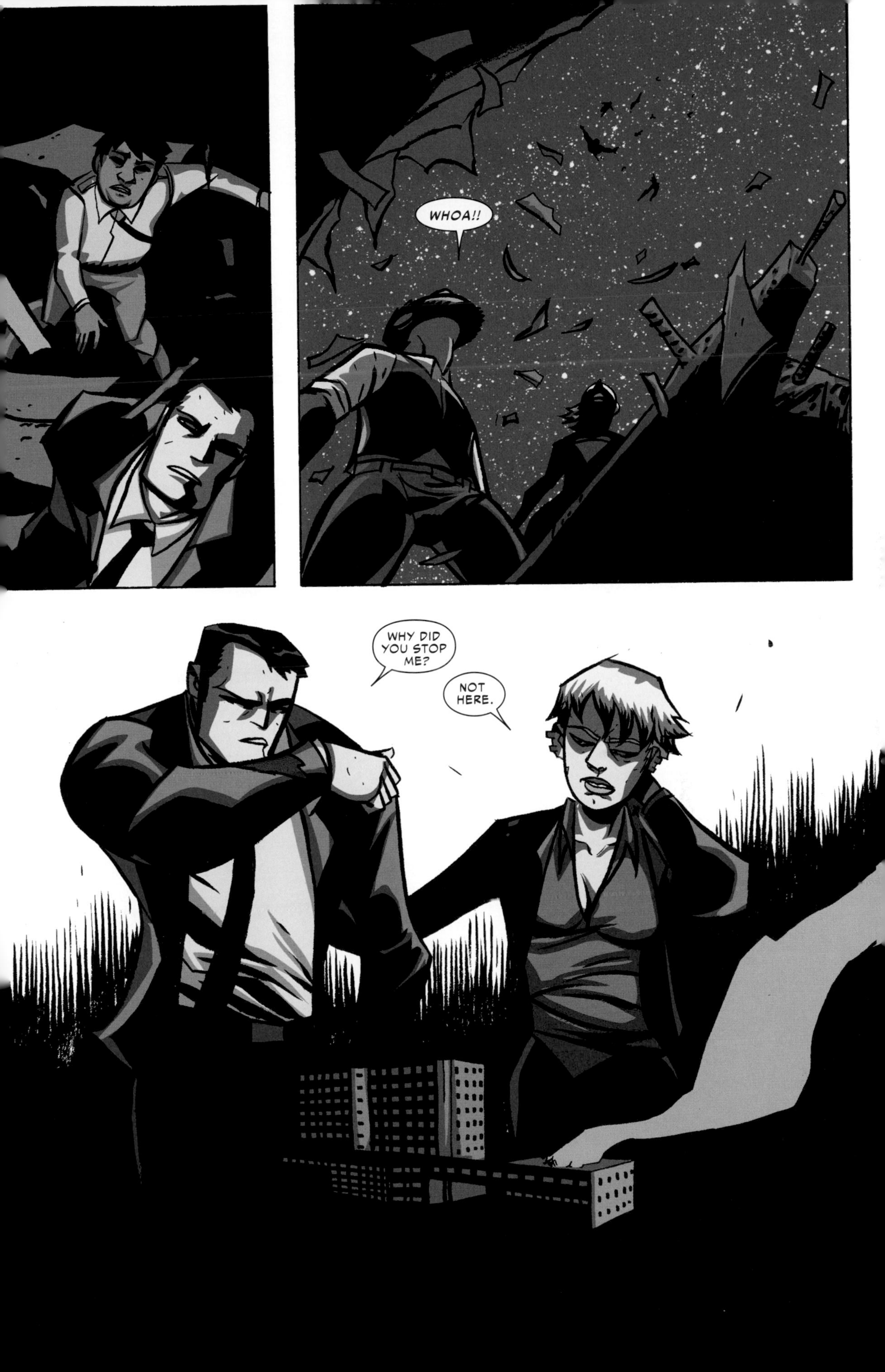
WHOA!!
WHY DID YOU STOP ME?
NOT HERE.

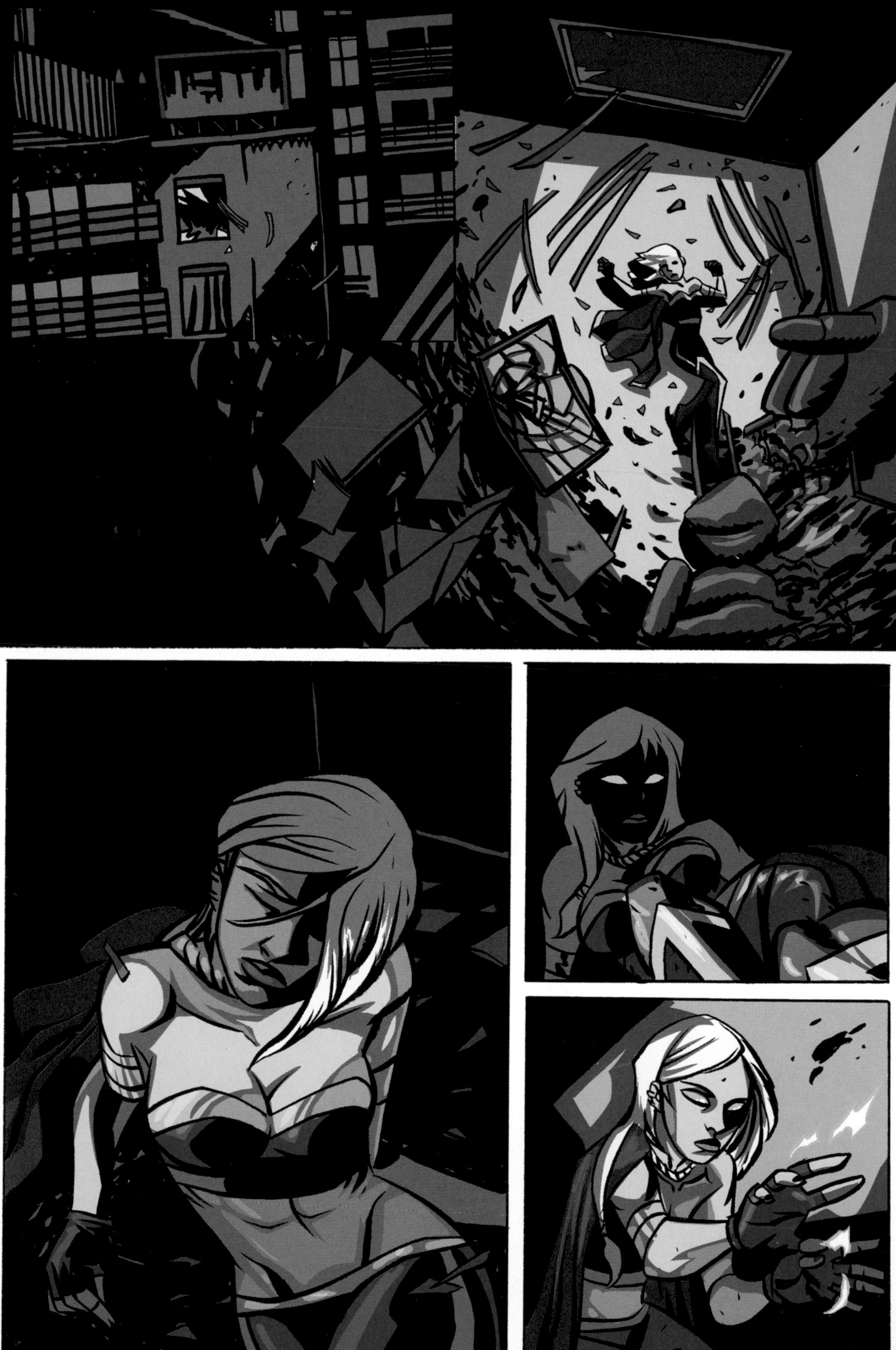

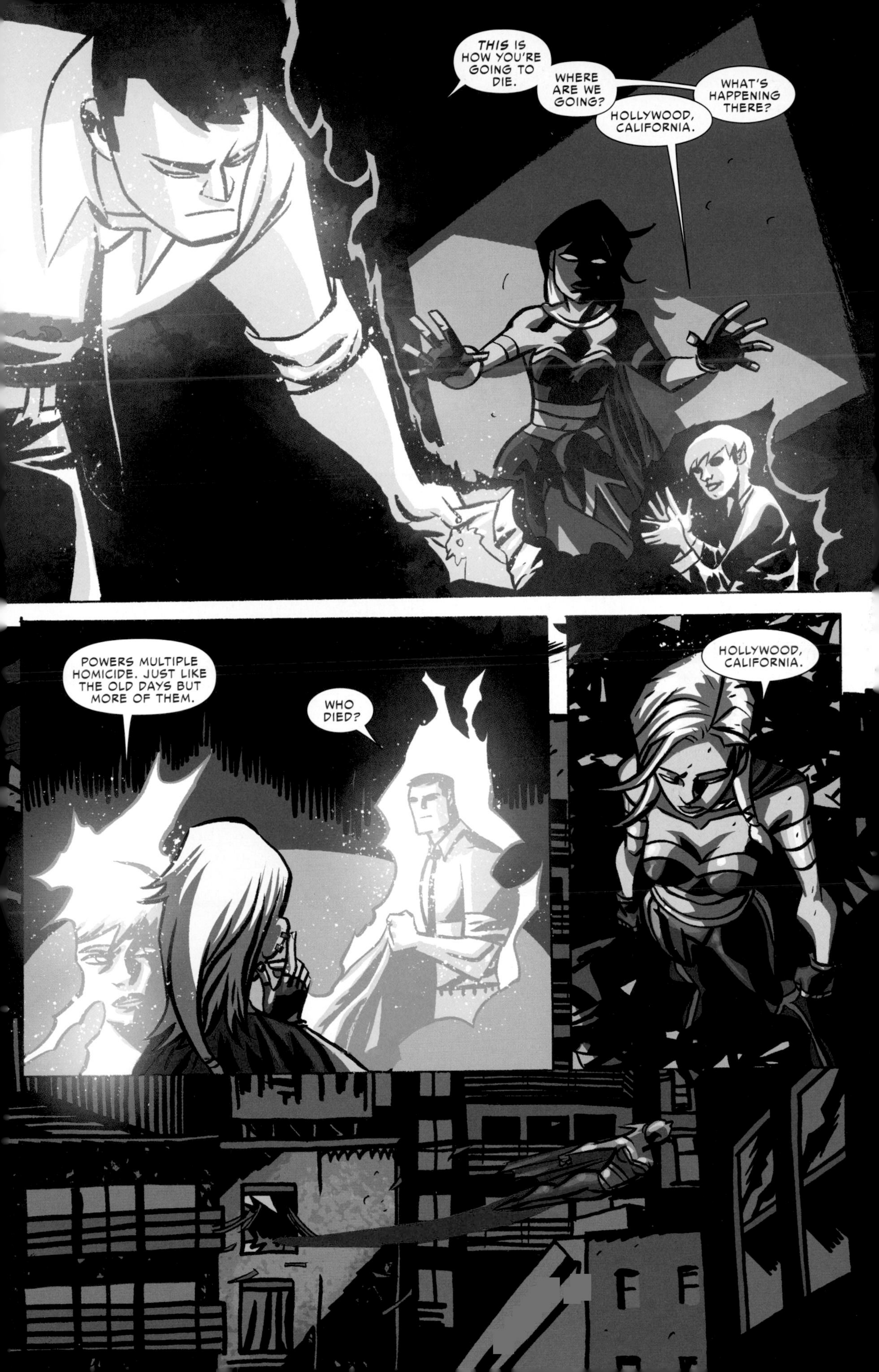
THIS IS HOW YOU'RE GOING TO DIE.
WHERE ARE WE GOING?
WHAT'S HAPPENING THERE?
HOLLYWOOD, CALIFORNIA.
POWERS MULTIPLE HOMICIDE. JUST LIKE THE OLD DAYS BUT MORE OF THEM.
WHO DIED?
HOLLYWOOD, CALIFORNIA.

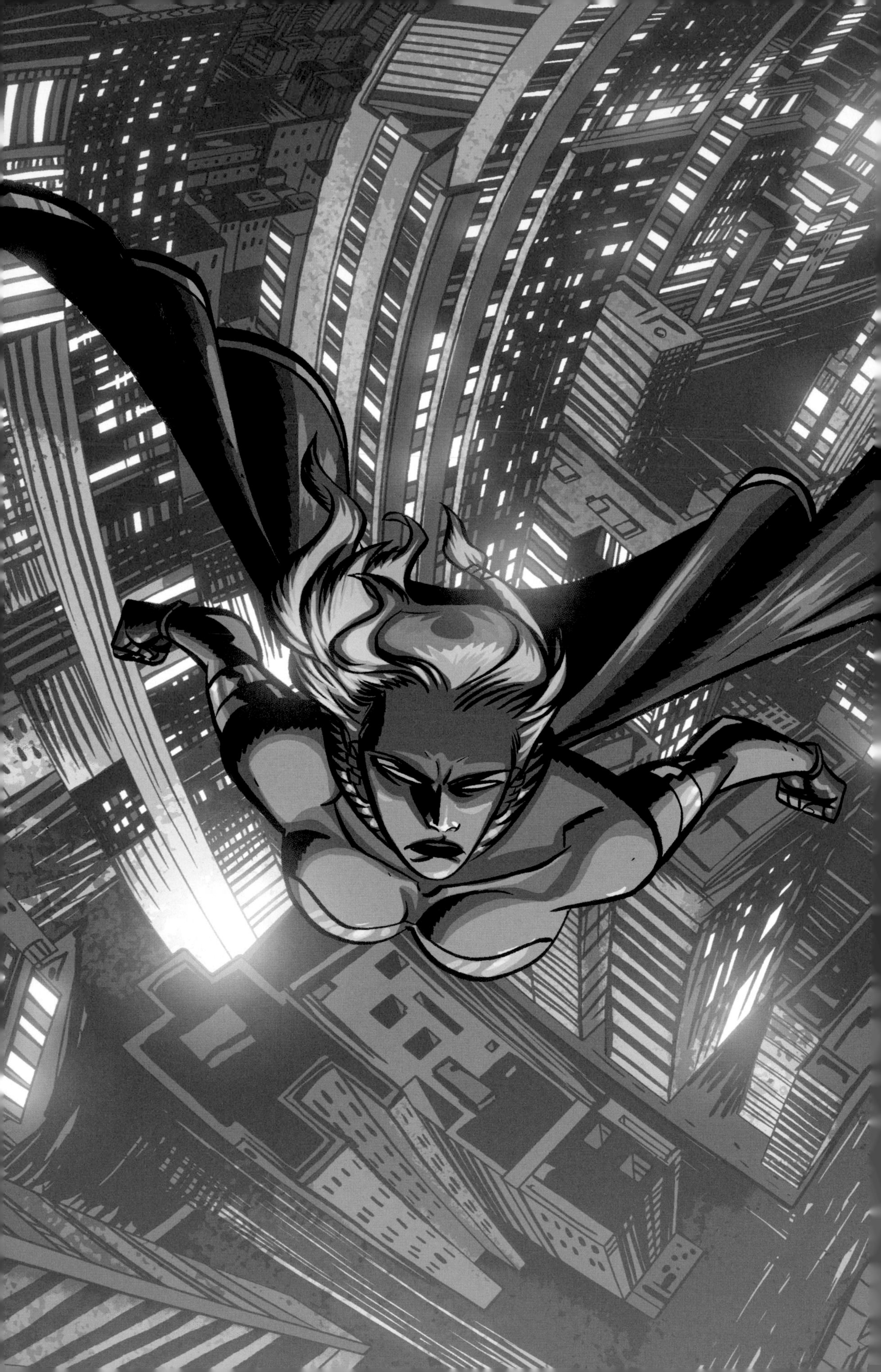

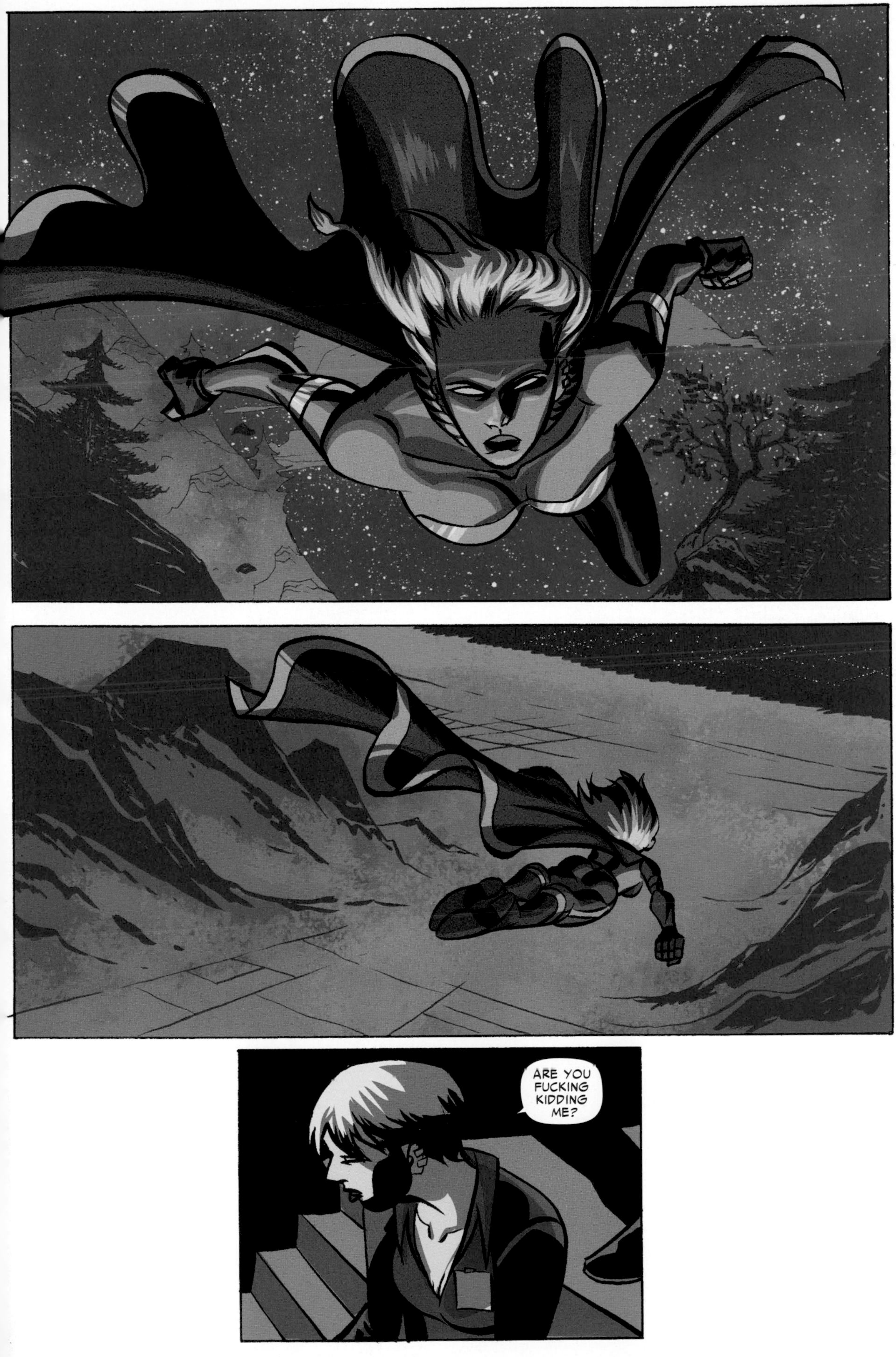
ARE YOU FUCKING KIDDING ME?

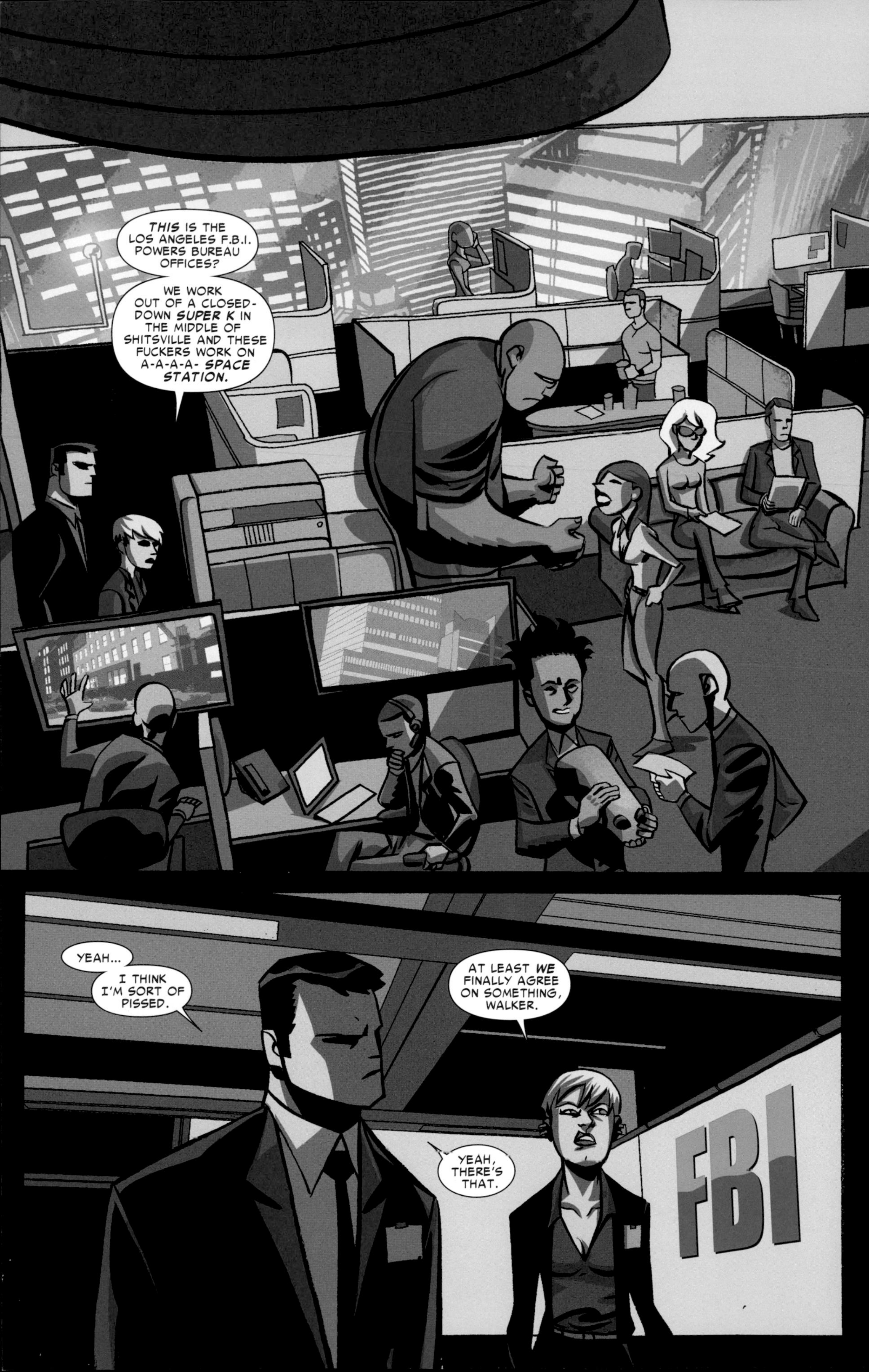
THIS IS THE LOS ANGELES F.B.I. POWERS BUREAU OFFICES?
WE WORK OUT OF A CLOSED-DOWN SUPER K IN THE MIDDLE OF SHITSVILLE AND THESE FUCKERS WORK ON A-A-A-A- SPACE STATION.
YEAH...
I THINK I'M SORT OF PISSED.
AT LEAST WE FINALLY AGREE ON SOMETHING, WALKER.
YEAH, THERE'S THAT.
FBI

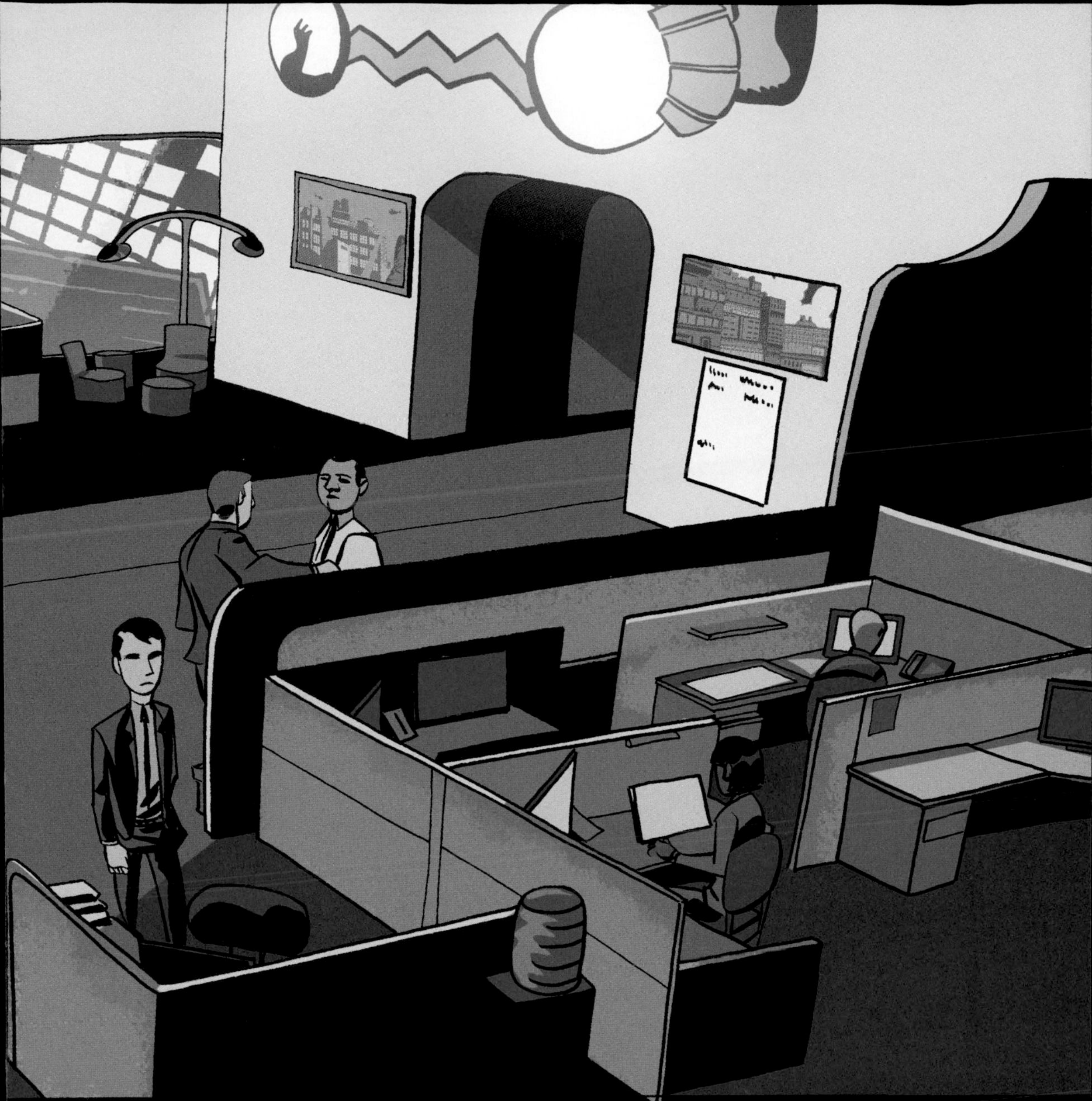

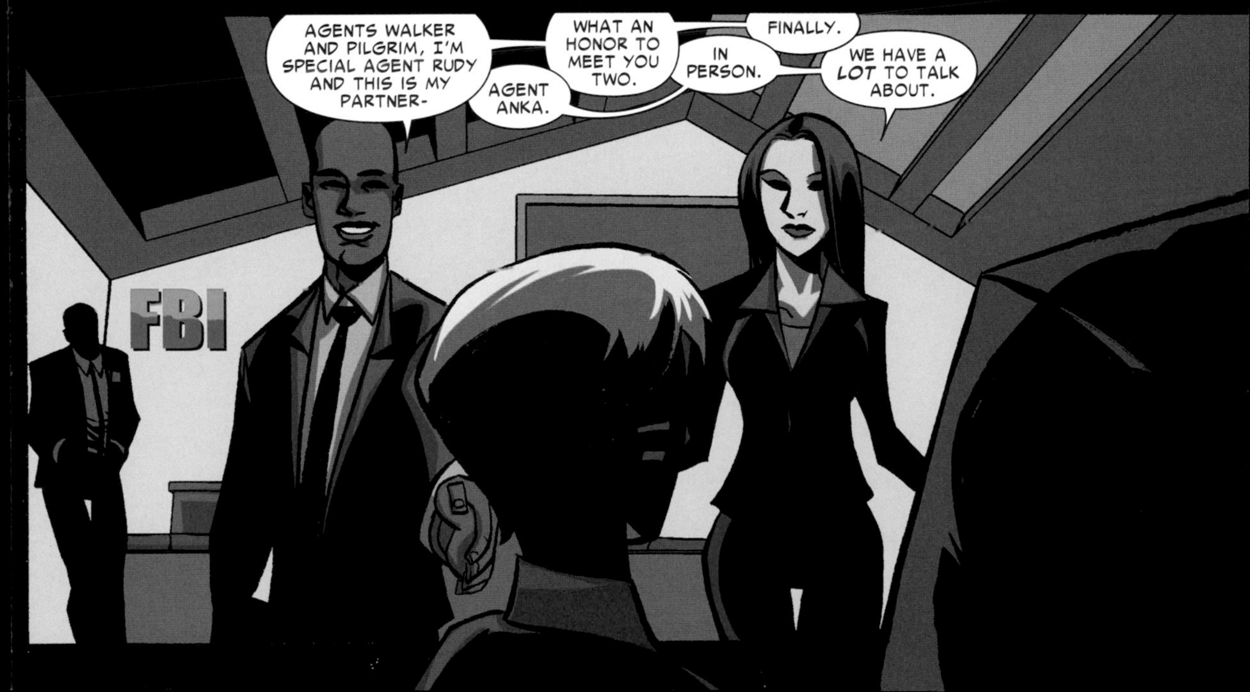
AGENTS WALKER AND PILGRIM, I'M SPECIAL AGENT RUDY AND THIS IS MY PARTNER-
AGENT ANKA.
WHAT AN HONOR TO MEET YOU TWO.
IN PERSON.
FINALLY.
WE HAVE A LOT TO TALK ABOUT.
FBI

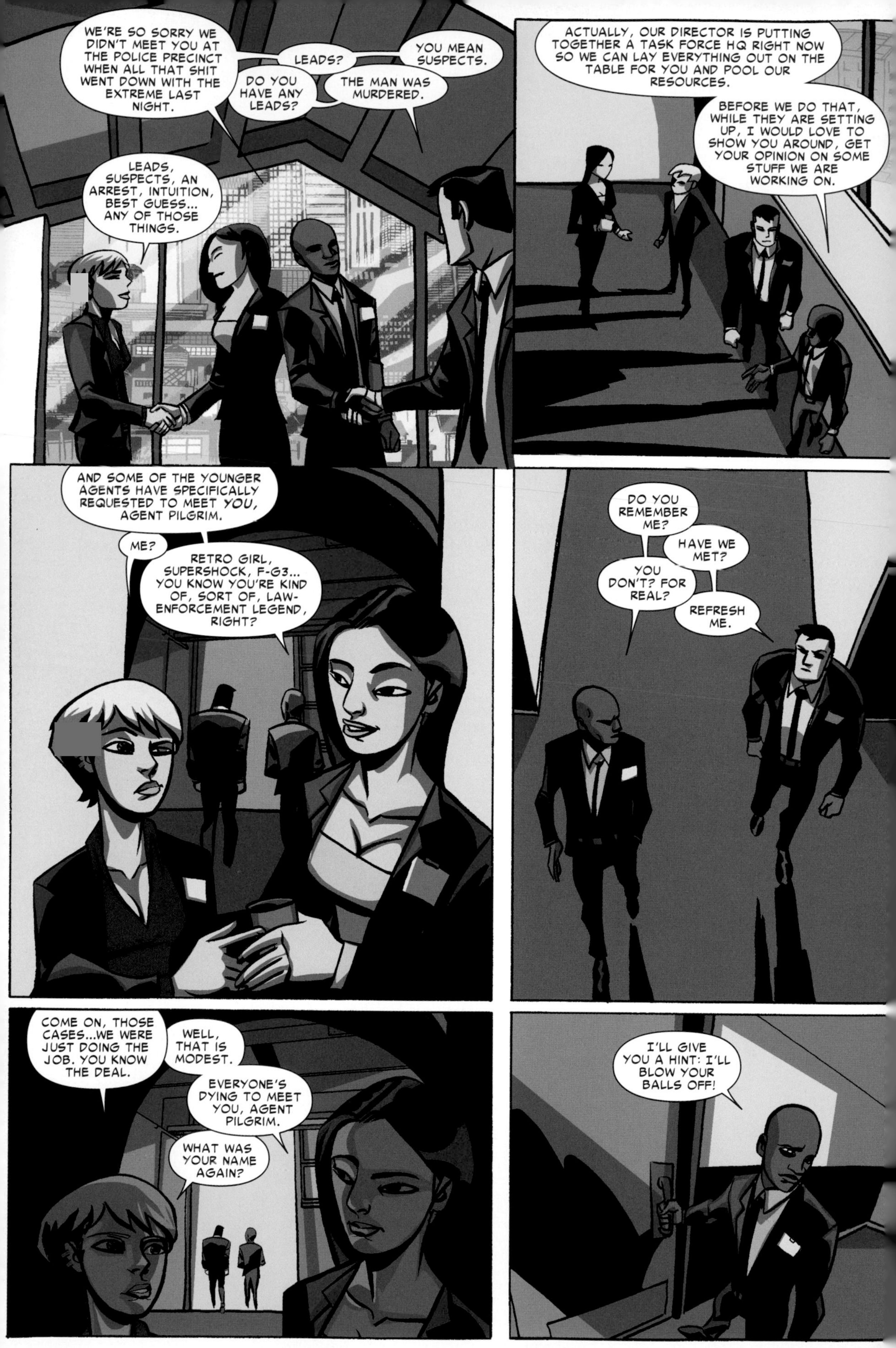
WE'RE SO SORRY WE DIDN'T MEET YOU AT THE POLICE PRECINCT WHEN ALL THAT SHIT WENT DOWN WITH THE EXTREME LAST NIGHT.
DO YOU HAVE ANY LEADS?
LEADS?
THE MAN WAS MURDERED.
YOU MEAN SUSPECTS.
LEADS, SUSPECTS, AN ARREST, INTUITION, BEST GUESS... ANY OF THOSE THINGS.
ACTUALLY, OUR DIRECTOR IS PUTTING TOGETHER A TASK FORCE HQ RIGHT NOW SO WE CAN LAY EVERYTHING OUT ON THE TABLE FOR YOU AND POOL OUR RESOURCES.
BEFORE WE DO THAT, WHILE THEY ARE SETTING UP, I WOULD LOVE TO SHOW YOU AROUND, GET YOUR OPINION ON SOME STUFF WE ARE WORKING ON.
AND SOME OF THE YOUNGER AGENTS HAVE SPECIFICALLY REQUESTED TO MEET *YOU*, AGENT PILGRIM.
ME?
RETRO GIRL, SUPERSHOCK, F-G3... YOU KNOW YOU'RE KIND OF, SORT OF, LAW-ENFORCEMENT LEGEND, RIGHT?
DO YOU REMEMBER ME?
HAVE WE MET?
YOU DON'T? FOR REAL?
REFRESH ME.
COME ON, THOSE CASES...WE WERE JUST DOING THE JOB. YOU KNOW THE DEAL.
WELL, THAT IS MODEST.
EVERYONE'S DYING TO MEET YOU, AGENT PILGRIM.
WHAT WAS YOUR NAME AGAIN?
I'LL GIVE YOU A HINT: I'LL BLOW YOUR BALLS OFF!

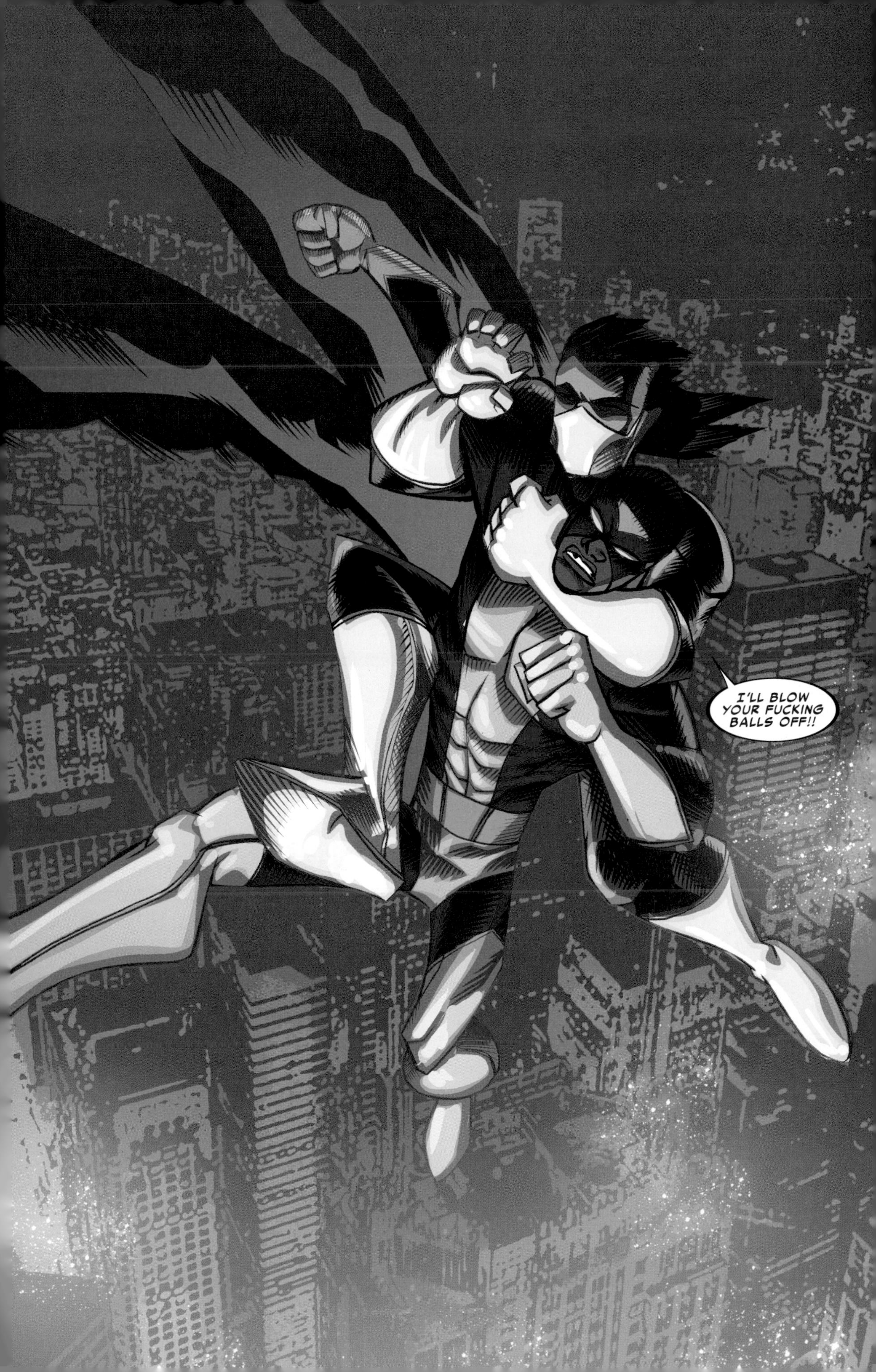
I'LL BLOW YOUR FUCKING BALLS OFF!!

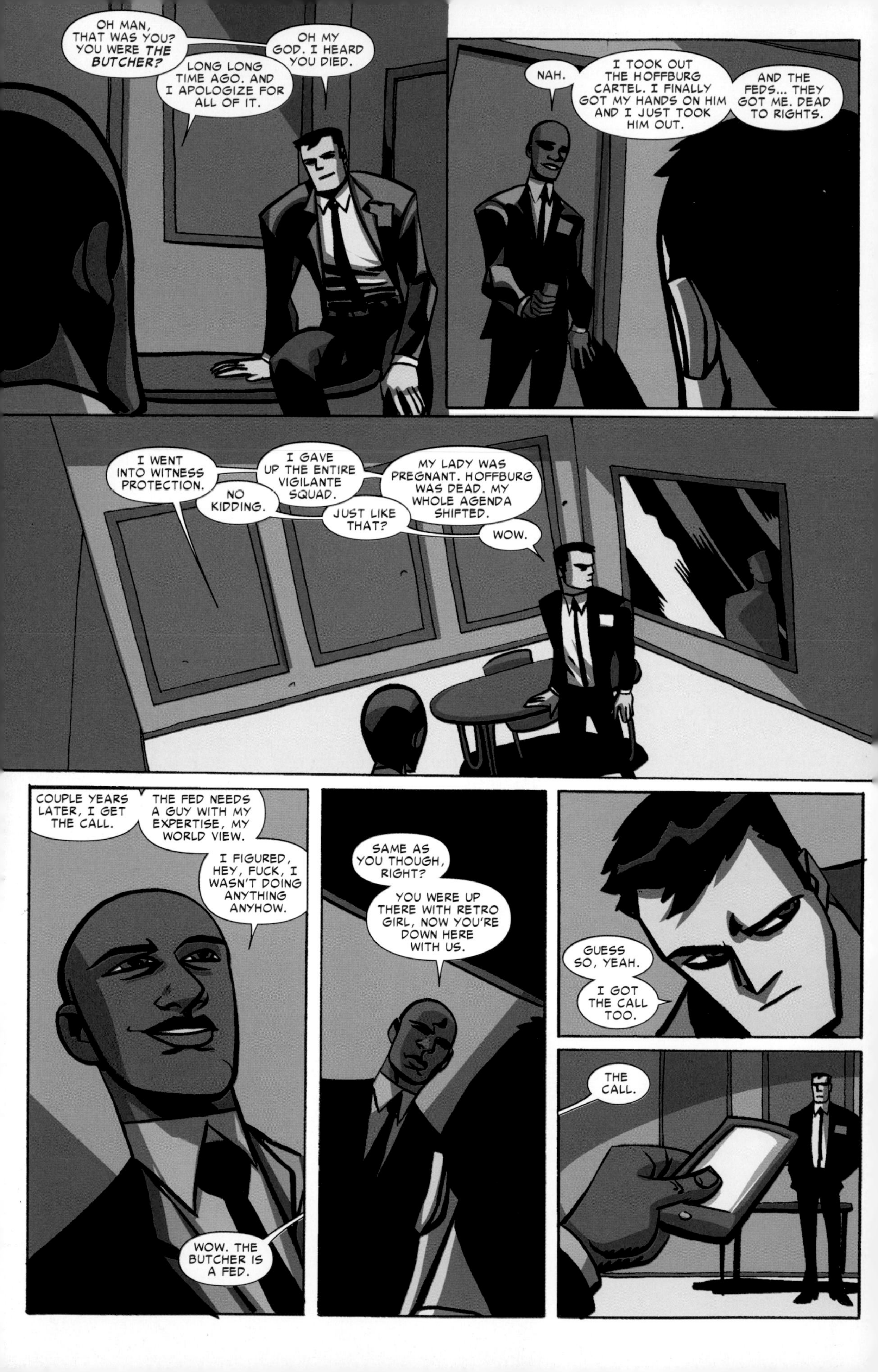
OH MAN, THAT WAS YOU? YOU WERE *THE BUTCHER?*
OH MY GOD. I HEARD YOU DIED.
LONG LONG TIME AGO. AND I APOLOGIZE FOR ALL OF IT.
NAH.
I TOOK OUT THE HOFFBURG CARTEL. I FINALLY GOT MY HANDS ON HIM AND I JUST TOOK HIM OUT.
AND THE FEDS... THEY GOT ME. DEAD TO RIGHTS.
I WENT INTO WITNESS PROTECTION.
I GAVE UP THE ENTIRE VIGILANTE SQUAD.
MY LADY WAS PREGNANT. HOFFBURG WAS DEAD. MY WHOLE AGENDA SHIFTED.
NO KIDDING.
JUST LIKE THAT?
WOW.
COUPLE YEARS LATER, I GET THE CALL.
THE FED NEEDS A GUY WITH MY EXPERTISE, MY WORLD VIEW.
I FIGURED, HEY, FUCK, I WASN'T DOING ANYTHING ANYHOW.
WOW. THE BUTCHER IS A FED.
SAME AS YOU THOUGH, RIGHT?
YOU WERE UP THERE WITH RETRO GIRL, NOW YOU'RE DOWN HERE WITH US.
GUESS SO, YEAH.
I GOT THE CALL TOO.
THE CALL.

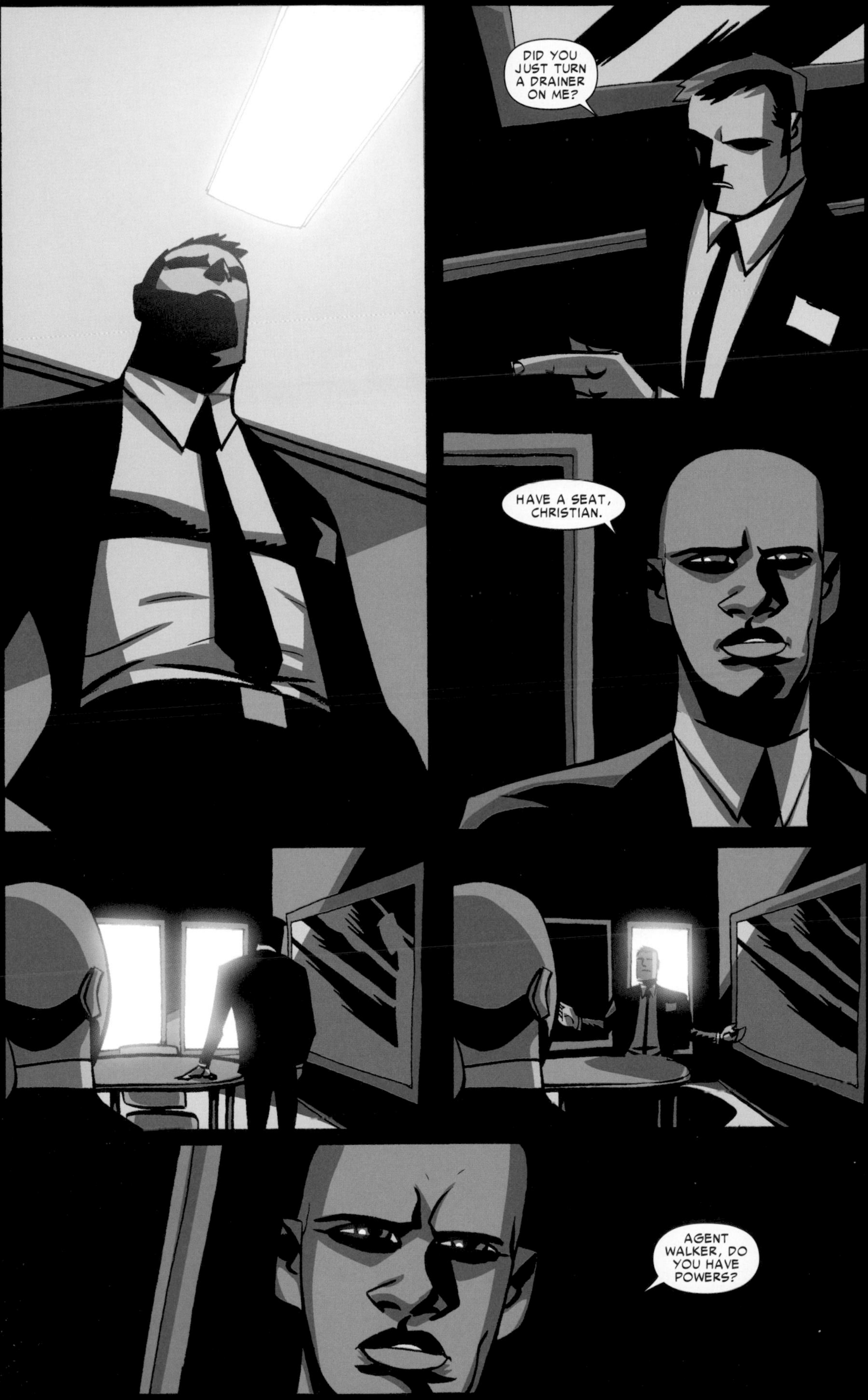
DID YOU JUST TURN A DRAINER ON ME?
HAVE A SEAT, CHRISTIAN.
AGENT WALKER, DO YOU HAVE POWERS?

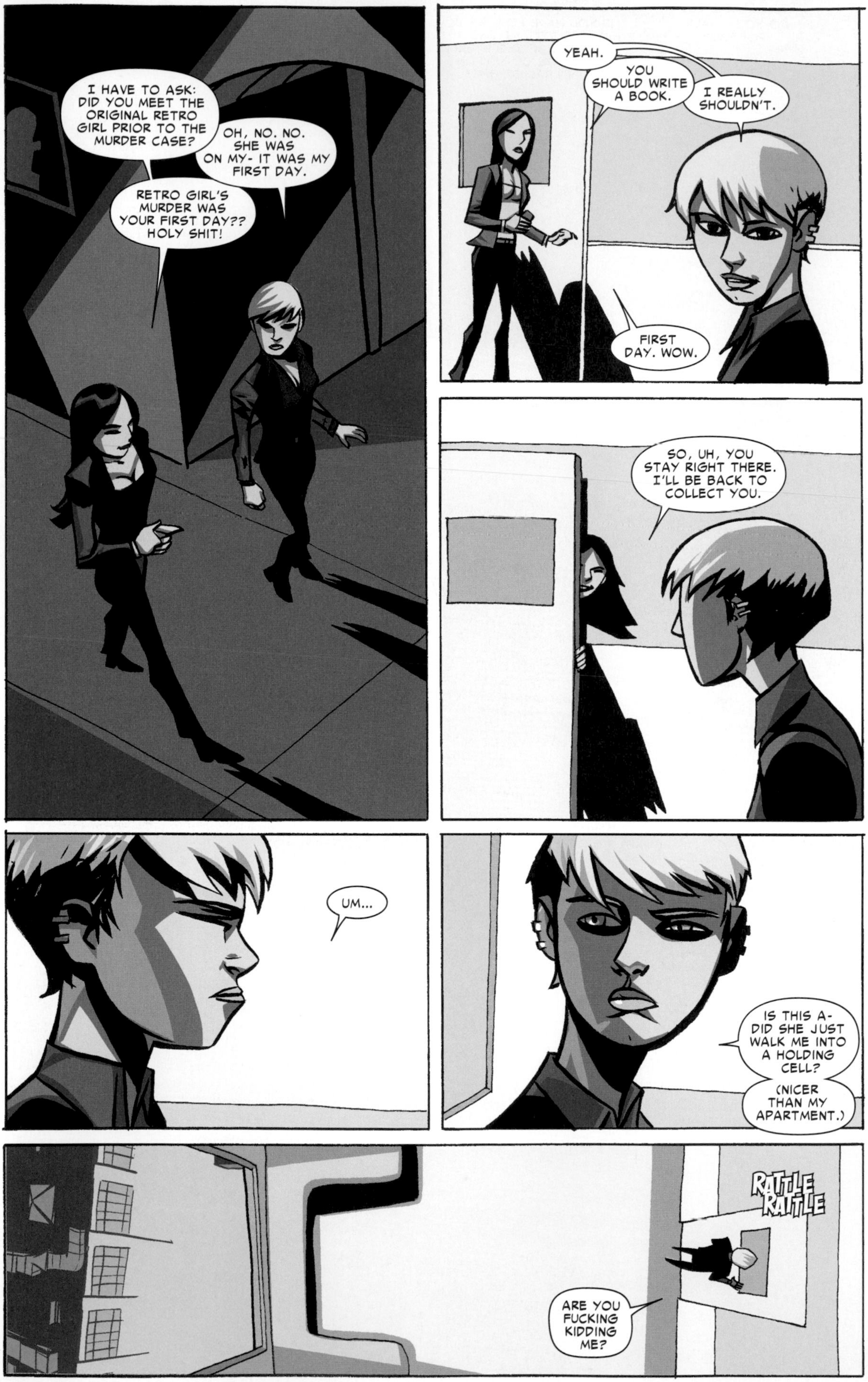
I HAVE TO ASK: DID YOU MEET THE ORIGINAL RETRO GIRL PRIOR TO THE MURDER CASE?
OH, NO. NO. SHE WAS ON MY- IT WAS MY FIRST DAY.
RETRO GIRL'S MURDER WAS YOUR FIRST DAY?? HOLY SHIT!
YEAH.
YOU SHOULD WRITE A BOOK.
I REALLY SHOULDN'T.
FIRST DAY. WOW.
SO, UH, YOU STAY RIGHT THERE. I'LL BE BACK TO COLLECT YOU.
UM...
IS THIS A- DID SHE JUST WALK ME INTO A HOLDING CELL?
(NICER THAN MY APARTMENT.)
RATTLE RATTLE
ARE YOU FUCKING KIDDING ME?

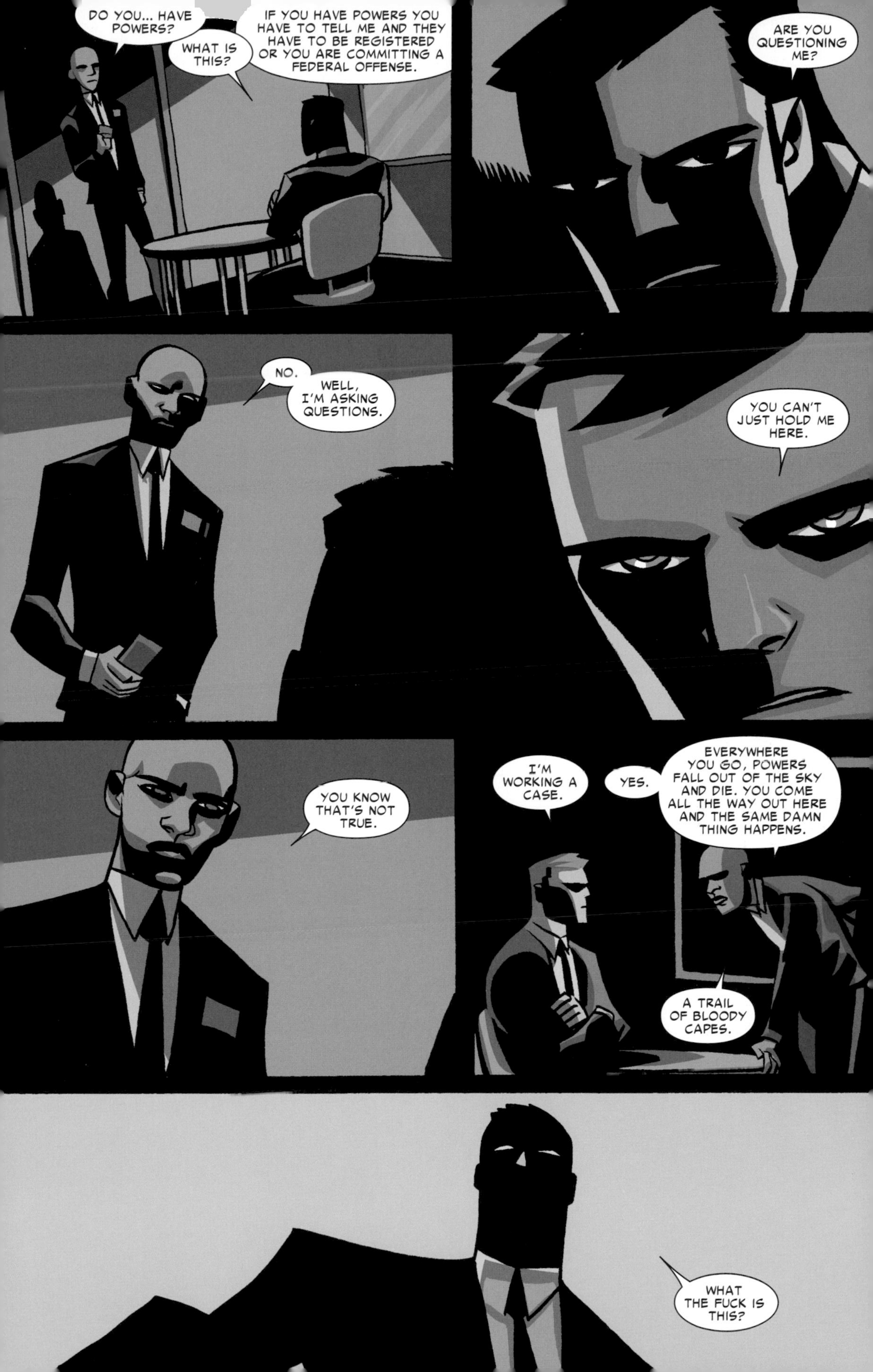
DO YOU... HAVE POWERS?
WHAT IS THIS?
IF YOU HAVE POWERS YOU HAVE TO TELL ME AND THEY HAVE TO BE REGISTERED OR YOU ARE COMMITTING A FEDERAL OFFENSE.
ARE YOU QUESTIONING ME?
NO.
WELL, I'M ASKING QUESTIONS.
YOU CAN'T JUST HOLD ME HERE.
YOU KNOW THAT'S NOT TRUE.
I'M WORKING A CASE.
YES.
EVERYWHERE YOU GO, POWERS FALL OUT OF THE SKY AND DIE. YOU COME ALL THE WAY OUT HERE AND THE SAME DAMN THING HAPPENS.
A TRAIL OF BLOODY CAPES.
WHAT THE FUCK IS THIS?

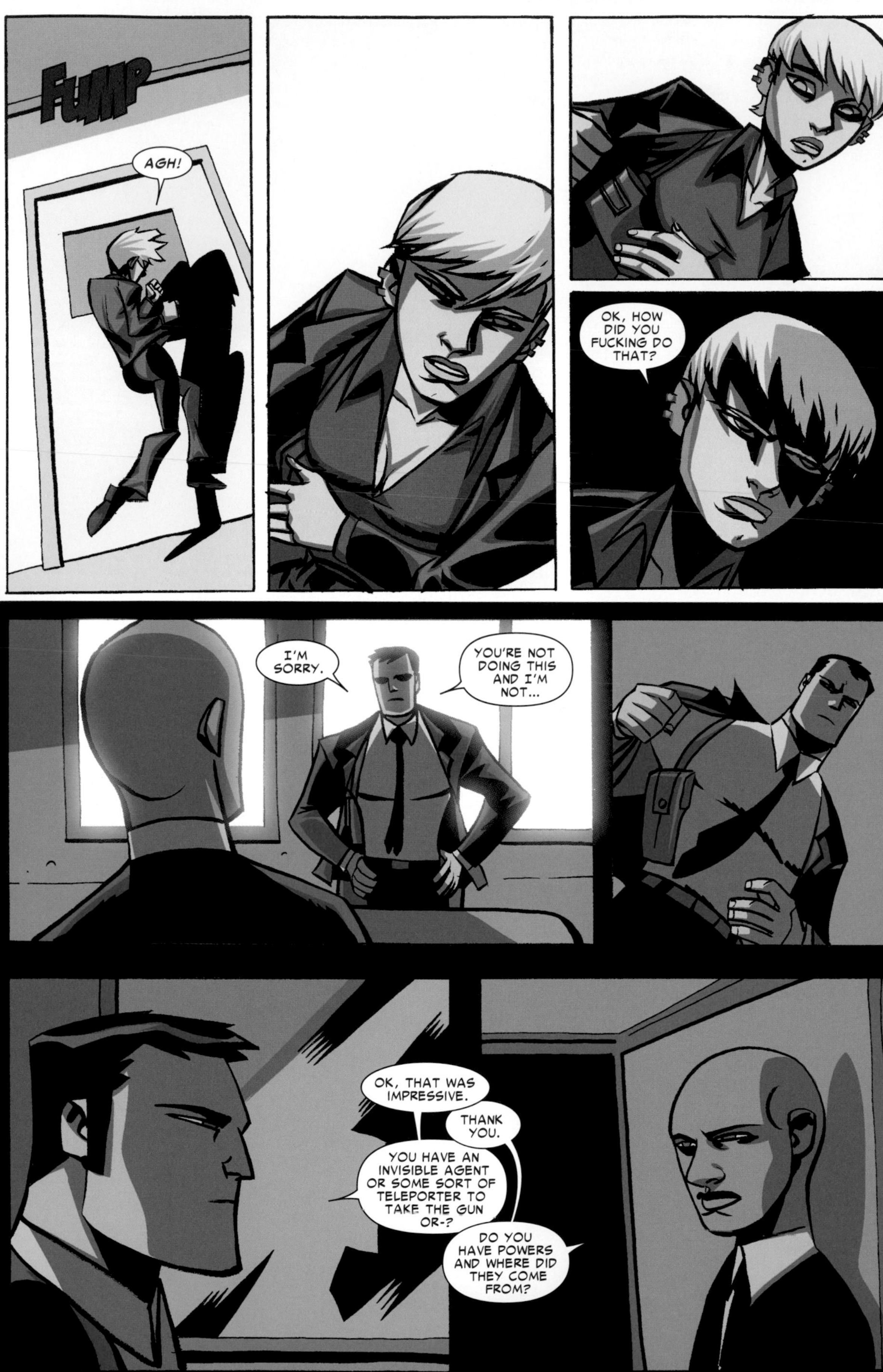
FUMP
AGH!
OK, HOW DID YOU FUCKING DO THAT?
I'M SORRY.
YOU'RE NOT DOING THIS AND I'M NOT...
OK, THAT WAS IMPRESSIVE.
THANK YOU.
YOU HAVE AN INVISIBLE AGENT OR SOME SORT OF TELEPORTER TO TAKE THE GUN OR-?
DO YOU HAVE POWERS AND WHERE DID THEY COME FROM?

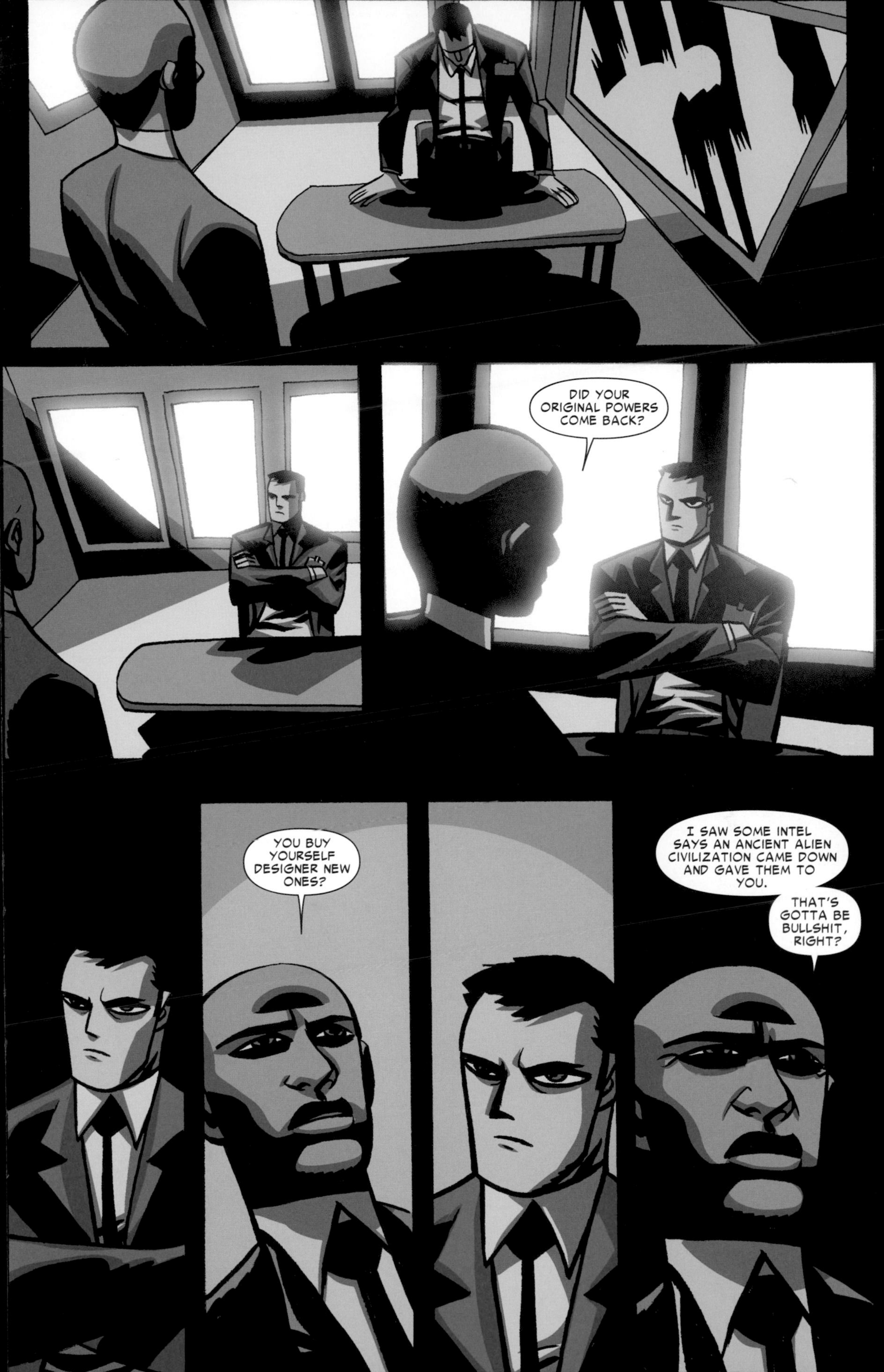
DID YOUR ORIGINAL POWERS COME BACK?
YOU BUY YOURSELF DESIGNER NEW ONES?
I SAW SOME INTEL SAYS AN ANCIENT ALIEN CIVILIZATION CAME DOWN AND GAVE THEM TO YOU.
THAT'S GOTTA BE BULLSHIT, RIGHT?

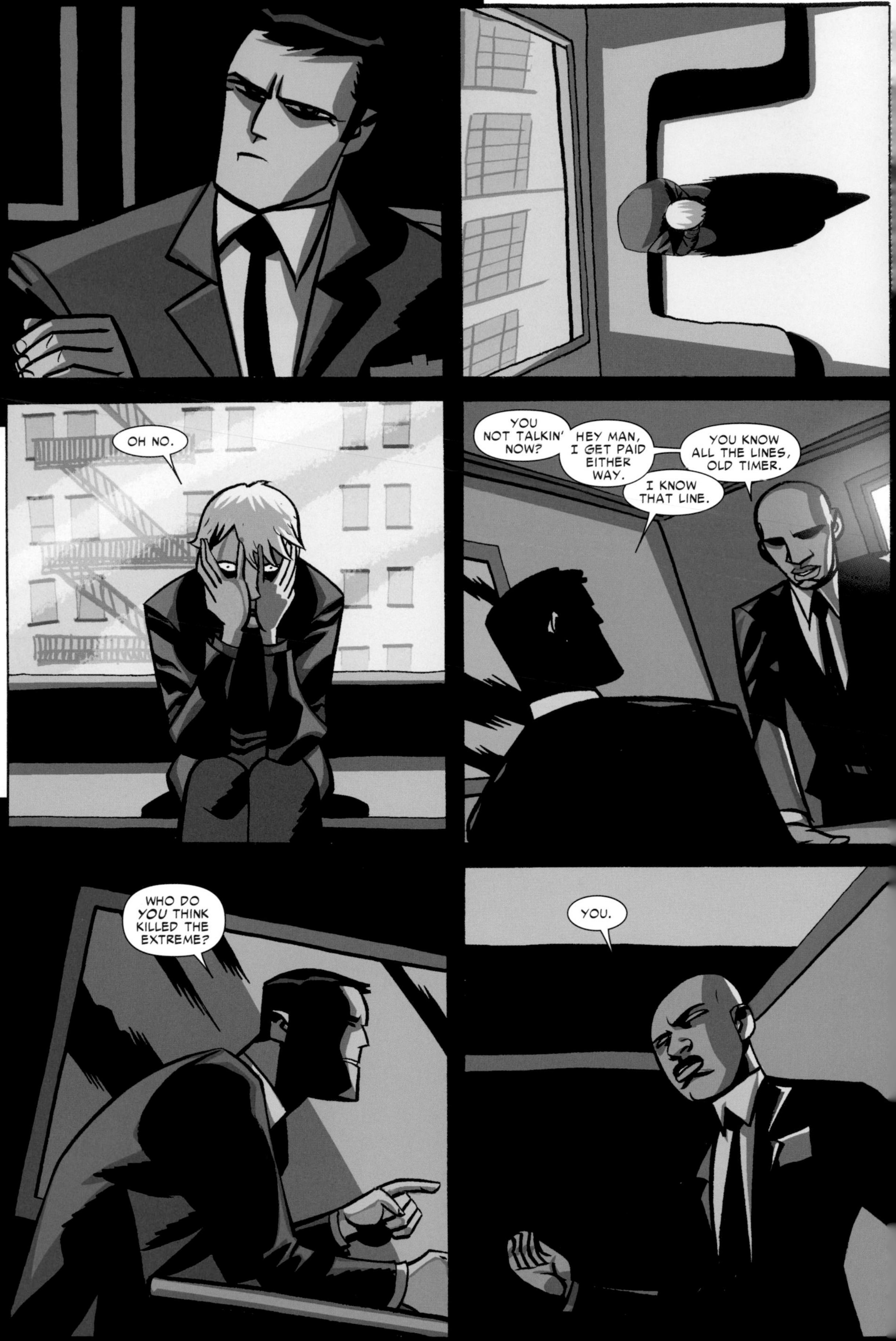
OH NO.
YOU NOT TALKIN' NOW?
HEY MAN, I GET PAID EITHER WAY.
I KNOW THAT LINE.
YOU KNOW ALL THE LINES, OLD TIMER.
WHO DO *YOU* THINK KILLED THE EXTREME?
YOU.

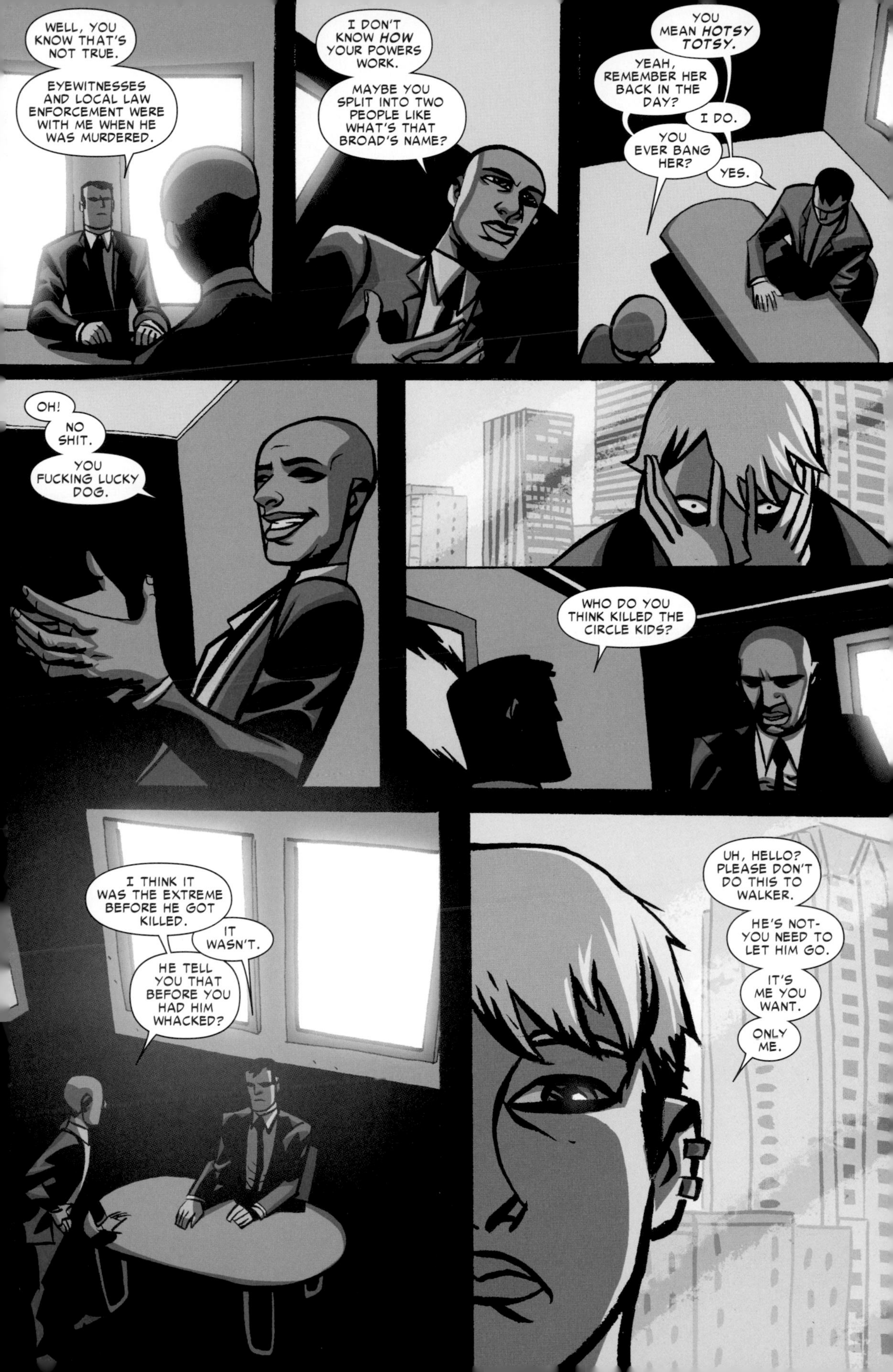
WELL, YOU KNOW THAT'S NOT TRUE.
EYEWITNESSES AND LOCAL LAW ENFORCEMENT WERE WITH ME WHEN HE WAS MURDERED.
I DON'T KNOW *HOW* YOUR POWERS WORK.
MAYBE YOU SPLIT INTO TWO PEOPLE LIKE WHAT'S THAT BROAD'S NAME?
YOU MEAN *HOTSY TOTSY.*
YEAH, REMEMBER HER BACK IN THE DAY?
I DO.
YOU EVER BANG HER?
YES.
OH!
NO SHIT.
YOU FUCKING LUCKY DOG.
WHO DO YOU THINK KILLED THE CIRCLE KIDS?
I THINK IT WAS THE EXTREME BEFORE HE GOT KILLED.
IT WASN'T.
HE TELL YOU THAT BEFORE YOU HAD HIM WHACKED?
UH, HELLO? PLEASE DON'T DO THIS TO WALKER.
HE'S NOT- YOU NEED TO LET HIM GO.
IT'S ME YOU WANT.
ONLY ME.

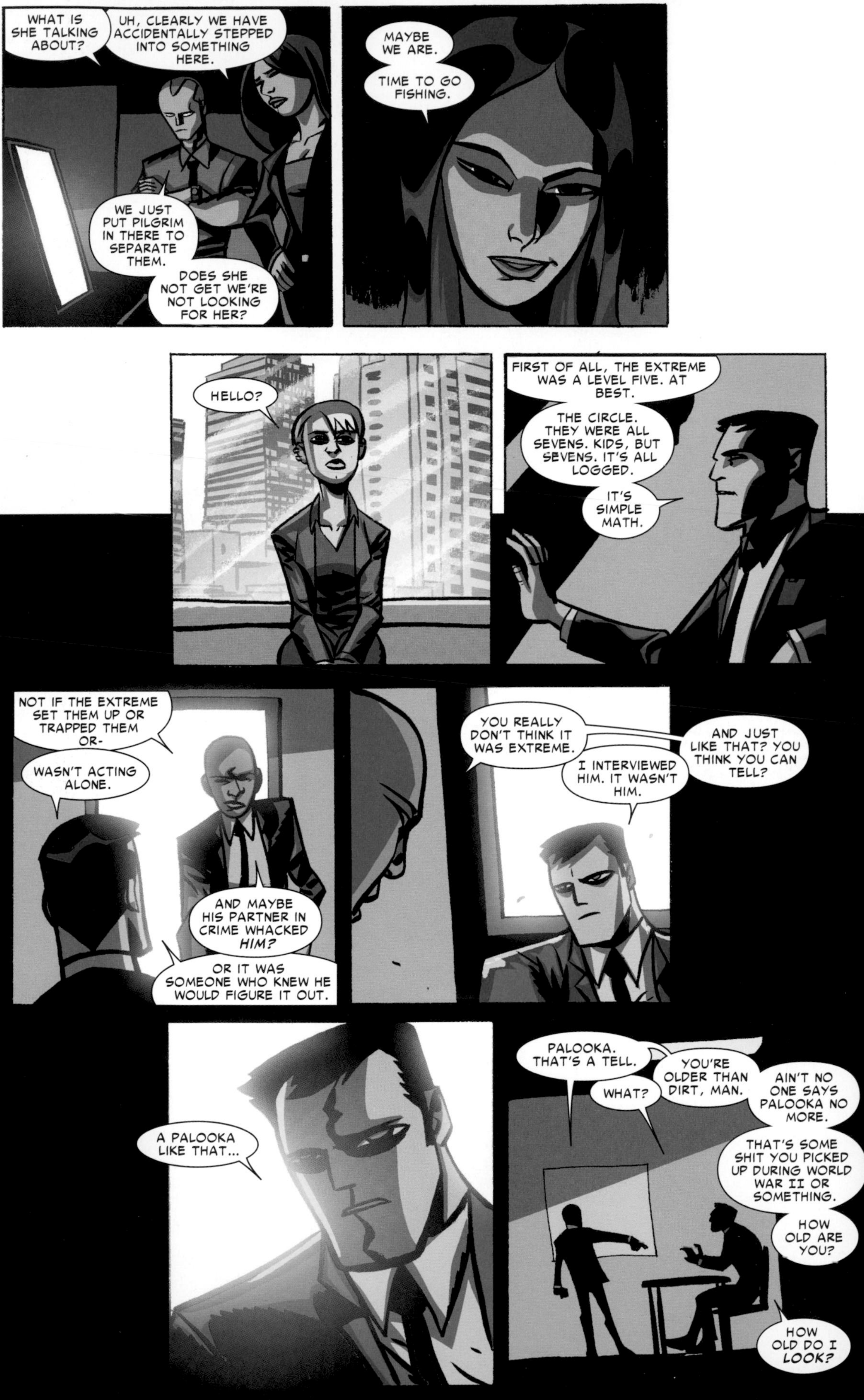
WHAT IS SHE TALKING ABOUT?
UH, CLEARLY WE HAVE ACCIDENTALLY STEPPED INTO SOMETHING HERE.
WE JUST PUT PILGRIM IN THERE TO SEPARATE THEM.
DOES SHE NOT GET WE'RE NOT LOOKING FOR HER?
MAYBE WE ARE.
TIME TO GO FISHING.
HELLO?
FIRST OF ALL, THE EXTREME WAS A LEVEL FIVE. AT BEST.
THE CIRCLE. THEY WERE ALL SEVENS. KIDS, BUT SEVENS. IT'S ALL LOGGED.
IT'S SIMPLE MATH.
NOT IF THE EXTREME SET THEM UP OR TRAPPED THEM OR-
WASN'T ACTING ALONE.
AND MAYBE HIS PARTNER IN CRIME WHACKED *HIM?*
OR IT WAS SOMEONE WHO KNEW HE WOULD FIGURE IT OUT.
YOU REALLY DON'T THINK IT WAS EXTREME.
I INTERVIEWED HIM. IT WASN'T HIM.
AND JUST LIKE THAT? YOU THINK YOU CAN TELL?
A PALOOKA LIKE THAT...
PALOOKA. THAT'S A TELL.
WHAT?
YOU'RE OLDER THAN DIRT, MAN.
AIN'T NO ONE SAYS PALOOKA NO MORE.
THAT'S SOME SHIT YOU PICKED UP DURING WORLD WAR II OR SOMETHING.
HOW OLD ARE YOU?
HOW OLD DO I *LOOK?*

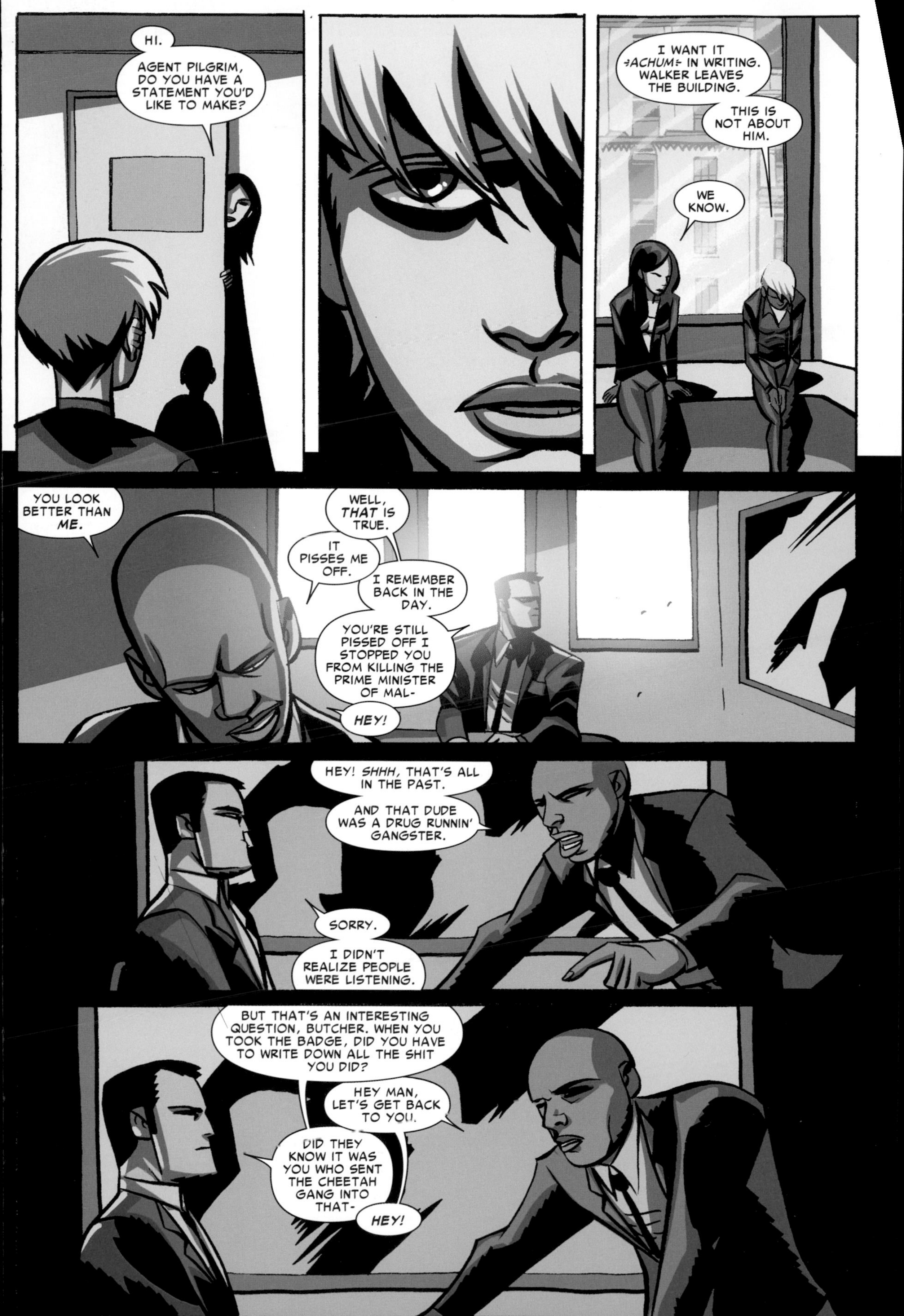
HI.
AGENT PILGRIM, DO YOU HAVE A STATEMENT YOU'D LIKE TO MAKE?
I WANT IT -ACHUM- IN WRITING. WALKER LEAVES THE BUILDING.
THIS IS NOT ABOUT HIM.
WE KNOW.
YOU LOOK BETTER THAN ME.
WELL, THAT IS TRUE.
IT PISSES ME OFF.
I REMEMBER BACK IN THE DAY.
YOU'RE STILL PISSED OFF I STOPPED YOU FROM KILLING THE PRIME MINISTER OF MAL-
HEY!
HEY! SHHH, THAT'S ALL IN THE PAST.
AND THAT DUDE WAS A DRUG RUNNIN' GANGSTER.
SORRY.
I DIDN'T REALIZE PEOPLE WERE LISTENING.
BUT THAT'S AN INTERESTING QUESTION, BUTCHER. WHEN YOU TOOK THE BADGE, DID YOU HAVE TO WRITE DOWN ALL THE SHIT YOU DID?
HEY MAN, LET'S GET BACK TO YOU.
DID THEY KNOW IT WAS YOU WHO SENT THE CHEETAH GANG INTO THAT-
HEY!

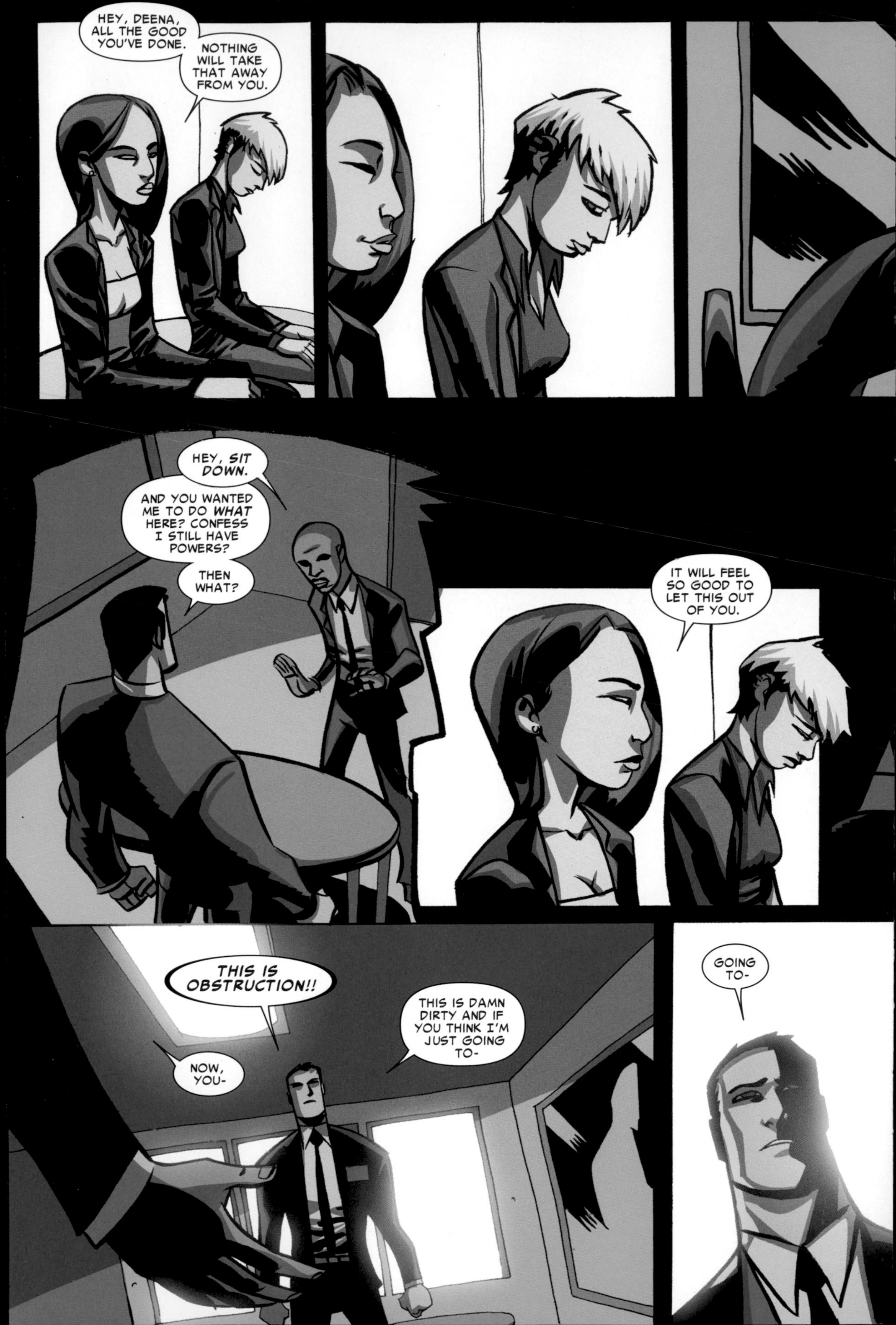
HEY, DEENA, ALL THE GOOD YOU'VE DONE.
NOTHING WILL TAKE THAT AWAY FROM YOU.
HEY, SIT DOWN.
AND YOU WANTED ME TO DO WHAT HERE? CONFESS I STILL HAVE POWERS?
THEN WHAT?
IT WILL FEEL SO GOOD TO LET THIS OUT OF YOU.
THIS IS OBSTRUCTION!!
NOW, YOU-
THIS IS DAMN DIRTY AND IF YOU THINK I'M JUST GOING TO-
GOING TO-

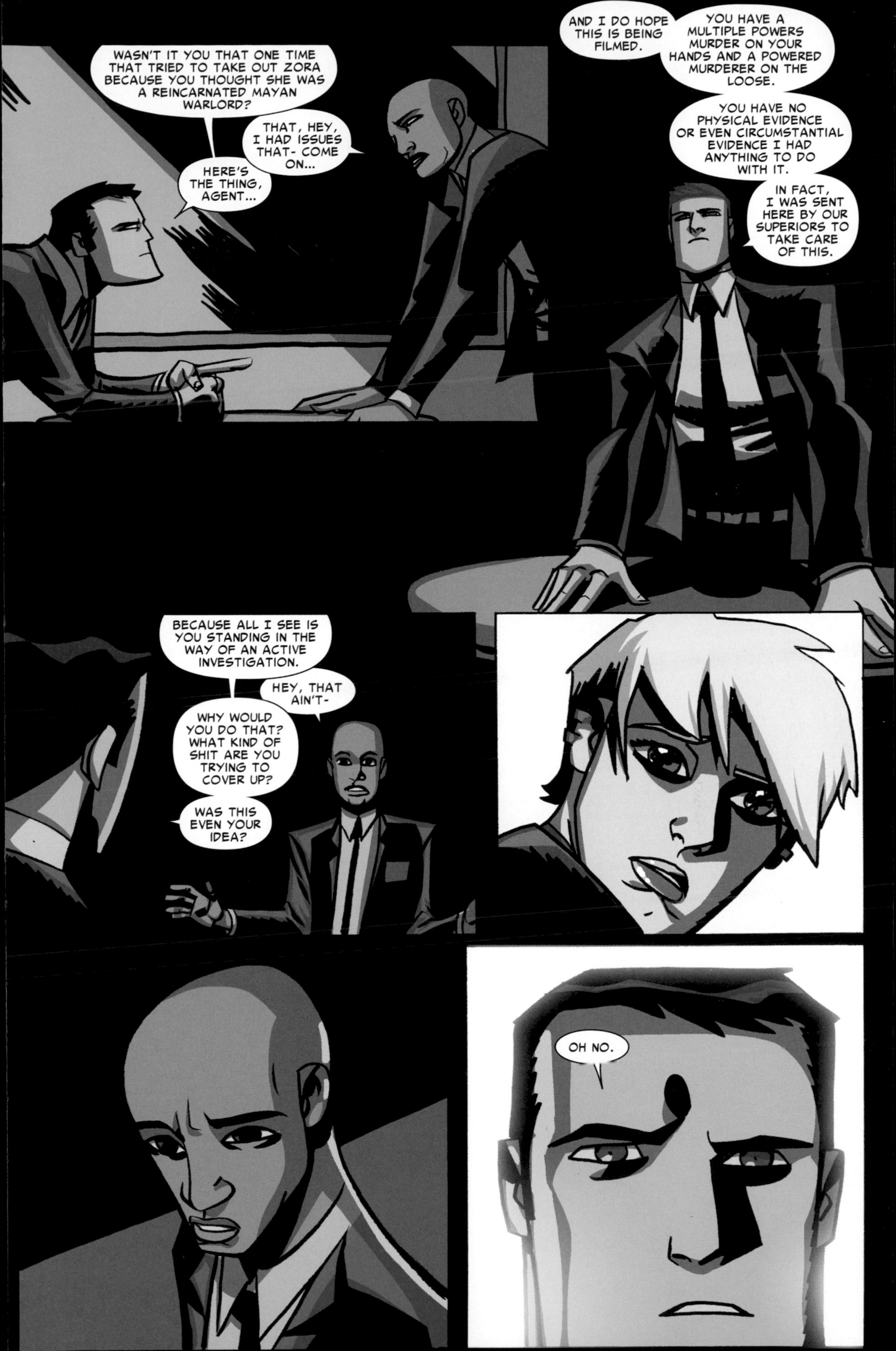
WASN'T IT YOU THAT ONE TIME THAT TRIED TO TAKE OUT ZORA BECAUSE YOU THOUGHT SHE WAS A REINCARNATED MAYAN WARLORD?
THAT, HEY, I HAD ISSUES THAT- COME ON...
HERE'S THE THING, AGENT...
AND I DO HOPE THIS IS BEING FILMED.
YOU HAVE A MULTIPLE POWERS MURDER ON YOUR HANDS AND A POWERED MURDERER ON THE LOOSE.
YOU HAVE NO PHYSICAL EVIDENCE OR EVEN CIRCUMSTANTIAL EVIDENCE I HAD ANYTHING TO DO WITH IT.
IN FACT, I WAS SENT HERE BY OUR SUPERIORS TO TAKE CARE OF THIS.
BECAUSE ALL I SEE IS YOU STANDING IN THE WAY OF AN ACTIVE INVESTIGATION.
HEY, THAT AIN'T-
WHY WOULD YOU DO THAT? WHAT KIND OF SHIT ARE YOU TRYING TO COVER UP?
WAS THIS EVEN YOUR IDEA?
OH NO.

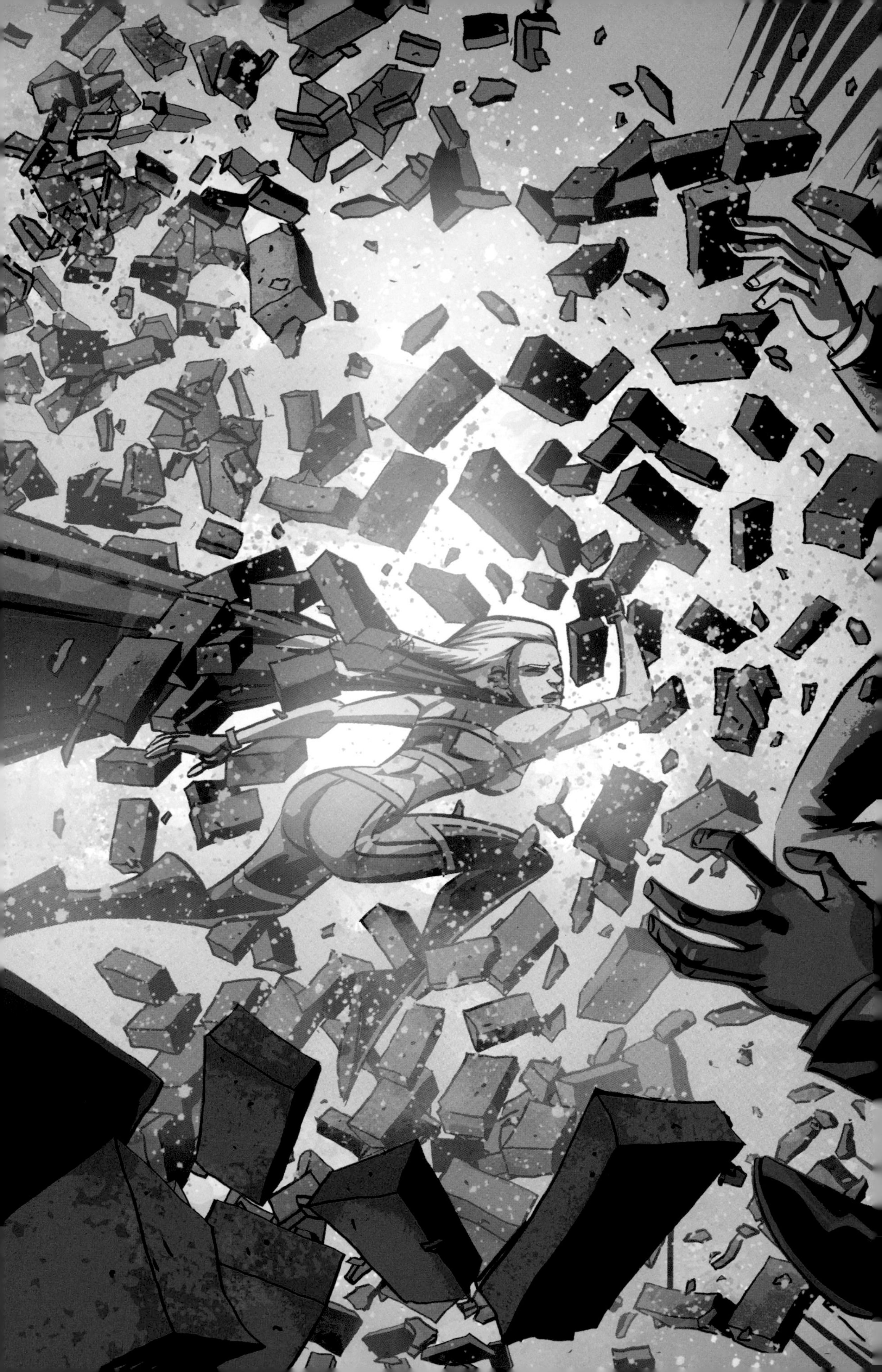

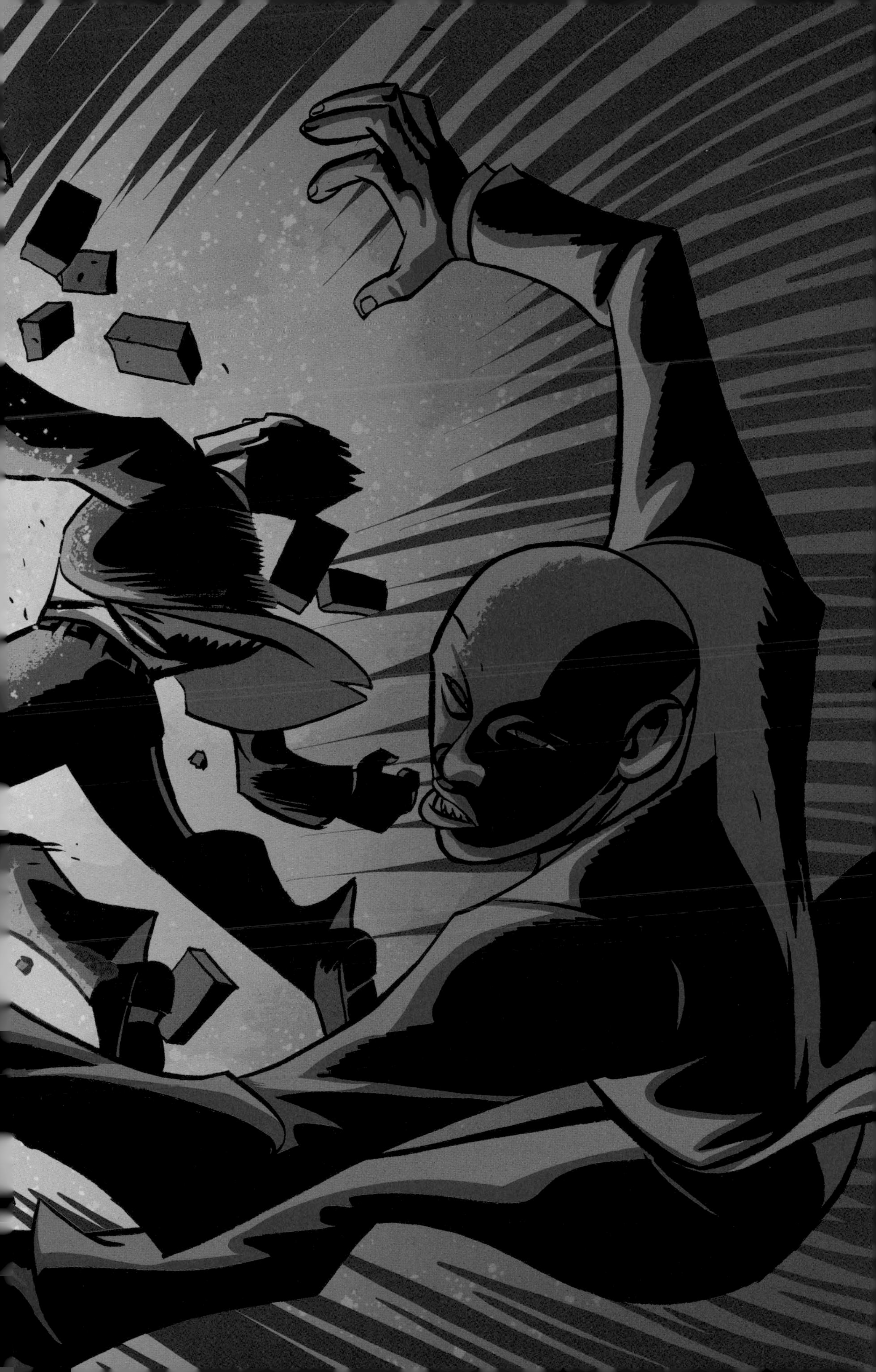

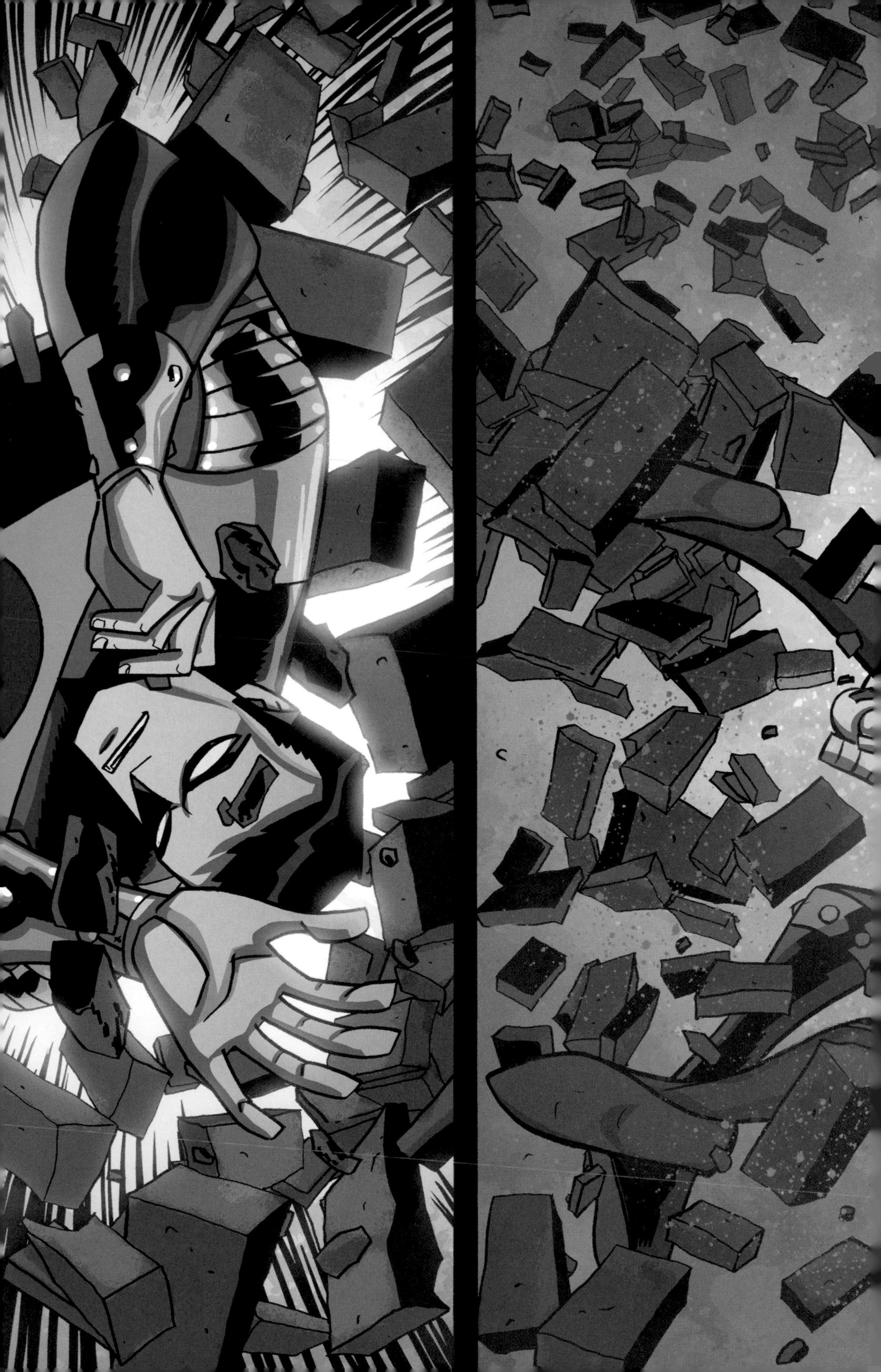

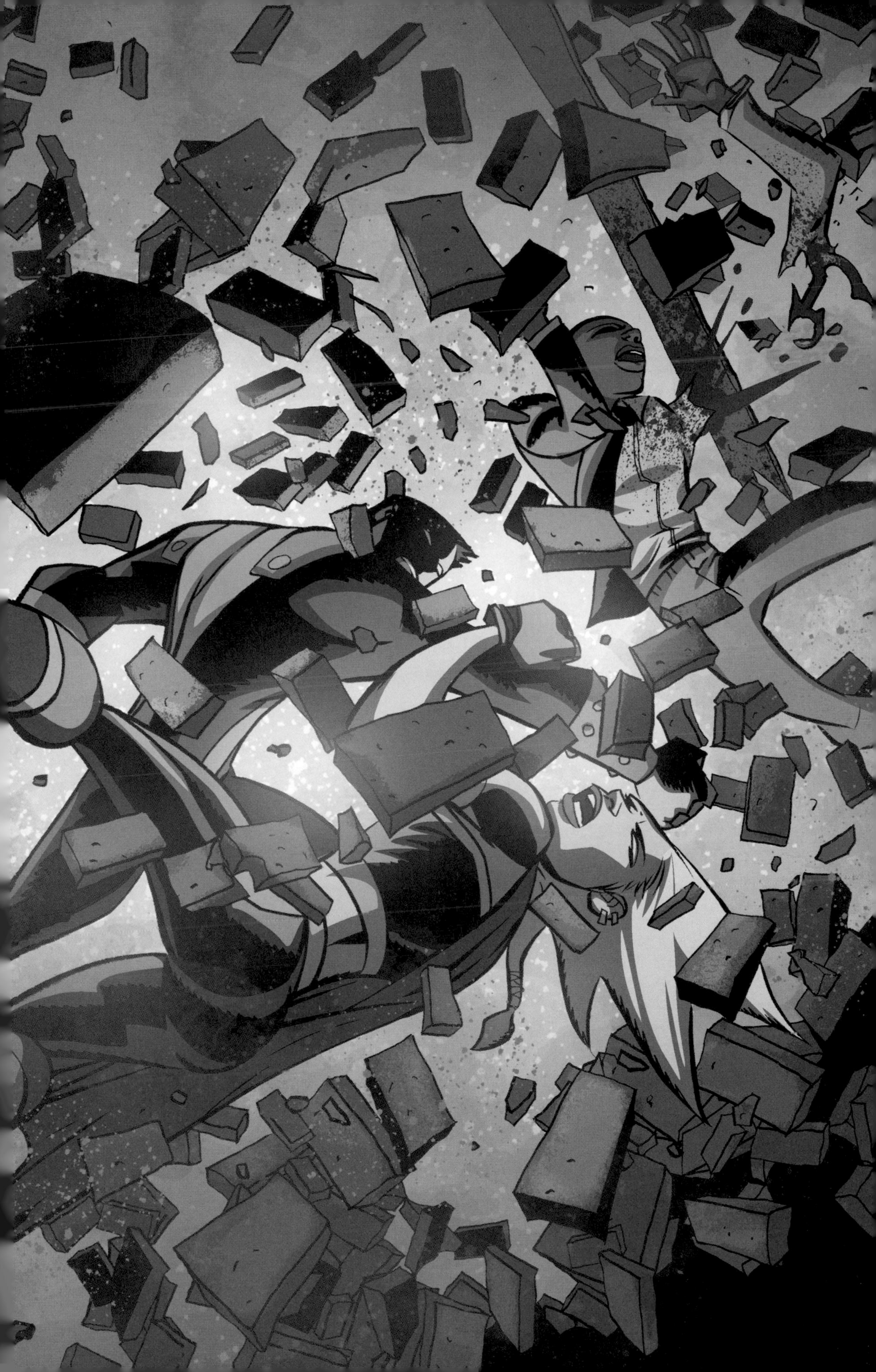

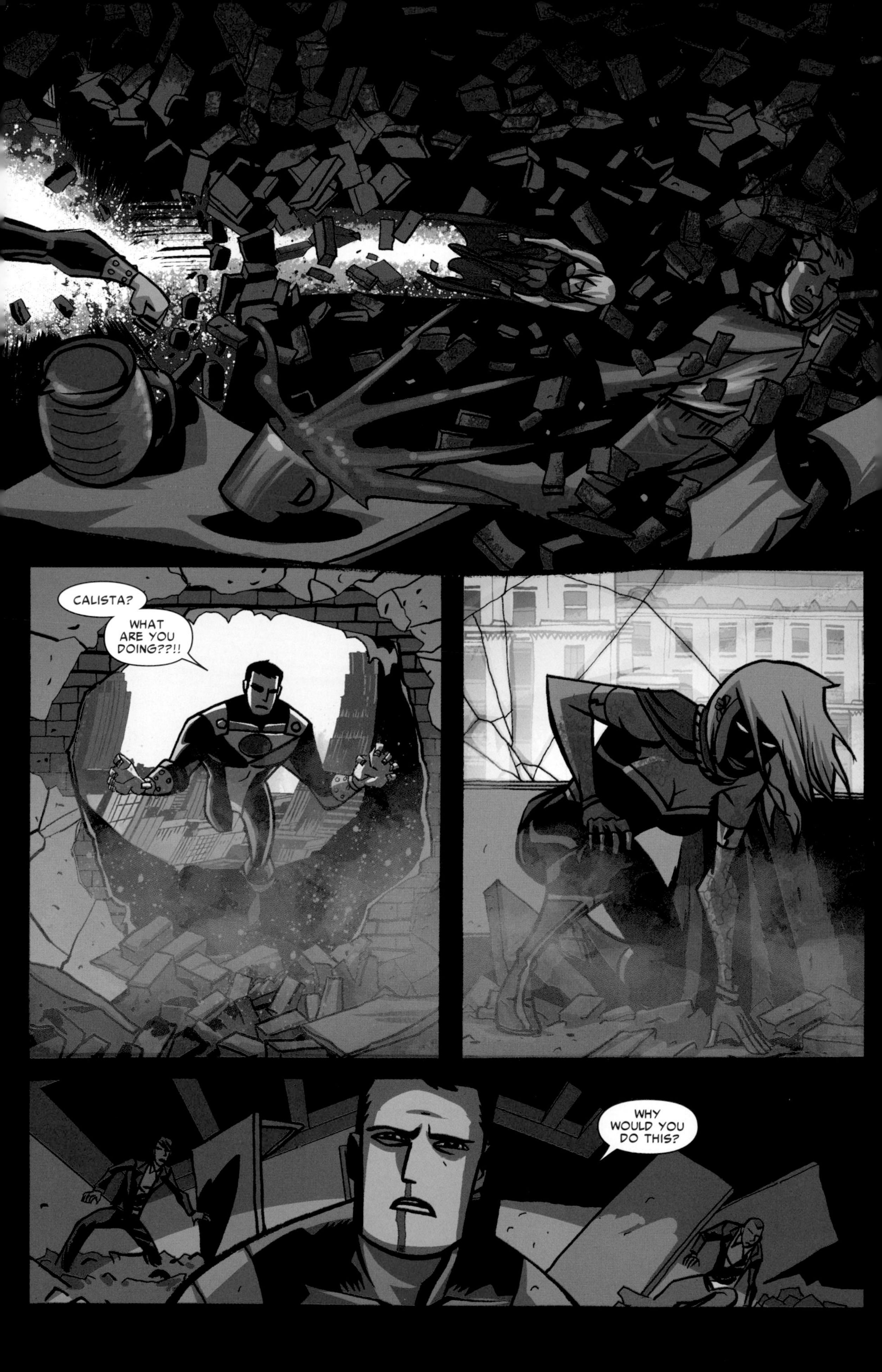
CALISTA?
WHAT ARE YOU DOING??!!
WHY WOULD YOU DO THIS?

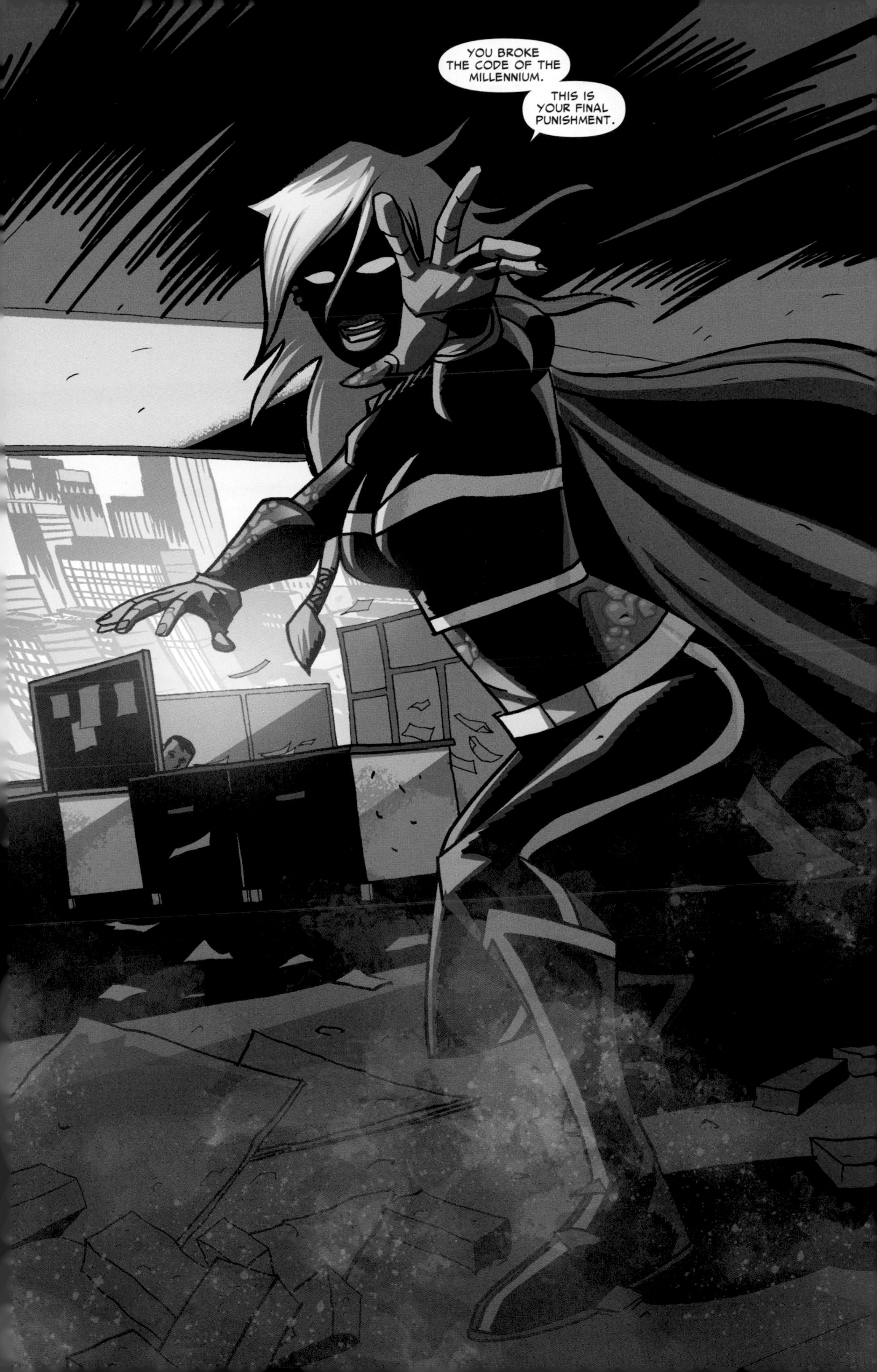
YOU BROKE THE CODE OF THE MILLENNIUM.
THIS IS YOUR FINAL PUNISHMENT.

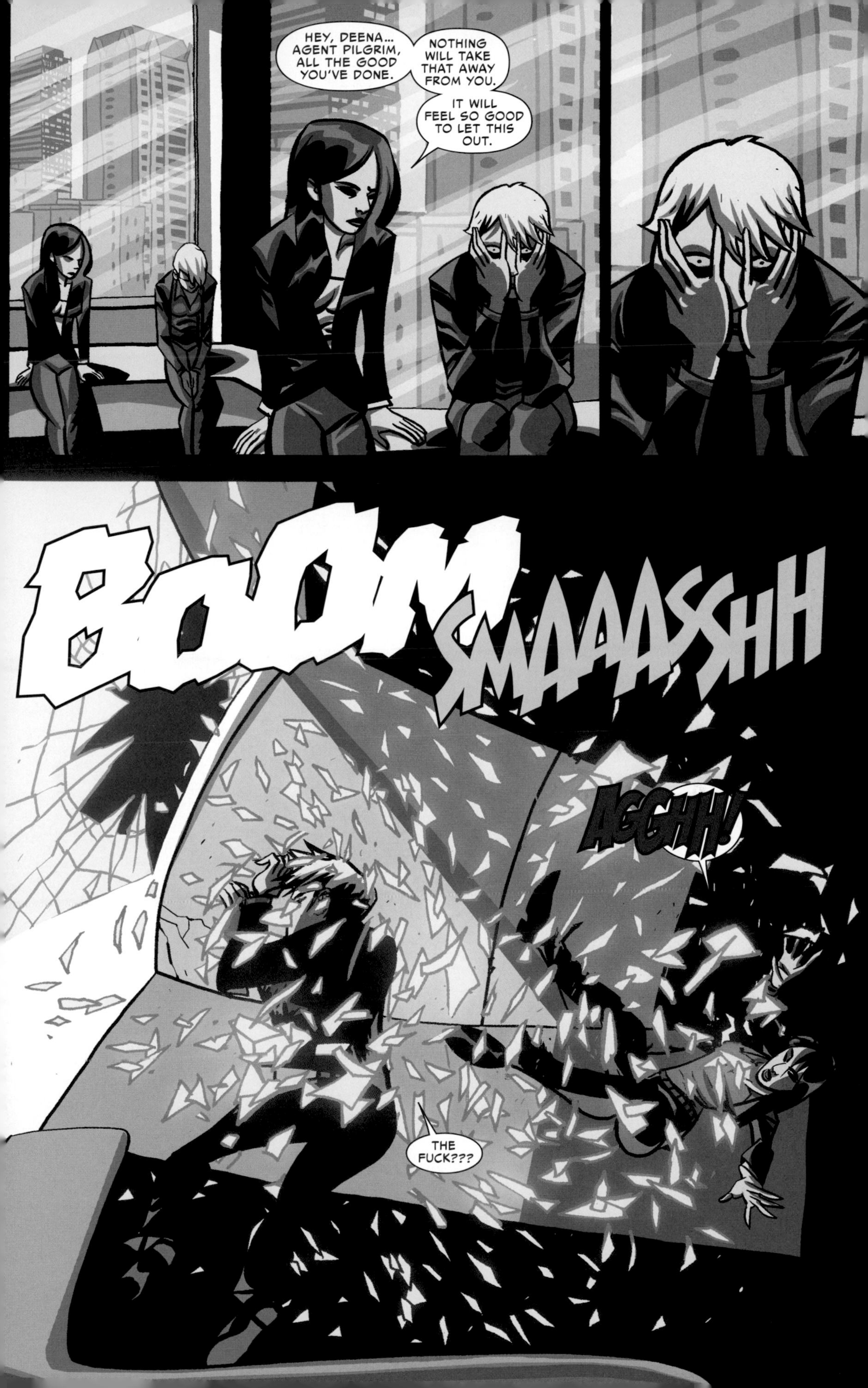
HEY, DEENA... AGENT PILGRIM, ALL THE GOOD YOU'VE DONE.
NOTHING WILL TAKE THAT AWAY FROM YOU.
IT WILL FEEL SO GOOD TO LET THIS OUT.
BOOM
SMAAASHH
AGGHH!
THE FUCK???

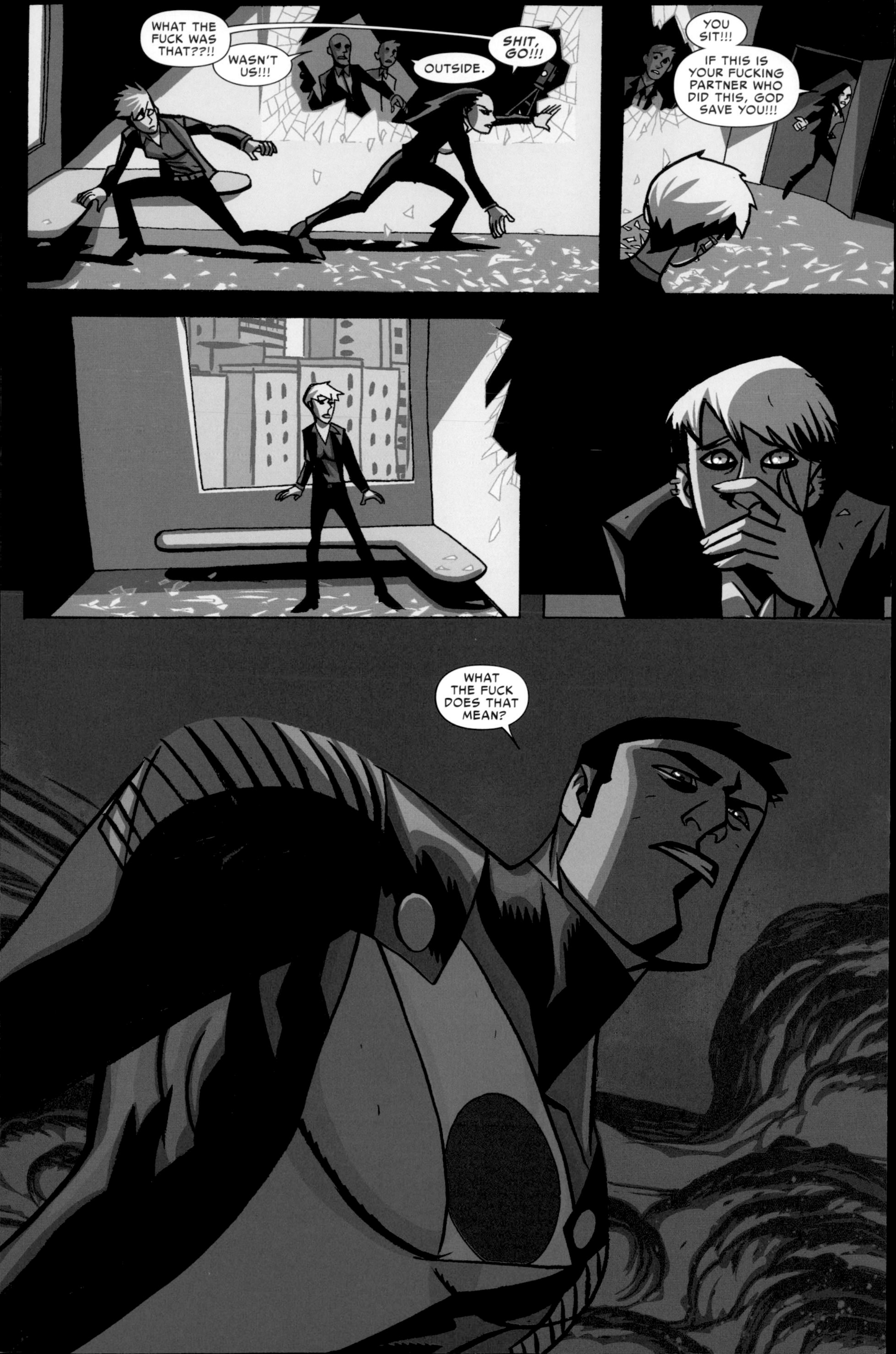
WHAT THE FUCK WAS THAT??!!
WASN'T US!!!
OUTSIDE.
SHIT, GO!!!
YOU SIT!!!
IF THIS IS YOUR FUCKING PARTNER WHO DID THIS, GOD SAVE YOU!!!
WHAT THE FUCK DOES THAT MEAN?

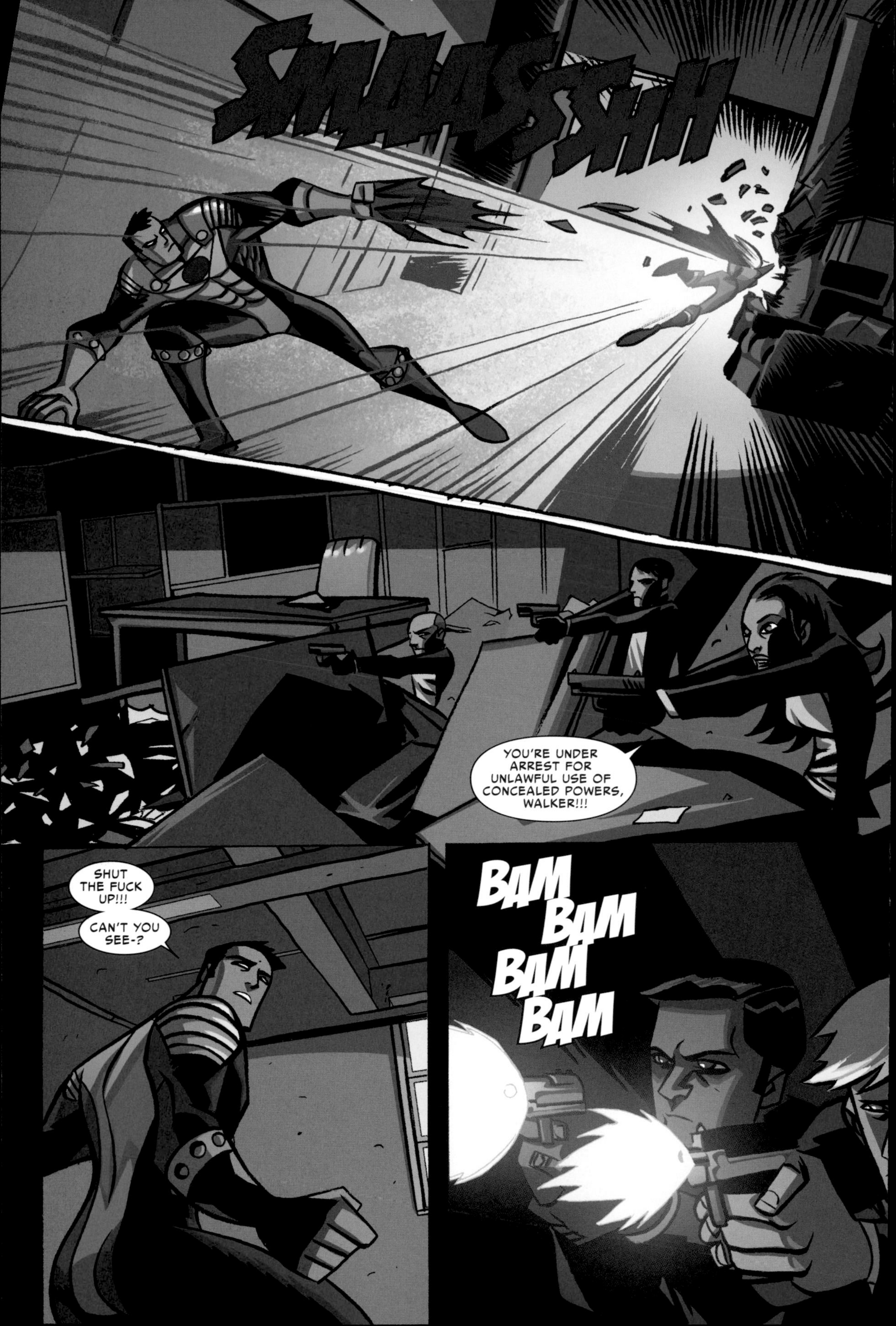
SMAASSHH
YOU'RE UNDER ARREST FOR UNLAWFUL USE OF CONCEALED POWERS, WALKER!!!
SHUT THE FUCK UP!!!
CAN'T YOU SEE-?
BAM BAM BAM BAM

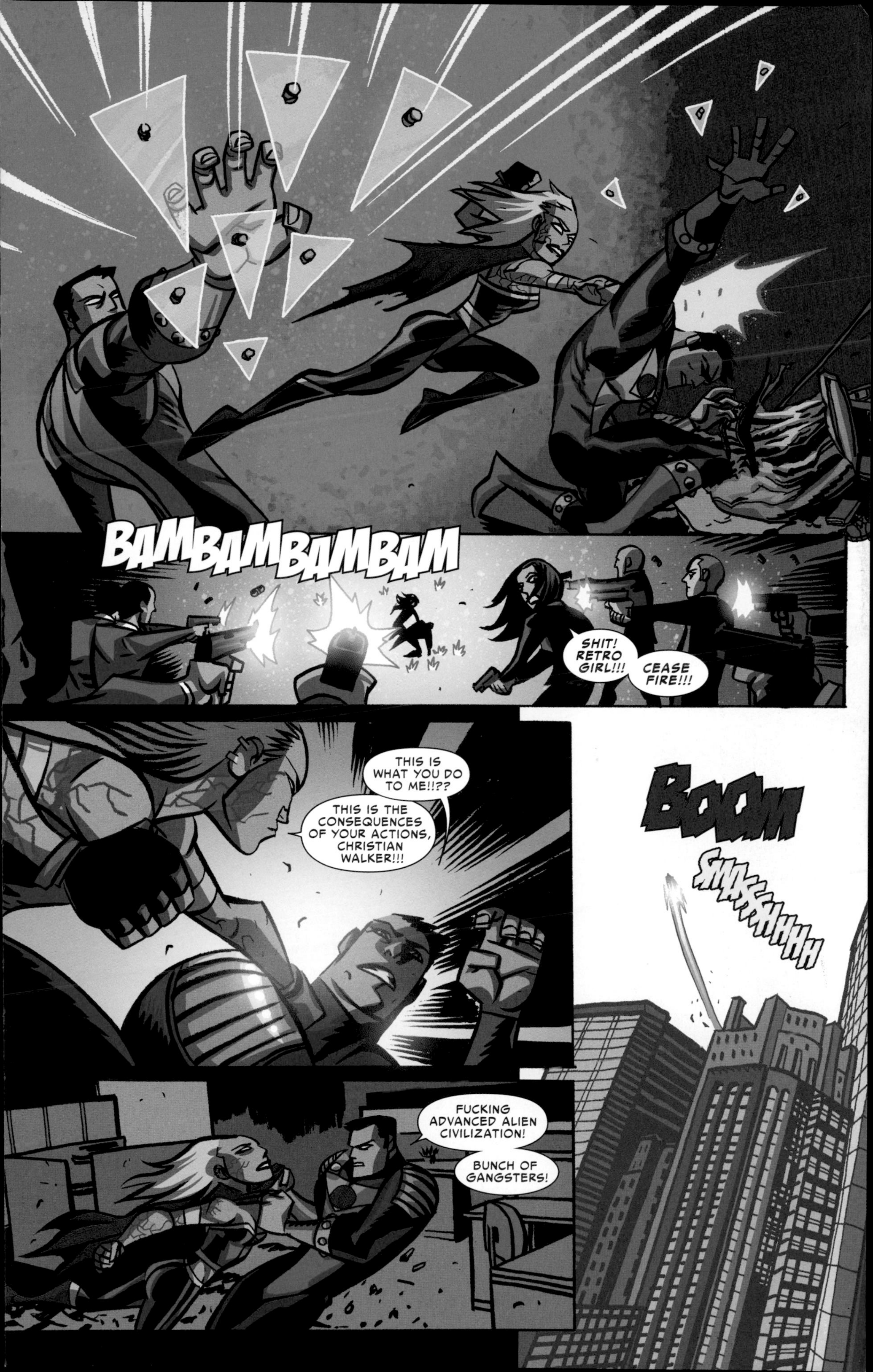
BAMBAMBAMBAM
SHIT! RETRO GIRL!!!
CEASE FIRE!!!
THIS IS WHAT YOU DO TO ME!!??
THIS IS THE CONSEQUENCES OF YOUR ACTIONS, CHRISTIAN WALKER!!!
BOOM
SMASSHHHH
FUCKING ADVANCED ALIEN CIVILIZATION!
BUNCH OF GANGSTERS!

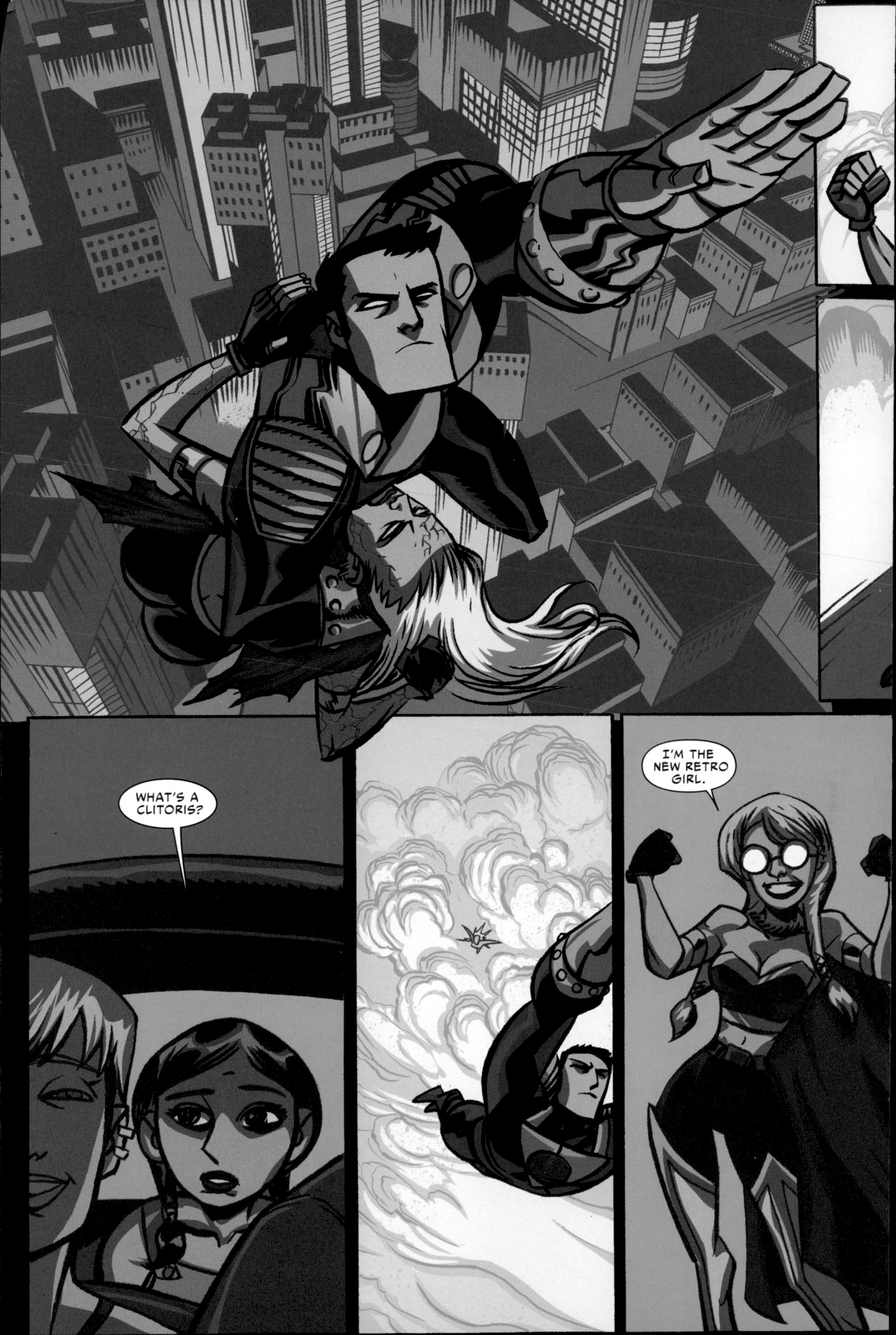
WHAT'S A CLITORIS?
I'M THE NEW RETRO GIRL.

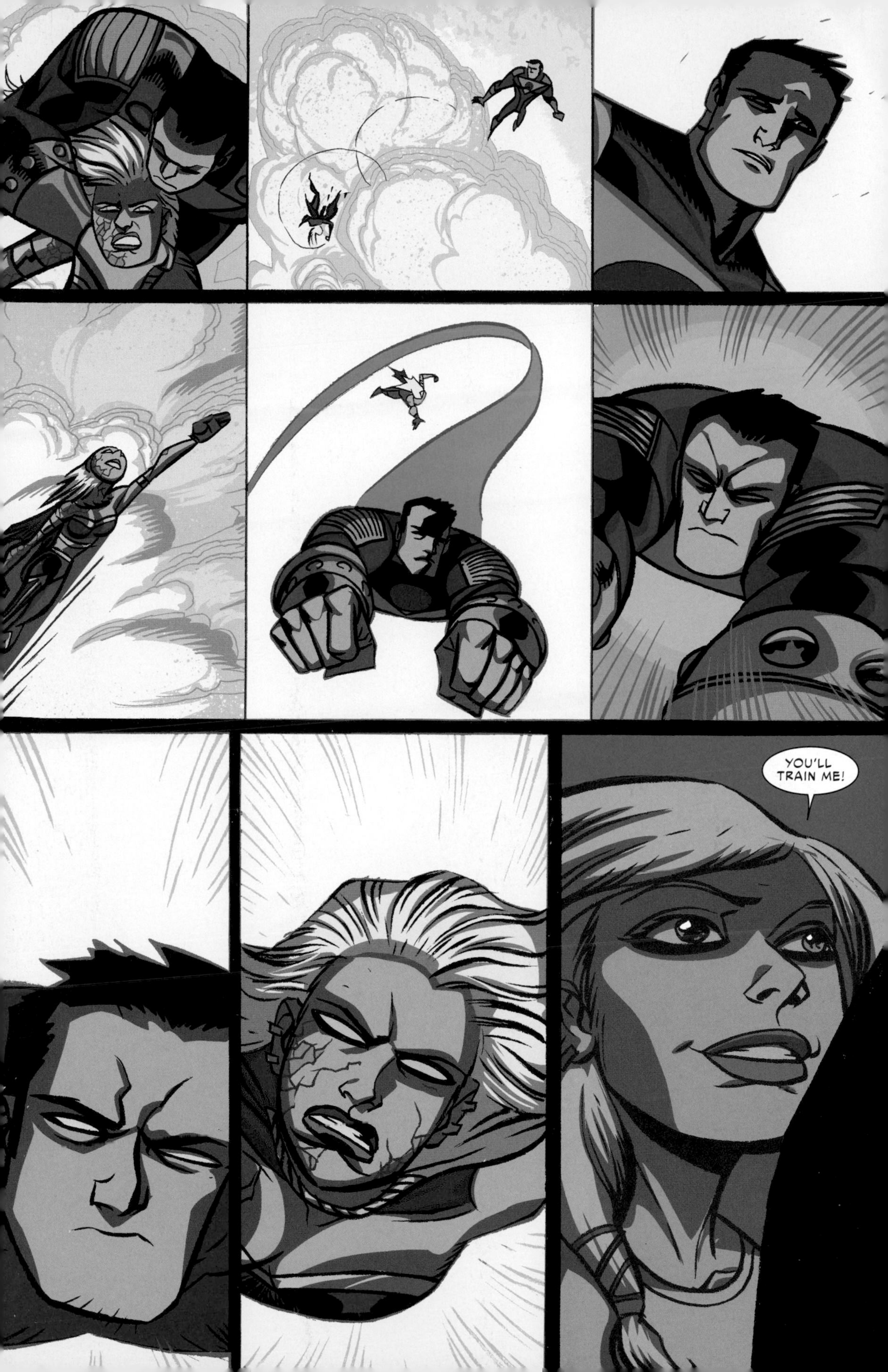
YOU'LL TRAIN ME!

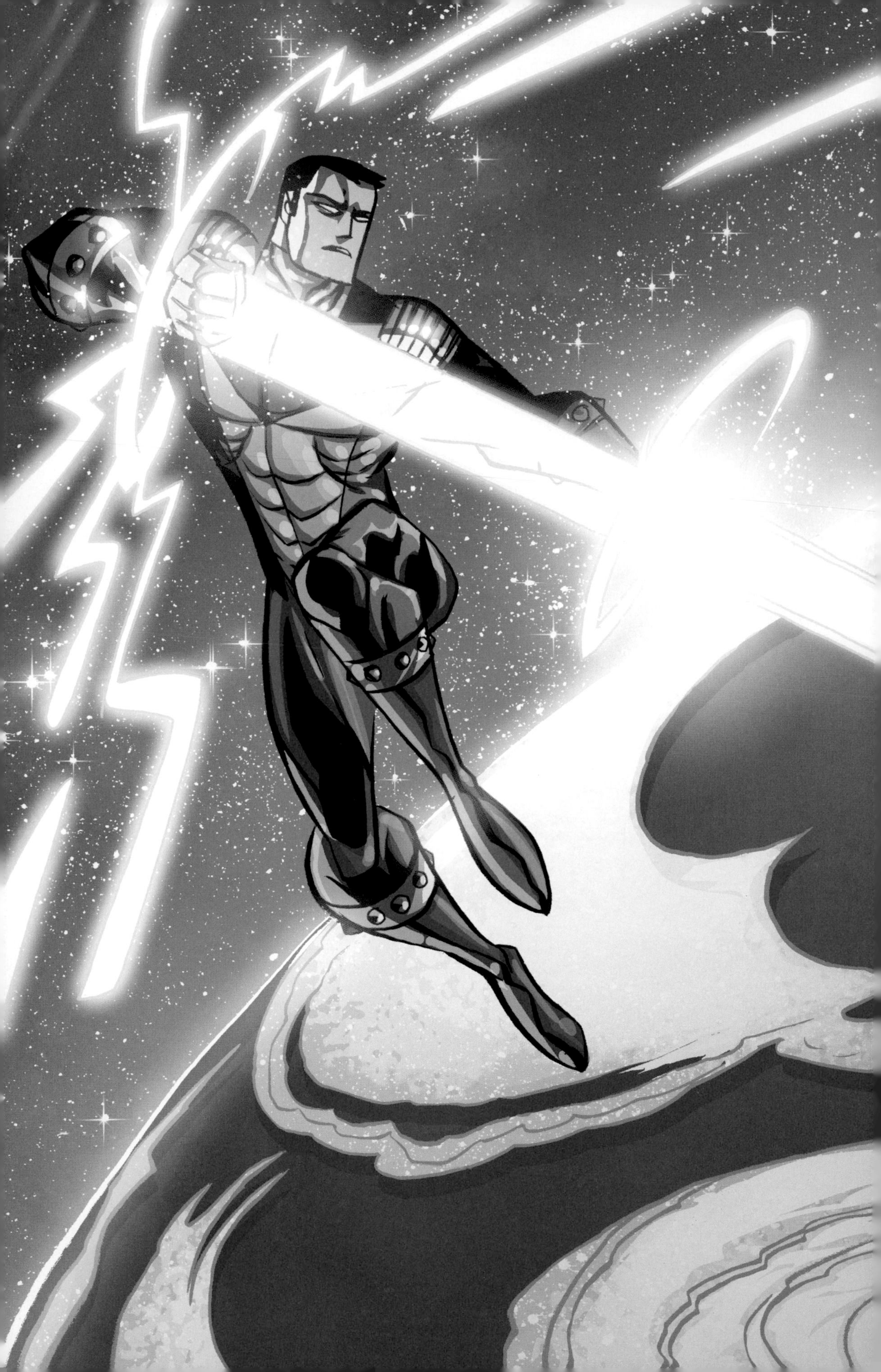

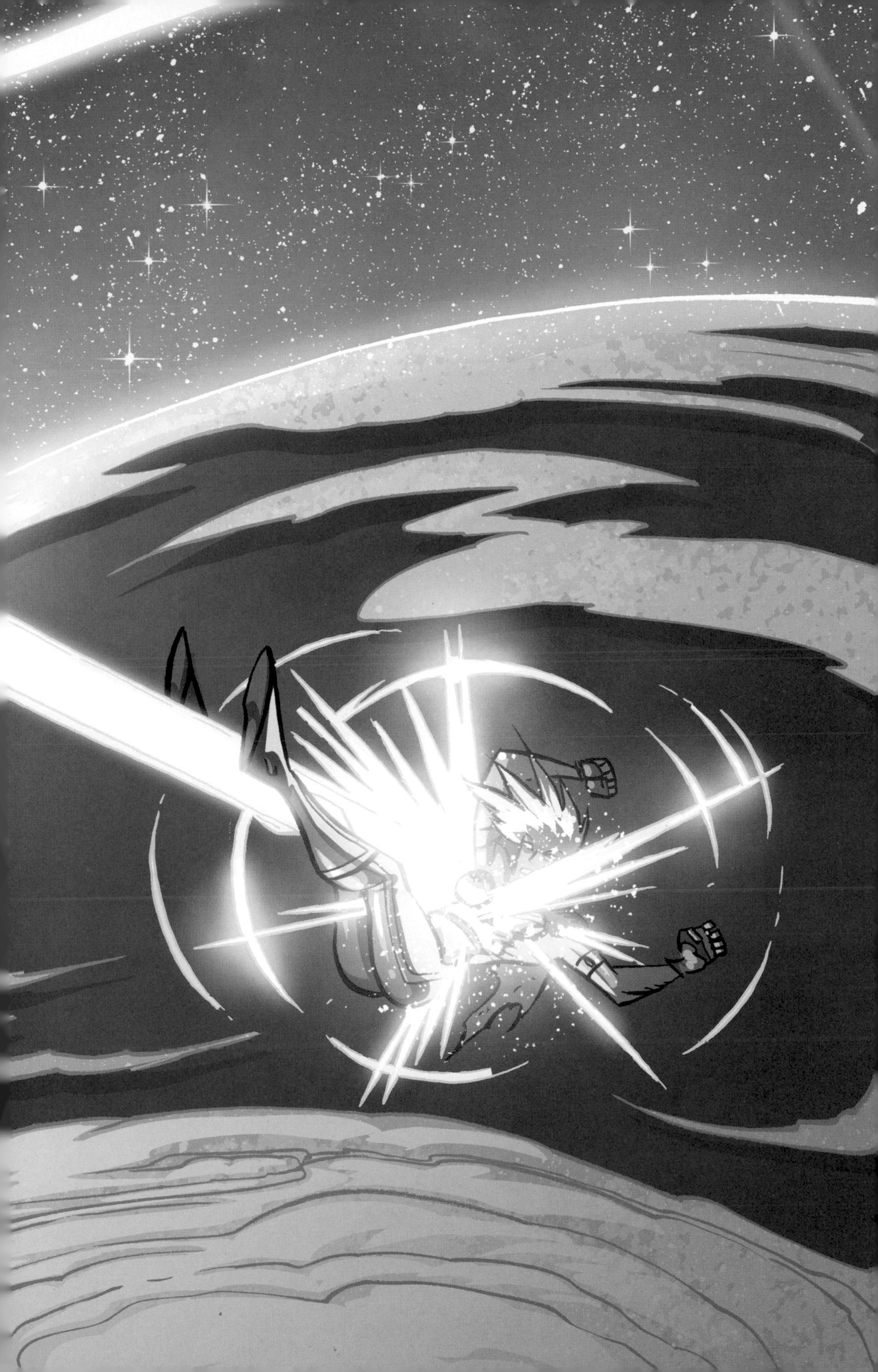

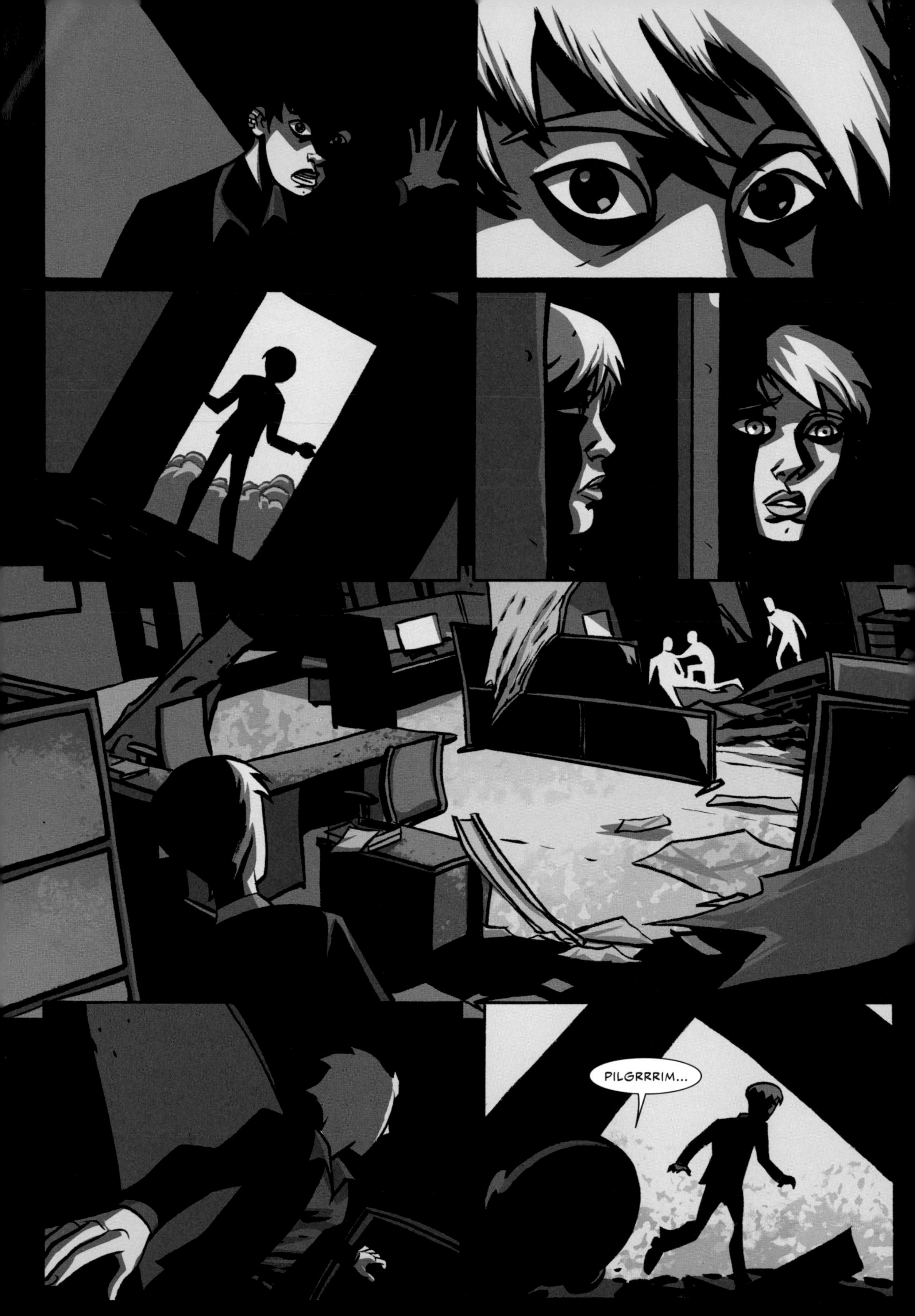
PILGRRRIM...

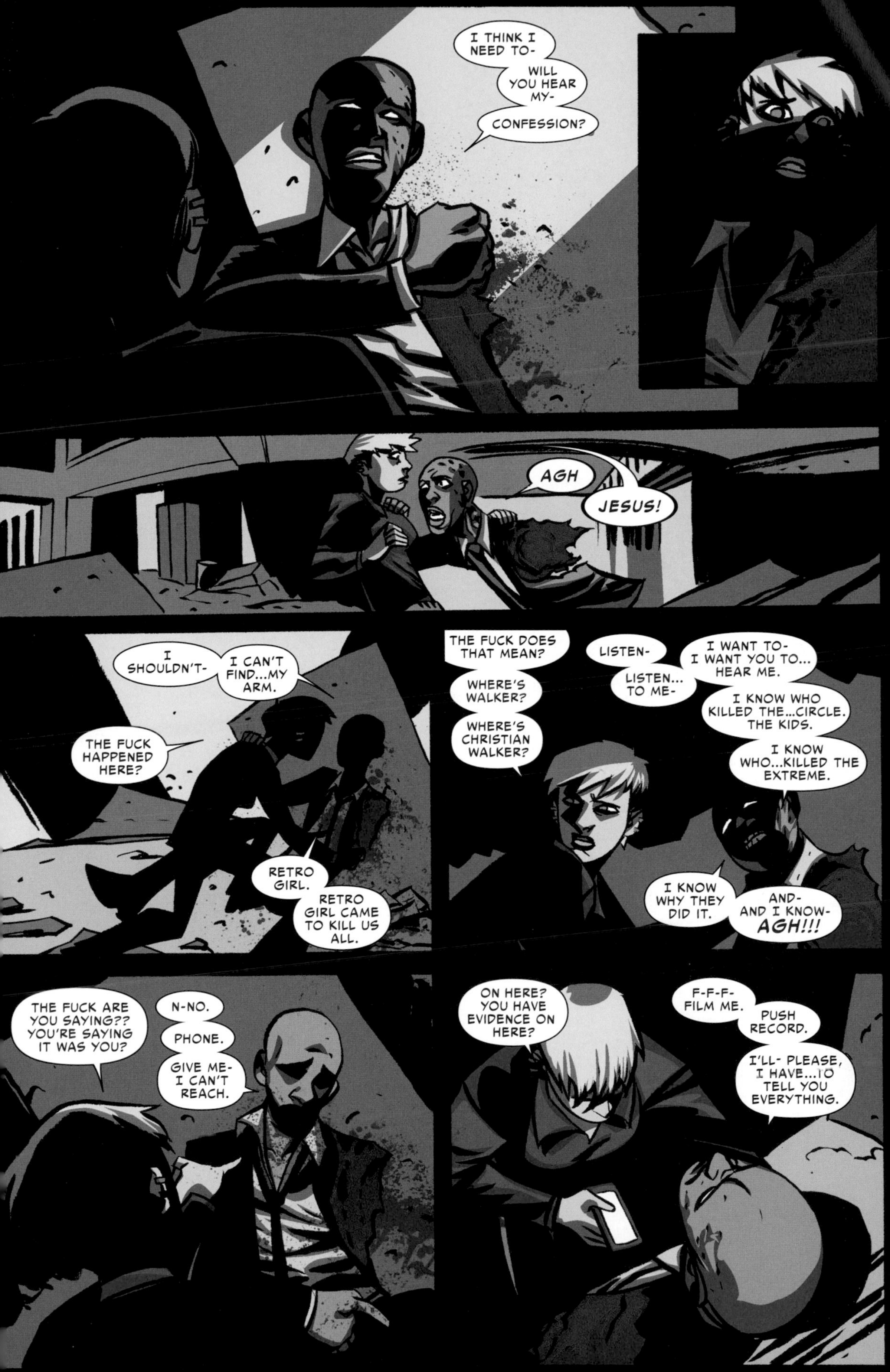
I THINK I NEED TO-
WILL YOU HEAR MY-
CONFESSION?
AGH
JESUS!
I SHOULDN'T-
I CAN'T FIND...MY ARM.
THE FUCK HAPPENED HERE?
RETRO GIRL.
RETRO GIRL CAME TO KILL US ALL.
THE FUCK DOES THAT MEAN?
WHERE'S WALKER?
WHERE'S CHRISTIAN WALKER?
LISTEN-
LISTEN... TO ME-
I WANT TO- I WANT YOU TO... HEAR ME.
I KNOW WHO KILLED THE...CIRCLE. THE KIDS.
I KNOW WHO...KILLED THE EXTREME.
I KNOW WHY THEY DID IT.
AND- AND I KNOW- AGH!!!
THE FUCK ARE YOU SAYING?? YOU'RE SAYING IT WAS YOU?
N-NO.
PHONE.
GIVE ME- I CAN'T REACH.
ON HERE? YOU HAVE EVIDENCE ON HERE?
F-F-F- FILM ME.
PUSH RECORD.
I'LL- PLEASE, I HAVE...TO TELL YOU EVERYTHING.

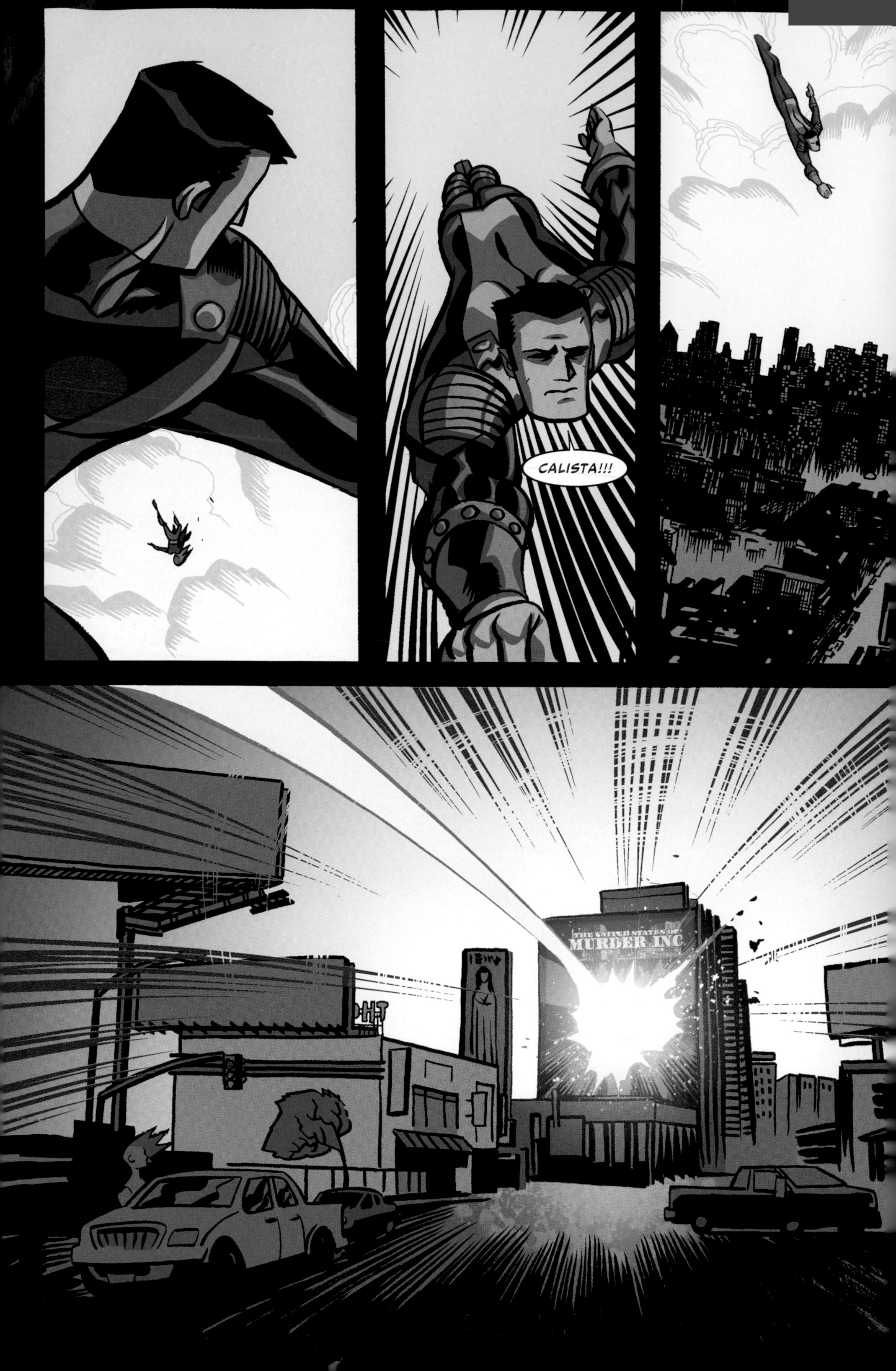
CALISTA!!!
THE UNITED STATES OF
MURDER INC

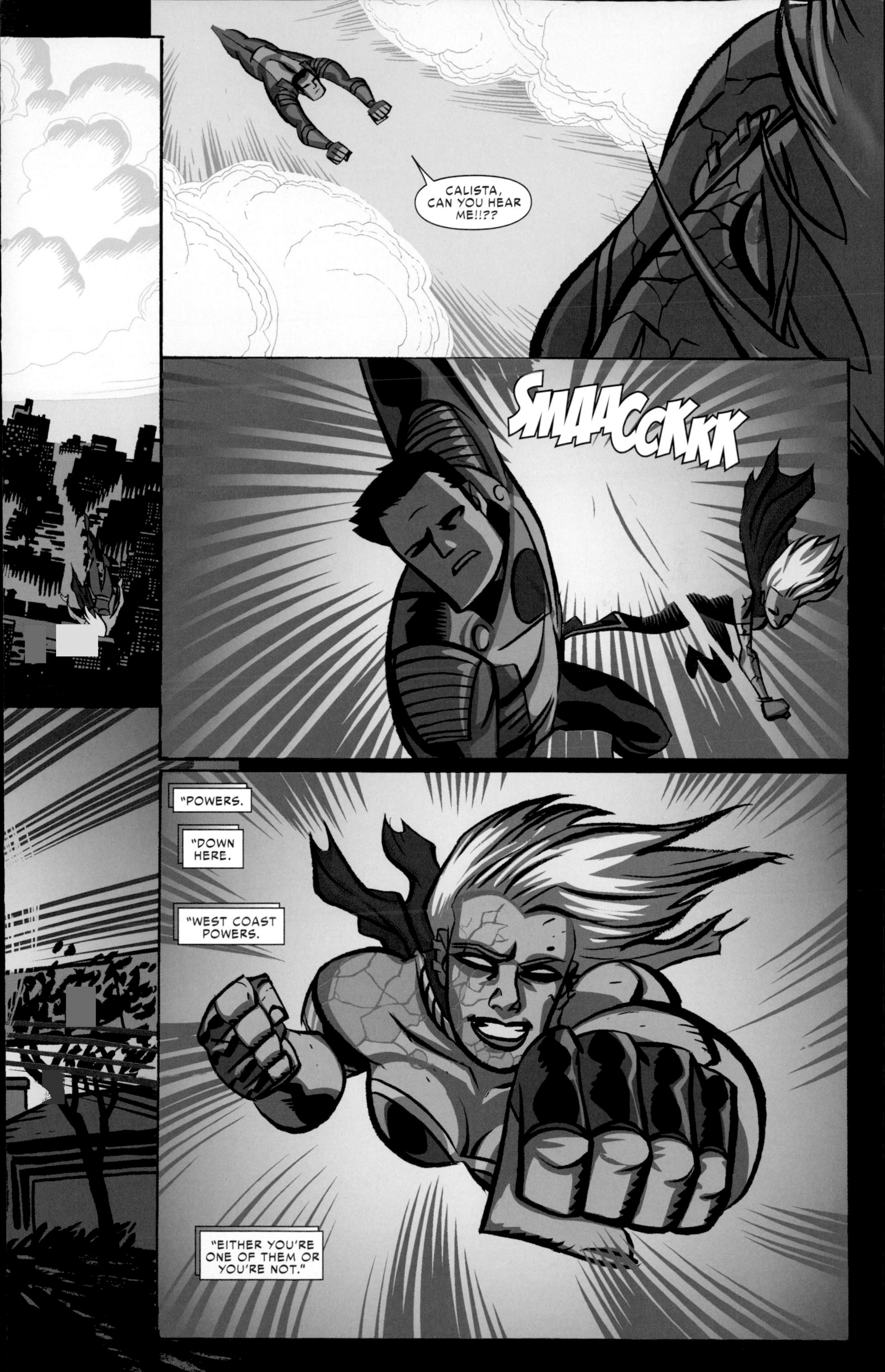
CALISTA, CAN YOU HEAR ME!!??
SMAAACCKKK
"POWERS.
"DOWN HERE.
"WEST COAST POWERS.
"EITHER YOU'RE ONE OF THEM OR YOU'RE NOT."

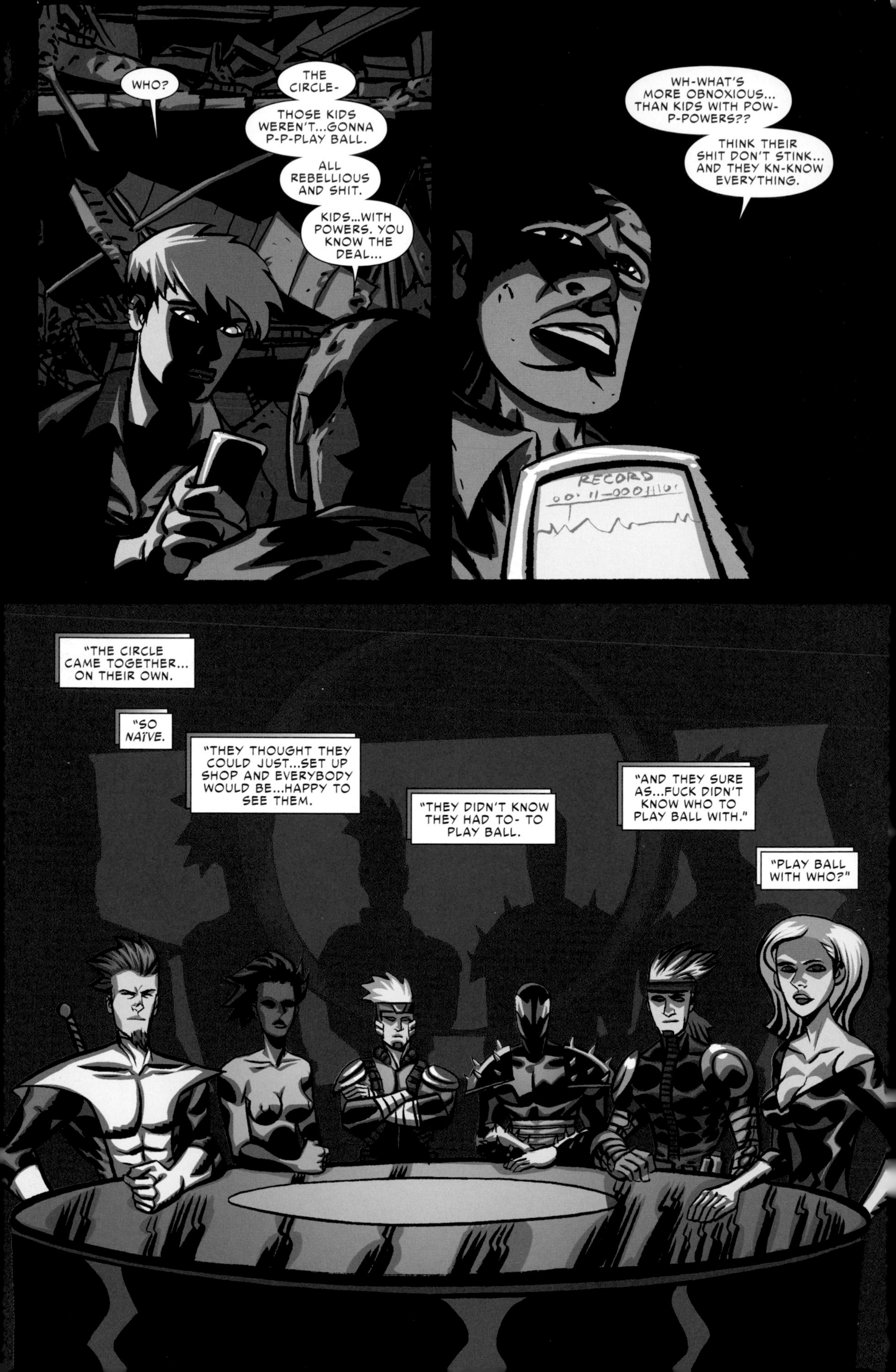
WHO?
THE CIRCLE-
THOSE KIDS WEREN'T...GONNA P-P-PLAY BALL.
ALL REBELLIOUS AND SHIT.
KIDS...WITH POWERS. YOU KNOW THE DEAL...
WH-WHAT'S MORE OBNOXIOUS... THAN KIDS WITH POW-P-POWERS??
THINK THEIR SHIT DON'T STINK... AND THEY KN-KNOW EVERYTHING.
RECORD
"THE CIRCLE CAME TOGETHER... ON THEIR OWN.
"SO NAÏVE.
"THEY THOUGHT THEY COULD JUST...SET UP SHOP AND EVERYBODY WOULD BE...HAPPY TO SEE THEM.
"THEY DIDN'T KNOW THEY HAD TO- TO PLAY BALL.
"AND THEY SURE AS...FUCK DIDN'T KNOW WHO TO PLAY BALL WITH."
"PLAY BALL WITH WHO?"

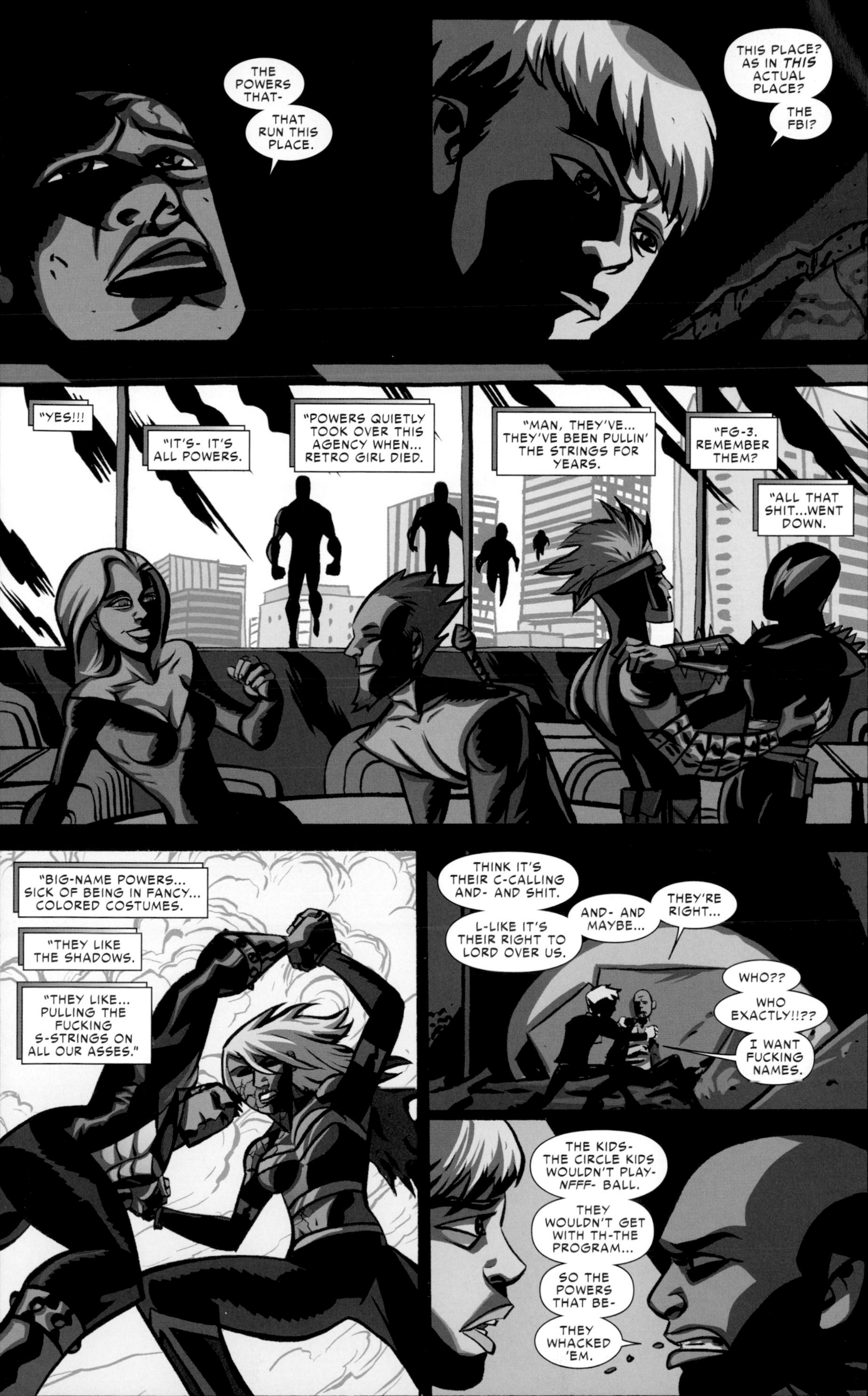
THE POWERS THAT-
THAT RUN THIS PLACE.
THIS PLACE? AS IN *THIS* ACTUAL PLACE?
THE FBI?
"YES!!!
"IT'S- IT'S ALL POWERS.
"POWERS QUIETLY TOOK OVER THIS AGENCY WHEN... RETRO GIRL DIED.
"MAN, THEY'VE... THEY'VE BEEN PULLIN' THE STRINGS FOR YEARS.
"FG-3. REMEMBER THEM?
"ALL THAT SHIT...WENT DOWN.
"BIG-NAME POWERS... SICK OF BEING IN FANCY... COLORED COSTUMES.
"THEY LIKE THE SHADOWS.
"THEY LIKE... PULLING THE FUCKING S-STRINGS ON ALL OUR ASSES."
THINK IT'S THEIR C-CALLING AND- AND SHIT.
L-LIKE IT'S THEIR RIGHT TO LORD OVER US.
AND- AND MAYBE...
THEY'RE RIGHT...
WHO??
WHO EXACTLY!!??
I WANT FUCKING NAMES.
THE KIDS- THE CIRCLE KIDS WOULDN'T PLAY- *NFFF*- BALL.
THEY WOULDN'T GET WITH TH-THE PROGRAM...
SO THE POWERS THAT BE-
THEY WHACKED 'EM.

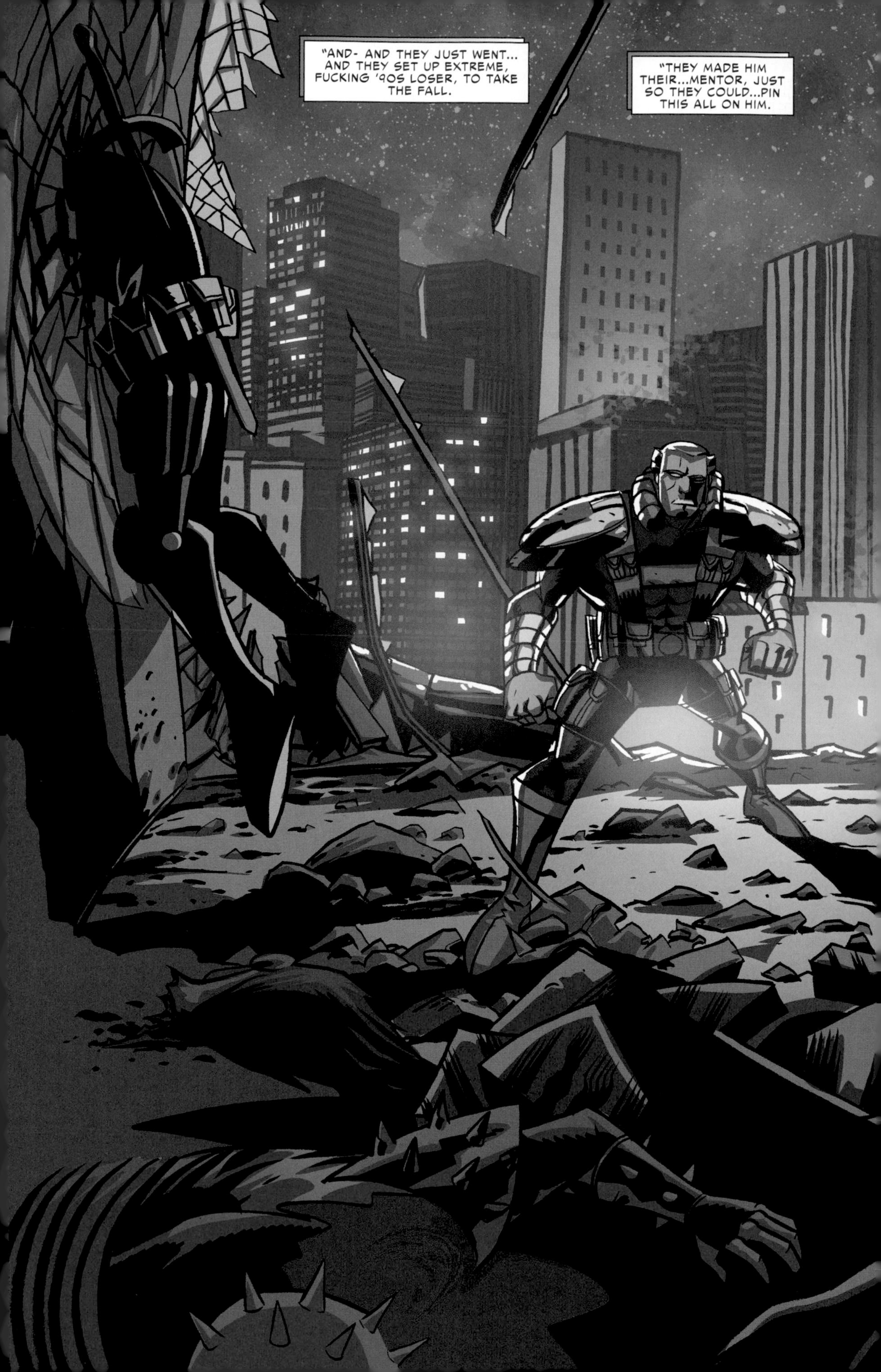
"AND- AND THEY JUST WENT... AND THEY SET UP EXTREME, FUCKING '90S LOSER, TO TAKE THE FALL.
"THEY MADE HIM THEIR...MENTOR, JUST SO THEY COULD...PIN THIS ALL ON HIM.

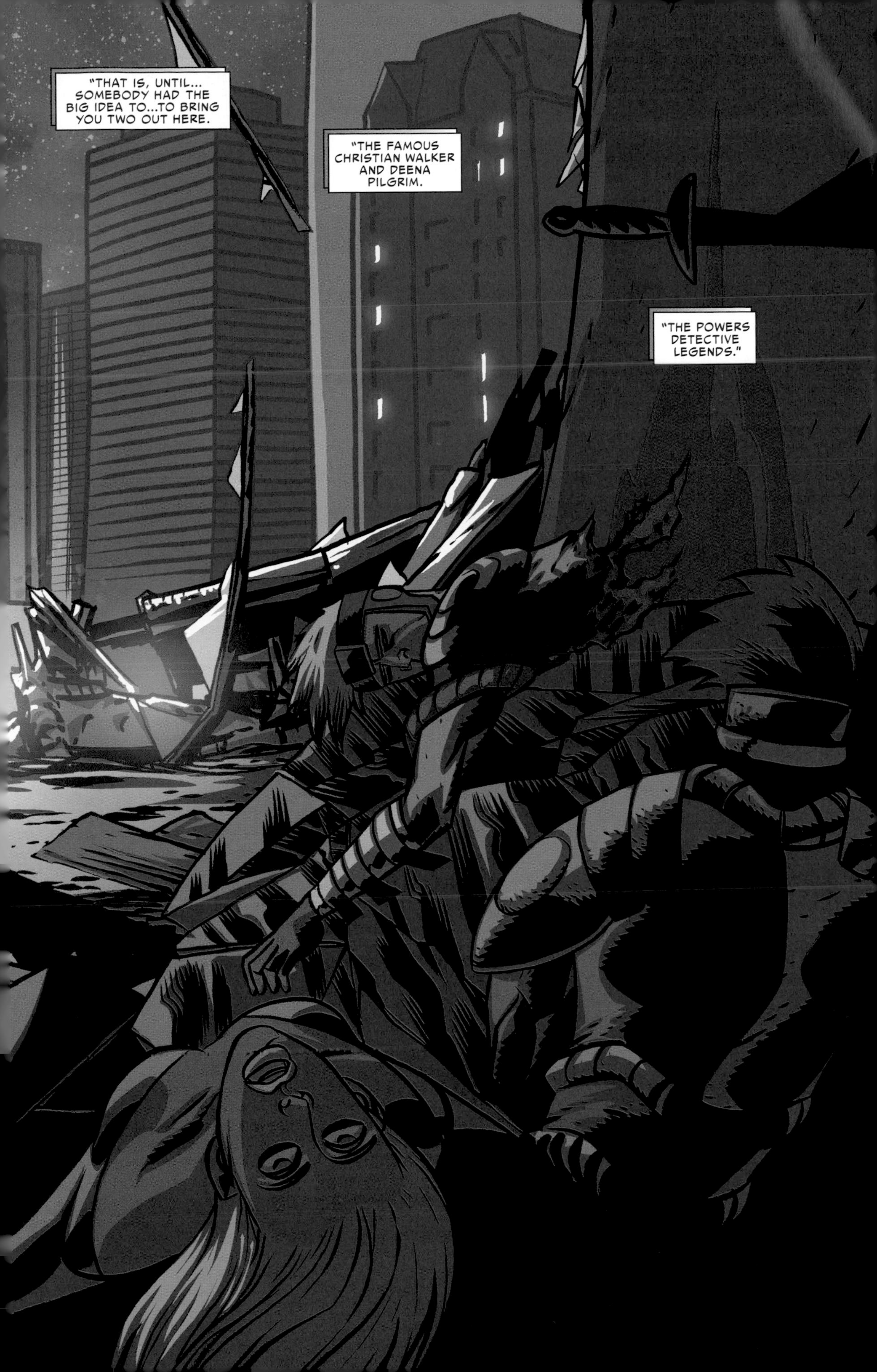
"THAT IS, UNTIL... SOMEBODY HAD THE BIG IDEA TO...TO BRING YOU TWO OUT HERE.
"THE FAMOUS CHRISTIAN WALKER AND DEENA PILGRIM.
"THE POWERS DETECTIVE LEGENDS."

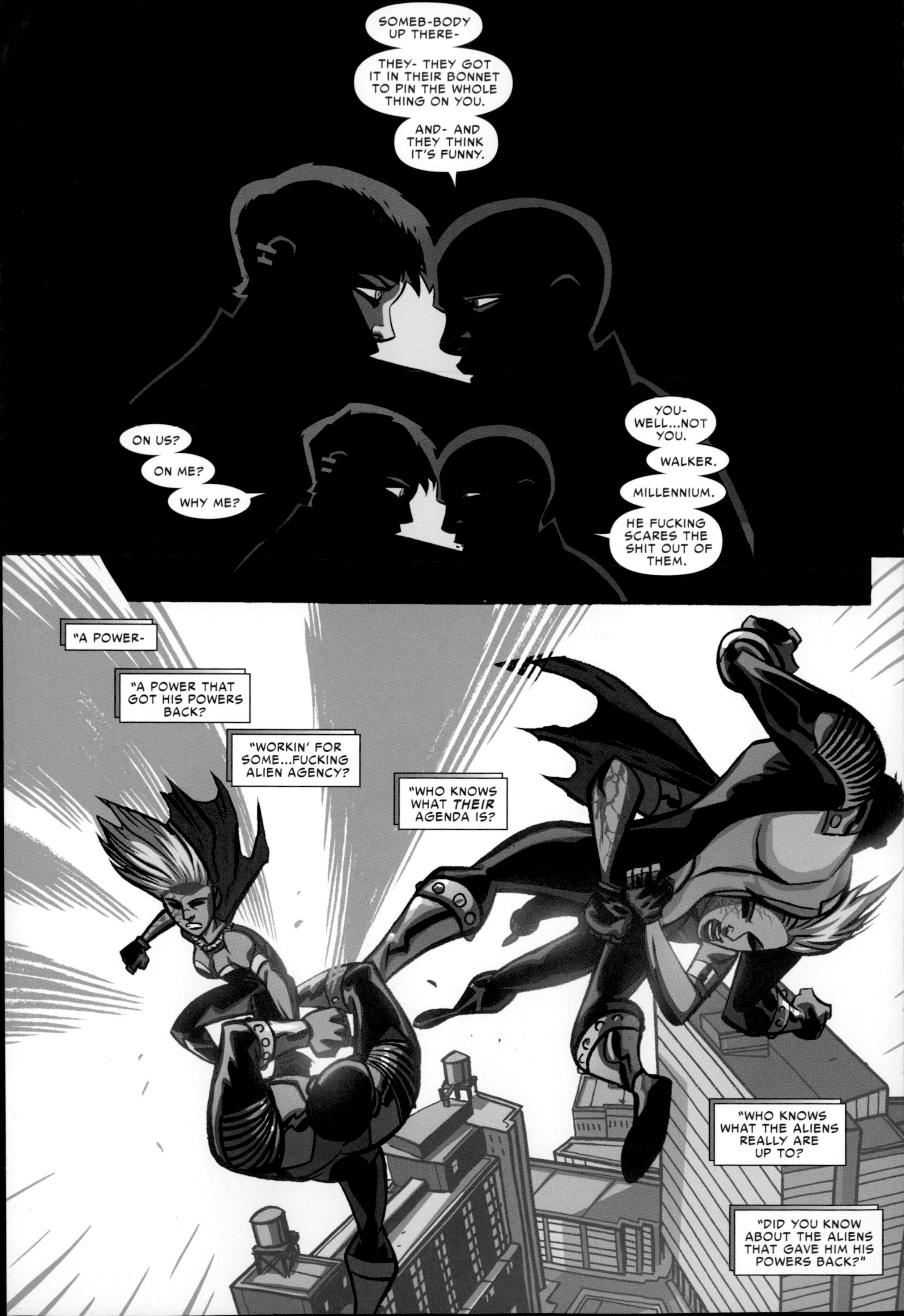
SOMEB-BODY UP THERE-
THEY- THEY GOT IT IN THEIR BONNET TO PIN THE WHOLE THING ON YOU.
AND- AND THEY THINK IT'S FUNNY.
ON US?
ON ME?
WHY ME?
YOU- WELL...NOT YOU.
WALKER.
MILLENNIUM.
HE FUCKING SCARES THE SHIT OUT OF THEM.
"A POWER-
"A POWER THAT GOT HIS POWERS BACK?
"WORKIN' FOR SOME...FUCKING ALIEN AGENCY?
"WHO KNOWS WHAT *THEIR* AGENDA IS?
"WHO KNOWS WHAT THE ALIENS REALLY ARE UP TO?
"DID YOU KNOW ABOUT THE ALIENS THAT GAVE HIM HIS POWERS BACK?"

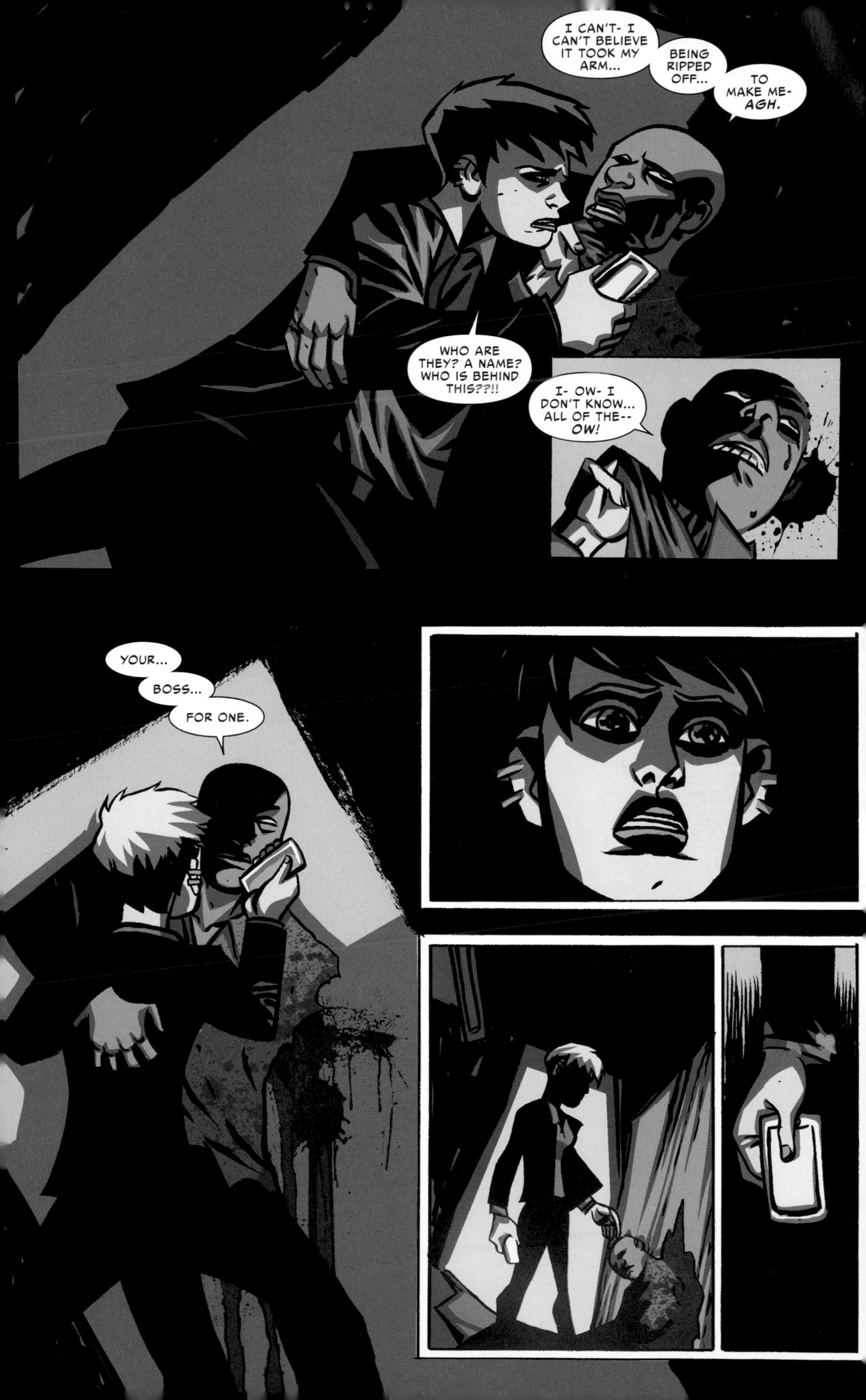
I CAN'T- I CAN'T BELIEVE IT TOOK MY ARM...
BEING RIPPED OFF...
TO MAKE ME- AGH.
WHO ARE THEY? A NAME? WHO IS BEHIND THIS??!!
I- OW- I DON'T KNOW... ALL OF THE-- OW!
YOUR...
BOSS...
FOR ONE.

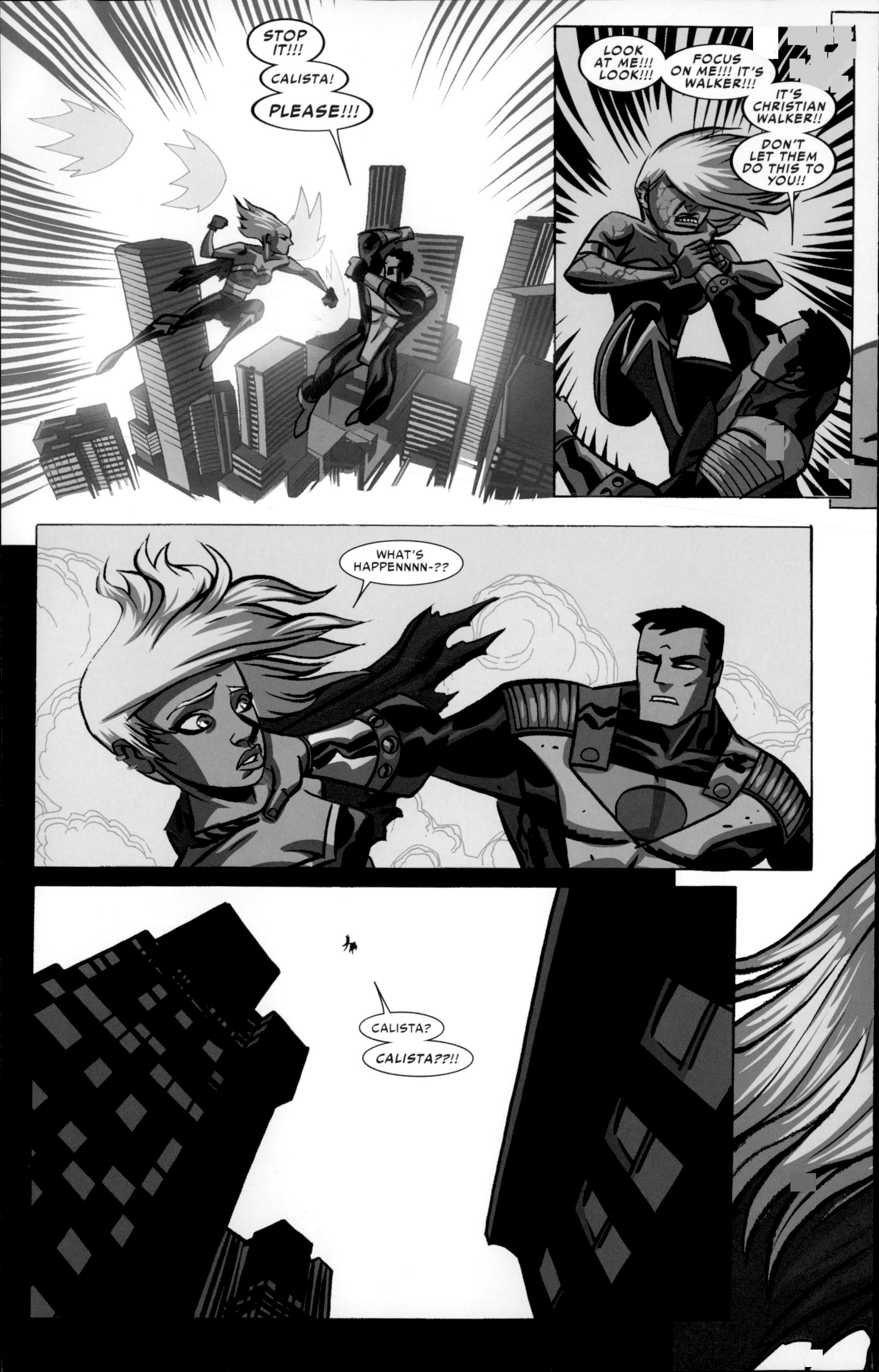
STOP IT!!!
CALISTA!
PLEASE!!!
LOOK AT ME!!! LOOK!!!
FOCUS ON ME!!! IT'S WALKER!!!
IT'S CHRISTIAN WALKER!!
DON'T LET THEM DO THIS TO YOU!!
WHAT'S HAPPENNNN-??
CALISTA?
CALISTA??!!

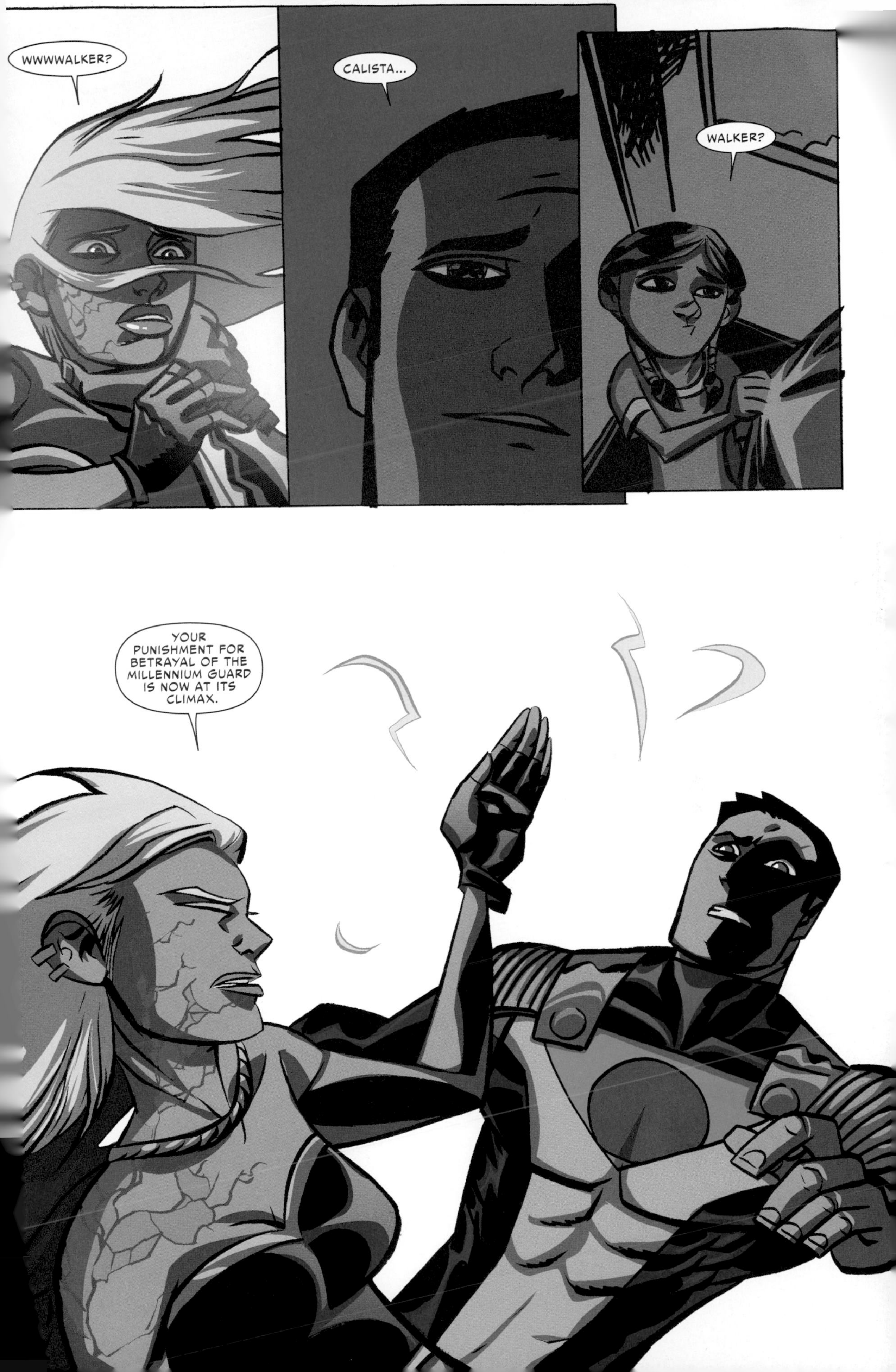
WWWWALKER?
CALISTA...
WALKER?
YOUR PUNISHMENT FOR BETRAYAL OF THE MILLENNIUM GUARD IS NOW AT ITS CLIMAX.

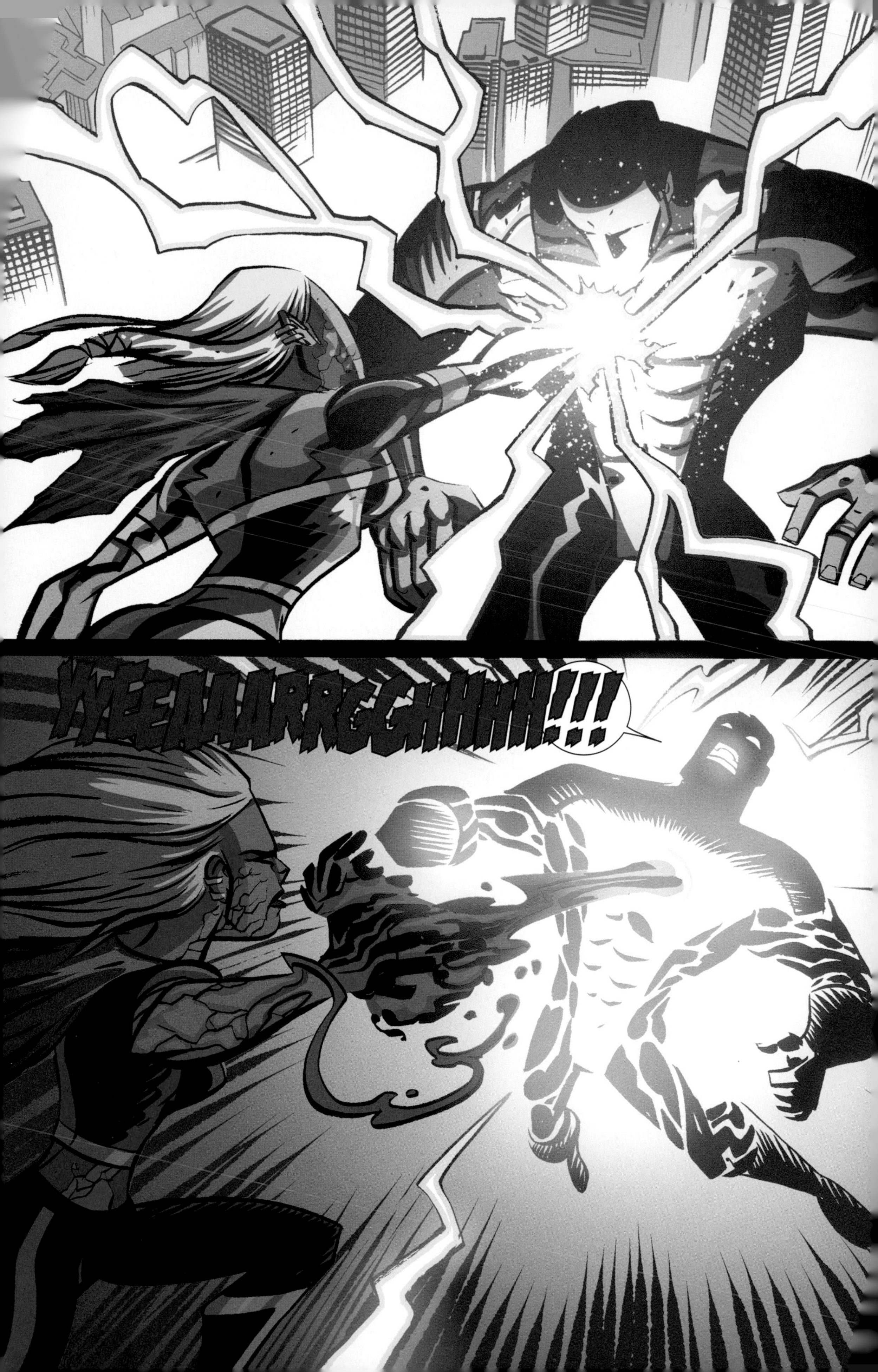
YYEEAAARRGGHHHHH!!!

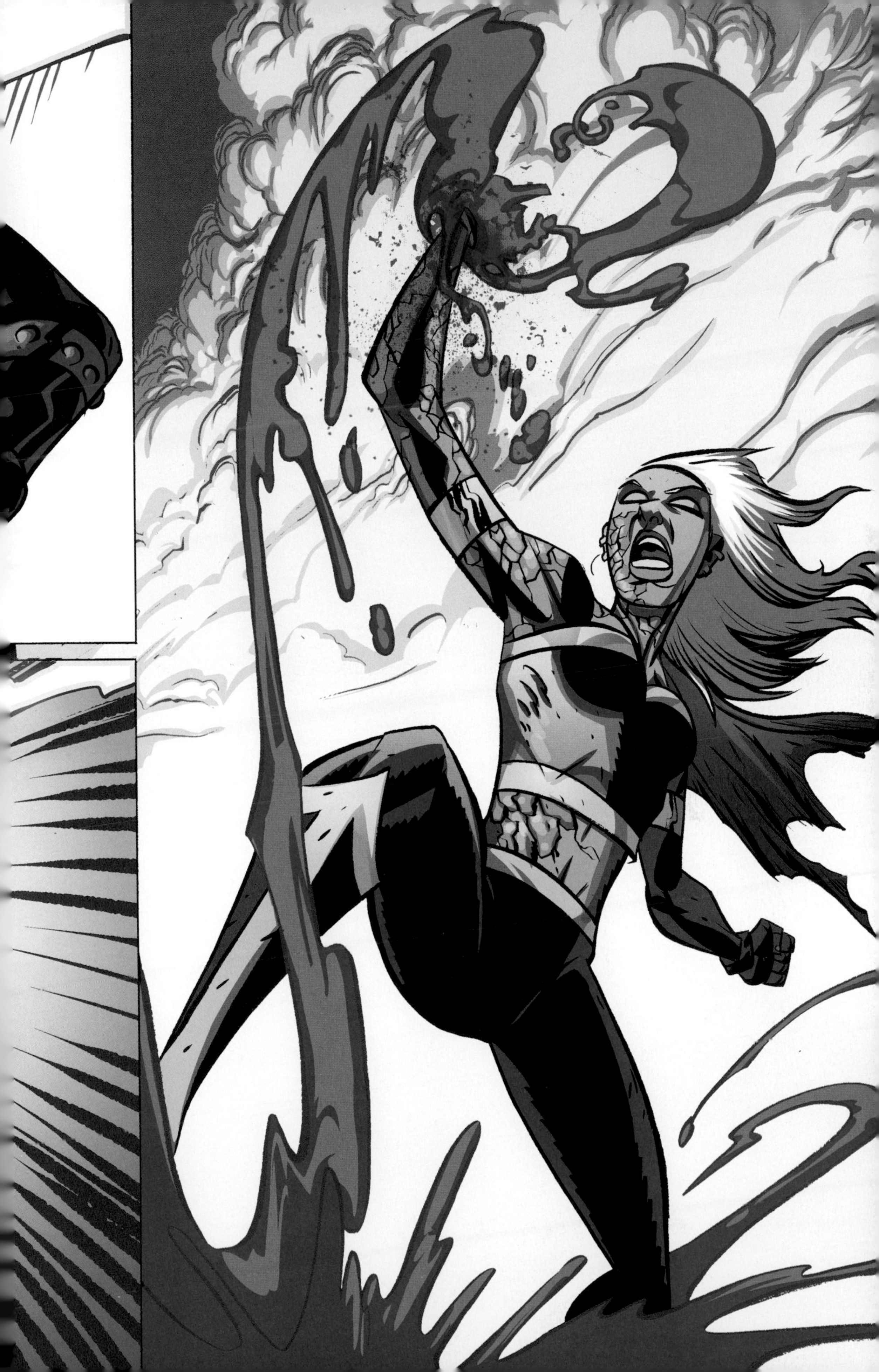

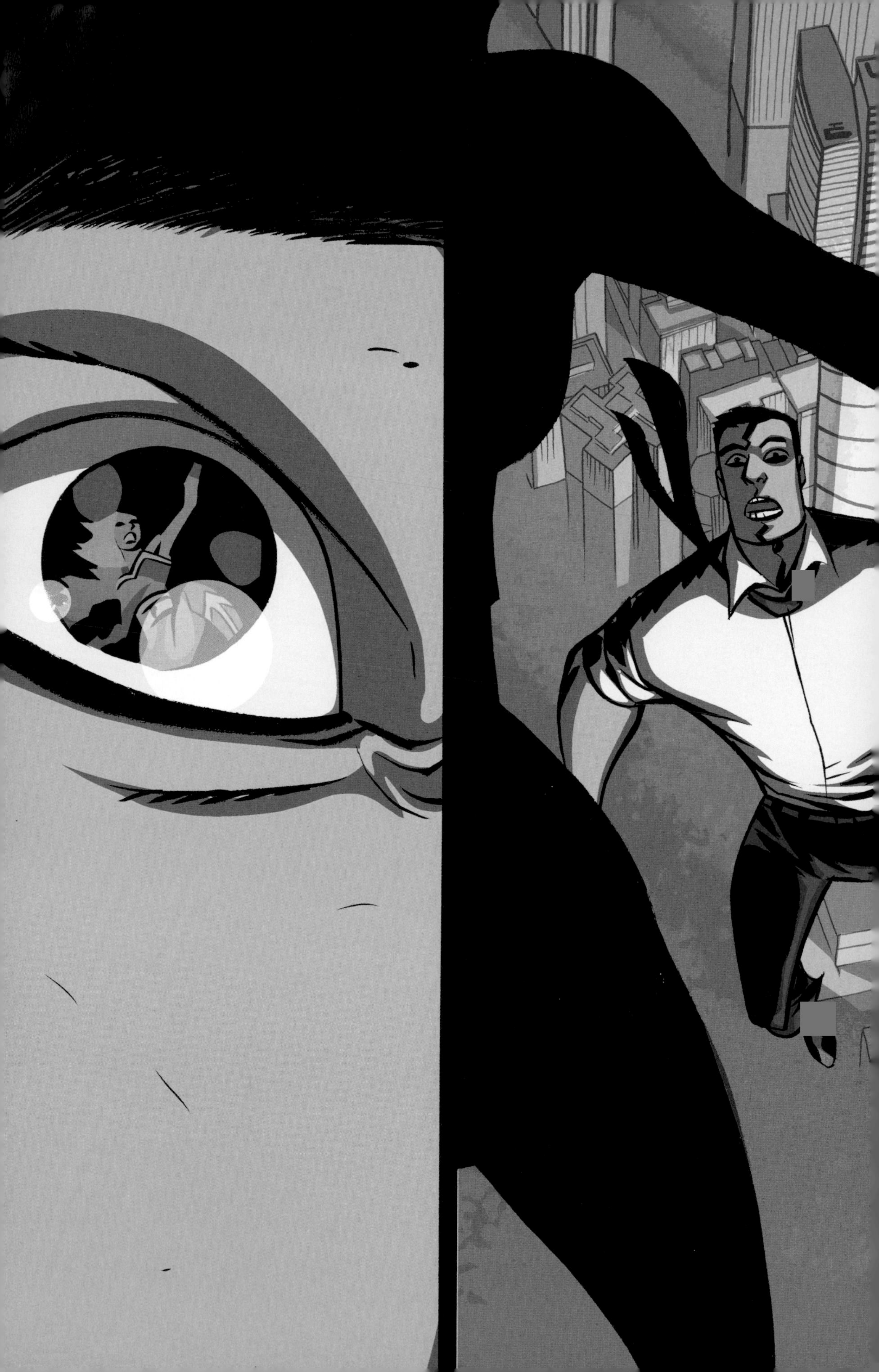

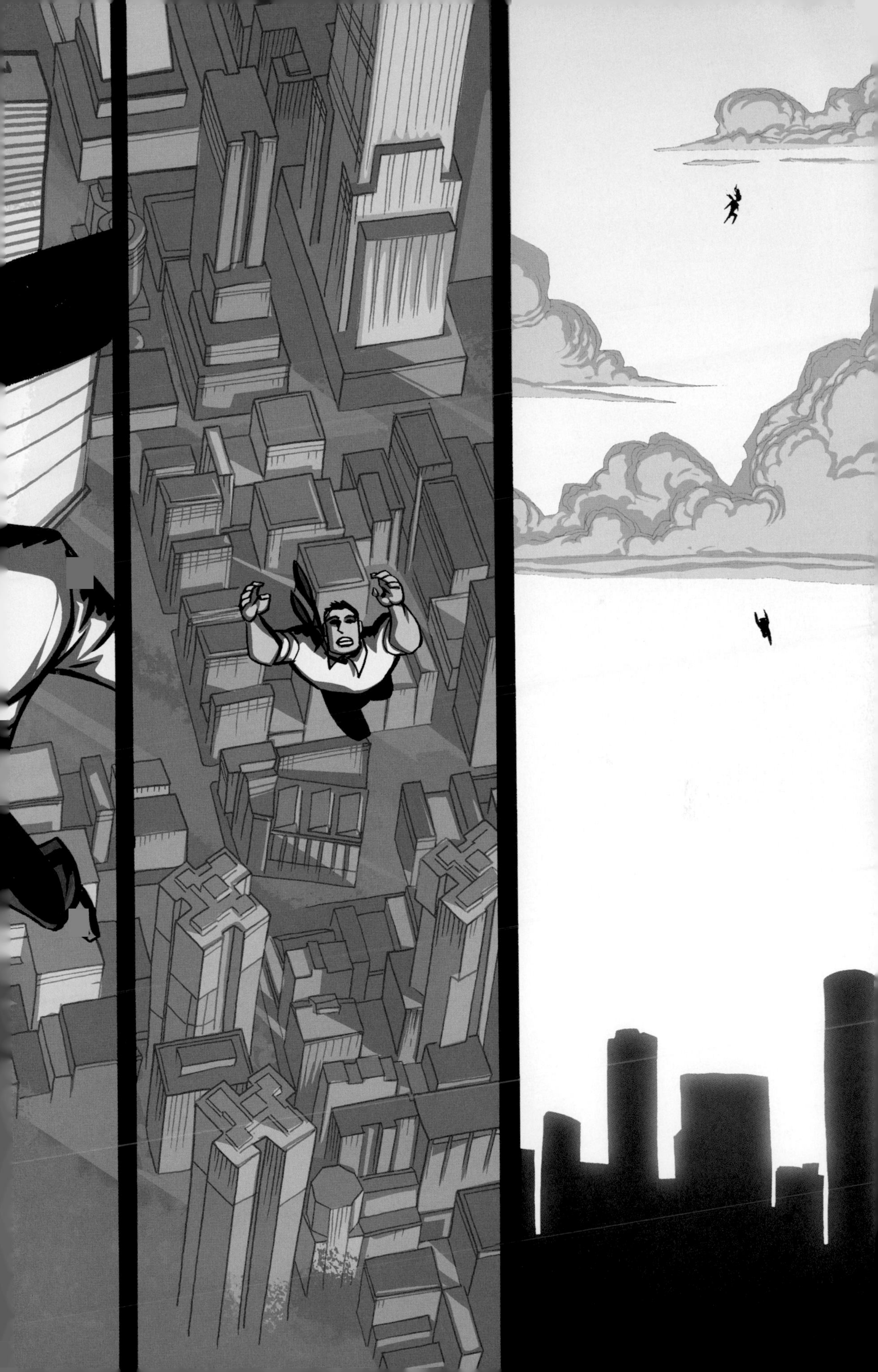

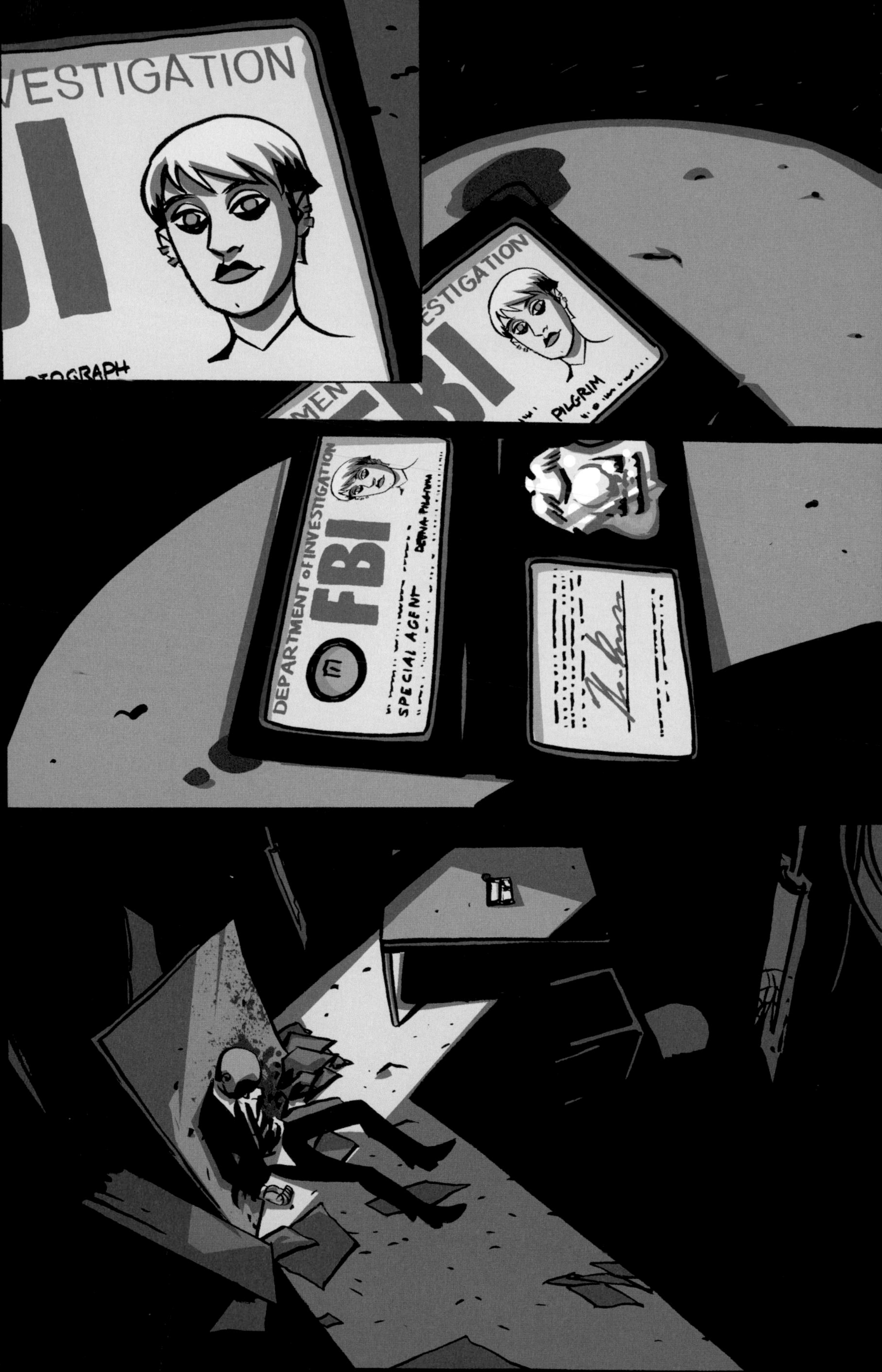

VESTIGATION
BI
ESTIGATION
PILGRIM
DEPARTMENT OF INVESTIGATION
FBI
SPECIAL AGENT

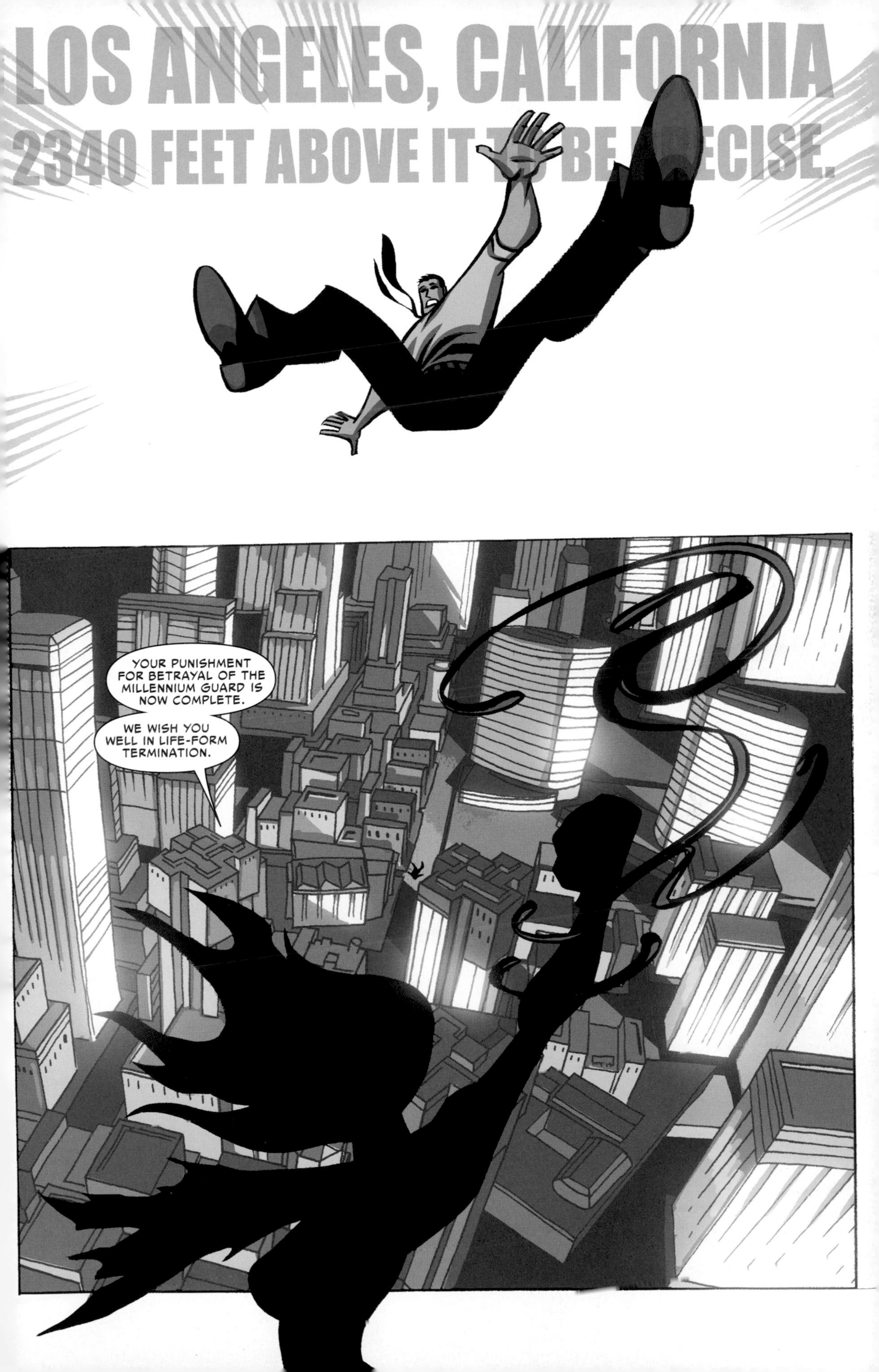
LOS ANGELES, CALIFORNIA
2340 FEET ABOVE IT TO BE PRECISE.
YOUR PUNISHMENT FOR BETRAYAL OF THE MILLENNIUM GUARD IS NOW COMPLETE.
WE WISH YOU WELL IN LIFE-FORM TERMINATION.

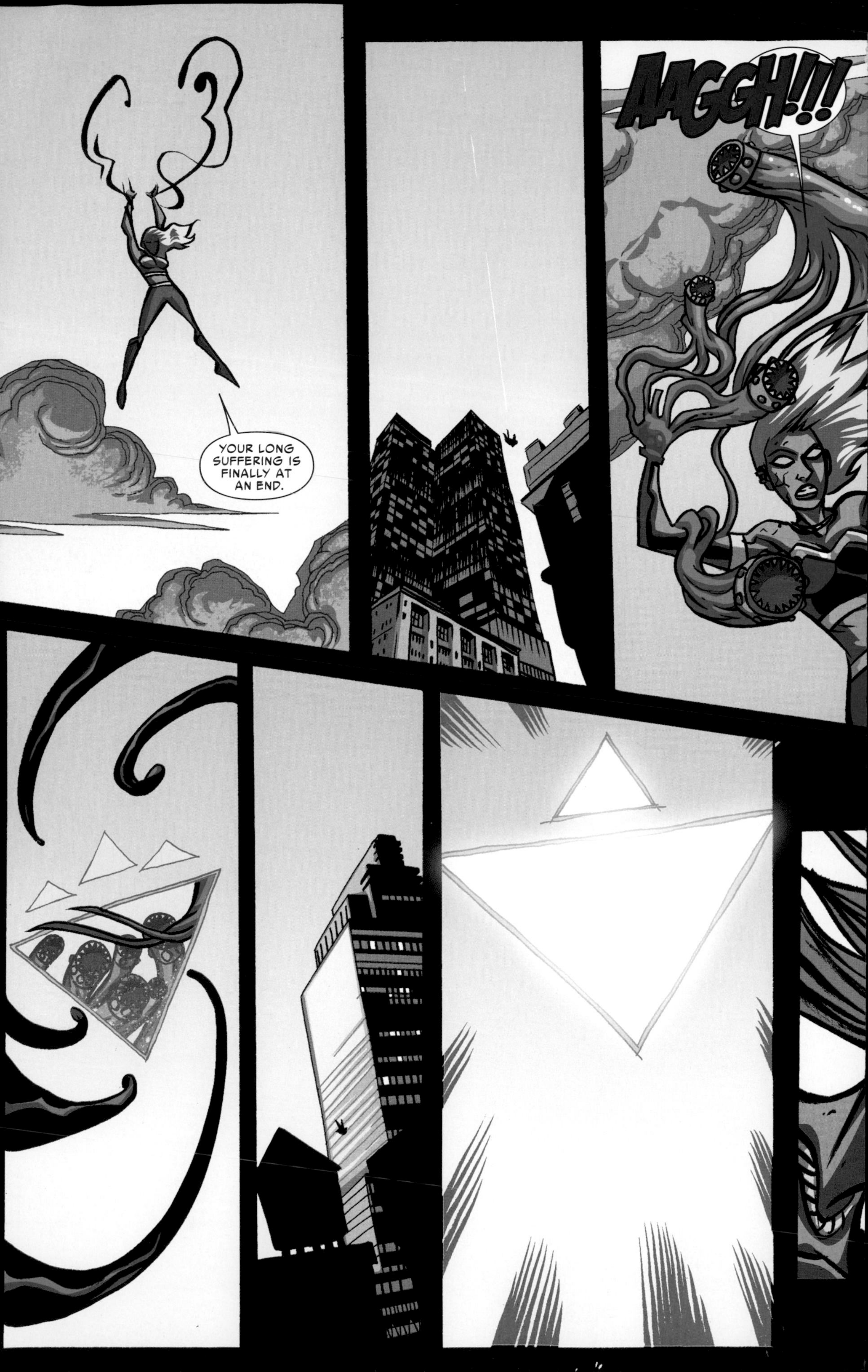
YOUR LONG SUFFERING IS FINALLY AT AN END.
AAGGH!!!

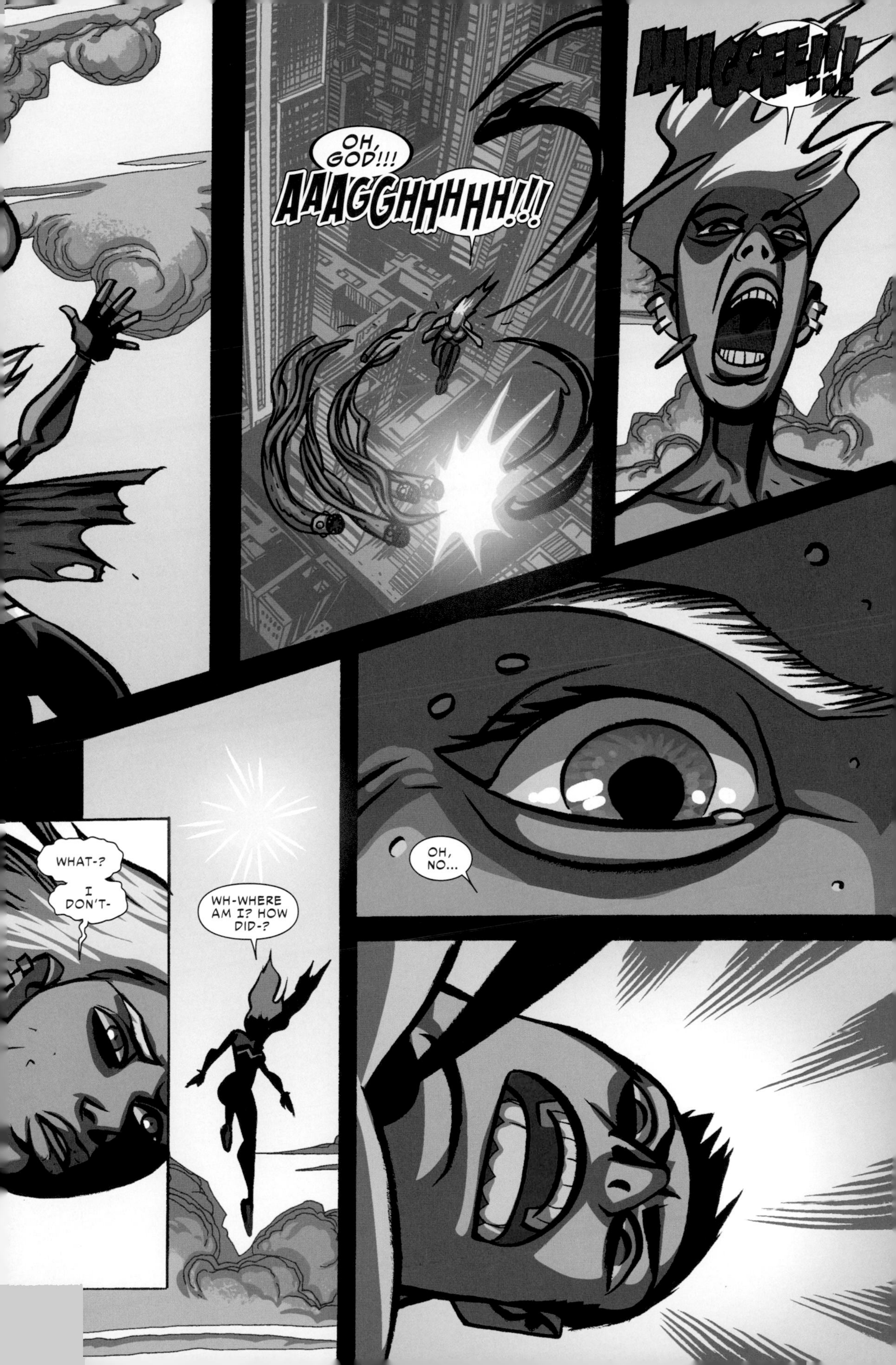
OH, GOD!!!
AAAGGHHHHH!!!
AAIIGGEE!!!
OH, NO...
WHAT-? I DON'T-
WH-WHERE AM I? HOW DID-?

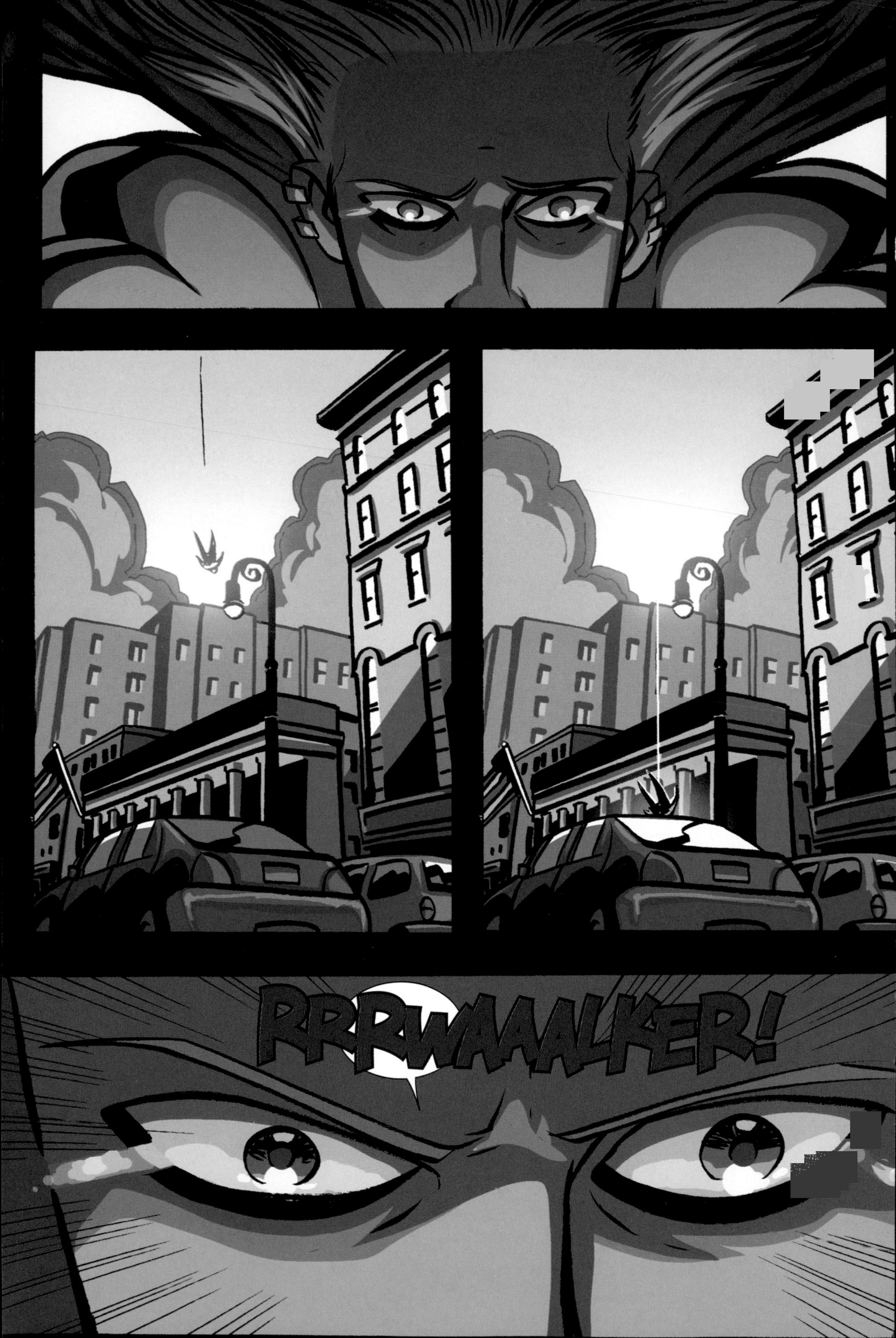
RRRWAAALKER!

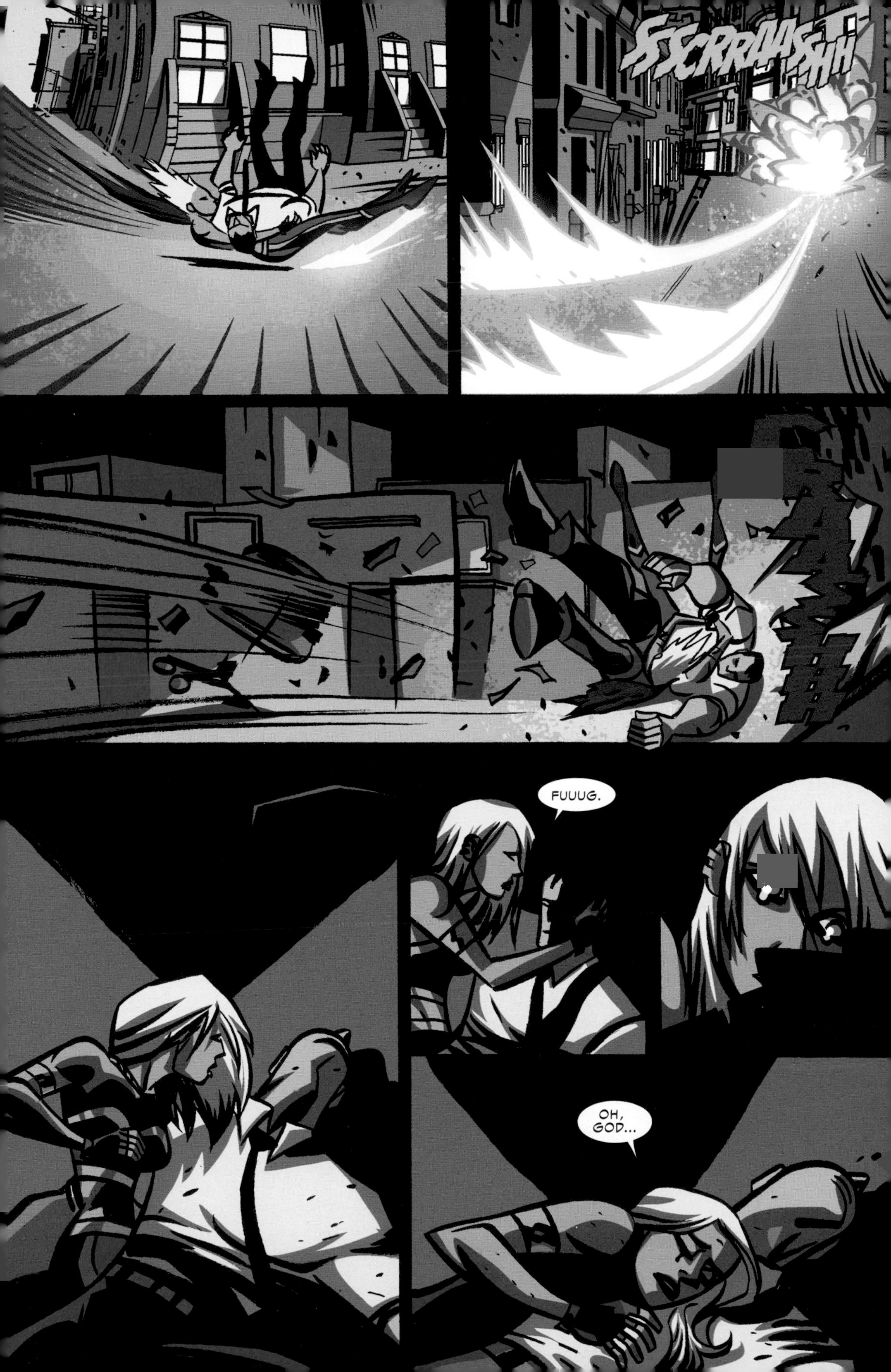
SSCRRAASHH
FUUUG.
OH, GOD...

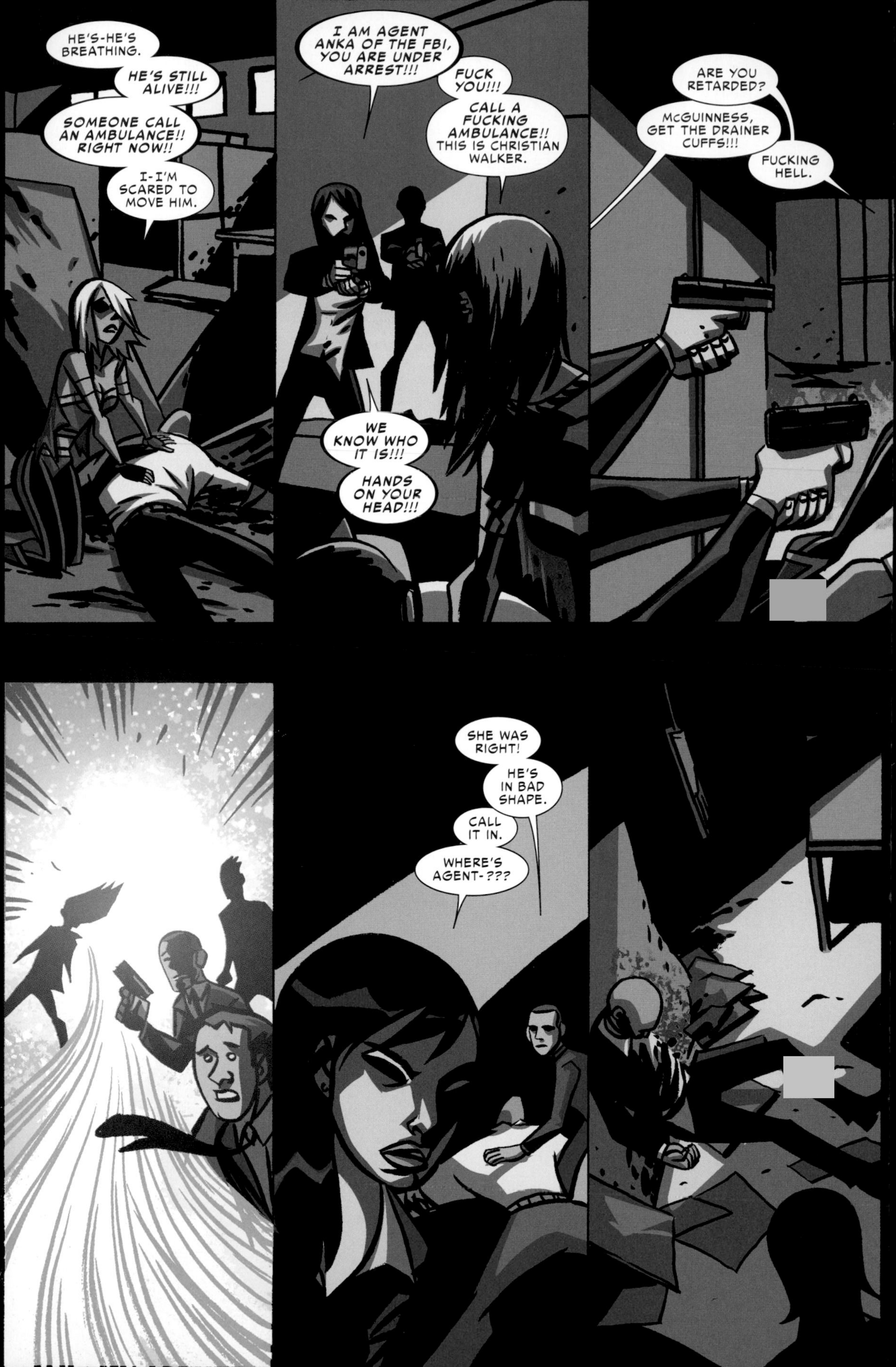
HE'S-HE'S BREATHING.
HE'S STILL ALIVE!!!
SOMEONE CALL AN AMBULANCE!! RIGHT NOW!!
I-I'M SCARED TO MOVE HIM.
I AM AGENT ANKA OF THE FBI, YOU ARE UNDER ARREST!!!
FUCK YOU!!!
CALL A FUCKING AMBULANCE!! THIS IS CHRISTIAN WALKER.
WE KNOW WHO IT IS!!!
HANDS ON YOUR HEAD!!!
ARE YOU RETARDED?
McGUINNESS, GET THE DRAINER CUFFS!!!
FUCKING HELL.
SHE WAS RIGHT!
HE'S IN BAD SHAPE.
CALL IT IN.
WHERE'S AGENT-???

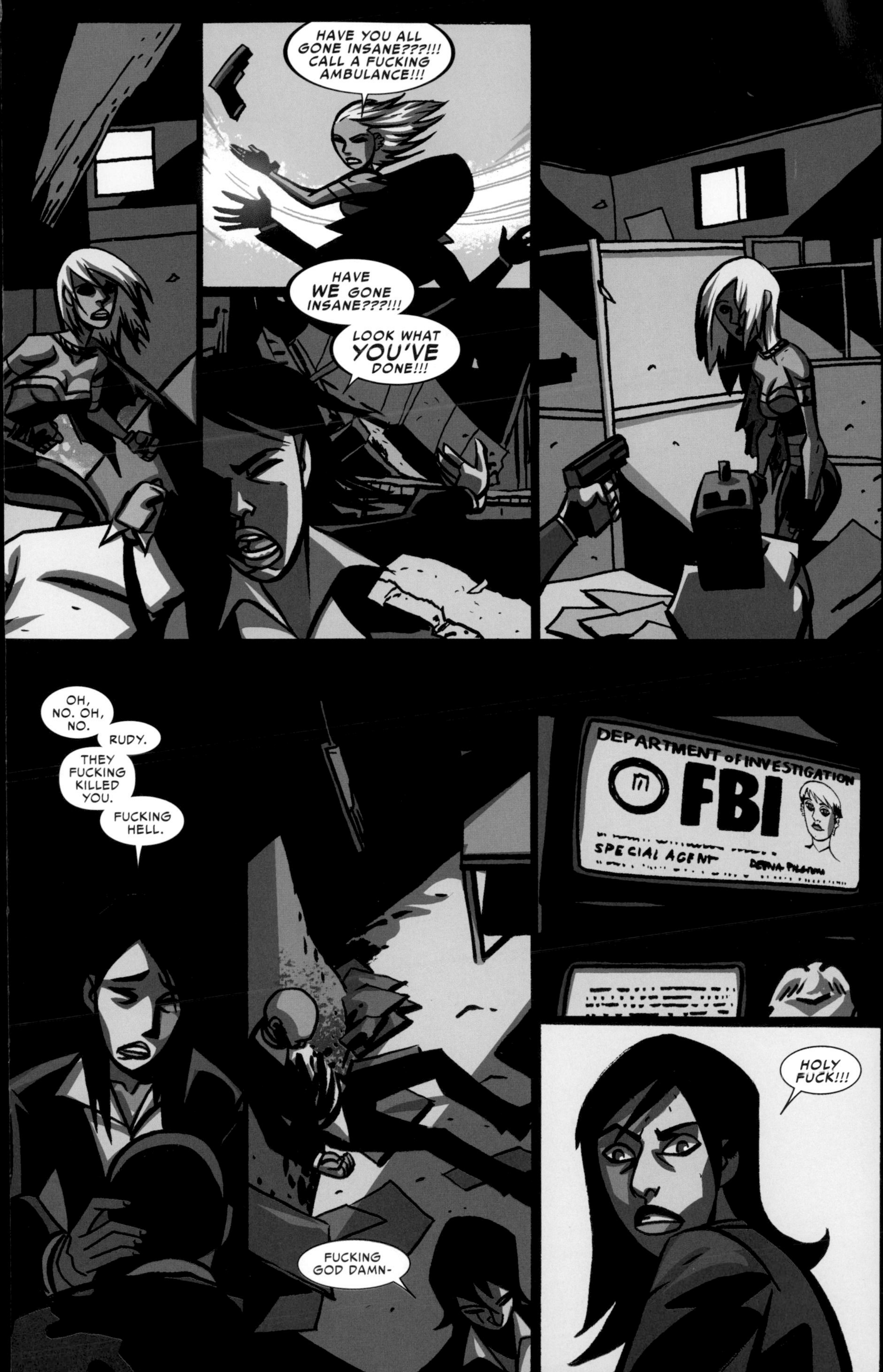
HAVE YOU ALL GONE INSANE???!!! CALL A FUCKING AMBULANCE!!!
HAVE WE GONE INSANE???!!!
LOOK WHAT YOU'VE DONE!!!
DEPARTMENT of INVESTIGATION
FBI
SPECIAL AGENT
OH, NO. OH, NO.
RUDY.
THEY FUCKING KILLED YOU.
FUCKING HELL.
FUCKING GOD DAMN-
HOLY FUCK!!!

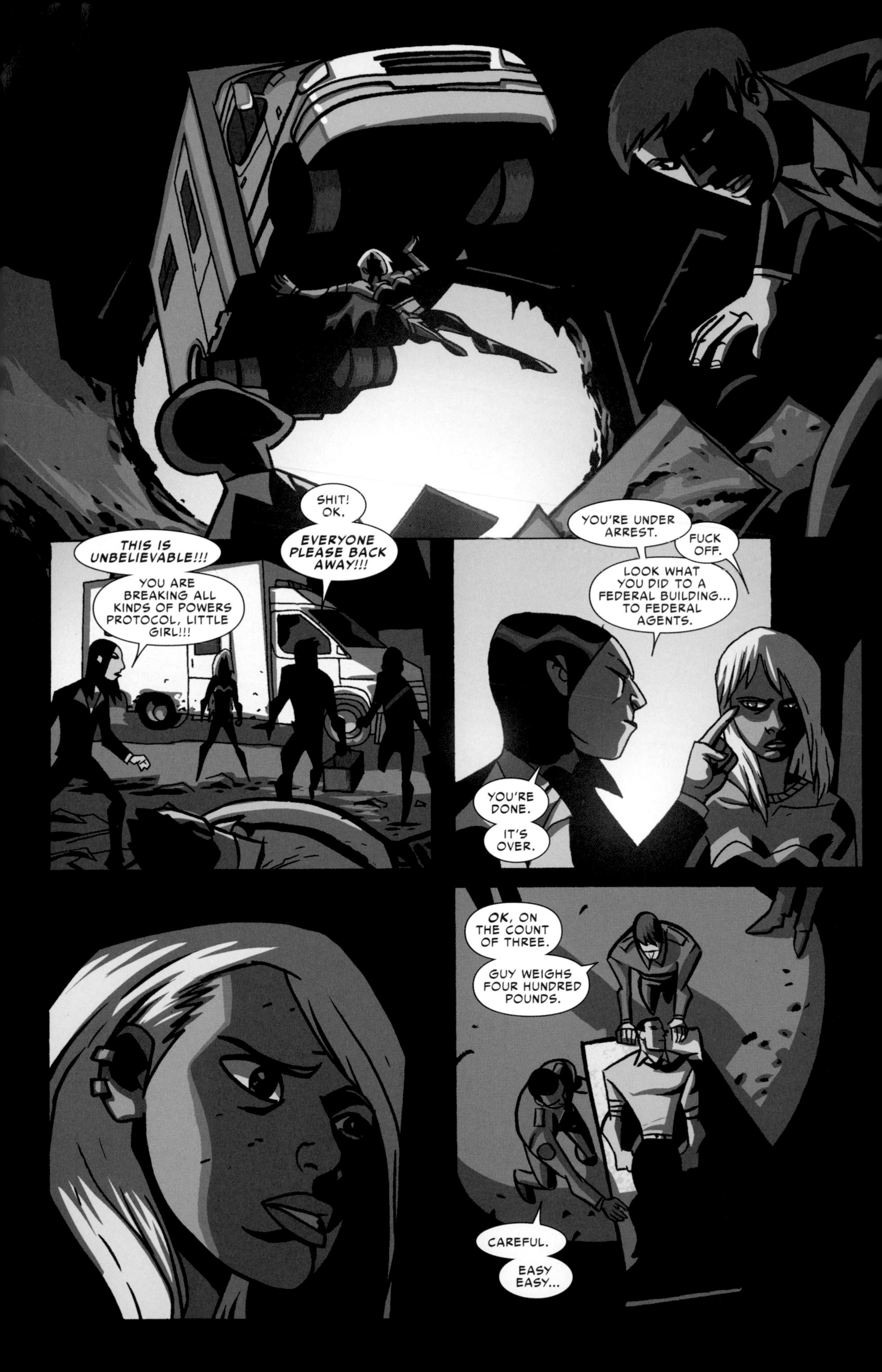

THIS IS UNBELIEVABLE!!!
YOU ARE BREAKING ALL KINDS OF POWERS PROTOCOL, LITTLE GIRL!!!
SHIT! OK.
EVERYONE PLEASE BACK AWAY!!!
YOU'RE UNDER ARREST.
FUCK OFF.
LOOK WHAT YOU DID TO A FEDERAL BUILDING... TO FEDERAL AGENTS.
YOU'RE DONE.
IT'S OVER.
OK, ON THE COUNT OF THREE.
GUY WEIGHS FOUR HUNDRED POUNDS.
CAREFUL.
EASY EASY...

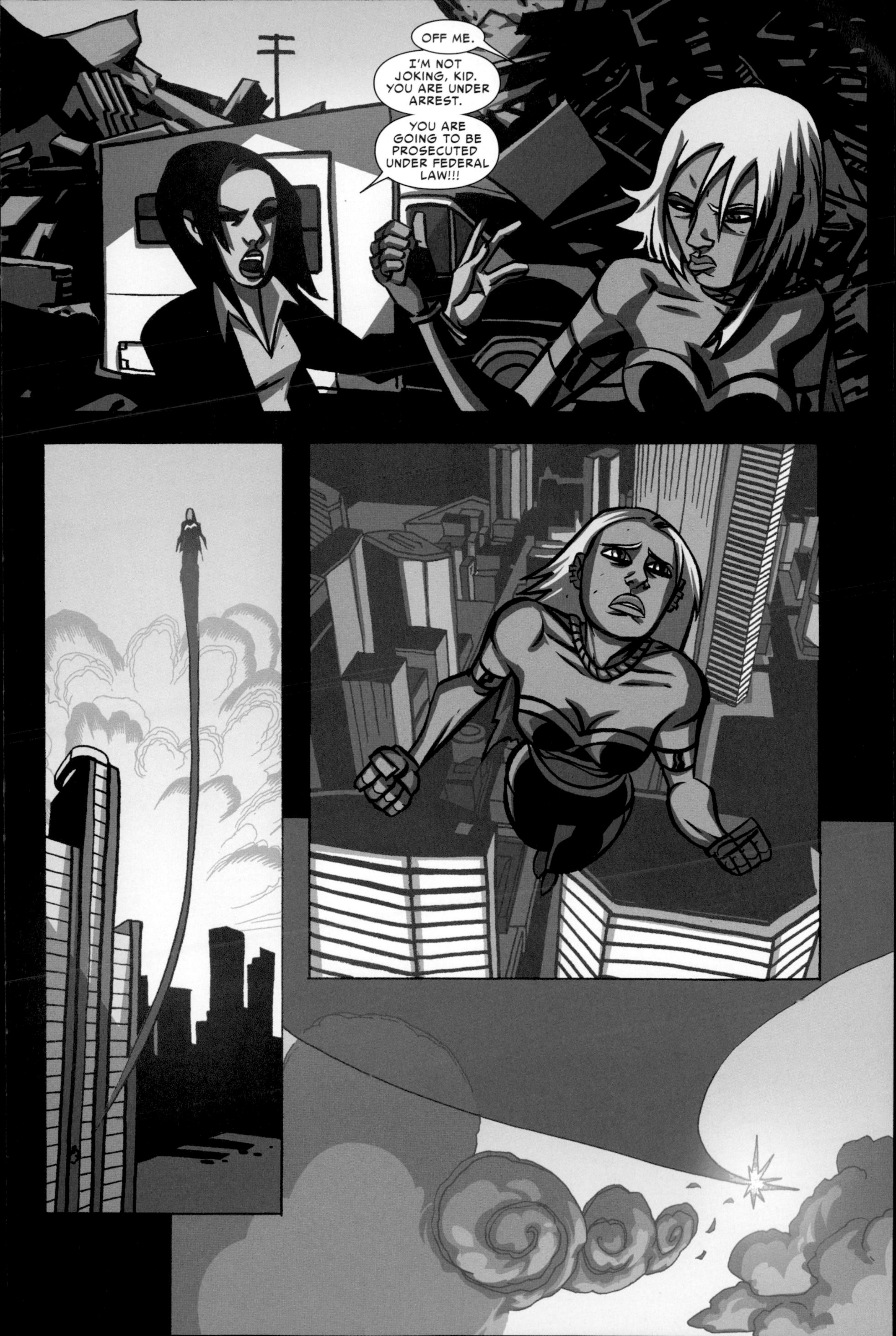
OFF ME.
I'M NOT JOKING, KID. YOU ARE UNDER ARREST.
YOU ARE GOING TO BE PROSECUTED UNDER FEDERAL LAW!!!

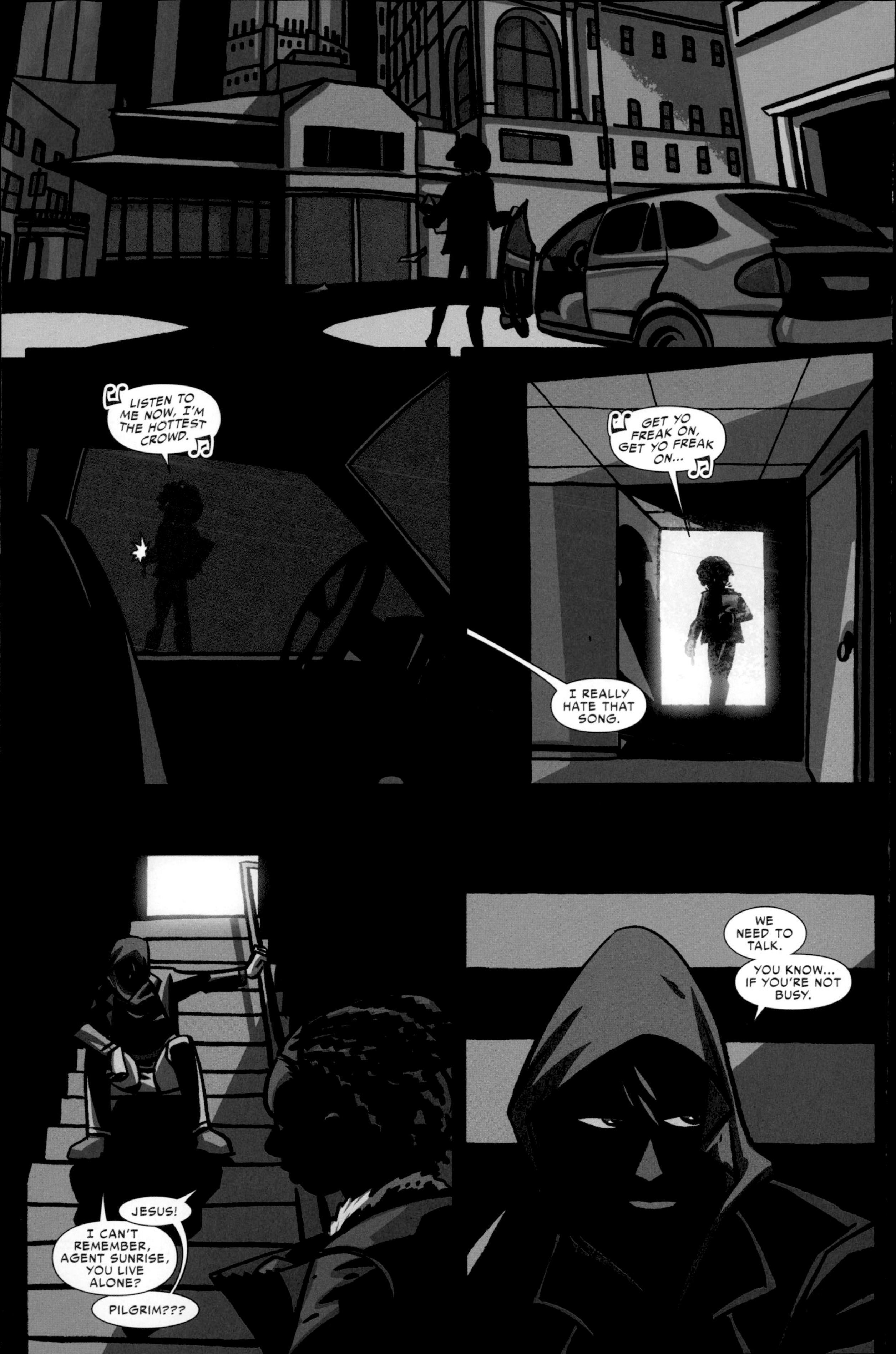

LISTEN TO ME NOW, I'M THE HOTTEST CROWD.
GET YO FREAK ON, GET YO FREAK ON...
I REALLY HATE THAT SONG.
WE NEED TO TALK.
YOU KNOW... IF YOU'RE NOT BUSY.
JESUS!
I CAN'T REMEMBER, AGENT SUNRISE, YOU LIVE ALONE?
PILGRIM???

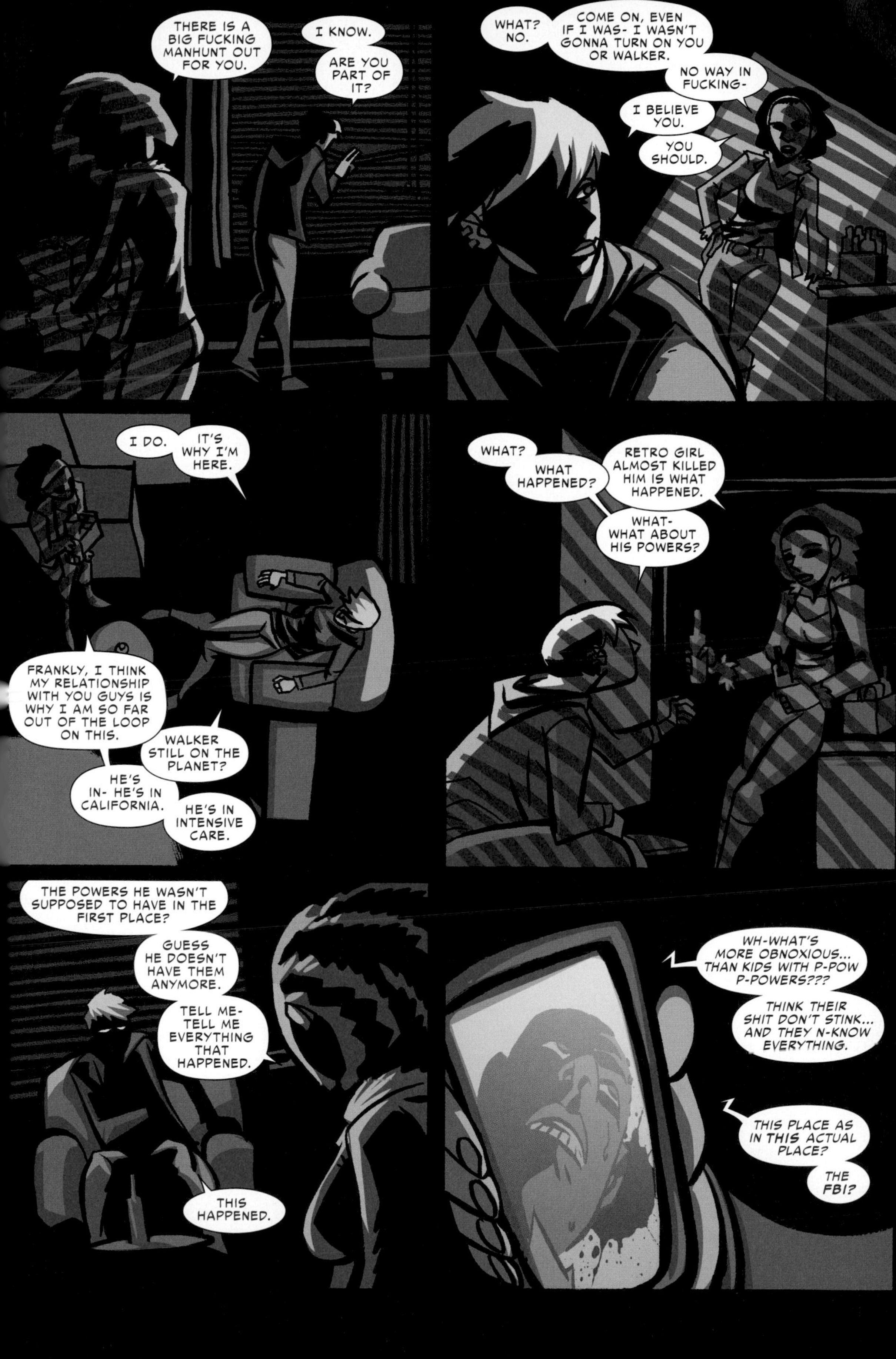
THERE IS A BIG FUCKING MANHUNT OUT FOR YOU.
I KNOW.
ARE YOU PART OF IT?
WHAT? NO.
COME ON, EVEN IF I WAS- I WASN'T GONNA TURN ON YOU OR WALKER.
NO WAY IN FUCKING-
I BELIEVE YOU.
YOU SHOULD.
I DO.
IT'S WHY I'M HERE.
FRANKLY, I THINK MY RELATIONSHIP WITH YOU GUYS IS WHY I AM SO FAR OUT OF THE LOOP ON THIS.
WALKER STILL ON THE PLANET?
HE'S IN- HE'S IN CALIFORNIA.
HE'S IN INTENSIVE CARE.
WHAT?
WHAT HAPPENED?
RETRO GIRL ALMOST KILLED HIM IS WHAT HAPPENED.
WHAT- WHAT ABOUT HIS POWERS?
THE POWERS HE WASN'T SUPPOSED TO HAVE IN THE FIRST PLACE?
GUESS HE DOESN'T HAVE THEM ANYMORE.
TELL ME- TELL ME EVERYTHING THAT HAPPENED.
THIS HAPPENED.
WH-WHAT'S MORE OBNOXIOUS... THAN KIDS WITH P-POW P-POWERS???
THINK THEIR SHIT DON'T STINK... AND THEY N-KNOW EVERYTHING.
THIS PLACE AS IN THIS ACTUAL PLACE?
THE FBI?

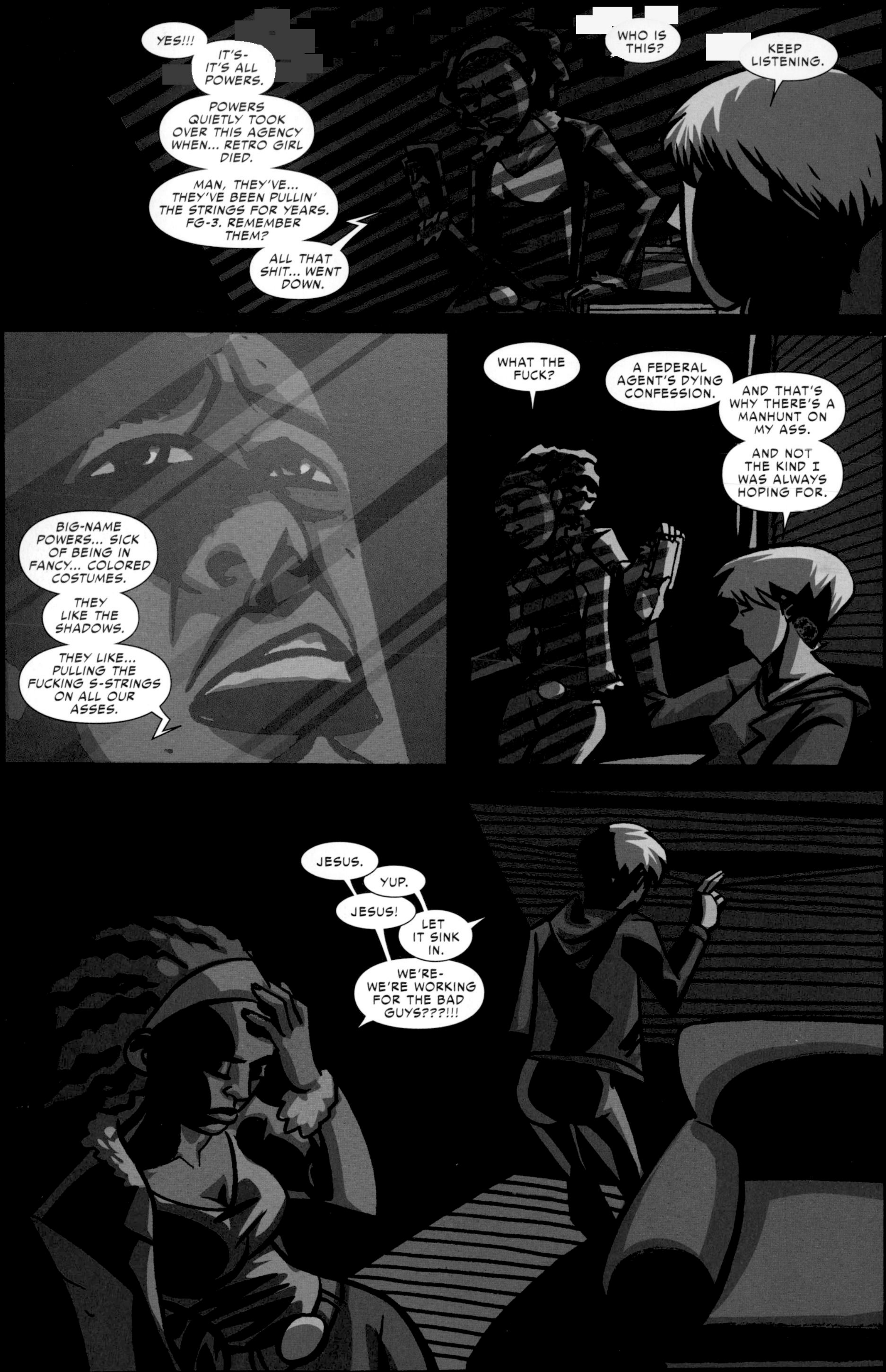
YES!!!
IT'S- IT'S ALL POWERS.
POWERS QUIETLY TOOK OVER THIS AGENCY WHEN... RETRO GIRL DIED.
MAN, THEY'VE... THEY'VE BEEN PULLIN' THE STRINGS FOR YEARS. FG-3. REMEMBER THEM?
ALL THAT SHIT... WENT DOWN.
WHO IS THIS?
KEEP LISTENING.
BIG-NAME POWERS... SICK OF BEING IN FANCY... COLORED COSTUMES.
THEY LIKE THE SHADOWS.
THEY LIKE... PULLING THE FUCKING S-STRINGS ON ALL OUR ASSES.
WHAT THE FUCK?
A FEDERAL AGENT'S DYING CONFESSION.
AND THAT'S WHY THERE'S A MANHUNT ON MY ASS.
AND NOT THE KIND I WAS ALWAYS HOPING FOR.
JESUS.
YUP.
JESUS!
LET IT SINK IN.
WE'RE- WE'RE WORKING FOR THE BAD GUYS???!!!

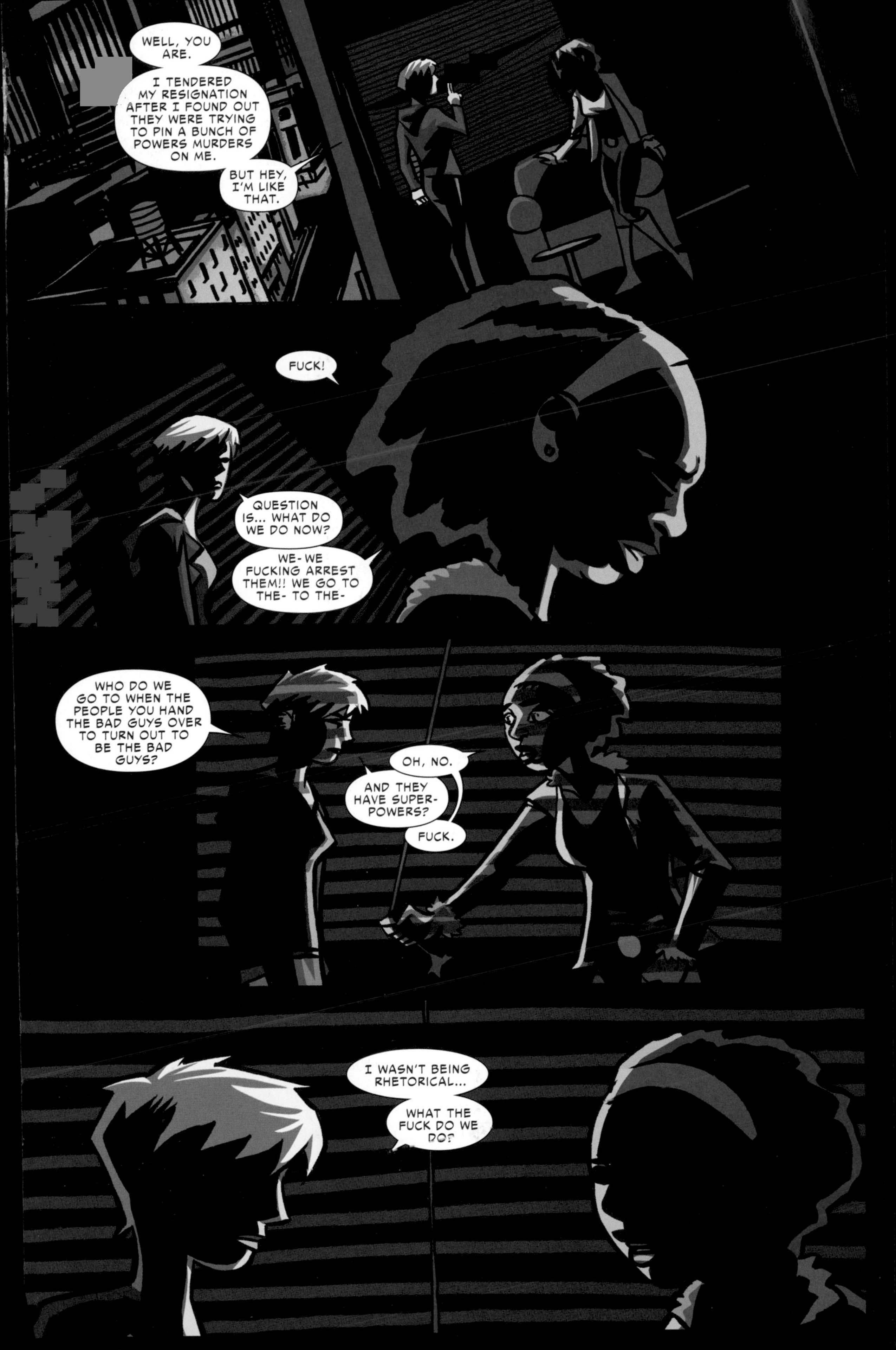
WELL, YOU ARE.
I TENDERED MY RESIGNATION AFTER I FOUND OUT THEY WERE TRYING TO PIN A BUNCH OF POWERS MURDERS ON ME.
BUT HEY, I'M LIKE THAT.
FUCK!
QUESTION IS... WHAT DO WE DO NOW?
WE- WE FUCKING ARREST THEM!! WE GO TO THE- TO THE-
WHO DO WE GO TO WHEN THE PEOPLE YOU HAND THE BAD GUYS OVER TO TURN OUT TO BE THE BAD GUYS?
OH, NO.
AND THEY HAVE SUPER-POWERS?
FUCK.
I WASN'T BEING RHETORICAL...
WHAT THE FUCK DO WE DO?

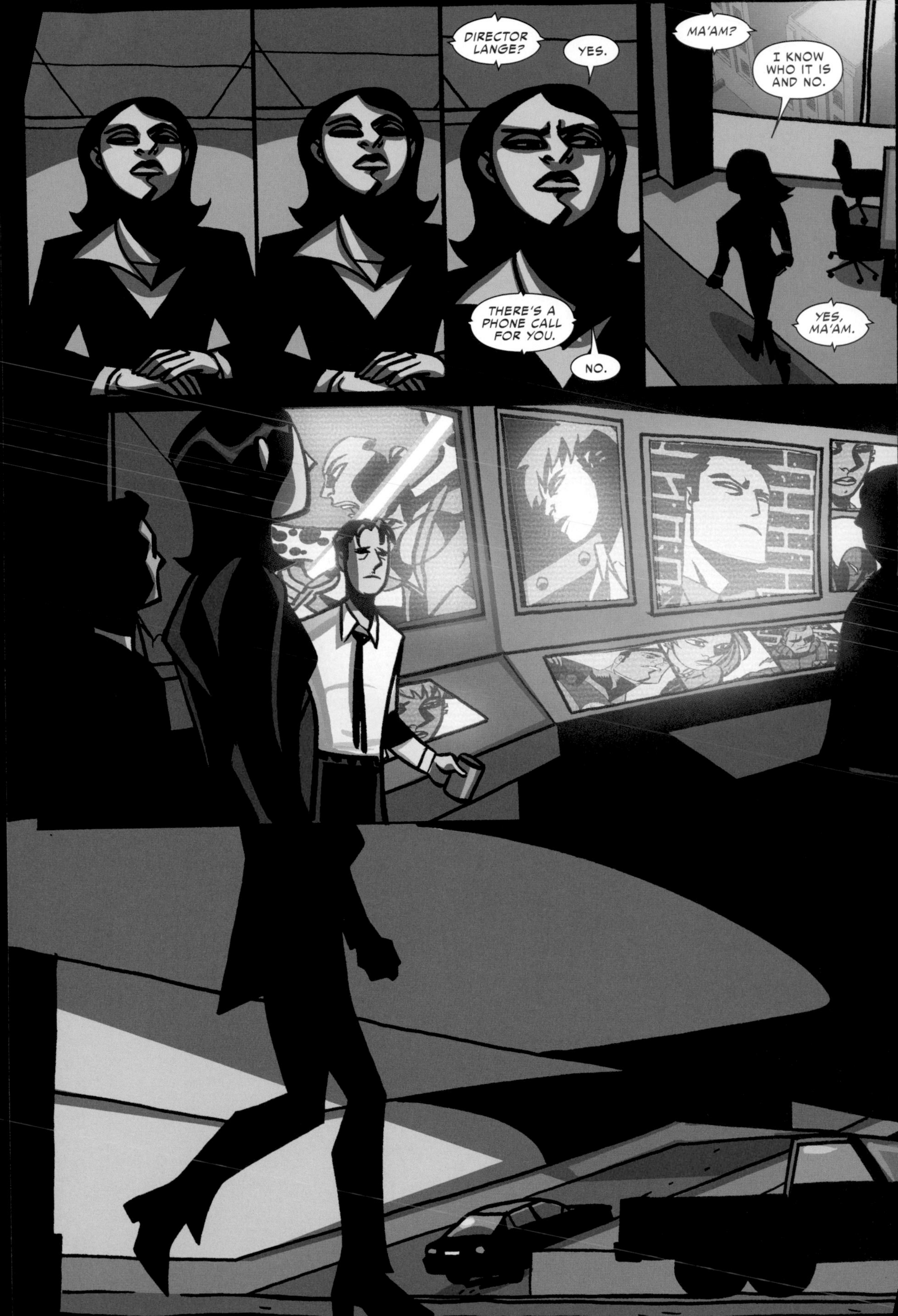
DIRECTOR LANGE?
YES.
THERE'S A PHONE CALL FOR YOU.
NO.
MA'AM?
I KNOW WHO IT IS AND NO.
YES, MA'AM.

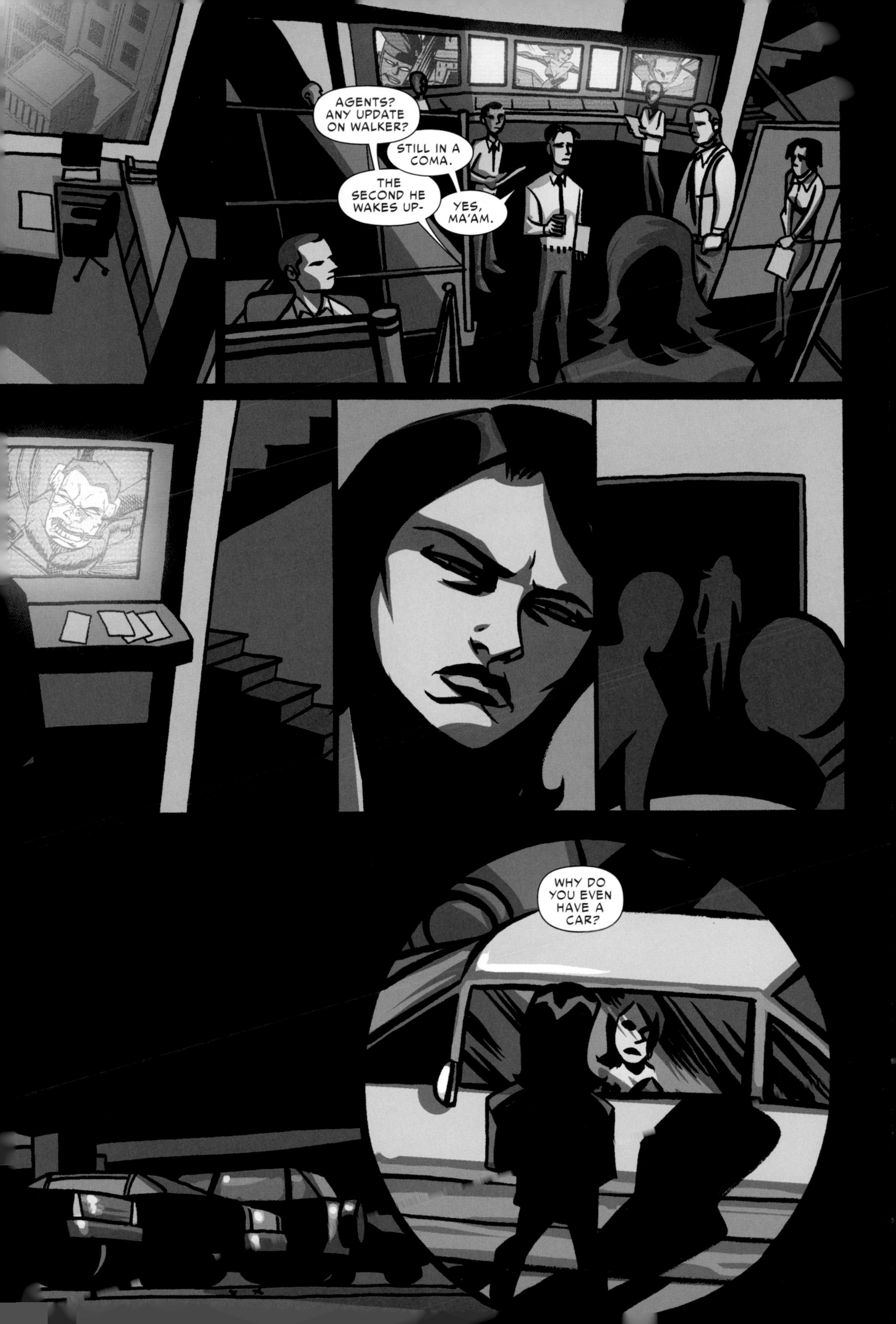
AGENTS? ANY UPDATE ON WALKER?
STILL IN A COMA.
THE SECOND HE WAKES UP-
YES, MA'AM.
WHY DO YOU EVEN HAVE A CAR?

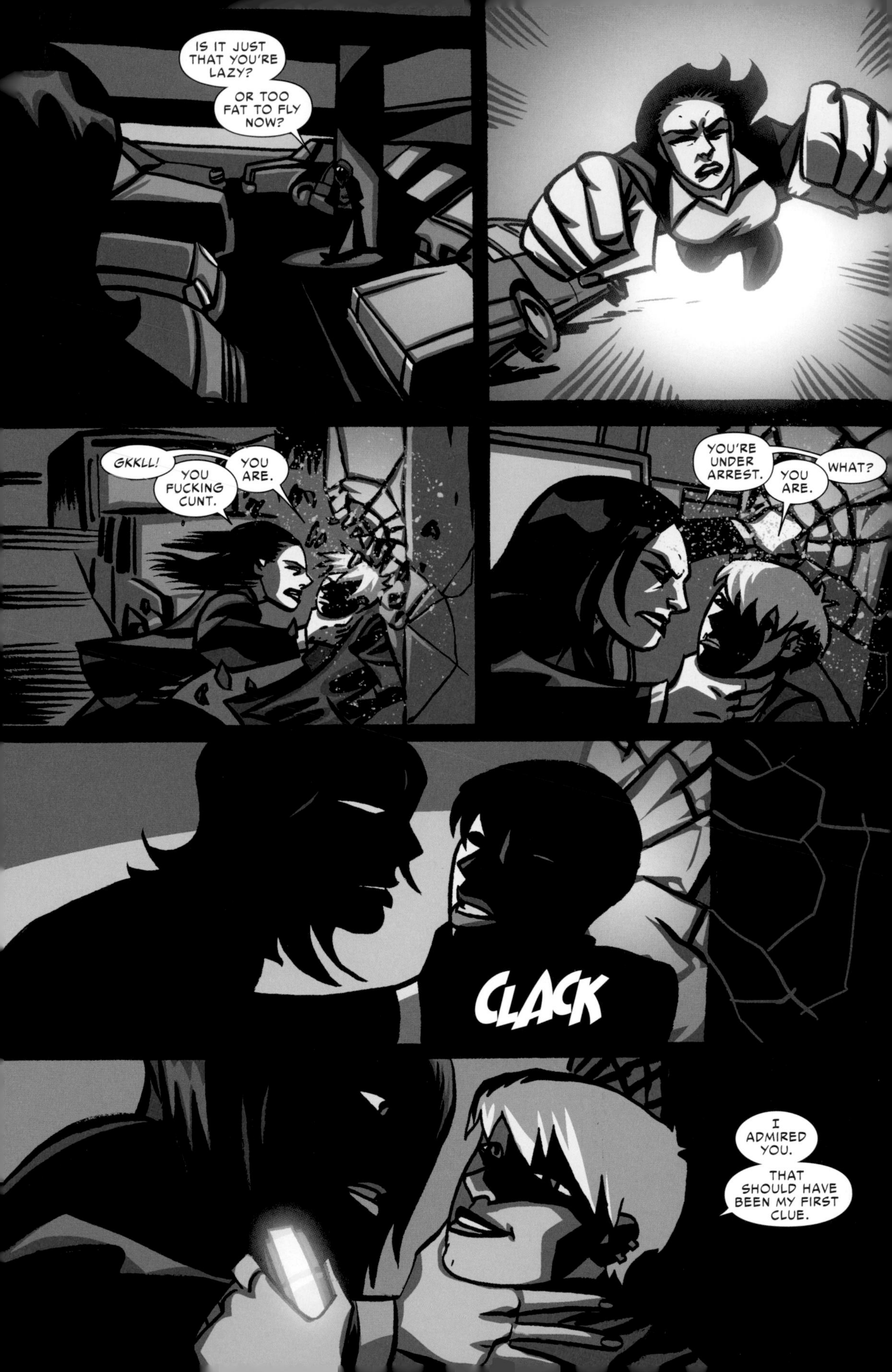
IS IT JUST THAT YOU'RE LAZY?
OR TOO FAT TO FLY NOW?
GKKLL!
YOU FUCKING CUNT.
YOU ARE.
YOU'RE UNDER ARREST.
WHAT?
YOU ARE.
CLACK
I ADMIRED YOU.
THAT SHOULD HAVE BEEN MY FIRST CLUE.

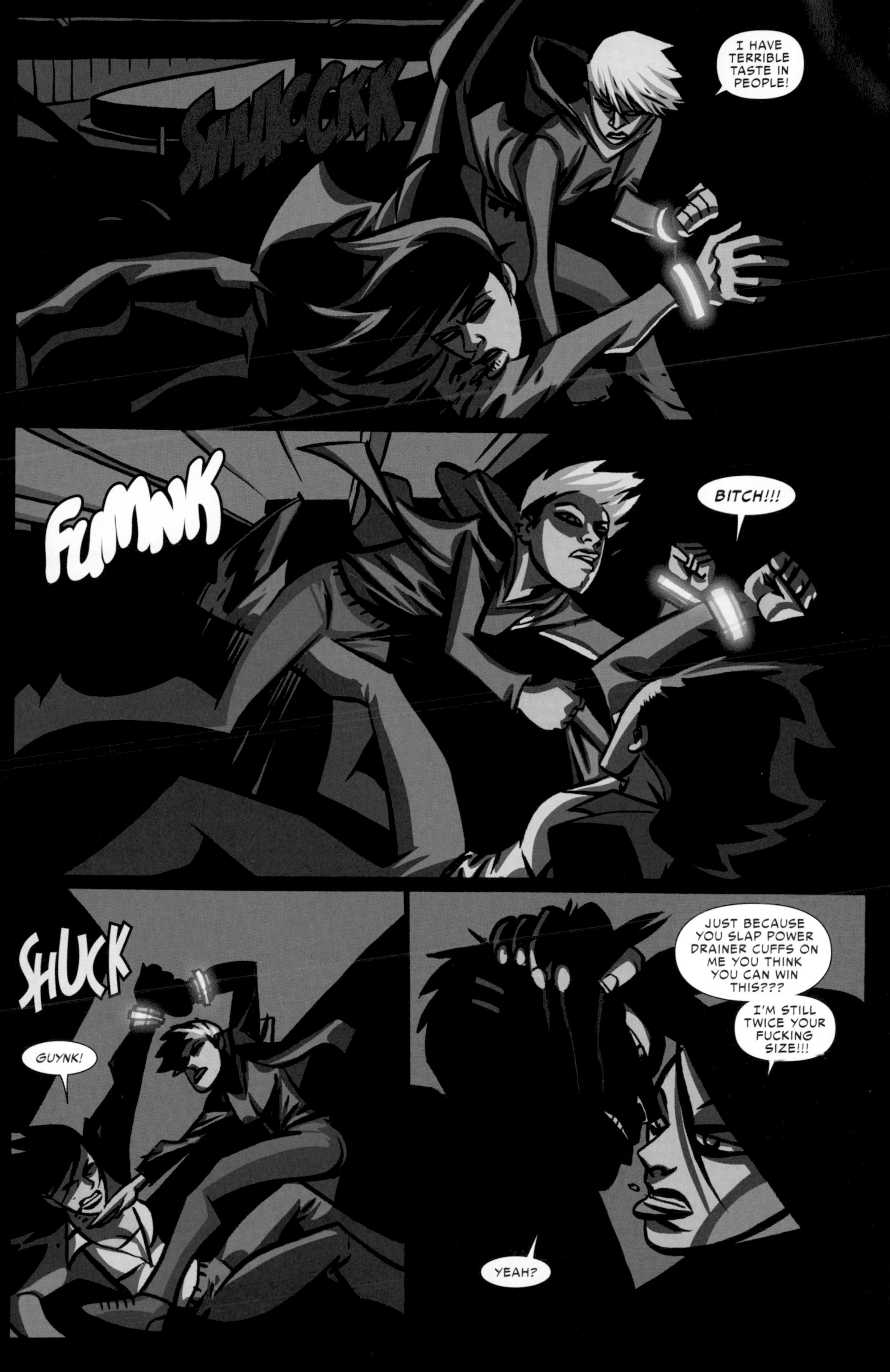
I HAVE TERRIBLE TASTE IN PEOPLE!
SHACCKK
FUMNK
BITCH!!!
SHUCK
GUYNK!
JUST BECAUSE YOU SLAP POWER DRAINER CUFFS ON ME YOU THINK YOU CAN WIN THIS???
I'M STILL TWICE YOUR FUCKING SIZE!!!
YEAH?

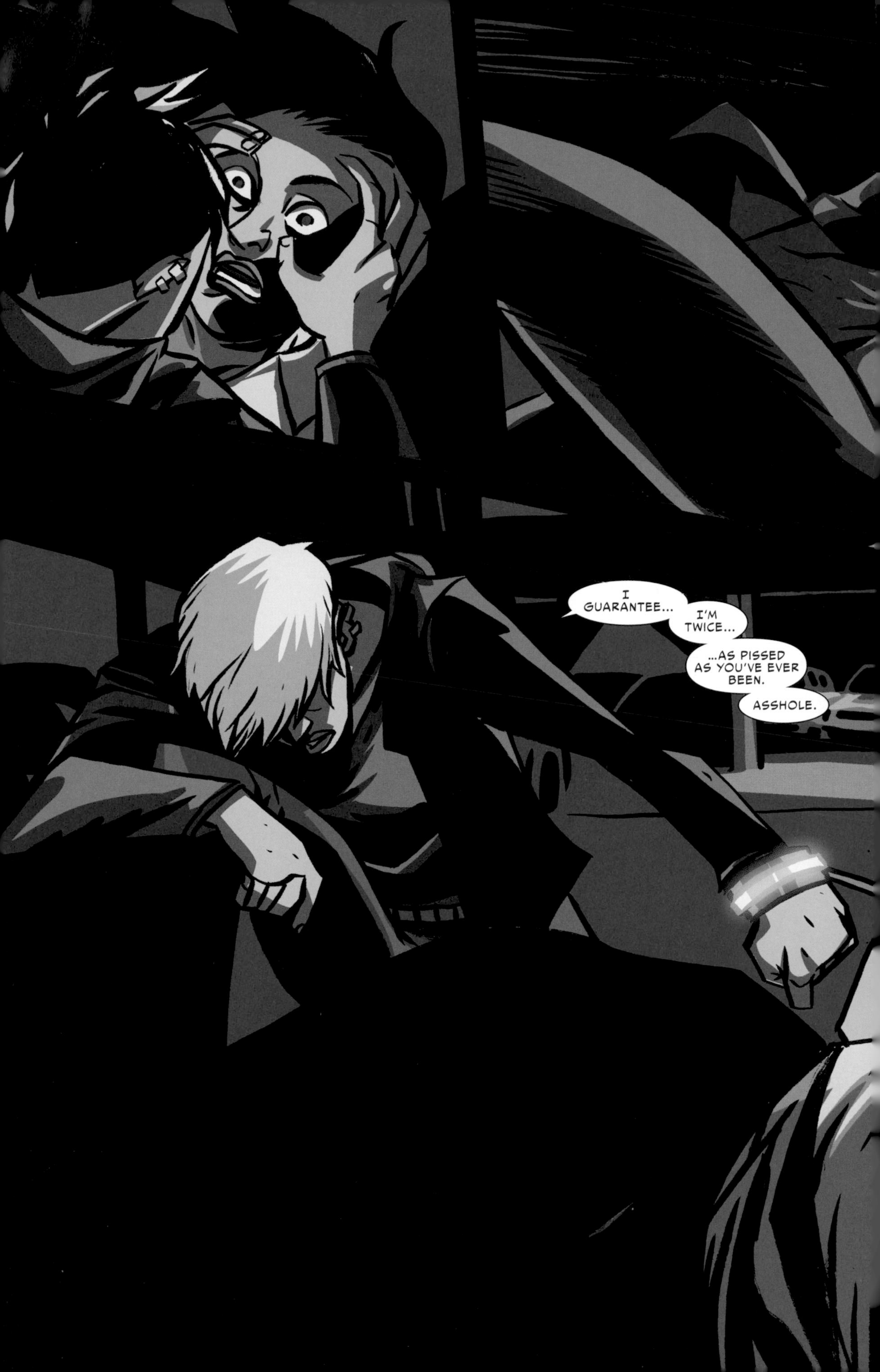
I GUARANTEE...
I'M TWICE...
...AS PISSED AS YOU'VE EVER BEEN.
ASSHOLE.

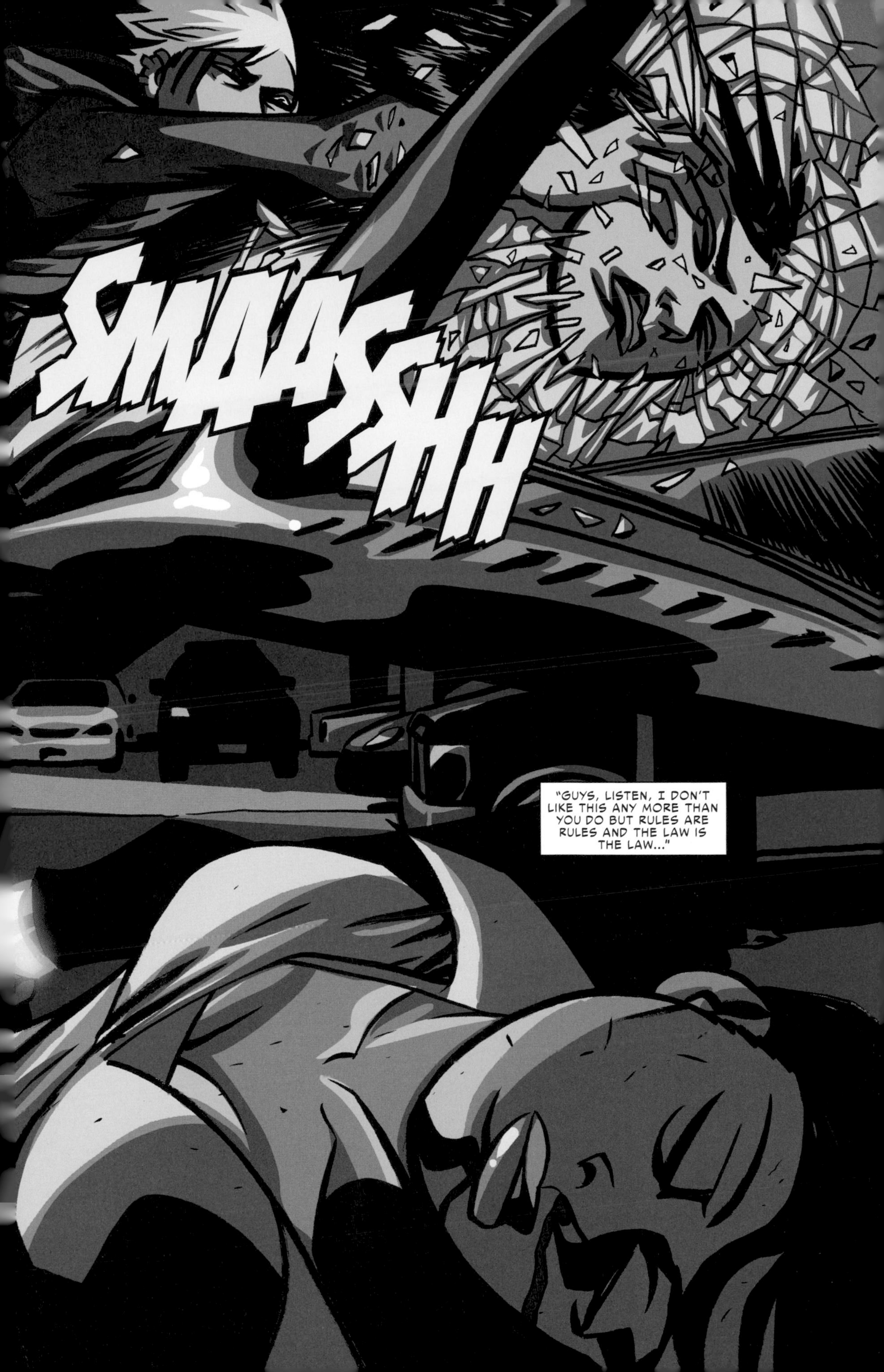
SMAASHH
"GUYS, LISTEN, I DON'T LIKE THIS ANY MORE THAN YOU DO BUT RULES ARE RULES AND THE LAW IS THE LAW..."

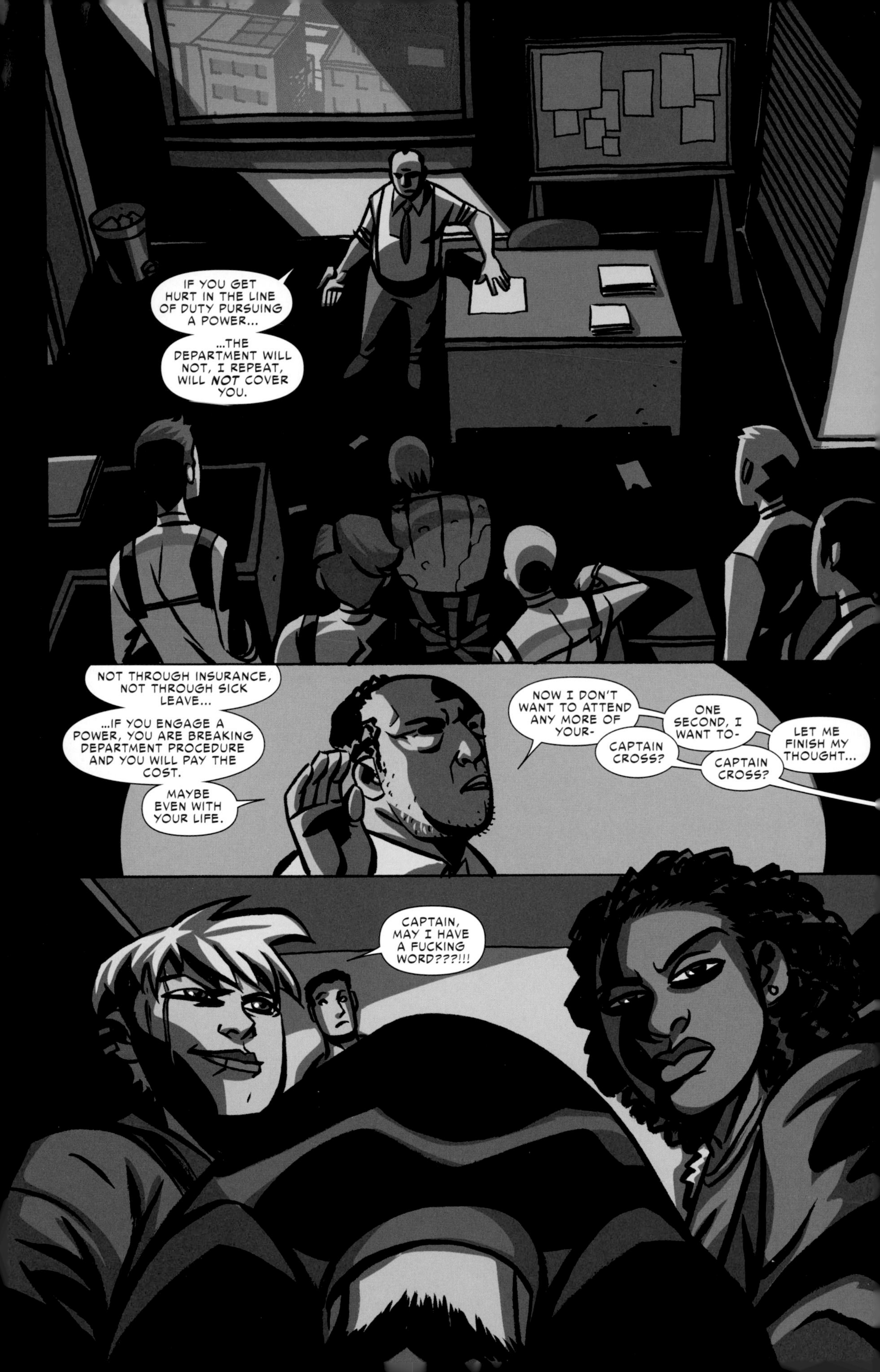
IF YOU GET HURT IN THE LINE OF DUTY PURSUING A POWER...
...THE DEPARTMENT WILL NOT, I REPEAT, WILL *NOT* COVER YOU.
NOT THROUGH INSURANCE, NOT THROUGH SICK LEAVE...
...IF YOU ENGAGE A POWER, YOU ARE BREAKING DEPARTMENT PROCEDURE AND YOU WILL PAY THE COST.
MAYBE EVEN WITH YOUR LIFE.
NOW I DON'T WANT TO ATTEND ANY MORE OF YOUR-
ONE SECOND, I WANT TO-
CAPTAIN CROSS?
LET ME FINISH MY THOUGHT...
CAPTAIN CROSS?
CAPTAIN, MAY I HAVE A FUCKING WORD???!!!

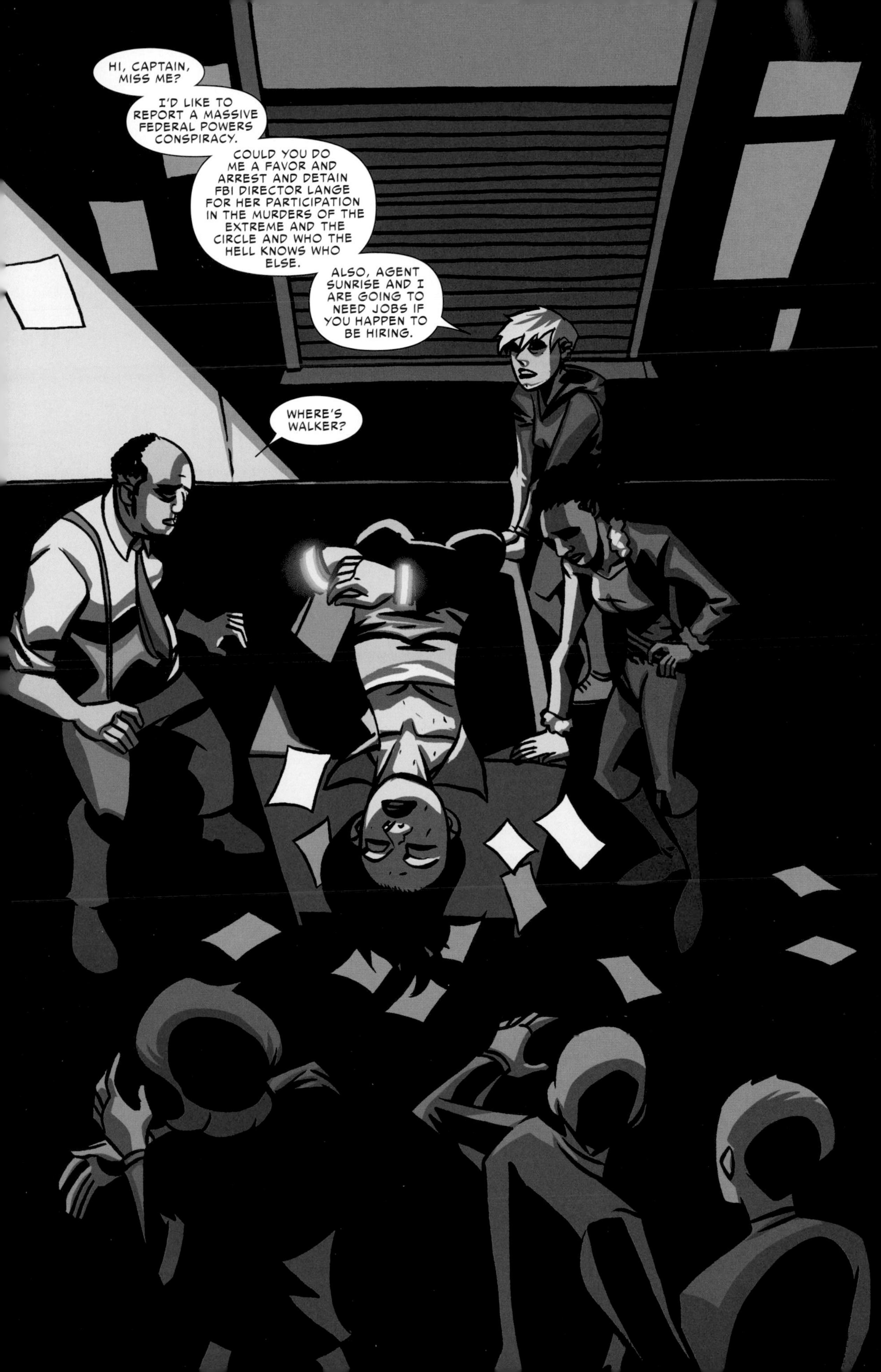
HI, CAPTAIN, MISS ME?
I'D LIKE TO REPORT A MASSIVE FEDERAL POWERS CONSPIRACY.
COULD YOU DO ME A FAVOR AND ARREST AND DETAIN FBI DIRECTOR LANGE FOR HER PARTICIPATION IN THE MURDERS OF THE EXTREME AND THE CIRCLE AND WHO THE HELL KNOWS WHO ELSE.
ALSO, AGENT SUNRISE AND I ARE GOING TO NEED JOBS IF YOU HAPPEN TO BE HIRING.
WHERE'S WALKER?

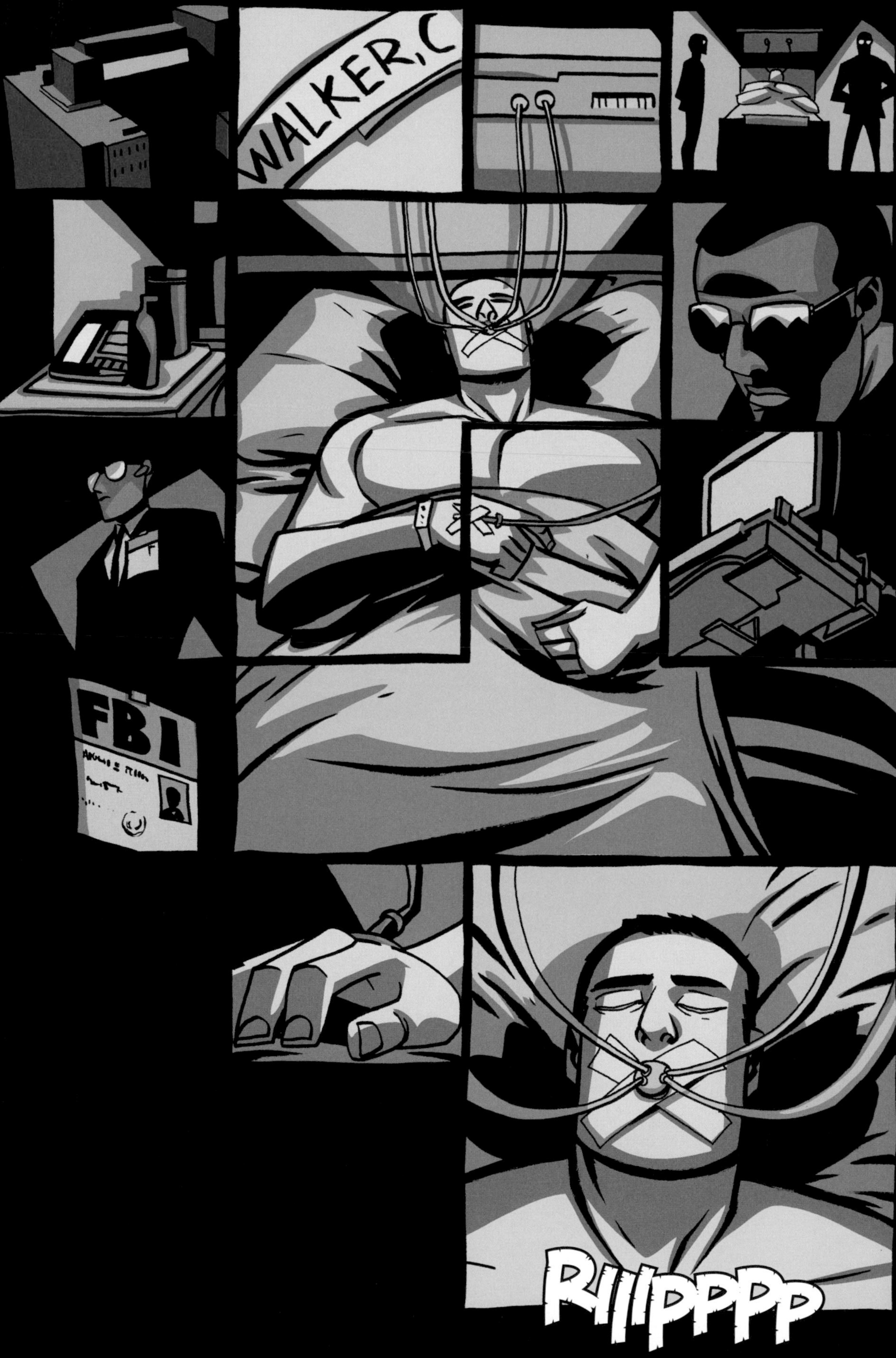
WALKER, C
FBI
RIIIPPPP

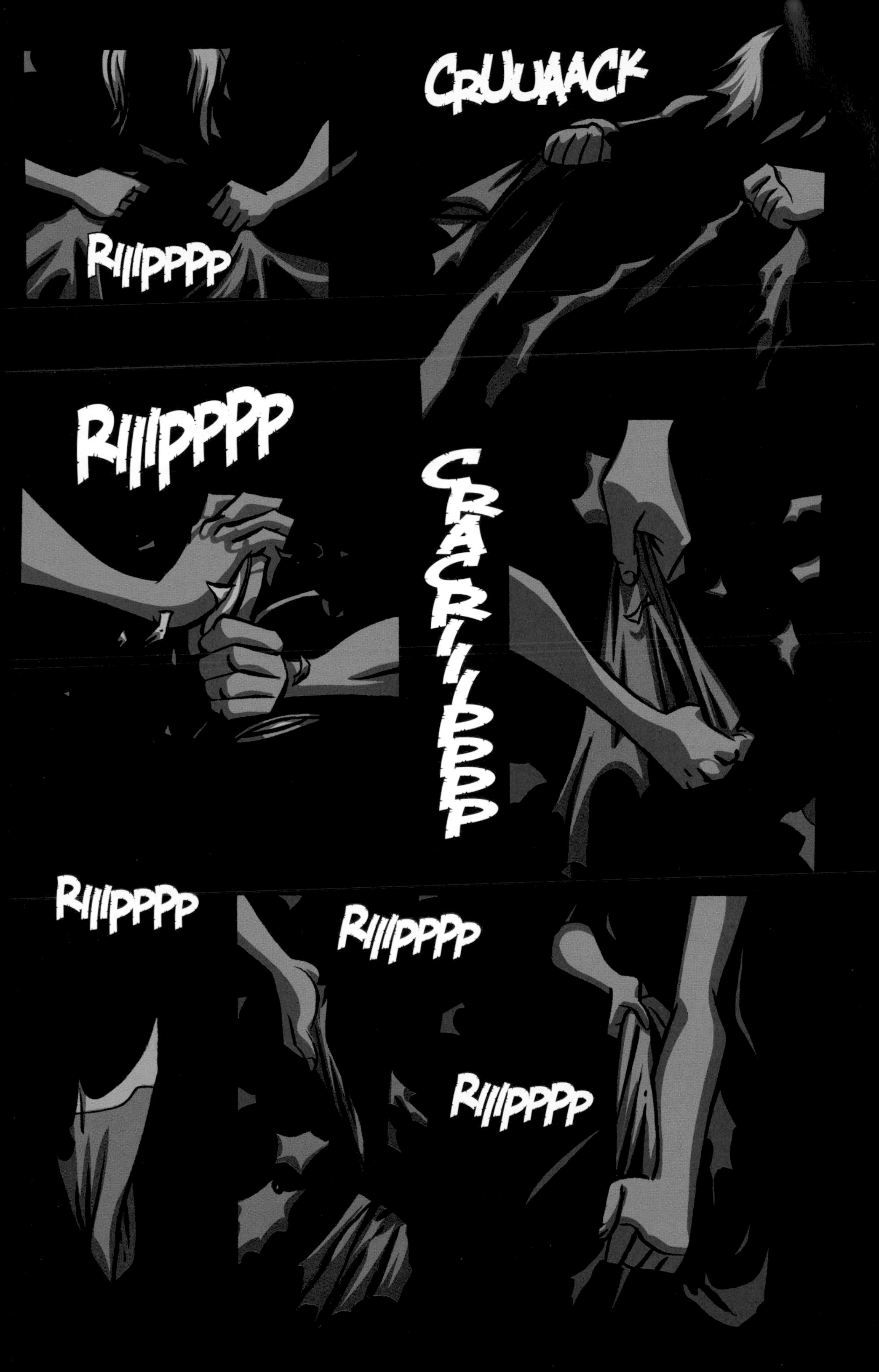
RIIIPPPP
CRUUAACK
RIIIPPPP
CRACRIIIIPPPP
RIIIPPPP
RIIIPPPP
RIIIPPPP

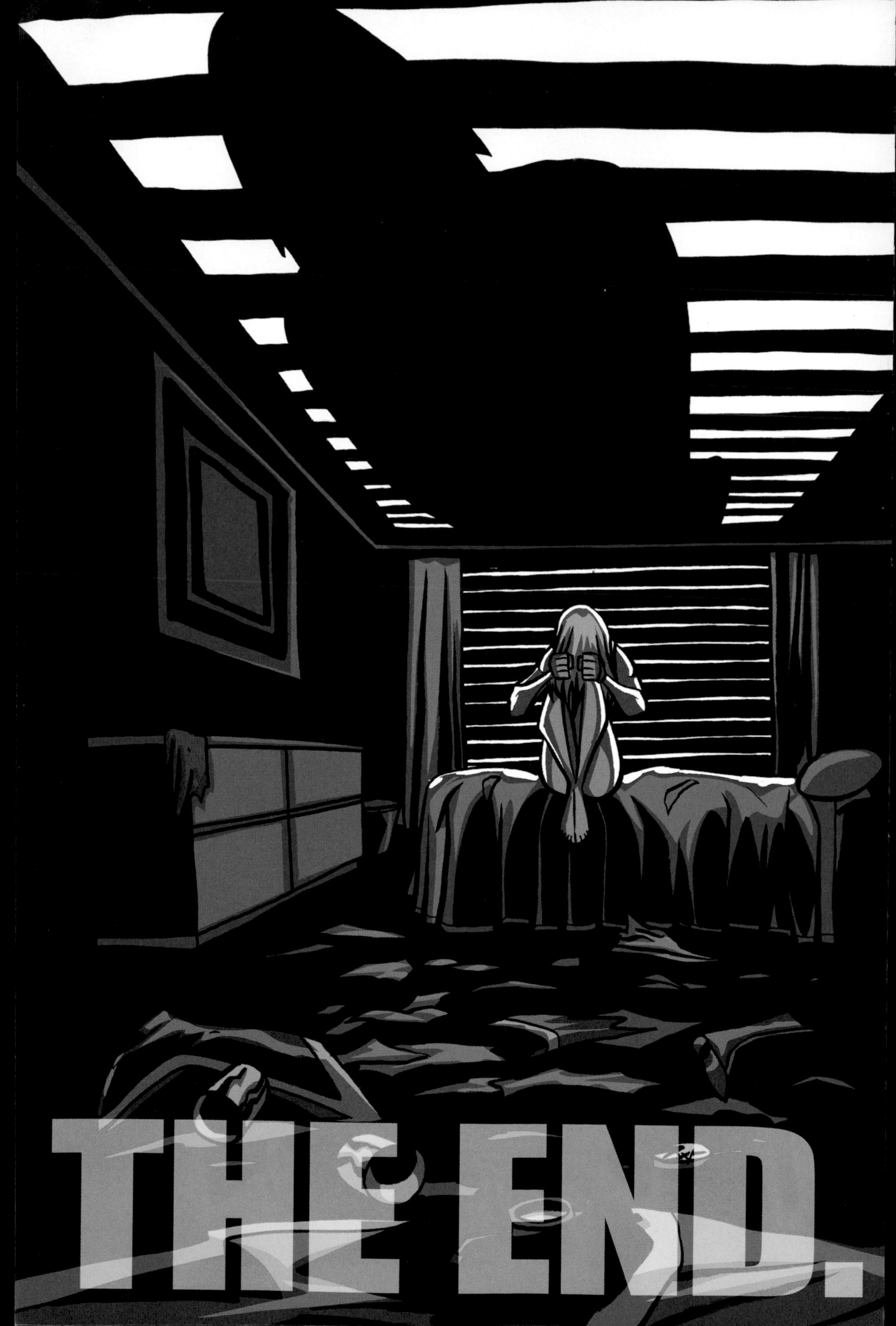
THE END.

POWERS

COVER GALLERY

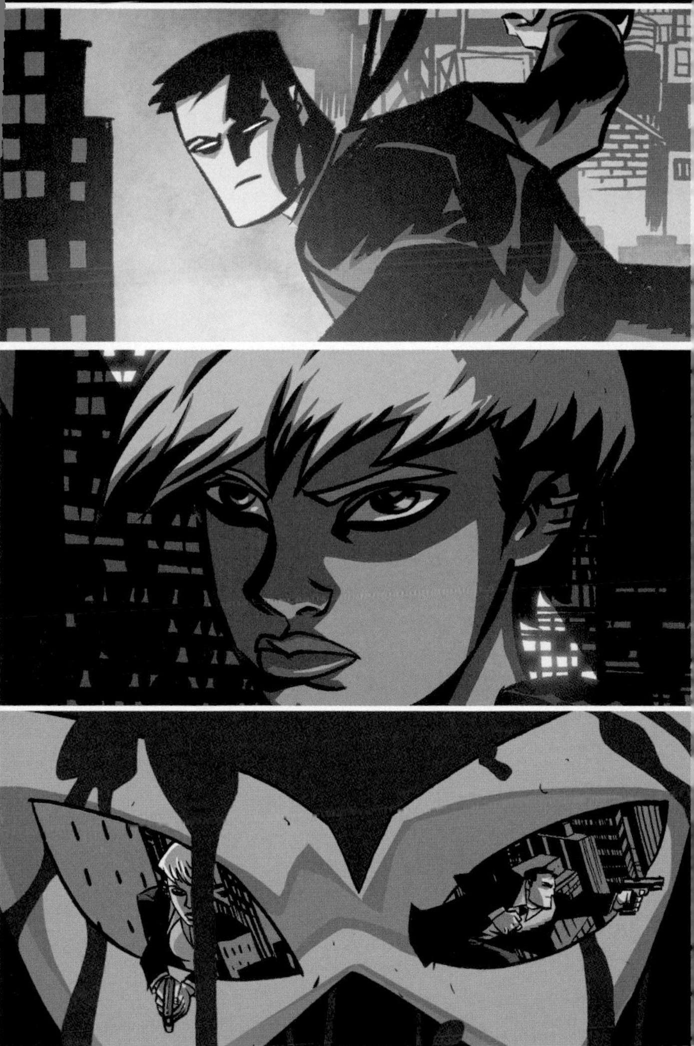

POWERS: BUREAU #7 – Cover Process

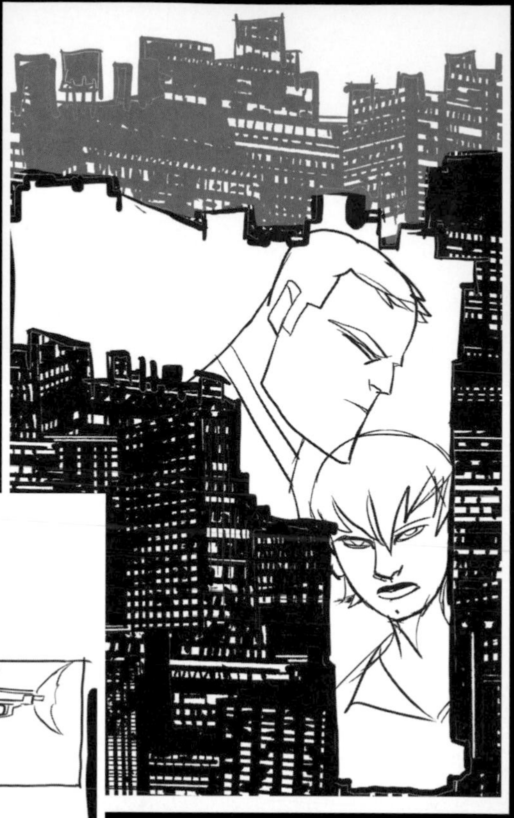

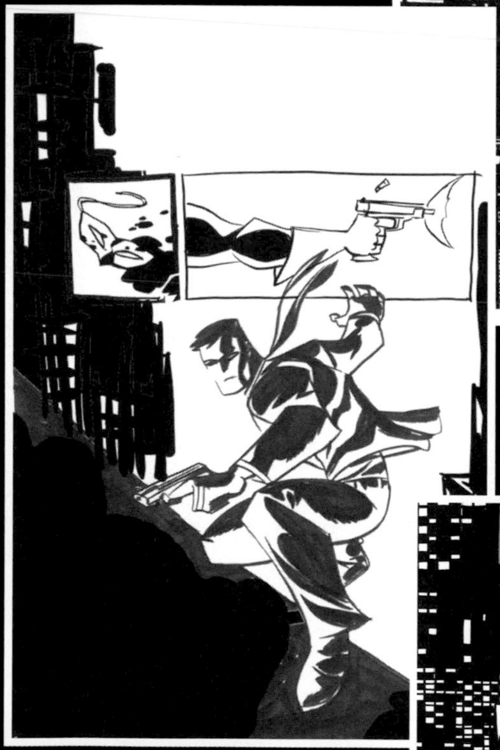

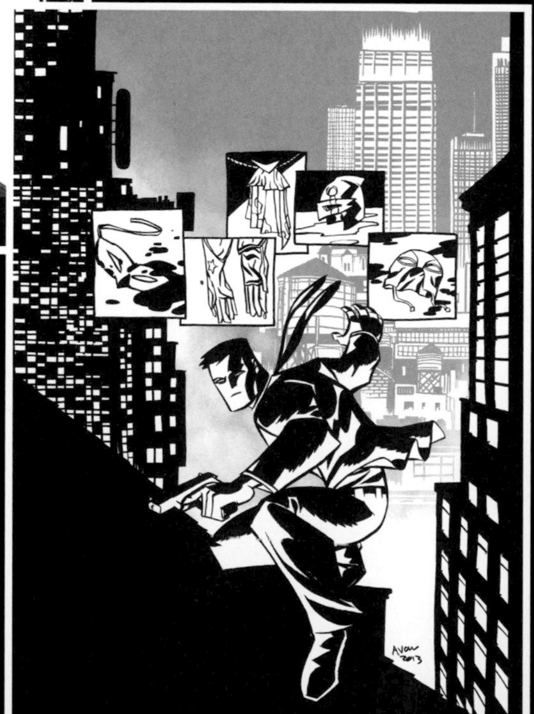

POWERS: BUREAU #7

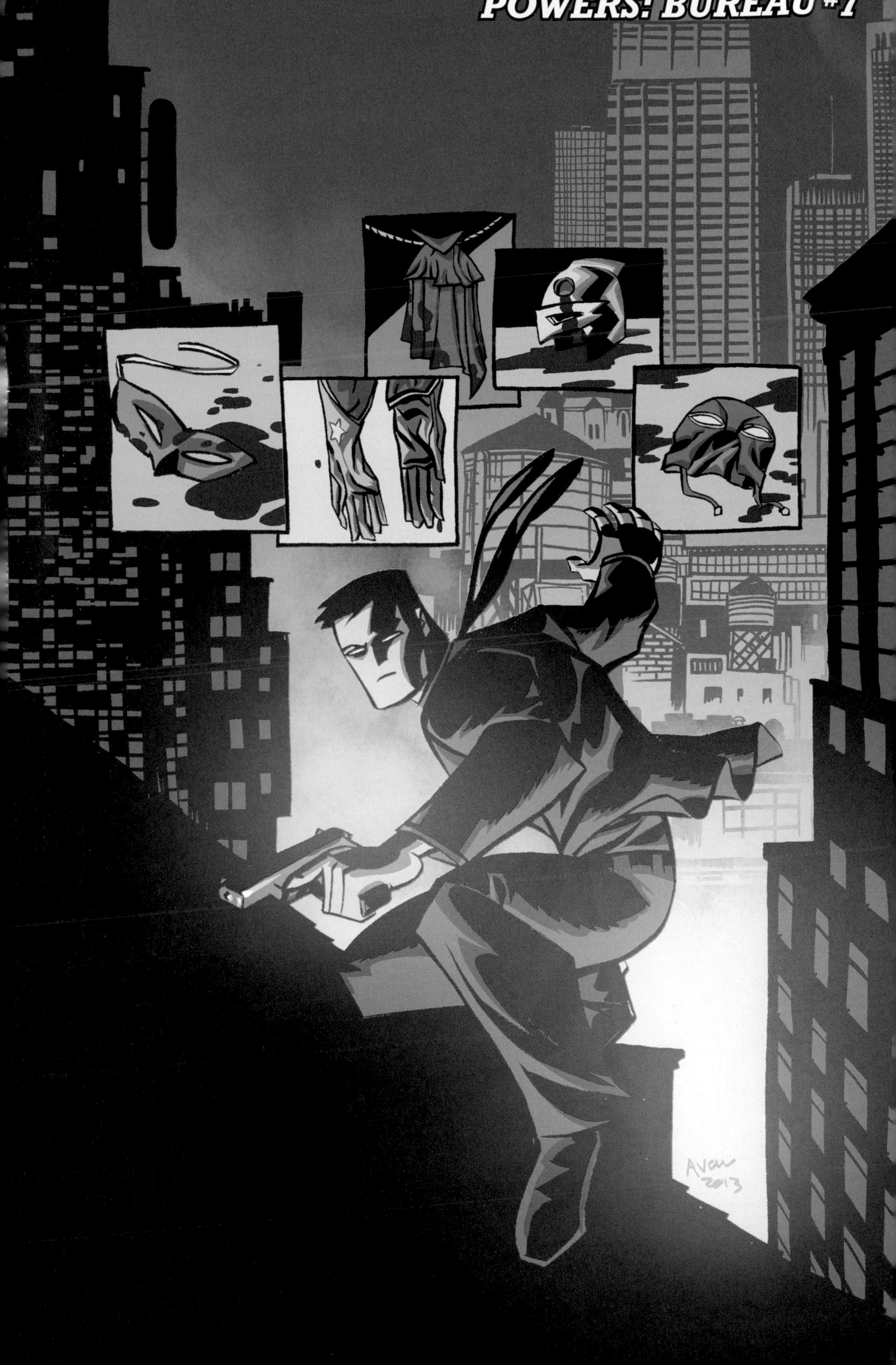
AVON
2013

POWERS: BUREAU #8

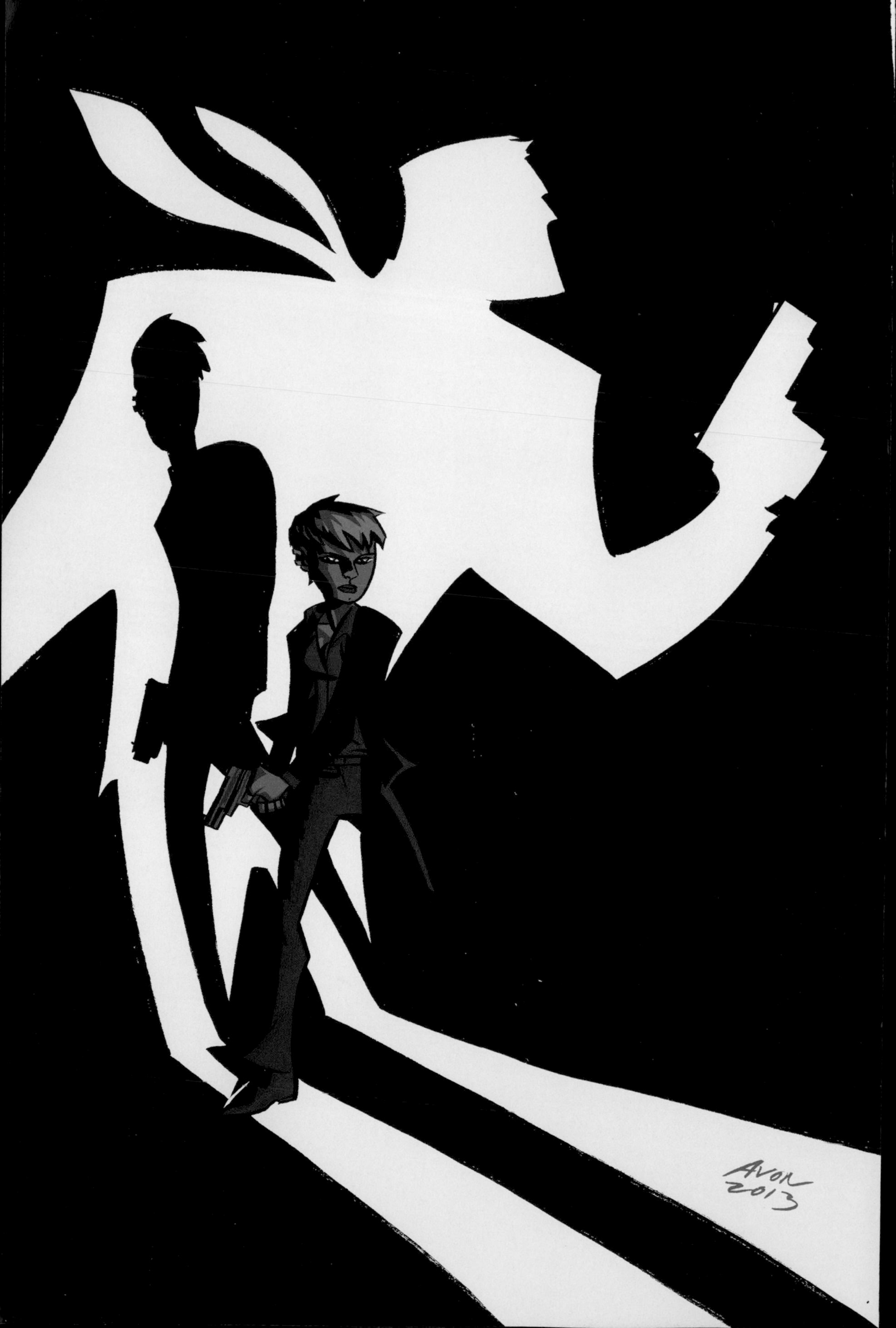

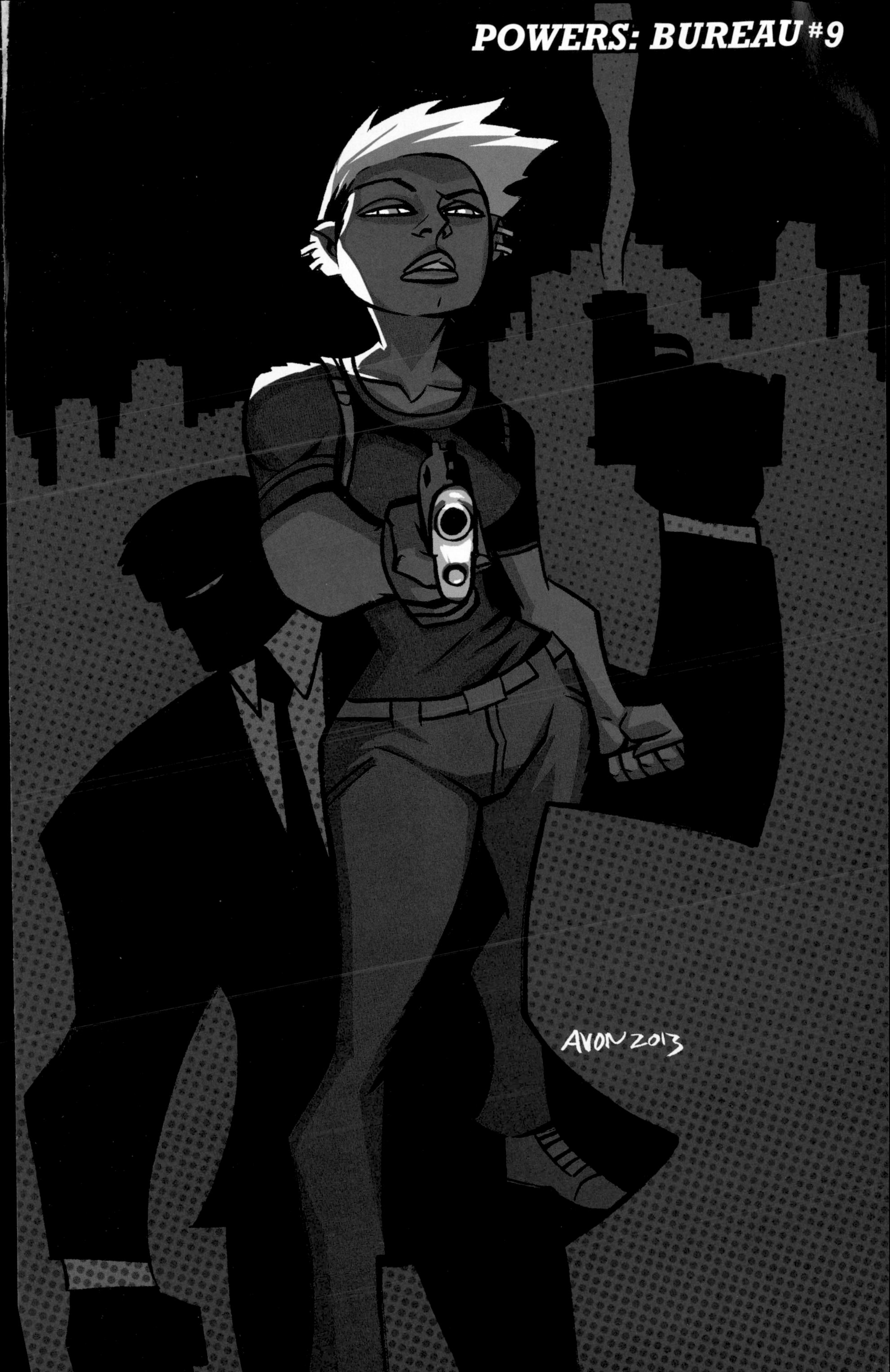
POWERS: BUREAU #9
AVON 2013

POWERS: BUREAU #10

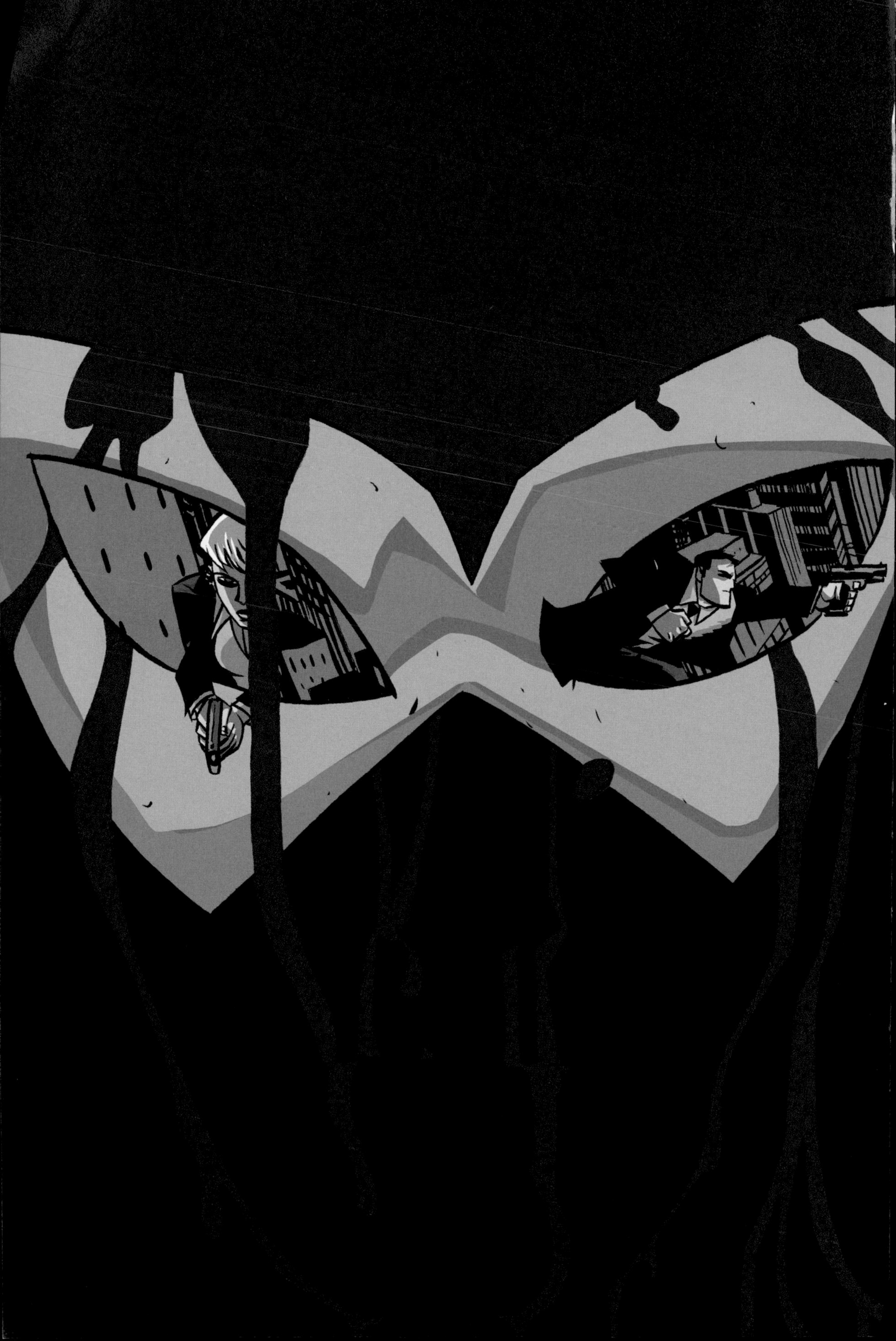

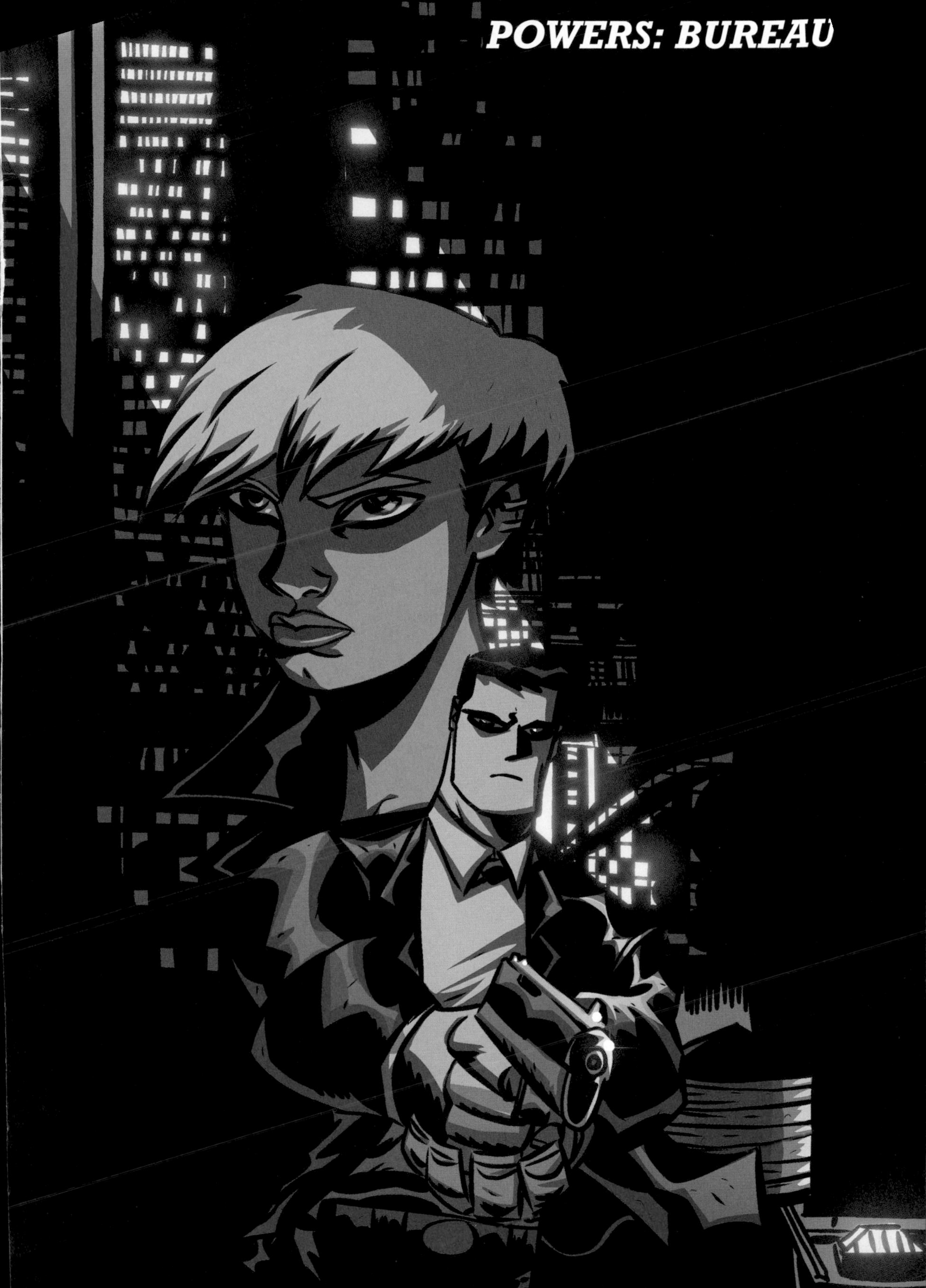
POWERS: BUREAU

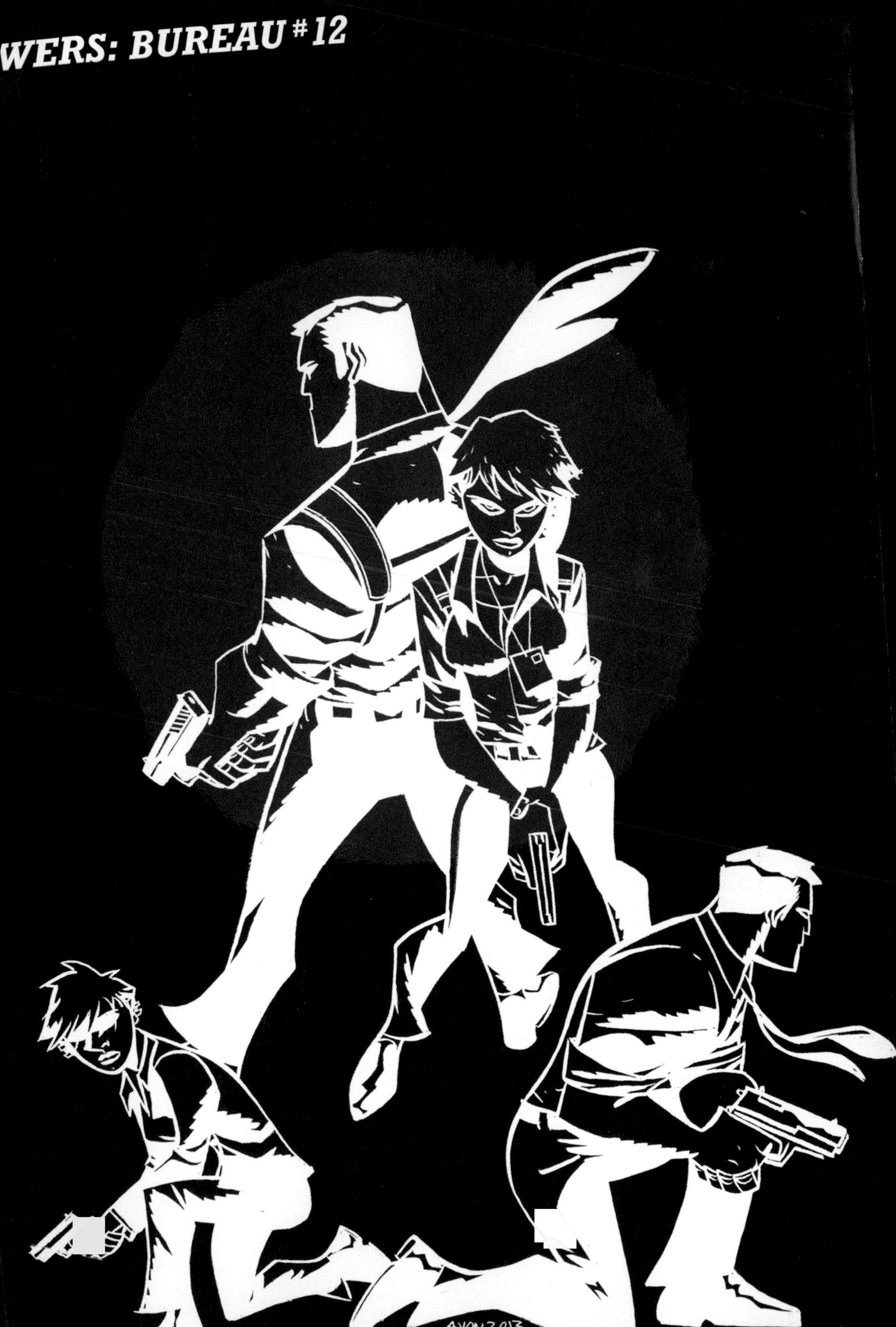
WERS: BUREAU #12

POWERS BUREAU

SKETCHBOOK

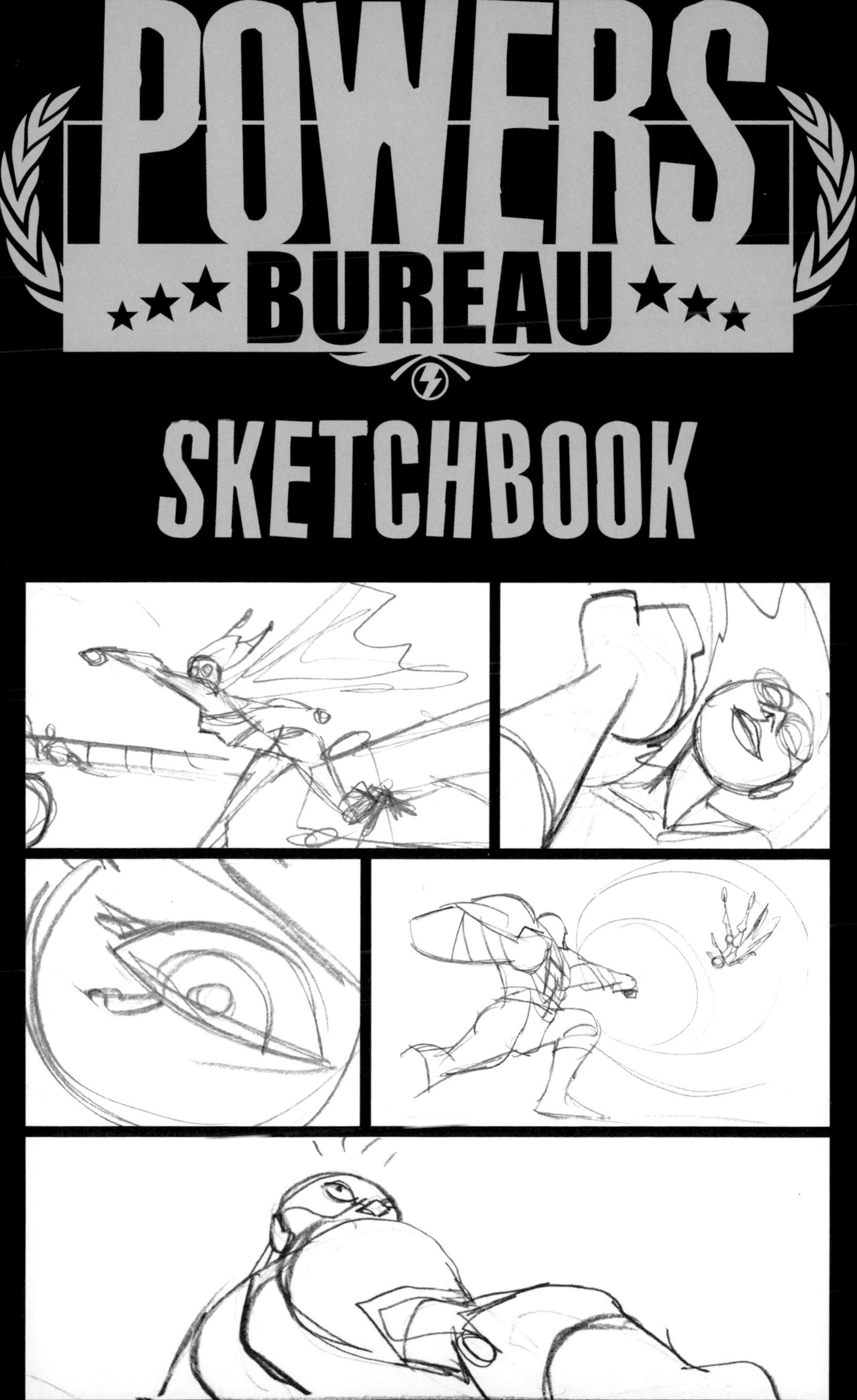

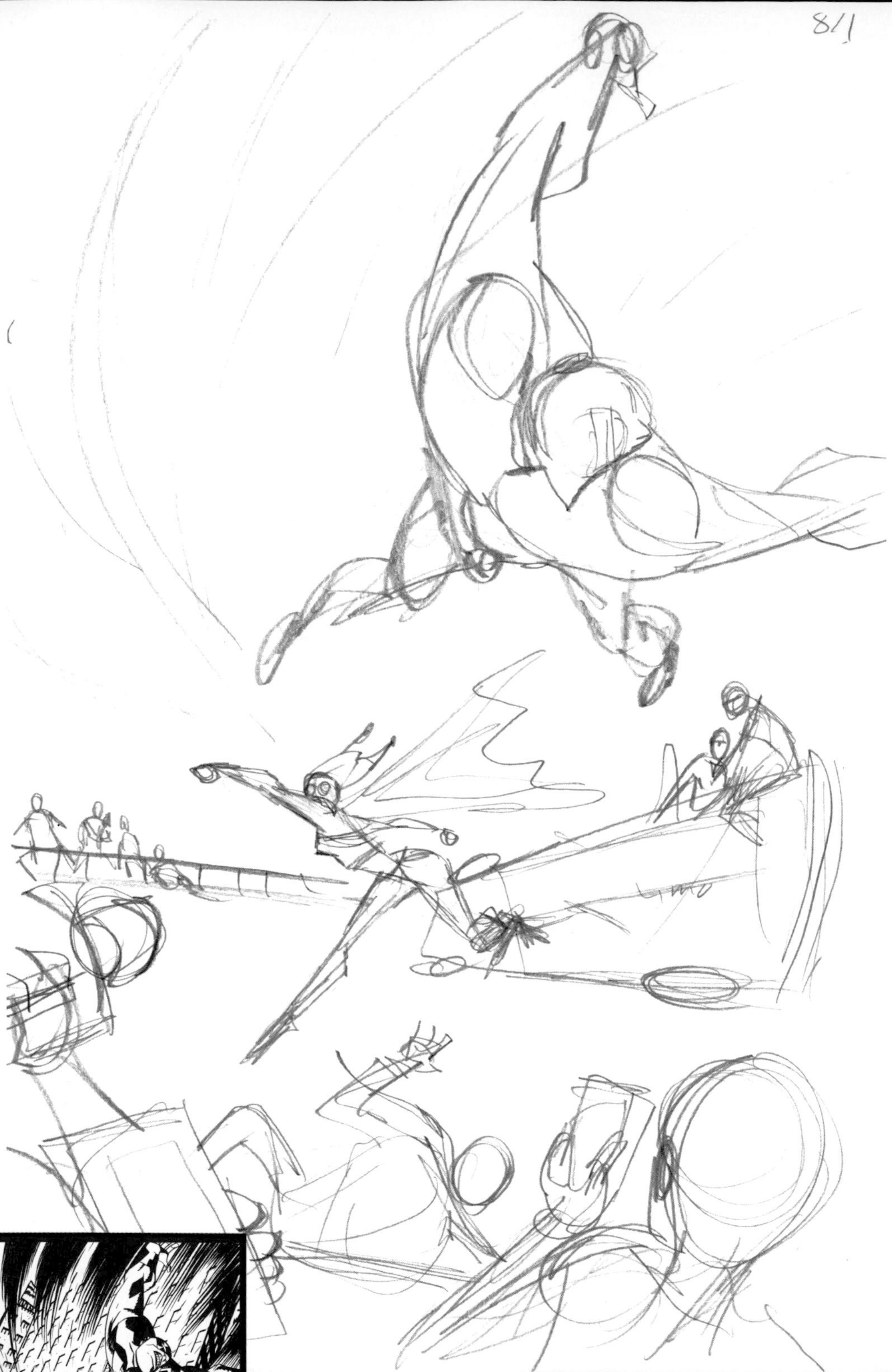

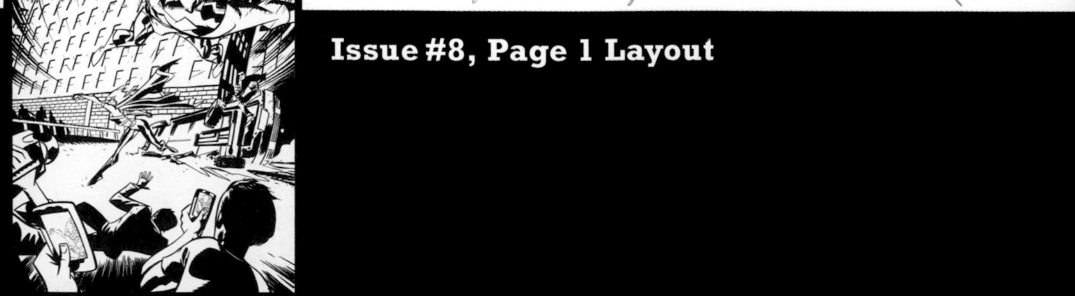

Issue #8, Page 1 Layout

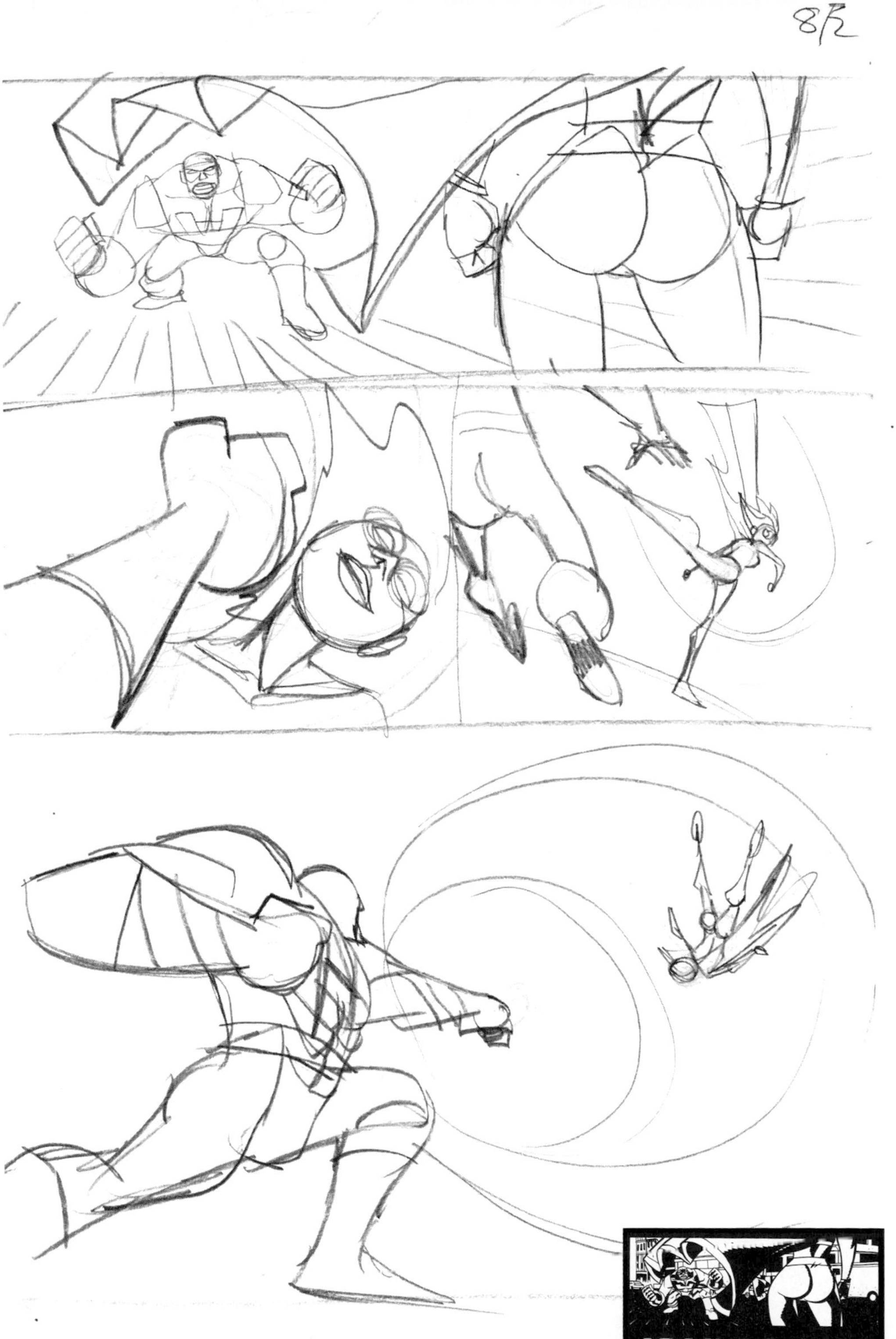

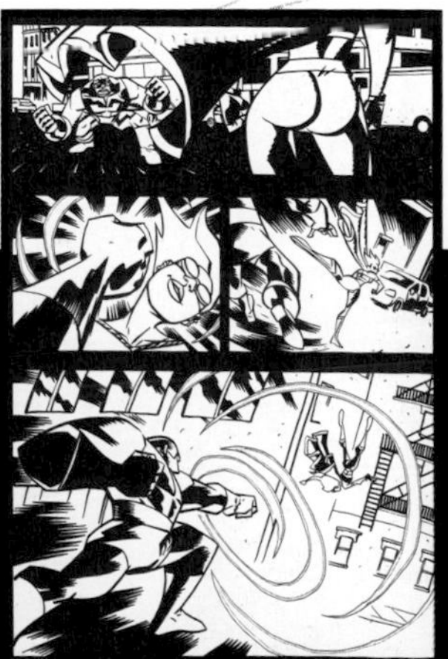

Issue #8, Page 2 Layout

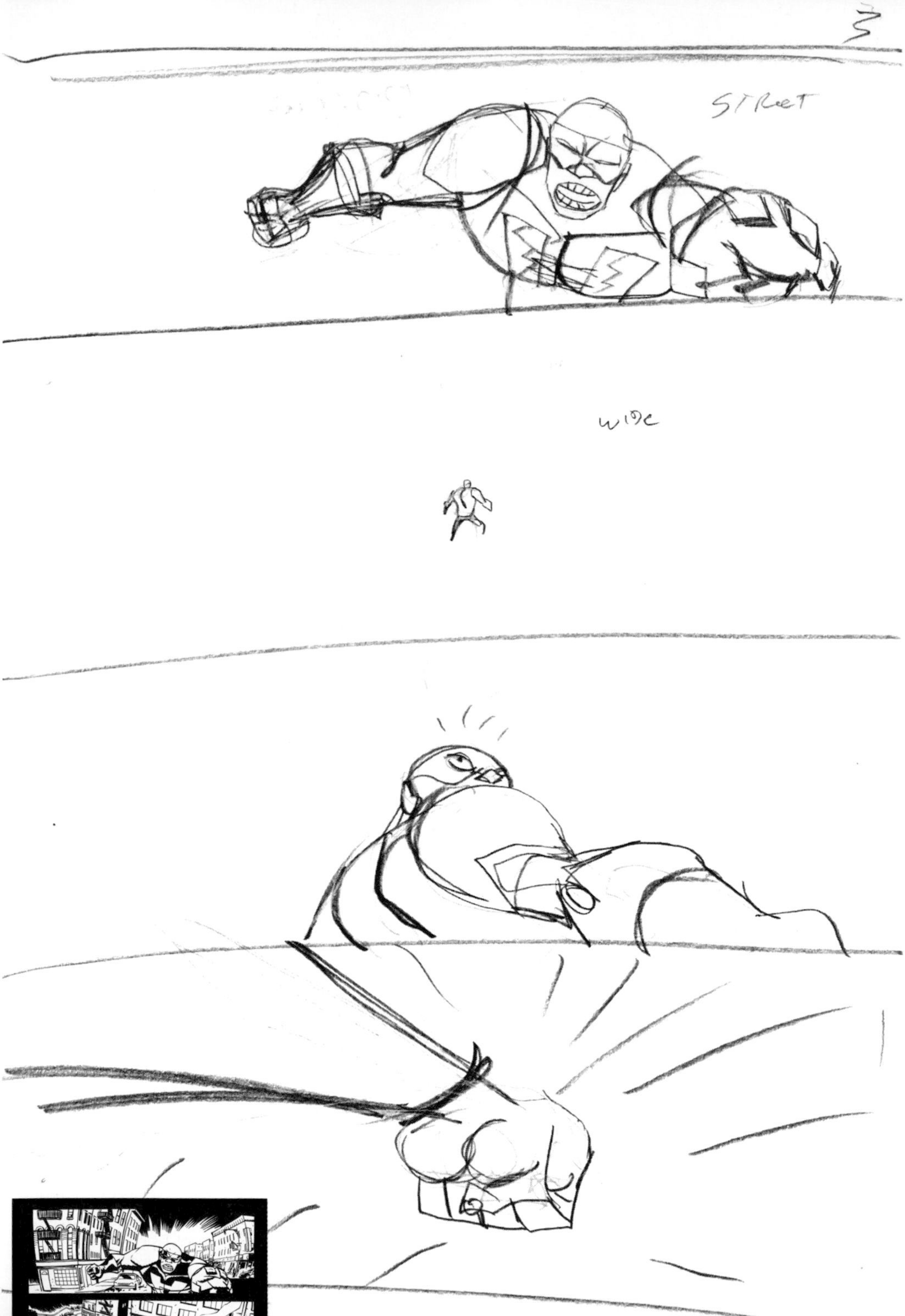
3
STREET
WIDE

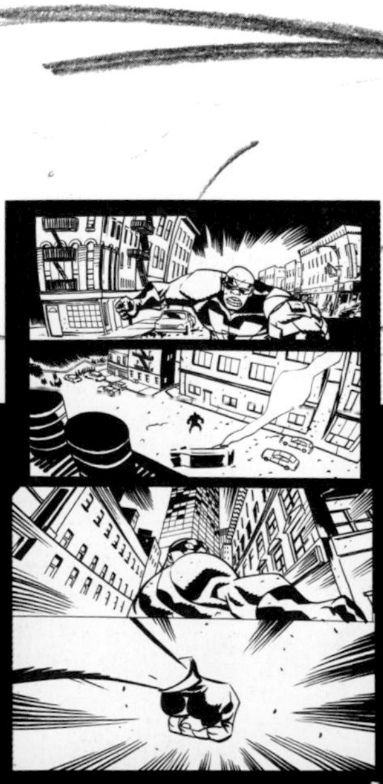

Issue #8, Page 3 Layout

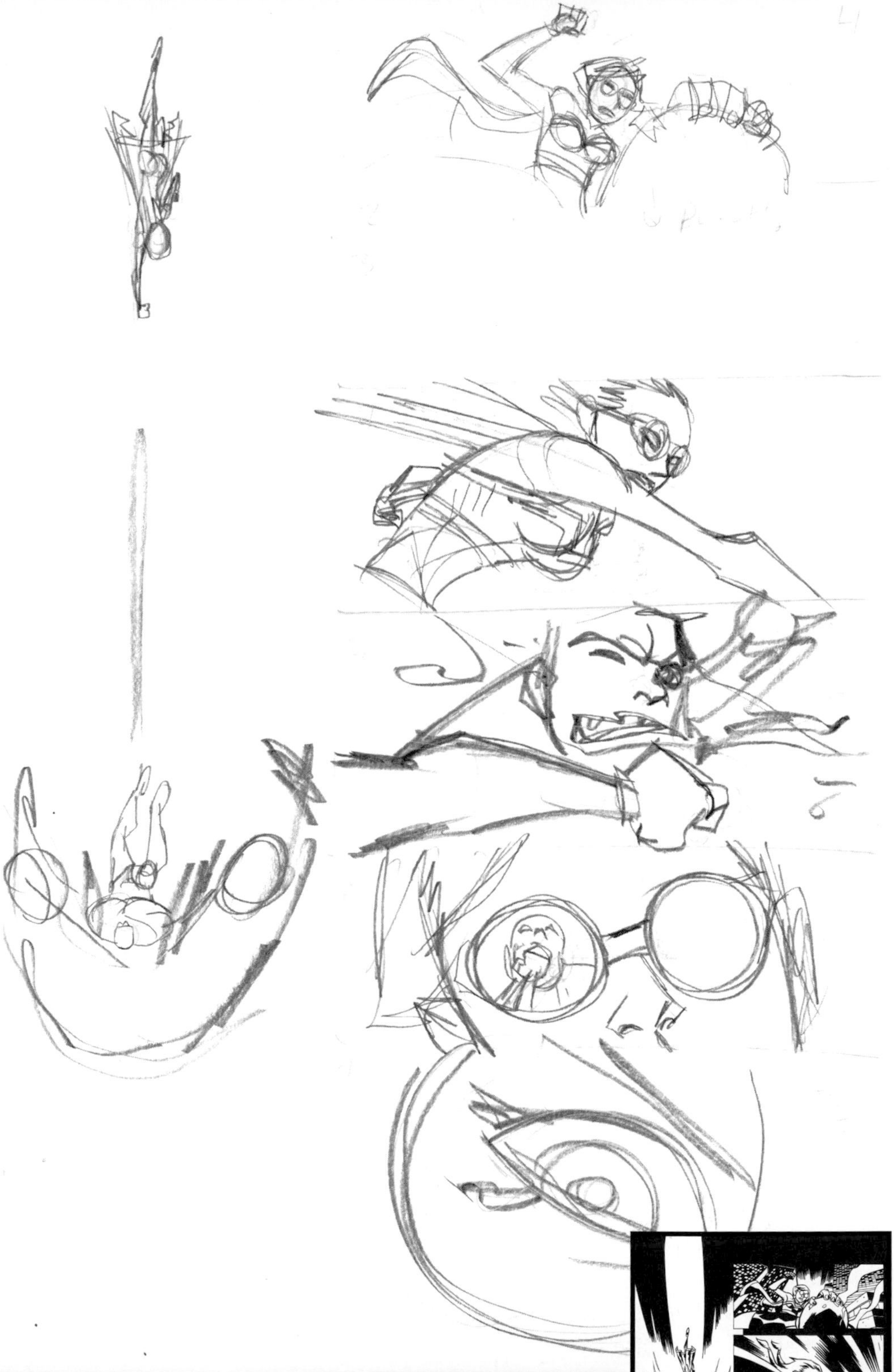

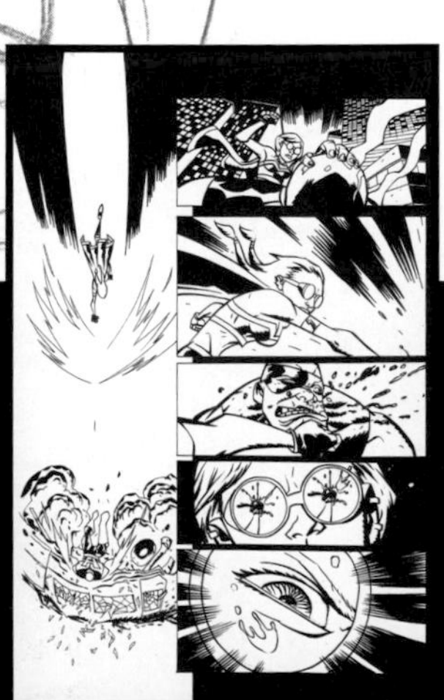

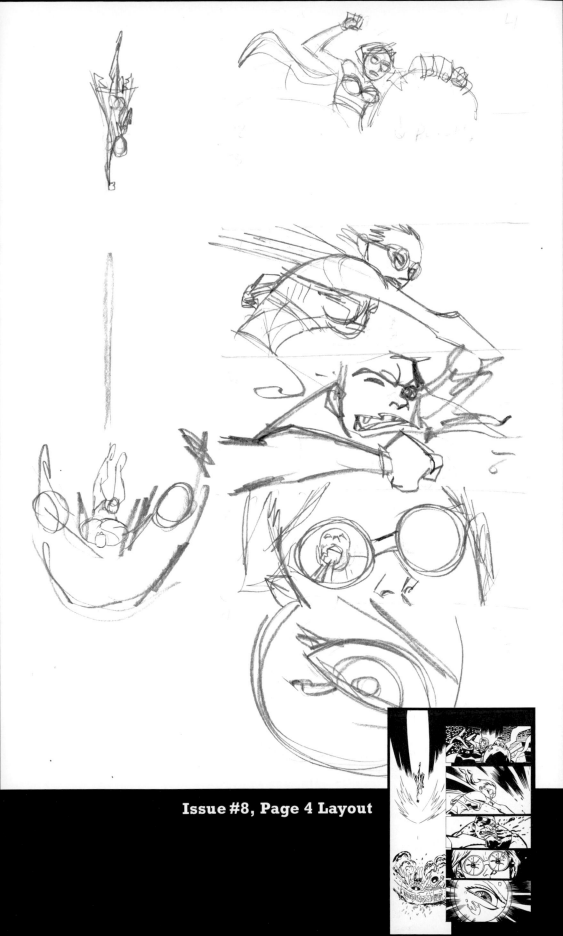

Issue #8, Page 4 Layout

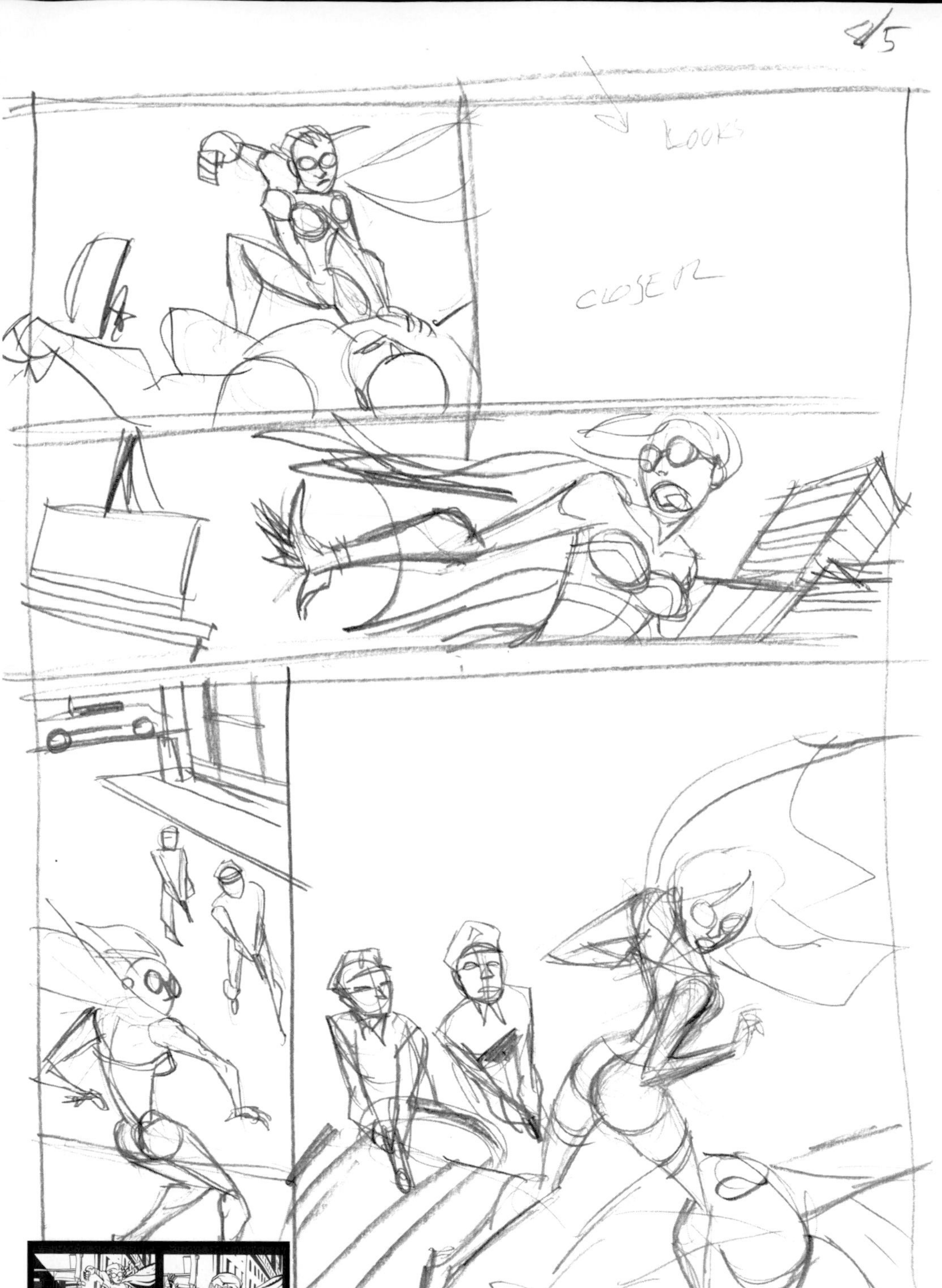
LOOKS
CLOSER

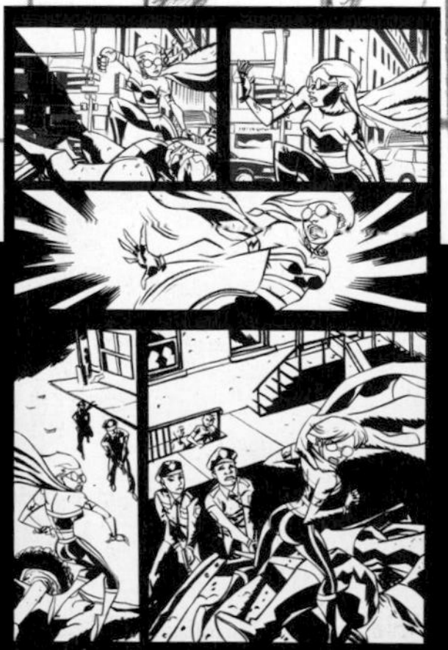

Issue #8, Page 5 Layout

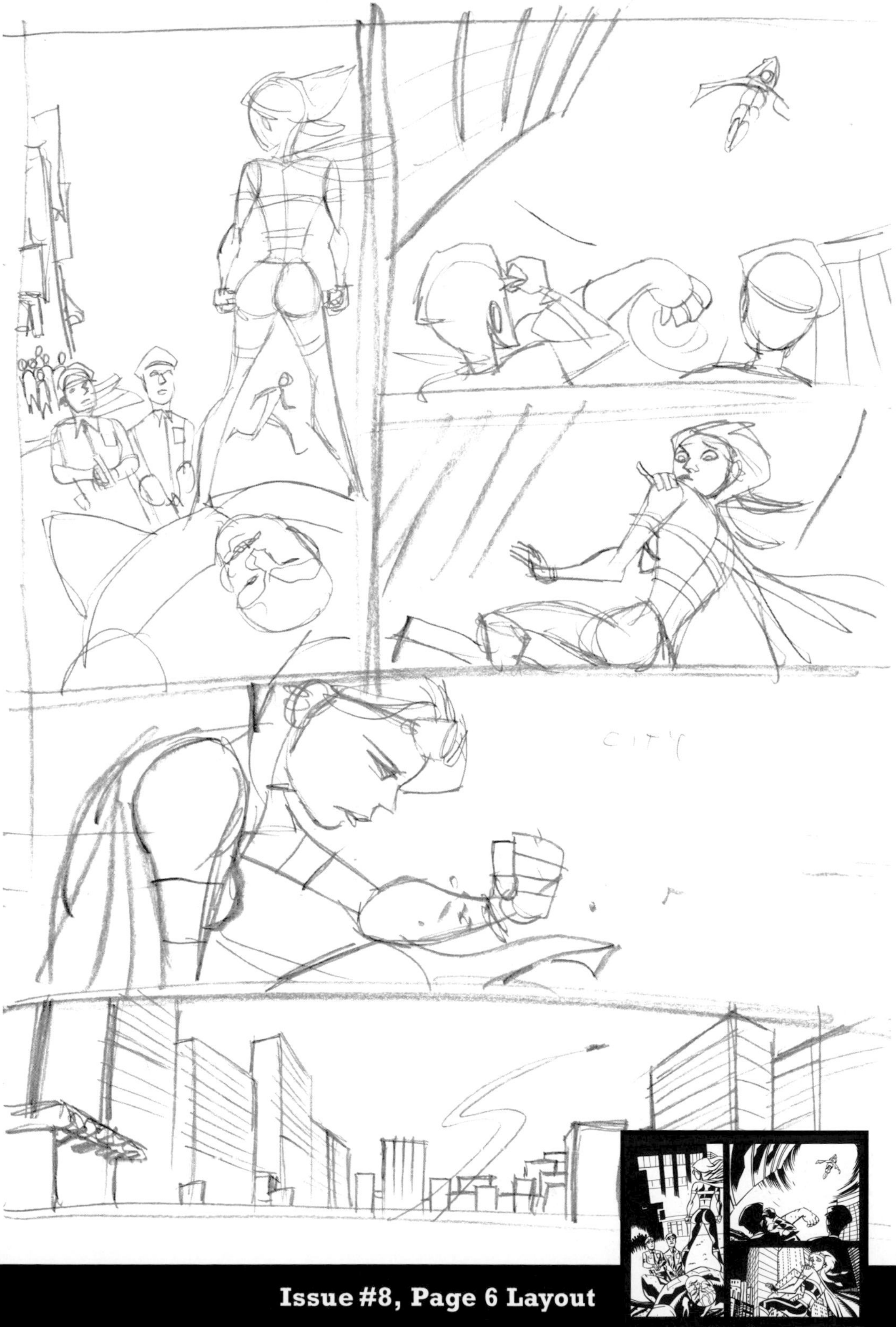
CITY

Issue #8, Page 6 Layout

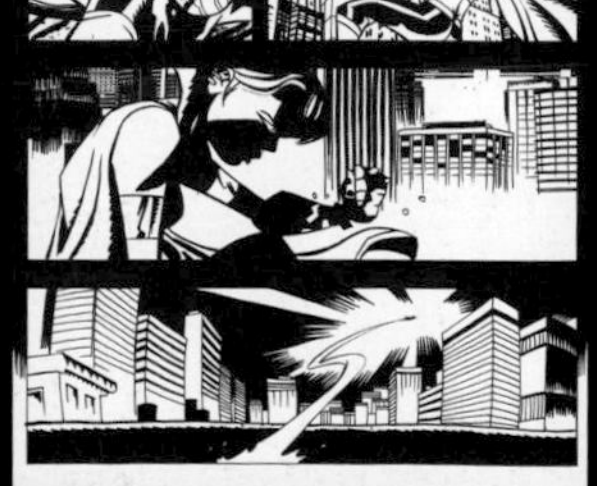

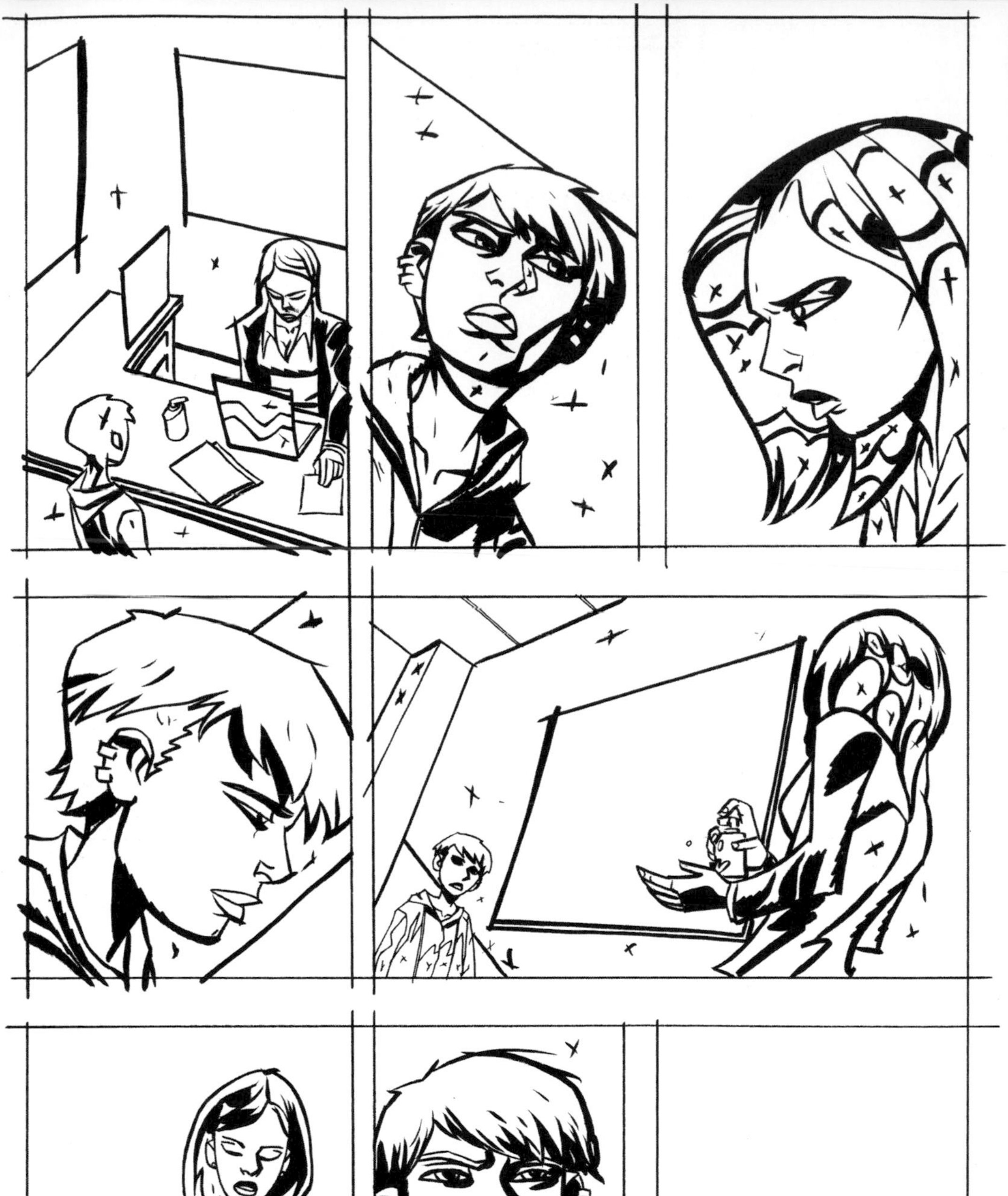

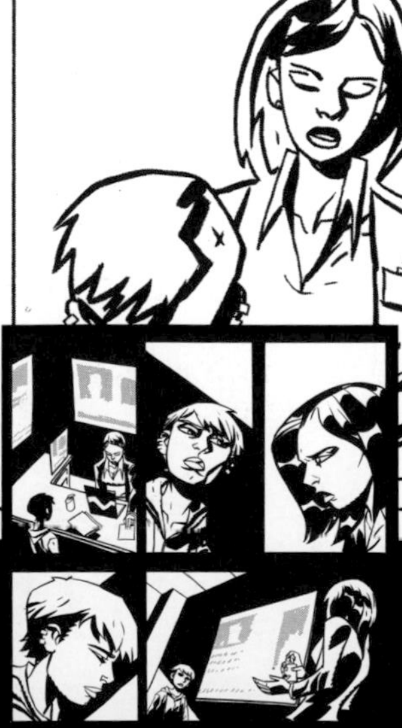

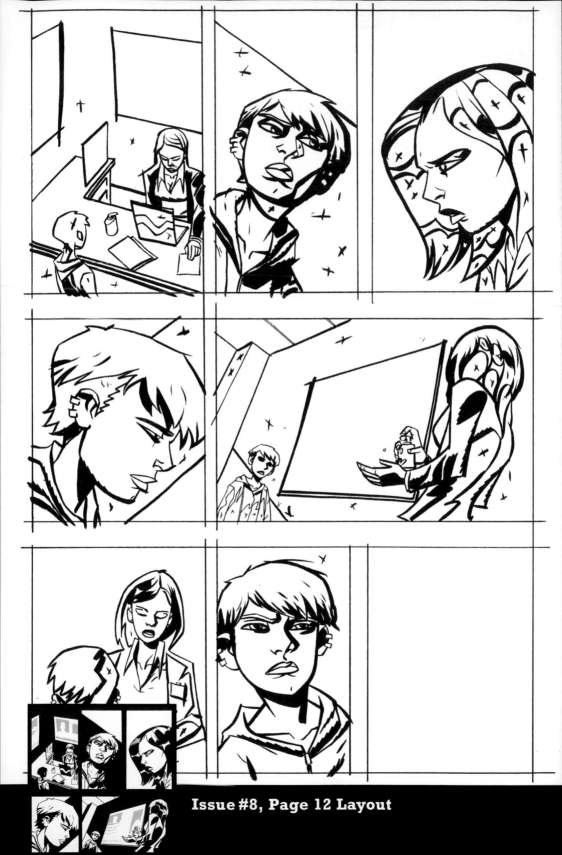

Issue #8, Page 12 Layout

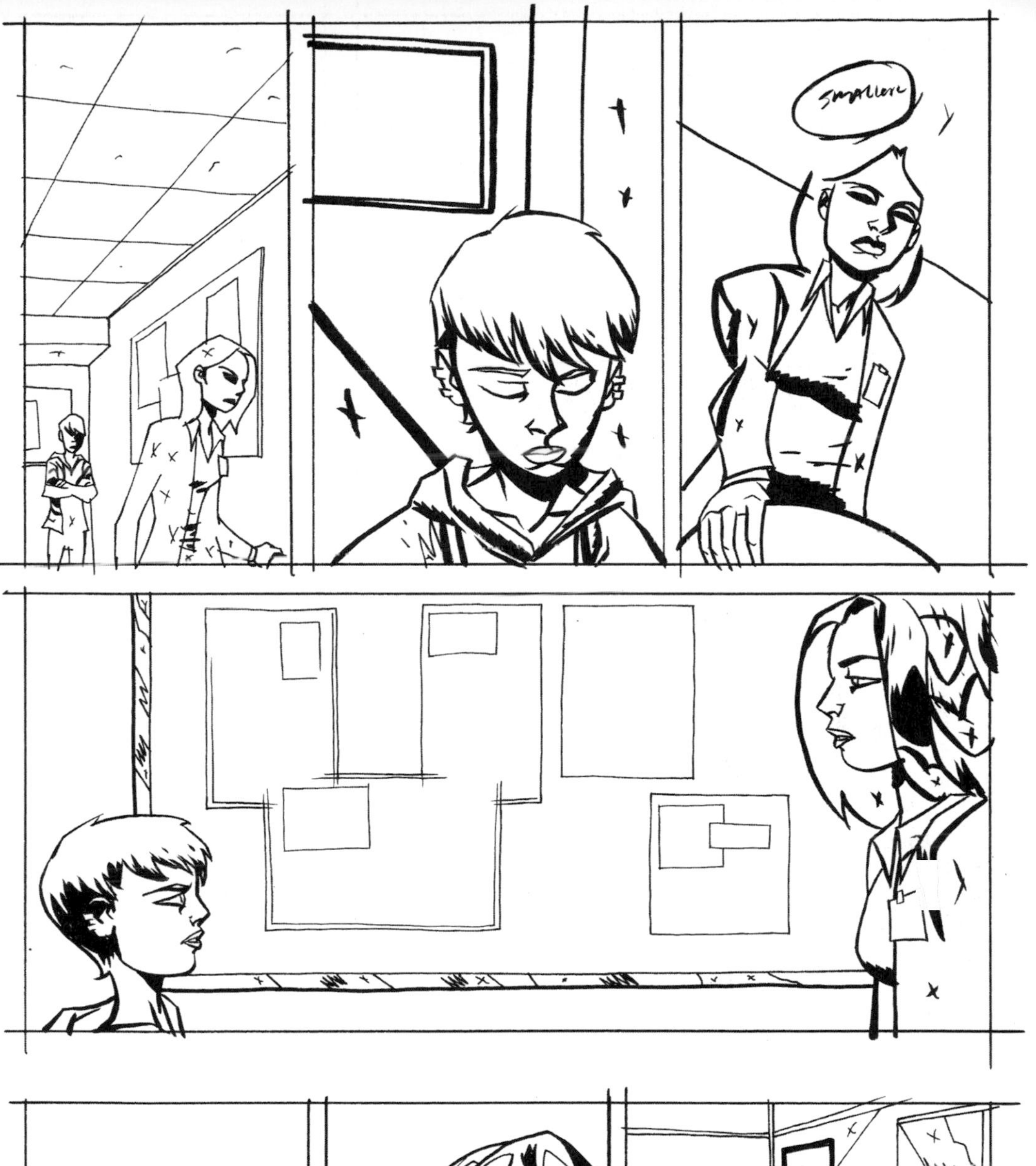

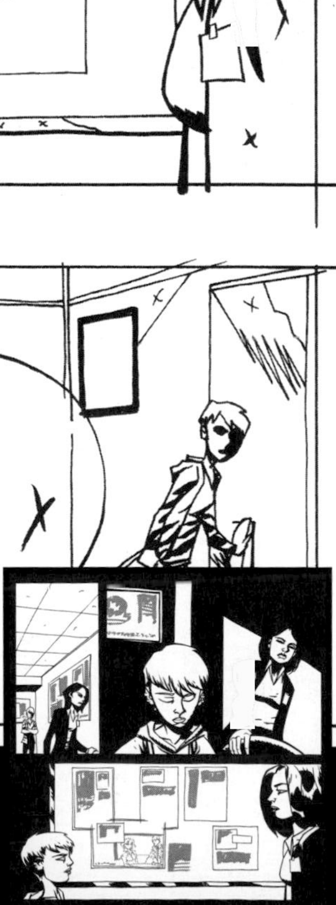

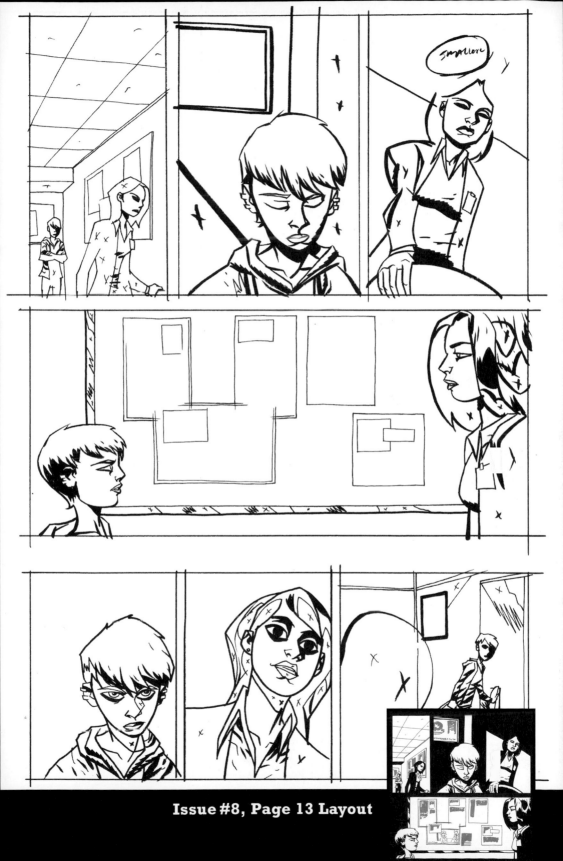

Issue #8, Page 13 Layout

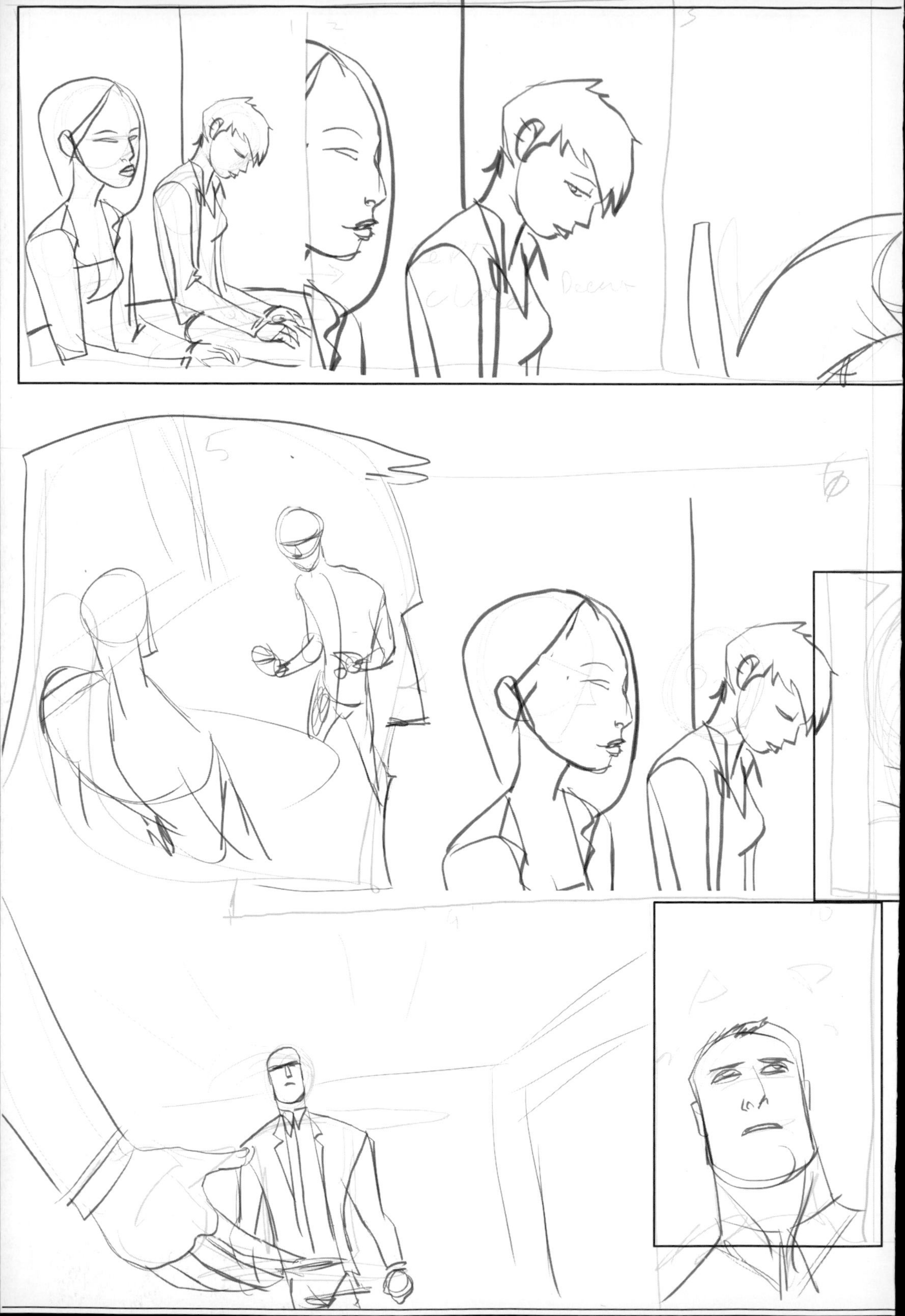

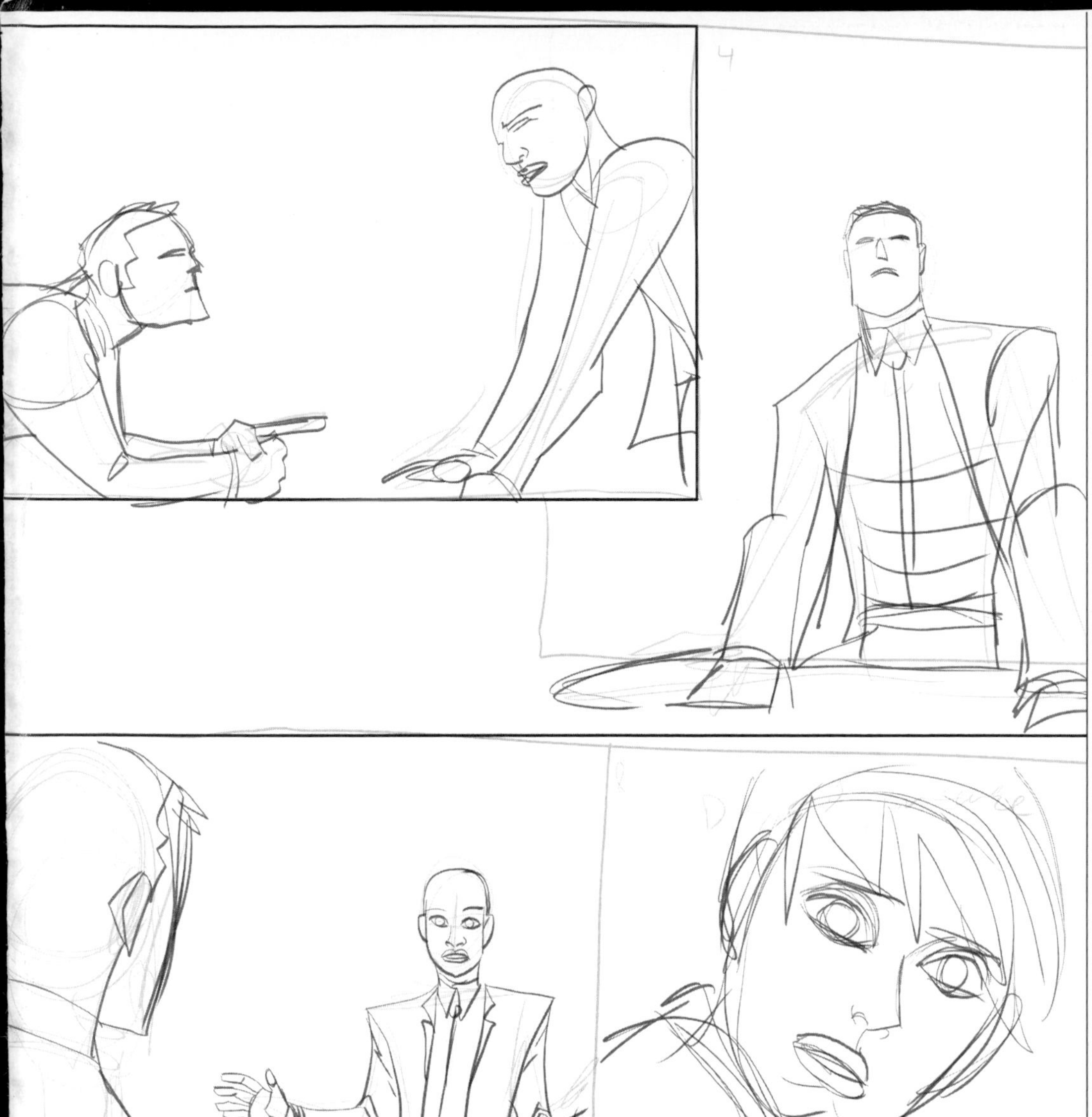

Issue #10, Pages 16-17

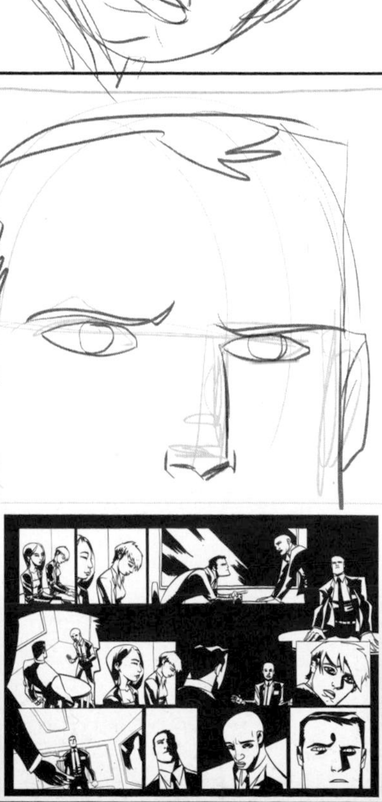

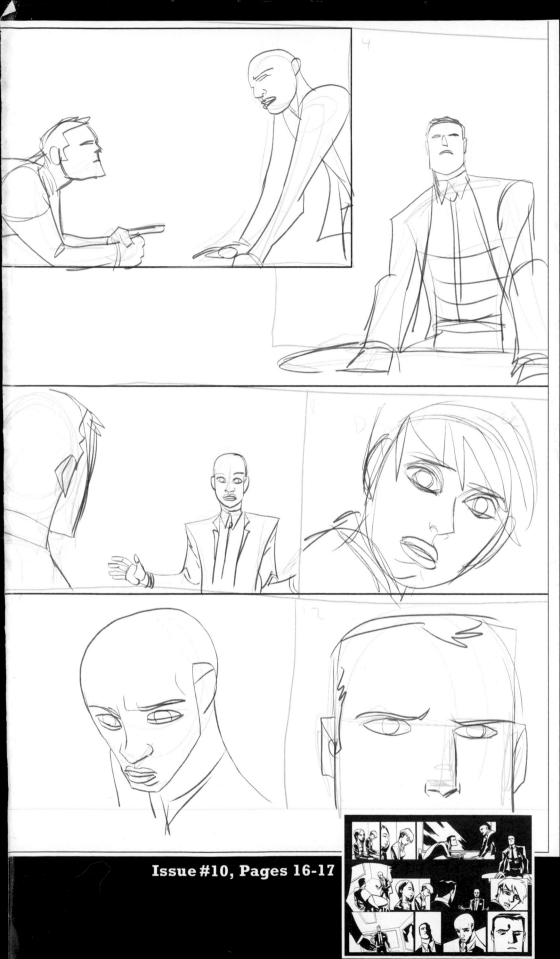

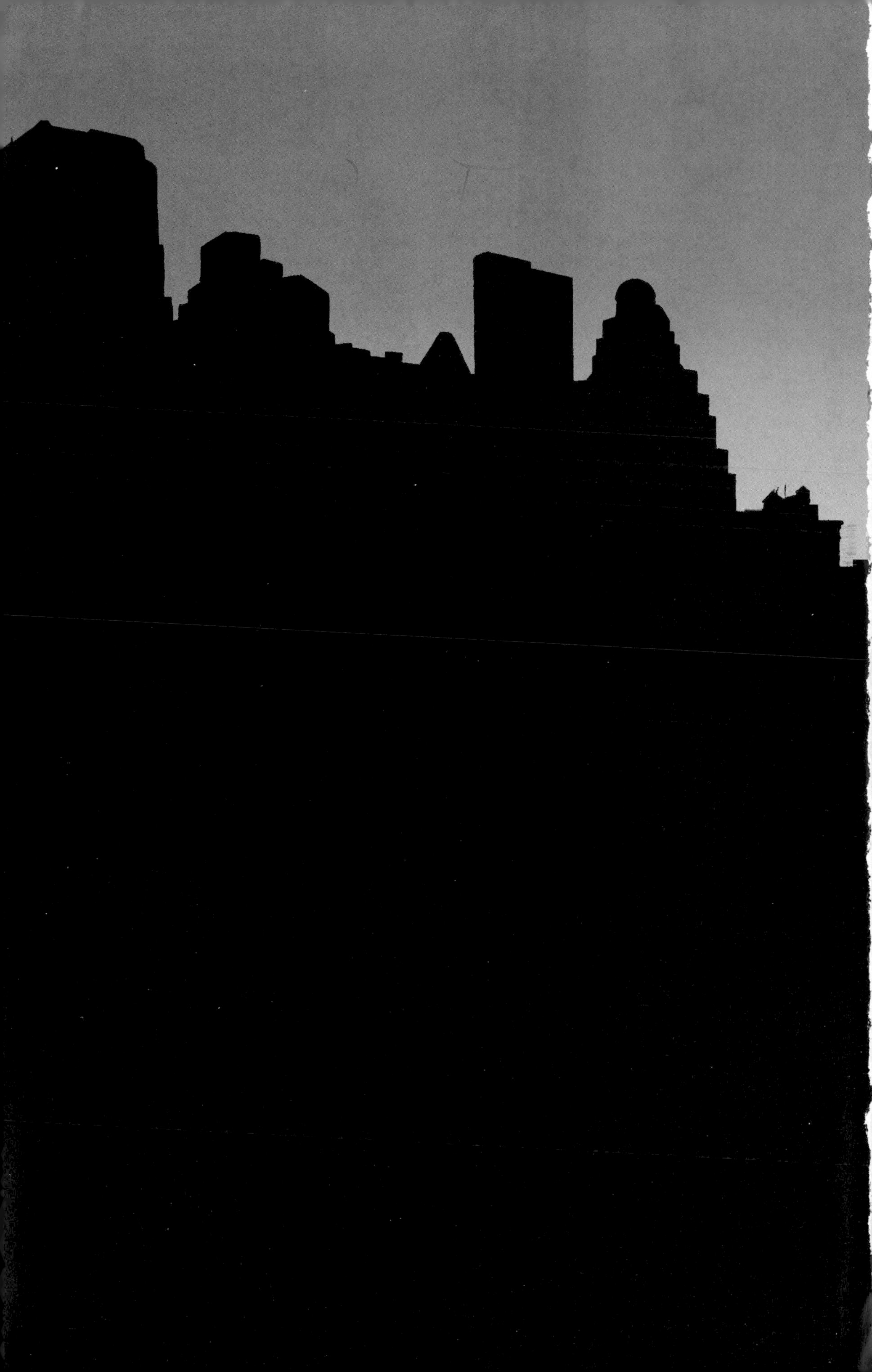